GLEE-WOOD

Speech is God's gleeman and a game of heaven.

GLEE-WOOD

*"With them is mirth manifold,
Glee-wood and game."*

Passages from Middle English Literature
from the Eleventh Century *to the* Fifteenth

Translated and Arranged by

Margaret Williams

Full-page Pictures by Amalia Suarez

Chapter-headings and Tail-pieces by Katherine Kiernan

GREENWOOD PRESS, PUBLISHERS
NEW YORK   1968

Prologue

IN ANGLO-SAXON TIMES the harp was called "glee-wood," for a maker of song is a maker of joy. It was a small harp that the roving *scop* could carry in his hands; it hummed to his words even when his song was sad. There is a passage in *Beowulf* that tells of a man's loneliness at the passing of the heroic days of his clan:

> There is no more harp-joy,
> game of the glee-wood,   nor does the good hawk
> swing round the hall,   nor the swift steed
> beat his hooves in the courtyard;   for the war-horror
> sends living men   far away.

Glee-wood was silenced in the harsh passing of an age upon which the light of Revelation had not yet risen, but its voice broke out again when Christianity sublimated the heroic spirit, lifting it out of gloom. There is a passage in *The Christ* that tells how "God's Bairn," after His Ascension, pours out His gifts upon men from heaven itself, filling the arts and crafts of earth with a more than earthly beauty:

> A man with his fingers   stirs well the harp;
> loudly before heroes   he can touch the glee-wood.

This is the spirit of Anglo-Saxon literature.

The Norman Conquest imposed a brief silence on English song, but soon the bright, melodic strains of the newcomers blended with the graver tones of old. The

men of the Middle Ages, too, "stirred well the harp."
This present book calls itself by the harp's name, *Glee-Wood*. Like its predecessor, *Word-Hoard,* it is an attempt to let our early English literature speak for itself.
The two books form a continuous story; *Word-Hoard*
covered the Old English epoch, from the sixth century
to the eleventh, *Glee-Wood* covers the Middle English
epoch, from the eleventh century to the fifteenth. The
method used in both is the same; representative passages, in translations as close as possible to the original
in form and spirit, are set against that background of
religious, political and literary history which alone can
truthfully interpret them. The task of the compiler
has been more difficult in the case of *Glee-Wood*.
Extant works in Middle English are more numerous
and lengthy than those in Old English; verse forms
that rhyme are less easily modernized than the older
cadences. The range of Middle English is wider, its
forms more contrasting, its spirit more complex. Booklovers who are not professional scholars cannot easily
find their way through such a harvest-heavy field. It is
for them that *Glee-Wood* has been compiled, and for
this reason passages have been selected, for the most
part, from works not easily obtainable in modern
English.

In its attitude towards the Middle Ages the twentieth
century has come a long way from the condescending
"Gothic enthusiasms" of the eighteenth, and from the
Pre-Raphaelite languors of the nineteenth. It has
blown away the smokescreen set up by the Renaissance
classicists who could find little to say for the "monkish
writers," whose Latin they thought barbarous and
whose English they could not understand. It has be-

come aware of the challenge of an age in which men were healthy of body and mystical of soul. It finds reflections of its own thoughts, and possibly answers to its own questions, in such things as the Holy Roman Empire (a Christian experiment in United Nations) and the craft guilds (gracious and peaceable trade unions). This new insight is largely due to scholars whose critical research is restoring mediaeval literature, and who find it not childish but towering in its strong simplicity.

There is another reason for listening to the glee-wood. As chasms open and fears beset our time, it is good to come closer to the joy of a time when God was very much at home in His world and men were—rudely or reverently—very familiar with Him. In no time, perhaps, has the supernatural outlook been more natural. The Middle Ages had wars and troubles of their own, but it was taken for granted that peace would conquer in the end. Today, when magnified wars and troubles have forced upon us a sense of global solidarity and deepened our understanding of the Mystical Body that draws all into one, we may well dare to be joyous. We may even hope for a spontaneous Christian literature once again, sung in our modern tempo and key. Such a literature will be once more aware of heaven, for, as Piers the Plowman knew, "speech is God's gleeman, and a game of heaven." Glee-wood is the harp of the pilgrim, and those who have found their way home still hold it in their hands. The forgotten author of *The Good Orison of Our Lady* has said so:

Thy dear Son is their King;   thou art their Queen again

vii

There be they never troubled   with wind nor with
    rain;
With them is ever more   day without night,
Song without sorrow,   and peace without fight.
With them is mirth manifold   without pain or fray,
Glee-wood and game enough,   life's will and
    endless play.

Manhattanville College of the Sacred Heart
Feast of the Immaculate Conception, 1947

Contents

List of Illustrations

GLEE-WOOD

The Silent Century

*The more a man knows,   the more
worthy he is.*
THE GLOUCESTER CHRONICLE

"THEN BEGINNING THE SONG OF ROLAND, the standard was raised and waved, the trumpets and bugles
sounded, and, invoking the aid of the heavenly powers,
they began the battle."

With these words from *The Old English Chronicle*
the book called *Word-Hoard* came to an end, and the
book called *Glee-Wood* begins. The battle was the
Battle of Hastings, where the trumpets and bugles of
the English were silenced in defeat. The Anglo-Saxon
time ended, apparently, under the Norman rule; its
standard was not raised again. Yet, as time went on,
the Saxon songs that rang out so bravely under that
fallen banner were lifted high once more. They blended
with the beat of the *Song of Roland,* and a new literature was formed, not in the French tongue but in Eng-

3

lish. This Middle English,[1] rich, varied, alive and constantly changing, was spoken, written, sung for five hundred years. Old English had "suffered a sea-change," as had England.

With the coming of the dark on October 12, 1066, King Harold lay dead; like Edward before him he had "sent his sooth-fast soul to Christ." Those of his soldiers who still lived had fled to the woods; the road to London town lay open before the men of William. These men were the Normans, whose doings run like veins of quicksilver through mediaeval Europe, bright, swift, elusive. The ranks marching inland from Hastings drew after them a thread of history already long and richly spun.

Only one hundred and fifty years had passed since the ancestors of these feudal knights, Christian and French-speaking, had been Vikings of the open boat, pirates and ravagers against whom the whole of Christendom had prayed in an invocation added to the Litany of the Saints: "From the peril of the Northmen, O Lord, deliver us." In 912 Rollo the Ganger took Rouen in his stride, and the surrounding province was divided among his followers. But he did homage—ungracefully, says legend—for his new fief, and this act drew him into the orbit of the Christian Empire. Soon the Northmen were Normans who changed their Teutonic tongue for that of the folk they had conquered, but who kept the keen and restless spirit of the North. With the faith of Rome they took the new culture that was forming in the light of the cross; they brought to it their own brave inheritance, blended their stark and active power with the beauty-seeking sensitiveness of the Romanized Celts. The blend was good; the Normans were lighthearted.

[1] Cf. Appendix I., p. 520.

Gradually the new people so formed became an integral part of the French kingdom as it shaped from the loose empire of Charlemagne. It was Richard the Fearless who helped Hugh Capet to his throne, and it was in Normandy that the French spirit flashed out first and best in poems, in buildings, in the graces of chivalry. But the Viking restlessness was still strong. Already this fair-haired race was ruling the capital of the new, dark Russian kingdom, led there by Ruric in 862. Robert and Roger Guiscard had already drawn Italians, Saracens, and Greeks under Norman rule in Sicily and in Naples by the time William the Conqueror, great-grandson of the Fearless, turned his eyes towards England.

We can watch his coming in the Bayeux tapestry[2] where embroidered ships of Viking pattern carry the gay Duke and his angular men on their blue, green and yellow horses over a wavy worsted sea onto land, where he moves through a storm of arrows to final victory. The *Anglo-Saxon Chronicle* tells of his crowning, briefly and sullenly: "William over-ran the land, and came to Westminster, and Ealdred the Archbishop hallowed him King, and men paid him tribute, and gave him hostages, and after bought their land."[3] In the century that followed, French language and laughter were heard at court, while the long and ample accounts of Norman chroniclers told in complacent Latin how the iron Duke bent England to his will.

[2] This extraordinary piece of needlework is almost contemporary with the events it records. It was probably worked by Bayeux craftsmen for Bishop Odo, and is connected by an obscure tradition with Queen Matilda. Seventy-two scenes depicting the Norman Conquest are worked in colored worsted on a strip of unbleached linen, 230 ft. long by 20 in. wide. It contains 1,512 figures, with Latin inscriptions. Bands at the top and bottom contain symbolic figures.

[3] MS Bodleian Laud 636, anno 1066. Rolls Series 43, p. 337.

That century was a century of silence for native
English literature, yet here and there a voice is heard
speaking, either in the tongue of the conquered or in
the universal Latin. These voices are resentful of the
inevitable blend that must come about as more and more
men of foreign blood are born on English soil, and as
the lives of both peoples are thrown together and shaped
by the unifying forces of a common faith and common
endeavor. Yet these sparse writings are already
changing their old beauty to a new. The *Doomsday
Book* is record enough of the subduing of the land; it
is accurate, but it is not literature. It has no soul, no
pride in its conquest comparable to the despairing
pride and passion of the men who lost their lands.

Among these men there were some who neither paid
tribute nor gave hostages. In the fens and open moors
where it was hard to enforce law on the unwilling, a
few raised armed resistance and others rallied around
them. One such leader was Hereward. He was of the
stuff of which popular heroes are made, about whom
cycles of songs are formed after their dearly paid defeat. Says Ingulf the Chronicler, writing about 1100:
"He underwent numerous perils, and showed the most
undaunted prowess, as we still hear sung in our
streets."[4] If none of these songs have come down to us,
it is because the roughened and lordless *scops* of those
days found no scribes to take down their sayings in
lettered leisure. The accounts of this unmistakably
Saxon hero, in which the gaps say more than the brief
and extravagant episodes, are in every current lan-

[4] Ingulf's *History of the Abbey of Croyland,* p. 136. This chronicle is
of doubtful authenticity but gives valuable evidence of many drifting traditions.

For the sources of the Hereward Cycle, see: Freeman, *The Norman
Conquest,* Vol. IV, 808 ff., and Appendix, Note DD.

guage but his own. They are sprinkled through Latin Chronicles, and developed in an extravagant *Gesta Herewardi incliti cœulis et militis*. According to these Latin sources, Hereward, son of a problematic Leofric of Brunne, was "a youth tall in person and of singular beauty."[5] What more was needed to make him a hero except to be outlawed, like Robin Hood? Outlawed he speedily was, for sheer overexuberance, and while wandering in foreign parts he killed a huge bear from Norway, fought with a giant in Cornwall, rescued a princess, and married the fair Turfrida, who was "skilled in mechanical art."[6] He returned to England and was knighted in time to raise rebellion in the fenlands against King William. That such a man lived and owned land we know from the *Doomsday Book,* that he was mighty, *"vir strenuissimus,"* we know from reputable sources such as Florence of Worcester. The *Anglo-Saxon Chronicle* testifies that his people watched his brave and futile resistance with dumb admiration and that the outlaws at Ely all surrendered to the King "but Hereward alone, and those who willed to be with him, and he led them boldly out."[7] All the prose accounts, even the fervid *Gesta,* say that he died at peace in the end. Not so the most spirited tale of the whole cycle. *L'Estori des Engles,* a long French poem by Geoffrey de Gaimar, of the race of the Conqueror, gives unstinted praise to the bravest Saxon of them all.[8]

[5] Ingulf, p. 135.
[6] *Gesta Herewardi,* in *L'Estori des Engles,* Rolls Series 237, p. 356.
[7] Bodleian Laud 363, anno 1071, Rolls Series 43, p. 347.
[8] This poem is a compilation by an unknown Anglo-Norman, c. 1185. It was drawn from many French, English and Latin sources, but its rough-and-ready style suggests that it was influenced by "the songs sung in our streets." It has the authentic ring of popular hero-worship, and although written in French is the closest extant echo of the lost Hereward Cycle of English poetry.

Already literature was busy at its work of harmonizing all differences into song:

HISTORY OF THE ENGLISH, ACCORDING TO THE
TRANSLATION OF MASTER GEOFFREY GAIMAR

Of outlaws there were many abroad; 5467
One noble man was their lord.
Hereward was his name,
Of the best men in that land he came;
Normans disinherited him.
Now there were gathered with him
Earl Morkere and his barons,
The Bishop and his companions.
They took back much land again
That the Normans had taken from them,
They went thence to Island Ely,
And feared not the enemy.

King William, hearing of this, besieged the coast and built a bridge into the fens so that the outlaws could not escape him.

When they knew this at Ely 5497
They put themselves at his mercy.
All went crying, "Mercy, save,"
All but Hereward who was right brave.
He escaped with a few men;
Gert his kinsman was there then,
And five companions true of his.
Then a man who sold fish
To the guards along the fen
Was most courteous to them then.
Into his boat he let them pass,
Hid them with reeds and tall grass.
Towards the guards he began to row

As the evening dark fell low;
Close to their camp he went.
The Frenchmen were in a tent.
Guy the Viscount was their captain;
Well he knew the fisherman.
They were sure that it was he,
And so the guards all let him be;
They let come near the fishing fleet.
It was night, they sat at meat.
Forth from the ship came Hereward,
In hardihood like a leopard . . . .[9]
What shall I say? The knights were caught   5525
At their supper, without thought.
The others entered, axe in hand;
They struck and missed not, all the band.
Twenty-six Normans they killed so,
And a dozen English fell dead too.

After this feat, English fighting men from the whole
countryside joined Hereward. They fought for years
till a truce was set and their leader was about to make
peace with the King.

When this the Normans heard, their men   5615
Broke the peace and assailed him then.
At his meat he was assailed;
Had he been warned he would not have failed
To make cowards of them all.
Aliward his chaplain did not call.
He had been set a watch to keep,
But on his rock he fell asleep.
What shall I say? He was unaware;

[9] . . . . in this and in all other passages quoted, whether poetry or prose, indicate omissions due either to defects in the manuscript or to the necessity of shortening the selections.

But nobly he resisted there.
He fought as bravely as a lion,
He and Winter, his companion.

The unequal combat lasted long, so hardy was this
champion of a hopelessly lost cause. With four lances
in his body he could still hurl his shield with force
enough to break a man's neck.

But Halselm at last struck dead   5691
This Hereward, and cut off his head.
He swore by God and by His power,
And others who saw him in that hour
Swore many times good oaths and round,
That a braver man could not be found,
That if there had been three such men
The French would not have conquered then.
If Hereward had held his stand
He would have driven them from the land.

In the meantime, standing close to the throne, there
were Anglo-Saxons who accepted the new order without losing the virtues of the old. These were men of
prayer and learning, more farseeing than the patriots
of the sword alone. Wulfstan, Bishop of Worcester, had
been a fervent monk and a wise abbot, according to the
heart of Saint Dunstan, during the confusing days of
the Danish dominion in England. After the Conquest
he was one of the first to submit to William, but in
such wise that he was none the less honored by his English brethren. Things of the spirit counted more with
him than mere temporal dominion, and while he allowed
political changes to take their course, he so lived that
men could not forget the traditions of English Bishops
in the past. At Worcester, during his rule, some un-

known versifier put into heartfelt words and rough,
alliterative metre a lament for the good old days:[10]

THE WORCESTER FRAGMENT

Sanctus Beda was born   here in Britain with us,
and he wisely   changed writings
so that English people   through him were taught.
And he undid the knots   of the questions asked
    him,
pierced their dim darkness;   he was dear-worthy.
Aelfric the Abbot   whom we call Alcuin,
he was a bookman   who changed five books,
Genesis, Exodus, Deuteronomy, Numbers,
    Leviticus.
Through these books were our people   taught in
    English.
These were the Bishops who proclaimed
    Christendom:

Wilfrid of Ripon, John of Beverley, Cuthbert of Dun-
holm, Oswald of Worcester, Egwin of Evesham,
Aldhelm of Malmesbury, Swithin, Aethelwold, Aidan,
Birinus of Winchester, Paulinus of Rochester, Saint
Dunstan, Saint Alfeah of Canterbury.

These all taught   our people in English;
not dark was their light,   but it glowed fair.
Now is their light lost,   the folk is forlorn.
Now there be other people   that teach our folk.
Many lore-thanes perish,   and the folk with them.
Now saith Our Lord thus: "As the eagle entices
its young to fly, and hovers over them . . ."
This is God's word   to the world sent;
and we should full fasten   our faith to Him.

[10] Cf. Appendix II., p. 523.

As though to show that the great line remained un-
broken, Wulfstan ruled his see with the sagacity of a
feudal lord and the humble openhandedness of a saint,
and at his death Coleman, his secretary, wrote the story
of his life, miracles and all. This *Vita* was translated
into Latin some fifty years later by no less an historian
than William of Malmesbury, good Anglo-Norman
that he was, and throughout the Middle Ages it recalled
to men's minds scenes of serene beauty in the turbulent
century of transition.

VITA WULFSTANI

He told his servants that he wished to celebrate
his Paschal banquet with good men. They interpreted this wrongly, and invited men at arms, and the
wealthy. So when Easter day dawned, and as many
poor people were crowded into the hall as it could
hold, the Bishop ordered them to be given seats at
his own table, and meat to be served to them. His
steward objected with mighty indignation; he mut-
tered through his clenched teeth; he blamed the
Bishop's condescension, saying that it would be more
fitting for him to dine with a few rich men than with
many poor. But the Bishop answered that the truly
rich are those who know and are able to fulfill the
will of God, and that they in whom God is received
and honored should be served. Scorning thus the
pomp and glory of the world he sat down and presided in the midst of the poor. Gaily he ate with them
thus, since in this humble place he again, as it were,
warmed the feet of Christ.

Thus the humble man honored the humble, yet was
he on his guard, for there was scarcely any wordly
glory which did not follow after him as he fled from

it, unwilling. For there was a strife between this man and honor which, the more he sought to escape it, pursued him the more constantly. The fame of his sanctity reached to the ends of the earth; King Malcolm of Scotland and the King of Ireland recommended themselves to his prayers; they set free captives at his request. Thus our wonderful Wulfstan became known to barbarous peoples. The Pope of Rome, the Archbishop of Bari, the Patriarch of Jerusalem, in their letters which later reached him, asked his intercession with God.

In the same fenlands that witnessed Hereward's exploits stood some of the oldest and story-richest of the monastic foundations of the Heptarchy. Ely watched on the edge of the Isle where the fighting was fiercest. Beyond waited Crowland, where the hermit Saint Guthlac had first come to live in the eighth century, seeking "smooth life-ways."[11] Here, in William's time, lived Abbot Ingulf, the problematical author of the Chronicle which gives both sides of the stormy picture of the Conquest. Further inland, at the head of Canute's Dyke, stood Peterborough, which Hereward had ravaged on the grounds that the monks were national traitors. Yet here, for many more years, faithful scribes continued the *Anglo-Saxon Chronicle* in the tongue in which it had been begun in King Alfred's day. They carried the story of the Conquest into the reign of Stephen until, at the date of its abrupt ending, 1154, the French words and forms that had slipped into it were as a sign that the two cultures could no longer hold apart.

[11] *Word-Hoard*, p. 268.

THE PETERBOROUGH CHRONICLE

1137—When King Stephen came to England he made his gathering at Oxford. And there he took Bishop Roger of Salisbury, and Alexander, Bishop of Lincoln, and the Chancellor Roger, his nephews, and put them all in prison till they gave up their castles. When the traitors understood that he was a mild man, and soft and good, and did not inflict justice, then they all did terrible things. They had paid him homage and sworn him oaths, but no man held to truth. They were all forsworn and their troths broken, for every powerful man made castles and held out against him, and filled the land full of castles.

They made the wretched men of this land toil with their castle-works. When the castles were made then they filled them with devils and evil men. Then they took the men who they thought had any goods, both by night and by day, men and women, and put them in prison for their gold and silver, and tormented them with untellable torments. For there were never martyrs tormented as they were. They were hung up by the feet and filled full of smoke. Some were hung up by the thumbs and others by the head, and burning things were hung under their feet. And knotted strings were put about their heads and twisted till they went to the brains. They were put in dungeons where snakes and toads were, and so killed. They put some in the "crucehus," that is, a box that was short and narrow and undeep, and they put sharp stones therein, and squeezed the men in them till they broke all their limbs. In many of the castles were things loathly and grim, that is, chains that two or three men had enough to bear together; it was so made that it was fastened to a beam, and a sharp iron was put about the man's throat and his neck so that he might no-whither sit nor lie, nor sleep, but bear all that iron. Many thousands they killed with hunger. I cannot and may not tell all the dreadful things, nor all the torments that they did to the wretched men in this land, and that lasted the nineteen winters that Stephen was king, and ever it was worse and worse. They laid tribute on the town from time to time, and called it protection money. When the wretched men had no more to give them they ravaged and burned all the towns, and thou mightest well fare all a day's faring and thou wouldst never find a man sitting in his farm nor the land tilled.

Then was corn dear, and flesh and cheese and butter, for there was none in the land. Wretched men died of hunger, some went on alms who were once great men, some fled from the land. There was never yet more wretchedness in the land nor did ever heathen men worse than they did. For they spared neither church nor churchyard, but took all the goods that were therein and afterwards burnt the church and all together. Nor did they spare Bishop's land nor Abbot's nor priest's but they robbed monks and clerks and every man whom they could overcome. If two men or three came riding into a town, all the township fled from them, for they thought they were robbers. The Bishops and the learned men cursed them ever, but that was nought to them, for they were already cursed and forsworn and lost. Wherever men tilled, the earth bore no corn, for the land was spoiled with such deeds, and they said openly that Christ slept and His Saints. Such and more than we could say we suffered nineteen winters for our sins. . . .

1140—In this year the King Stephen wanted to take Robert Earl of Gloucester, the son of King Henry, but he could not, for he was aware of it. Thereafter in the springtime the sun grew dark, and at about noontide of the day, when men eat, they lit candles to eat by, and that was the thirteenth day before the Kalends of April. Men wondered greatly. Thereafter William the Archbishop of Canterbury died, and the King made Theobald Archbishop, who was Abbot of Bec.

1154—In this year was King Stephen dead, and buried where his wife and son were buried at Feversham; they built that minster. When the King was dead, then there was the Earl beyond the sea, and no man durst do aught but good, for great awe of him. When he came to England he was received with great worship, and blessed as King in London on the Sunday before mid-winter's day, and held there great court.

With the passing of time, men were anxious to forget the drastic nature of the Conquest, and another Robert of Gloucester, writing his doggerel Chronicle at the end of the thirteenth century, looked back on it as something remote, out of which a new people had at last been formed.

THE RHYMING CHRONICLE

Much sorrow has there been often in English land,

7395

As you must ever more hear and understand;

Many battles there have been, for land men made
    their home.
First, as you have heard, of the Emperor of Rome,
Then the Saxons and Englishmen with their battles
    strong,
And after they of Denmark, who held it all so long,
And lastly they of Normandy who yet are masters
    here
Won it and held it; in what way I now will tell
    you clear. . . .

A vivid account of the Battle of Hastings leads to a
sensible conclusion:

And thus lo! the English folk for nought to ground
    had come,   7564
For a false king that had no right to hold the
    kingdom,
And came to a new lord that more in right was,
Yet neither of them, as men may see, in pure right
    was. . . .
So William was fair received as King of this land,
                            7605
Thus came lo! England into the Norman's hand.
And the Normans then could speak nought but their
    own speech,
And speak French as they did at home, and so their
    children teach.
So that high men of the land all of their blood came,
And held to the same speech that they had of them.
For unless a man know French small praise will he
    get;

But low men hold to English and to their own speech
 yet.
I think that in the world there are other countries
 none
That hold to their own speech, save England alone.
But men try to know both, for so well it is;
For the more a man knows the more worthy he is.

II

Court and Country

*And priests in upland places sing
When light of day begins to spring.*

THE OWL AND THE NIGHTINGALE

THE SILENT CENTURY came to an end in 1154 when
Henry II,[1] broomplant in hat, came from overseas to
unite his divided kingdom. The blood of English
aethelings in his veins made the old thanes look to him
with relief, while they looked askance at his queen,
Eleanore, whose Aquitaine blood made her listen more
readily to the troubadours with their warm songs than
to English singers of a war long since lost. A gay and
sophisticated life, shot through with family tragedy,
began at court, where wit and wealth, cynicism and
learning, led to the writing of books heavy with worldly
wisdom. Winds from the broader fields of Europe were

[1] For historic events, see Chronological Tables, pp. 539-40.

moving over England. A renaissance was on foot,
comparable in importance and in character to the later
movement that has taken that name exclusively to
itself. Towns were consolidating, universities forming,
crusaders and pilgrims coming home from the East.
Every phase of this rich life was echoed at court in the
French or Latin tongue.

But the court was surrounded by the country, and
here the English tongue had not been forgotten. It is
the unknown English people whom we first hear speaking in the twelfth century, and the poetry into which
their speech fell so easily was both old and new. In the
villages men paid less attention to the Norman Kings
than to a king of their own who had been dead for
many centuries, but who still lived for them in their
own wise sayings. Middle English literature really
opens with the name of King Alfred the Great, while
the Normans were invoking King Arthur.

THE PROVERBS OF ALFRED

The literatures of all ancient peoples have collections
of wise sayings. The Wisdom Books of the Bible are
full of pondering reflections that echo the thoughts of
the unknown man, the man of the street and of the
farm: "Thy eye desireth favor and beauty, but more
than these green, sown fields."[2] We are warned: "Tell
not thy secret to a stranger,"[3] yet bidden speak, for
"To speak a word in due time is like apples of gold on
beds of silver."[4] The Chinese, the East Indians, the
Assyrians, all built pyramids of lore from loose pebbles,
such as the saying of Confucius, "Virtue is the root,

[2] *Ecclesiasticus* 40.20.
[3] *Proverbs* 25.11.
[4] *Ibid.*, 25.9.

wealth the fruit." People thought to be less civilized,
like our own North American Indians, were wise
enough to say: "Do not stand wishing for a fish in the
water; go home and make a spear." In the days of the
late Roman Empire an unknown Cato compiled a little
book of *Distiches* which became the pocket companion
of Europe through the Middle Ages and beyond into
the seventeenth century, so well do men like to be re-
minded, for instance, that: "He is a god who keeps
silence well." In the heyday of sophisticated classicism
the process was reversed. The brittle philosophy of the
arch-satirist, Alexander Pope, broke down into a series
of sayings dear to people who are looking for an apt
expression for their own thoughts, and who will repeat
without knowing the source: "A little learning is a
dangerous thing."[5] There is no end to proverb-making.

Anglo-Saxon England had its *Gnomic Verses,*[6] pondering thought-dreams flowing through sun and rain,
pictured lines in which "wise men share their sayings."
The Danes who had broken England's peace had their
Havomal, where it is said:

A measure of wisdom shall each man have,
But never too much to know.

But whether such classic collections come to be written
down or not, each age has its people who say: "A stitch
in time saves nine." So it happened that popular proverbs long adrift in southern England floated together
in the silent century of conquest, and found expression
in the following years of awakening. It was a renaissance different from the one at court. By the year 1180
The Proverbs of Alfred were caught on parchment, in

[5] *Essay on Criticism* II, 15.
[6] Cf. *Word-Hoard,* p. 167.

the southern dialect, and in a rough popular metre in
which the Anglo-Saxon alliterative line tends to fall
apart into rhyming couplets under the influence of the
new French metres. All these bits of wisdom, so thought
the people, had come once from the lips of Alfred
himself, less a king and warrior in their inherited memories than a father and a lover of books. It had happened,
they said, in this wise:

> At Sifford   sat thanes many,
> many Bishops,   many book-wise men,
> proud earls,   bold knights.

> There was earl Alfrich,   very wise in the law,
> and also Alfred,   Englishmen's shepherd,
> Englishmen's darling.
> In Englishmen's land   he was king.
> Them he would teach,
> so you may hear,
> how they their life   ought to lead.
> Alfred, he was   in Englishmen's land,
> and a king he was,   very strong.
> He was king and clerk,
> well he loved God's work.
> He was wise in his word,   and wary in his work.
> He was the wisest man
> that was in England.

> Thus quoth Alfred,   Englishmen's comfort:
> "Would ye, my people,   now listen to your lord,
> he would teach you   wise-seeming things,
> how you may wield   honor in the world,
> and also your souls   make one with Christ."
> Wise were the words   that said King Alfred:
> "Mildly I warn you,   my dear friends,
> poor and rich,   my people,

that ye all be adread   of our Lord Christ.
Love Him and please Him   for He is Lord of life.
He is good alone   over all goodness,
He is glee alone   over all gladness,
He is bliss alone   over all blisses.
He is of all men   the mildest master,
His folk's only   Father and comfort,
He is one most righteous,   and so great a king
that nought shall be wanting   to the will of one
who in this world   thinks to honor Him."

Thus quoth Alfred,   Englishmen's comfort:
"No king can be righteous   —save Christ
      Himself—
but if he be   learned in books,
and knows well in his wit   the things that are
      written,
nor can he look to himself   unless he knows letters,
how he may hold   his land with laws."

Thus quoth Alfred:
"The earl and the aetheling   must under a good
      king
lead the land   in law to stand.
Both clerk and knight   must judge always aright;
the poor and the rich   they shall judge alike.
As a man shall sow   thus shall he mow,
and every man's doom   turneth back on
      himself.". . .

Thus quoth Alfred: **78**
"Without wisdom   wealth is worthless
for though a man had   seventy acres,
and he had sown it   all with red gold,
and the gold grew   as grass does on earth,

for all his wealth   he were never the worthier
but if he had made   a friend of the stranger.
For what is gold but a stone   unless a wise man
    owns it?"

Thus quoth Alfred: 150
"If thou hast sorrow,
say it not to thy foe;   say it to thy saddle bow,
and ride thee singing forth.
Then will he think   who knows not thy case,
that thou likest   it well enough.
If thou hast a sorrow,   and thy enemy knows it,
before he will trouble thee,
behind he will mock thee.
If thou say it to such a man
he grants thee as a favor
that without any mercy   he will lay on the more.
So hide it in thy heart   lest thou afterwards
    smart. . . ."
Thus quoth Alfred: 310
"Wise child is father's bliss.
If so it betide   that thy bairn abide,
while he is little   teach him good ways. . . .
For better is a child unborn   than unobedient. 326
The man who spares the yard   and the young
    child,
and fails to rule him   till he cannot bend him,
he in his old age   shall rue his sorrow."

Expliciunt dicta Regis Alfredi.

THE BESTIARY

Not quite so rough, in form, but as hearty in tone, is
the *Bestiary.* If not by the people, like the *Proverbs,*
it was popular, as much at home in the country as in

the court, a product of the monasteries that faced upon
both worlds. By the highways of translation and the
byways of storytelling, not to mention the loose winds
of popular tradition, wisdom from the East had long
been finding its way into English literature. The
Church habitually seized upon anything interesting or
beautiful, seeing in it a symbol of some spiritual truth,
and thus helped to transmute ancient lore into Christian
commonplaces.

As early as the second century a Greek book appeared at Alexandria, called—out of deference to Aristotle—*Physiologus,* "The Naturalist." Forty-nine actual or mythical beasts, birds and fish are described.
Their appearance and habits are seen in the light of
Egyptian nature symbolism and of a loose form of
Judaeo-Christian theology. The book was translated
into many Eastern tongues, and of course into Latin,
which assured its popularity for twelve hundred years.
Allegory revelled in the picturesque interpretations;
uncritical eyes could easily see the significance behind
the sign; preachers and poets plundered the animal
kingdom for the adornment of their works, as the
carved forms of the beasts themselves adorned every
cathedral. Even in the days of the Heptarchy a number
of them had found their way into Anglo-Saxon poetry,
in a Bestiary of which only three sections are extant,
those on the Panther, the Whale and the Partridge.[7]
Then at Monte Cassino, c. 1130, a monk named Theo-
baldus made a Latin version of some thirteen of them,
with elaborate moralizations added to each. Early in
the next century an unknown poet in East Anglia
translated this work into English, using a variety of
metres ranging from the Old English alliterative line to

[7] Cf. *Word-Hoard*, p. 263.

the new verse forms derived from the classical system.
Aesop before him and Uncle Remus after him have also
proved how enjoyable is morality revealed in an animal
story, and here were doctrine and piety as well:

Natura Leonis:

The lion stands on the hill   and he hears men
    hunting,
Or through his nose's smell   smacks that they draw
    near;
By whatever way that he will   wend to the nether
    dale,
Each of his footsteps   after him he fills,
Drags dust with his tail   where he down steps,
Either dust or dew   so they cannot be found;
He drives down to his den   where he will defend
    him.

Another way he has.   When he is first born
Still lies the lion   and stirs not from his sleep
Till the sun has shone   three days about him;
Then his father raises him   with the roar that he
    makes.

A third law has the lion.   When he lies to sleep
He shall never lock   the lids of his eyes.

Significacio:

Well high is the hill   that is heaven's kingdom;
Our Lord is the lion   that lives there above.
So when it pleased Him   to light here on earth,
The devil might never know,   though darkly he
    hunted,
How He down came,
Nor how He denned Him   in that deft maiden,

The lion hears men hunting or through his
nose's smell smacks that they draw near.

NATURA LEONIS

Mary by name   who bore Him to man's kind.
When Our Lord dead was,   and buried as His will
      was,
In a stone still He lay   till it came to the third day;
His Father helped Him so   that He rose from the
      dead though,
To bring us to life.
He stays awake, as His will is,   as a shepherd for
      his fold;
He is shepherd, we are sheep;   shield us He will,
If we obey His word,   that we may stray no-where.

Natura Cathegrandie:

Cathegrande is a fish,
The greatest that in water is,
So that thou wouldst surely cry
If thou sawest it floating by,
That it was an island
Seated on the sea-sand.
This fish has an ugly side—
When he hungers he gapes wide;
Out of his throat a breath is hurled,
The sweetest thing in the wide world.
Other fishes come from afar;
When they feel it glad they are.
They come and into his mouth they swarm,
All unknowing of the harm.
Then this whale locks up his jaw,
Sucks the fish into his maw.
The small ones he can thus uptrip;
The great he can in no wise grip.
This fish dwells on the deep sea-ground,
And lives there ever hale and sound,
Till that time has come to be

When storms stir all the sea;
When summer and winter strive together
He cannot stay there in such weather.
So troubled is the sea's floor
He cannot stay there any more,
But stirs himself, and heaves up still
While the weather is so ill.
Then ships are driven on in fear,
Death is hateful, life is dear.
They look about and see the fish,
An island they think it is.
Thereof they are glad anew,
With all their might they draw thereto,
All their ships on it they fasten,
And then onto the island hasten.
Of stone and steel in the tinder
They make a fire burn on this wonder,
Warm them well, and eat and drink.
He feels the fire, begins to sink,
For soon he dives down to the ground
And kills them all without a wound.

Significacio:

The devil is great in might and will,
As are witches with their skill.
He makes men have hunger and thirst,
And many another sinful lust.
With his breath he draws men on;
Shame comes to him who thus has gone.
Little ones tricked by pleasure be,
The great ones not so easily,
The great, I mean the steadfast, most
In right belief, both flesh and ghost.
Who listens to the devil's lore

At long last he shall rue it sore;
Whoso fastens hope in him
Shall follow down to hell dim.

Natura Turturis:

In a book is the turtle's life   written in rhyme,
How loyally she holds   love all her life time;
If she has one mate   from him she will never
    wander.
Women, remember her life;   I will tell it you.
By her mate she sits at night,   in the day she goes
    and flies,
Whoso says that they are sundered,   I say that he
    lies.
But if her mate were dead,   and she a widow were,
Then flies she alone, and fares,   none other will she
    more,
But alone goes and alone sits
And waits for her old love,
In her heart she has him night and day,
As though he were alive alway.

Significacio:

Listen, believing man, hereto,   and hereof often
    think;
Our soul at the Church door   chose Christ for her
    mate,
He is our soul's spouse,   love we him with might,
And wend we never from Him   by day nor by
    night.
Though He be from our sight gone,   be we to Him
    all true,
None other Lord trust we,   nor other love new,
Believe we that he lives   for aye in heaven's realm,

Thence He shall after come   to be our life's helm,
For to judge all men,   but not with like doom,
Men hateful to Him shall fare to hell,   those dear
    to Him to His home.

THE OWL AND THE NIGHTINGALE

Towards the close of the twelfth century an unknown
poet living in a corner of Dorset wrote a bird-tale very
different from the *Bestiary*. Owls and nightingales had
long played a part in mythology and legend of all sorts,
but they were also to be heard on any summer night in
the woods around Portisham; it seems that a certain
young nightingale on her flowery branch had tried one
night to outsing an old owl on his stump, and the contest was overheard by a poet, who tuned his glee-wood
to the song. In his own homely language of the South,
and in the simple yet subtle metre that was just then
beginning to lend French grace to the more robust
English, he reported what he had heard, and left it to
others to interpret. He did not explain, and was probably too sympathetic with the arguments of both birds
to take sides. It may be that the poet was called Master
Nicholas of Guildford, for at the end of his poem he
unbashfully suggests that a man by that name should
receive a benefice, for he is wise enough to solve the
problems even of birds!

The Owl and the Nightingale is one of the greatest
of mediaeval debate-poems. The *contentio,* an art-form
going back through the *Eclogues* of Virgil to the
Pastorals of Theocritus, had been made popular during
the Carolingian Renaissance by the schoolmasters of
Europe, such men as Alcuin[8] and Sedulius Scotus.

[8] See *"Conflictus Veris et Hiemis"* in H. Waddell, *Mediaeval Latin
Lyrics.*

When summer and winter, or wine and water, extolled their own merits, allegory was bound to creep in. So too, this bird debate is allegorical, spontaneously so, in the sense in which all thoughtful relishing of life reveals deeper realities than at first appear. The Owl sings of what is grave, austere and traditional, the Nightingale of what is joyous, new and daring. On these two themes they run through the gamut of music, poetry, philosophy, love. With fine humor, and in the allusive way of the booklover who is innocent of pedantry, Master Nicholas draws upon his sources: animal lore, *The Proverbs of Alfred,* French *Fabliaux,* and the drifting, long-lived scholarship of the old monasteries and the new universities, all woven without effort into the country speech of Dorset. The whole of Europe, in the excitement of its first crusades and its first cathedrals, is reflected in this piece of local and even colloquial roadside gossip. As for settling the question as to whether it is better to be grave or gay, Nicholas was too wise to do that. If he was interested in getting a benefice for himself, he could hardly have given a better proof than this very poem that he was a man of his times: witty, beauty-loving, realistic and learned, with an eye to this world and to the next.

Incipit altercacio inter filomenam et bubonem:

> I was in a summer dale,
> In a deeply hidden vale;
> There I heard a great tale
> From an owl and from a nightingale.
> Their quarrel was stiff and stark and strong,
> Sometimes soft, then loud and long,
> And one against the other fought

And let out every evil thought.
And each one said of the other's way
The very worst that she could say;
And so about each other's song
They kept up a contention strong.
The nightingale began the speech
From the shelter of a beech,
And sat upon a fair bough,
All about were blossoms enow,
In a thick and lonely hedge,
Among the reeds and green sedge.
She was glad for the twigs to rise,
And sang in a very cunning wise.
The glad song rather seemed to play
From a harp or pipe than another way,
It seemed more that it gave a note
From a harp or pipe than from a throat.
There stood an old stock there beside
Where the owl sang at vesper-tide;
It was with ivy overgrown,
And there the owl dwelt alone.
The nightingale beheld her there
And began to look and stare.
She thought full evil of the owl,
For men called it loathly and foul.

Nightingale:

"Wretch," she said, "away now, fly!
I am the worse when thou art by.
Iwis, for thy foul face,
Well oft I cease my song a space,
My heart flies out, and fails my tongue,
When near me thy song is sung.
I would rather spit than sing

At thy wretched yodelling....
Thy body is short, thy neck is small,   **74**
Greater is thy head than all.
Thine eyes are both coal-black and broad,
As if they painted were with woad.
Thou starest as if thou wouldst soon bite
Everything thy claws could smite;
Thy bill is stiff and sharp and hook'd
Just like an awl that's made all crook'd
With it thou clackest oft and long,
That's all there is of thy one song. . . ."
The Owl listened thitherward,   **143**
And held her eyes down netherward,
Sat blown and swollen on her log
As though she'd swallowed down a frog....

Owl:

Then quoth the Owl: "Who is in sight   **187**
That can and will judge us aright?"

Nightingale:

"I know well," quoth the Nightingale,
"Thereof there can be no tale.
Master Nicholas of Guildford,
He is wise and ware of word.
He is of word so very wise,
Every wrong he will despise,
With insight into every song,
Who sings well, who sings wrong;
He can tell wrong things from right,
And the darkness from the light."
The Owl for a while bethought
And afterwards this word upbrought:

Owl:

"I leave it to him willingly,
Though he once was wild as he could be,
With the nightingale dear to him,
And other beings pretty and slim.
I know that he is now well cooled,
And by thee will not be fooled."

The two birds thus agree to submit their case to arbitration, but before flying off to their judge they continue the dispute, each defending her song and her aims.

Owl:

"My voice is bold and not forlorn,   **317**
It is like a great horn;
But thine is like a little pipe,
A small piece of wood unripe.
I sing better than thou dost—
Thou chatterest like an Irish priest.
I sing at eve the first time,
And after when it is bed time,
The third time is at midnight,
And so I sing my song aright
When I see arising far
Either dawn or the day-star.
I do good with my throat,
Warn men in need with my note,
But thou singest through the night
From eve until it is daylight,
And ever sayest thy one song
As long as the night is long...."

Nightingale:

"Owl," she said, "why dost thou so?   **411**

Thou singest a winter wolawo!
Thou singest like a hen in the snow,
All that she sings it is for woe.
In winter thou singest loud and long,
In summer dumb is all thy song.
For thy foul jealousy
Blithe with us thou canst not be.
Thou burnest like an angry brand
When our bliss is in the land,
As a man does who is ill,
All bliss is against his will;
Grouching and louring, he is sad
If he sees that men are glad,
And he would that he might espy
Tears in every man's eye;
He'd care not if people were
Pulling each other by the hair.
So dost thou on every side,
For when the snow lies thick and wide
And every man is full of sorrow
Thou singest from eve until the morrow.
But I all bliss with me bring,
All men are glad to hear me sing,
And bless the time when I have come
And still hope when I have not come.
Blossoms begin to spring and spread
Both on the tree and in the mead...."
The Owl listened, and laid in hoard   **467**
All this talk, word after word,
And afterwards thought how she might
Find an answer sound and right;
For he must think and then be quick
Who fears lest his foe may trick.

Owl:

"Thou askest me," the Owl said then
"Why in the winter I sing to men.
A custom of good men, they say,
From the world's beginning till today,
Is that each good man should greet his friend,
And blissful times with him should spend
In his house, at his board,
With fair speech and fair word,
At this time, till Christmas snow,
When the rich, the poor, the high, the low
Sing their carols night and day;
Then I help them as I may.
And yet I think of another thing
Than just to play and just to sing.
And so I have an answer meet,
Ready for you, plain and neat:
For summer is lush and over-wrought,
And so upsets man in his thought....
Answer me, if thou art right,   **555**
Tell me now, thou wretched wight,
Is there any other note
Hidden in thy shrill throat?
For thou art good for no other thing;
Thou knowest nought but chattering.
Thou art little and unstrong,
And thy garb is nothing long.
What dost thou of good to men?
No more than does a wretched wren.
Of thee no real good may be had;
Thou criest as if thou hadst gone mad,
And when thy piping is all past,
No more crafts hast thou at last.

Alfred said—and he was wise—
(Well he might, 'tis true advice)
'No man, for a mere song,
Is worthy of praise for very long,
For that man is a worthless thing
Who can nothing do but sing.'
So thou art but a worthless thing,
In thee is nought but chattering,
Dim thy hue, and foul withal,
Like a little sooty ball.
Thou art not fair, thou art not strong,
Thou art not thick, thou art not long;
Thou hast missed all fairhead
And little is thy goodhead....
Yet I do many a kind deed   605
That can help men in their need;
I catch a mouse from my barn-door perch
And at the dusk-hour in the church,
For dear to me is Christ's house;
I cleanse it from the foul mouse...."
The nightingale at this word   659
From her wits was well nigh stirred,
And deeply thought, in her heart's mood,
If aught else she understood,
If she could do aught but sing
That might help to another thing.
Hereto she must an answer find
Or withal be left behind.
It is very hard to fight
Against the truth, against the right....

Nightingale:

"Owl, thou askest me," she said,   707
"If I can do another deed

Save singing in the summer-tide
And bringing bliss thus far and wide.
Why ask me of this craft of mine?
Better it is than all of thine.
Better is one song that I sing
Than all thy kind could ever bring.
Listen while I tell thee more:
Man was born—knowest thou wherefore?
For the bliss of heaven's days
Where there is song and mirth always.
There a man will come with strife
Who does any good in life.
Therefore in Holy Church I sing
When songs of clerks begin to ring,
That a man may think through my song
Whither he goes and will be long.
That mirth he will not soon forget
But thereon think and ponder yet.
And there in Church he will learn this,
How merry is heaven with its bliss.
Canons, clerks and monks we see
Wherever holy houses be
Who in the middle of the night
Sing their praise of heaven's light,
And priests in upland places sing
When light of day begins to spring,
And I help them as I may,
I sing with them by night and day,
The gladder are they all for me
And their song will swifter be.
I warn men to their good
That they may be blithe of mood,
And bid them seek every day
The song that will not pass away.

Now must thou, Owl, sit and cling,
In this there is no chattering.
I grant that we go for doom
Before the very Pope of Rome. . . ."

Owl:

"Thinkest thou easily to bring   854
Men to heaven who only sing?
Nay, nay! For thou shalt soon know
Men must weep before they go
For their sins, ere they come there.
I counsel men to be aware,
And to weep before they sing
Who strive to come to Heaven's King.
There is no man without a sin,
Thus, if he would heaven win,
He must amend with bitter tears
And turn to sour the sweet of years.
Thereto I help him, God knows well,
No silly trifle will I tell.
For all my song is of longing,
And mingled somewhat with weeping,
So that by me a man begins
To groan, repenting of his sins.
So I urge him with my song
To groan for all his guilt and wrong.
So, if thou dispute this thing,
I weep better than thou canst sing. . . .
Why twittest thou me for my might,   1187
For my wit and my insight?
For I am witty and full wise,
I know what in the future lies,
I know of hunger and thieves strong,
And if a man shall yet live long,

If a wife shall lose her mate,
I know if wars and dangers wait.
I know who will soon be hung,
Or by some foul death downflung;
When men meet on the battlefield
I know then which side will yield.
I know if a tree shall blow,
I know if the corn shall grow,
I know if ships shall drown at sea,
I know if smiths smite evilly.... [9]
For Alfred said a wise word   1223
That every man should lay in hoard:
'If thou seest thy foe before he come,
All his strength is well nigh numb.' "

The dispute then turns upon the good that the two birds
do to women who are in distress. The Nightingale be-
friends young girls, the Owl comforts unhappy wives.[10]

Nightingale:

"I cannot from pity cease   1445
When I see the drawn face
That love brings on the youngling;
Of mirth to such I cannot sing,
But I teach them by my song
That wrong love will not last long.
For my song soon passes by
As love that does but lightly lie
On children, and as soon is dead
When the hot breath is fallen and fled.
I sing with them of time's swift flow,

[9] Blacksmiths were connected with magic in popular Teutonic tradition,
in which earth and iron were endowed with preternatural powers.
[10] This form of *contentio* between different classes of women, like arguments on the theme of the *mal-mariées,* was common in French poetry.

Beginning high and ending low,
And let my singing downward fall
A little while, then gone is all.
The maid knows by my silence long
That her love is like my song;
'Tis but a little breath, she knows,
That soon comes and soon goes.
That child, through me, has understood
And turns her folly into good,
She sees well, by my song,
That dizzy love will not last long...."

Owl:

"Many a merchant, many a knight   **1575**
Loves and holds his wife aright,
And so does many a bond man;
His good wife does the best she can
And serves him well at bed and board
With fair deed and fair word,
And eagerly she tries to find
The thing most pleasing to his mind.
The lord must then go far indeed
And fare abroad to serve their need.
Unblithe that good wife, troubling
For her lord's hard journeying,
Sits and sighs and grieves apart
In her sorrow-troubled heart.
And all is for her own lord's sake,
Her days of care, her nights awake.
Such is her longing all the while
That every step seems like a mile.
When all are sleeping round about
I listen there, alone, without,
And knowing of her sore mood

I sing at night, for her good,
And for her sake. Thus all my song
Is turned into a mourning long.
Of her sorrow I bear a share
So I am welcome to her there;
And so I help her as I may,
For she follows ever the right way...."

The Owl then makes the mistake of technically giving
the case away by admitting the validity of a former
argument of the Nightingale:

"Thou sayest men hate me heartily,   1607
And everyone is wroth with me;
With stones and sticks they threaten so
And beat and break me with a blow,
And when their knocks have slain me quite
On a hedge they hang me for a sight.
Then pies and crows I scare away
From the seed sown yesterday.
Though this be true, I do them good,
And for them I shed my blood;
I do them good by my death,
Wherefore thou dost waste thy breath.
When thou art dead and shrivelling
Thy death brings nought to anything;
I know not what good thou canst do,
Thou art nothing but a wretched shrew...."
The Nightingale heard all this now   1635
And hopped upon a blossomy bough,
She sat up higher than she did ere:

Nightingale:

"Owl," she said, "thou must take care,
For with thee I'll plead no more,

Thou hast mis-said true right and lore.
Thy boasting up to now has been
That thou art hateful to all men,
Thy crying and thy yodelling
Show that thou art a cursed thing.
Thou sayest that boys make thee a fool,
Catch thee and hang thee on a pole,
Pluck thee and shake thee shamefully,
And make a scarecrow out of thee.
I think that thou hast lost the game,
Thou boasteth of thine own shame;
I think that I have won the case,
Thou boastest of thine own disgrace."
Thereupon she raised her song
And sang so shrilly and so long
That far and near it might be heard.
And then to her flew every bird,
Thrush and throstle and woodewall,
All the birds both great and small.
They thought the nightingale had won,
That the Owl was all undone,
And so they sang with many an air;
Bliss among the leaves was there. . . .
The wren[11] was the wisest, so they said,   **1723**
For not in the woods had she been bred;
She had been brought up among men,
And their wisdom gathered then;
She might speak where'er she would,
Before the King himself she could.

Wren:

"Listen," quoth she, "let me speak. Cease!

[11] A widespread mediaeval tradition honored the wren as the king of birds, because he once outwitted the eagle.

What! Will you thus break the peace,
And do the King such a shame?
He is neither dead nor lame.
You both shall earn shame and harm
If you break the peace with your alarm.[12]
Let be, and both together come
Rightly now to meet your doom,
And with the doom let there be peace;
You promised that the feud should cease. . . ."

Nightingale:

"I have promised, true it is,   1745
That Master Nicholas, who is wise,
Shall judge the case between us two,
As I hope that he will do.
But where can we find him now?"
The wren sat on her linden bough.

Wren:

"What! Thou knowest not his home?
He dwelleth down at Portisham,
At a town in Dorsetshire,
On an outlet, where the sea is near,
And there he makes his dooms so true,
With wisdom frames and makes laws too,
And through his mouth and through his hand
'Tis better from here to the Scottish land,
To seek him is a little thing;
For he has only one living.
On his Bishop that is great shame

---

[12] Internal references such as this help us to date the poem. The King is probably Richard I, who was often rumored to be dead during his absence from England on the Crusade. The poet believes that he is living. The "peace" referred to may be the order established by Justiciar Hubert Walter, 1194. L.1091 refers to Henry I as already dead.

For all have heard of his name.
They have all heard of his deeds
Why will they leave him in his needs?
With them he should be more at home,
To teach them by his wisdom.
They should give him rents in many a place
That every man might see his face...."
With these words forth they fared,   **1789**
Without a horde, without a fyrd.
To Portisham they soon had come,
But how they fared, and of their doom
There's nothing more that I can say,
There's nothing more of my tale today.

Explicit.

COURTIERS' TRIFLES

The Owl and the Nightingale echoes as from far
away the sophistication of life at court. The whole court
itself is reflected in the personality of a single courtier,
that writer, trifler and churchman known as Walter
Mapes. He was witty, restless, passionate and elusive,
and so great was his reputation as a man of letters (or
poeta, as he called it, with typical indifference to mere
form) that books he probably never wrote are attributed to him, books as different from each other as the
stinging, raucous and often vile Goliardic verse satiriz-
ing the clergy, and the sprawling, gorgeous French
prose romances of the Arthurian cycle. One book alone
clearly bears his name, and it is enough.

De Nugis Curialium is an odd, glamorous micro-
cosm of the twelfth century as lived by men and women
who were caught in the meshes of the ephemeral while
still aware of the eternal. They are found in all ages, the

sophisticates who know better. Mapes' book, he says,
is to be read "for the sake of pastime or pleasure"; it is
made up of "savorless and sapless trifles," yet he is
writing in 1187, "a year cloudy with the cloud of the
times, and of the shadows of unhappiness, a year of fear
and of war, of sorrow and of burden, of blasphemy, of
grief." His work, like his thought, is a blend of fact and
fiction, of philosophy and necromancy, of history and
of legend, of sharp gossip and of dreamy wishful-think-
ing. He revels in legend, because "old copper is pre-
ferred to new gold," yet he prefaces many a tale with
the provoking claim: "I knew this man myself." Mapes
was a Welshman, and as such believed in fairies and
wrote *de apparitionibus fantasticis.*" He was a scholar
fresh from the schools of Paris; cool classical allusions
cross in his work with the tales brought by Crusaders
from the hot, fabulous East. The Cistercian Order was
the object of his fiercest hate, but he considered himself
none the less a churchman for that, or for his tainted
tales. He is as credulous as a child and as untouchable
as a cynic. He is sound even in his flippancy, and tragi-
cally aware of the true nature of his "trifles," for "our
Jerusalem is neither hence nor here." His light and
sarcastic pages are a strange blend of the lurid and the
sombre, and his gifts are the gifts of the storyteller. His
repertoire is wide. There is the charming fairy tale
(seriously believed) of Herla, the Welsh King, who
followed the pigmies into a mountainside and returned,
after a longer time than Rip Van Winkle, to find such
changes in the days of the Saxons that "he could scarce
sit his horse for wonder"; there is the gruesome and revolting tale of the enchanted cobbler of Constantinople
who did such deeds that "the very sea was sick with
loathing." Such contradictions are not astonishing in

a man who could write as follows of the court of Henry II:

Book I, Chapter 1: A Comparison of the King's Court to Hell

"I am in time, and I speak of time," said Augustine, and he adds, "I know not what time is." With a like wonder I can say that I am in the court, and I speak of the court, and I know not—God knows—what the court is. I know, however, that the court is not time, yet it is of time, mutable and various, local and erratic, never remaining in the same state. I know that when I go away I shall find when I return nothing, or almost nothing, of what I left behind; I am become a stranger abroad. The court is the same, but its members are changeable. If I describe the court as Porphyry defined genus, perhaps I shall not lie if I say that it is as a multitude having one principle. Surely we are an indefinite multitude, contending to please one another. Today we are one multitude; tomorrow we shall be another; the court has not changed, it is ever the same. It is the hundred-handed giant [Briareus] who though torn to pieces is still whole. It is the hundred-handed hydra of as many heads who scorns and brings to nought the labors of Hercules, who does not feel the hands of the invincible athlete, and—happier than Antaeus—has for its mother the earth, the sea, the sky, and multiplies its strength throughout the earth; it will not be dashed against the breast of Hercules; the universe multiplies its strength. When this Hercules wills, his will is done.

If we say concerning the court what Boethius truthfully said concerning Fortune, it is certain indeed that it alone is stable in the midst of change. To those alone is the court pleasing who seek its good graces. For it is she alone that bestows her grace; she loves not the lovable nor those who are deserving of love, and she gives her gifts to those who are unworthy of life. This is the favor that comes without cause, that remains without merit, that is present together with secret causes of shame. The just hand of the Lord, with His mystic fan, sifts out the wheat from the cockle, but the court no less carefully sifts out the cockle from the wheat. What the former prudently chooses the latter as imprudently rejects; and thus so many are the goads with which our master, Greed, drives us on, that laughter is banished by care. He who laughs is laughed at, and he who sits in sorrow seems wise.

III

A King of Four Castles

Here lies Arthur, once a
king, and a king to be.
MORTE ARTHURE

"LISTEN, LORDINGS, YOU SHALL HEAR . . ."; with these words the minstrel struck the strings, and Glee-wood spoke. Sometimes a gay promise followed, when "my tale is merrier than the nightingale"; more often a foreboding of tragedy, "if you would hear a high tale of life and death." Metrical romances were the people's entertainment, their moving-pictures thrown by the storyteller on the screen of unjaded imaginations, their radio-dials catching waves of feeling from east and west, from past and present. The traditional songs of the Anglo-Saxon *scop* almost faded from the air after the Conquest,[1] but the Norman troubadour set a new

---

[1] The old alliterative beat was, however, handed down by oral tradition, especially in the north, and the west where the inroads of the Danes had been less destructive. It revived with remarkable vigor in the fourteenth century, as will be seen in later chapters.

pattern. The easy, rapid, unending verses spread like a network from country to country, from town to village, from castle to cottage, and down the streets; they wove together the most divergent strands of a complex civilization in the simple process of providing enjoyment. "There was a king called Arthur," said a friar suddenly in the midst of an otherwise dull sermon, and his sleepy listeners were wide awake.

This Arthur, who is still overlord of the kingdom of romance, was once no king at all but a *dux bellorum,* champion of the British Celts against the invading Saxons in the sixth century. He owes his fairy-immortality to the fact that he lived in Wales, among a hero-worshipping people of vivid imagination, at a moment when old mythological magic was still alive and Christianity was a new inspiration. Arthur was the child of both realms. All that is known of him historically is found in a few baffling passages of the oldest chronicles. The first mention of him is in a ninth-century tangle of history and legend, the *Historia Britonum* of Nennius, in which the Roman patrician, Aurelius Ambrosius, is crossed with a Celtic magician to give us Merlin, and where Arthur is a Christian warrior of unlimited faith and prowess:

> Arthur and the Kings of Britain fought against them [the Saxons] strongly, and met them in twelve battles, but he himself was the leader of the armies. The first battle was at the mouth of the river which is called Glenni, the second, third, fourth and fifth battles were near another river called Duglas by the Britons, in the region of Linius; the sixth battle was on the river Bassas, the seventh in the wood Celidon, that is, Cat Coit Celidon. The eighth battle was near

Gurnion Castle in which Arthur carried the image of
the Blessed Mary ever Virgin upon his shoulders,
and the pagans were put to flight that day, and there
was great slaughter made of them through the power
of Our Lord Jesus Christ, and through the power
of the Blessed Virgin His Mother. The ninth battle
was at the City of Legion. The tenth battle was on
the bank of the river which is called Tribuit. The
eleventh battle was fought on the mountain which is
called Agned. The twelfth battle was fought on
Mount Badon in which nine hundred and sixty men
fell in one day at one attack of Arthur, and none
overthrew them save he alone, and in all battles he
was the victor.

In the *Annales Cambriae*, a Welsh Chronicle compiled
in the twelfth century but dating back to the fourth,
the note of tragic finality is touched:

Anno 516—The Battle of Mount Badon, in which
Arthur carried the cross of Our Lord Jesus Christ
for three days and three nights on his shoulders, and
the Britons were victorious.

Anno 537—Gueith Camlann, in which Arthur and
Medraut [Mordred] fell.

This is restrained and sober enough, but already the
Welsh love of the marvellous had invested its hero with
more than mortal qualities. The *Mirabilia* appended to
Nennius' history relates that:

There is another marvel in the region which is
called Buelt. There is a pile of stones, and one stone
on top of the heap with the footprint of a dog on it.
When they hunted the pig Troynt, Cabal, who was

the dog of the warrior Arthur, set his footprint in
the stone and Arthur afterwards gathered a pile of
stones under the stone in which was the footprint of
his dog, and it is called Carn Cabal. And men come
and carry away the stone in their hands for the space
of a day and a night, and the next day it is found
again upon its heap.

There is another marvel in the region which is
called Ercing. There is a burial-place near a foun-
tain, and the name of the man who is buried in the
mound is Licar Anir. He was the son of a soldier of
Arthur, and he himself killed him there and buried
him. And men come to measure the mound, sometimes
six feet in length, sometimes nine, sometimes twelve,
sometimes fifteen. Whatever length you measure it
at one time, you will not find it again of the same
measure. And this I have myself tried.

To the Norman chroniclers who began in the twelfth
century to record the history of the land they had so
lately made their own, Arthur was an enigma. William
of Malmesbury tried to divest him of myth, and to
leave him in his simple historic dignity, but even he was
unable to resist the fascinating supposition that Arthur
had not died at all. He relates in *De Rebus Gestis
Regum Anglorum*:

> On the death of Vortimer the strength of the
> Britons grew faint, their dwindled hopes shrank,
> and they would have been ruined had not Ambrosius,
> the last survivor of the Romans, who reigned after
> Vortigern, repressed the over-weening barbarians,
> through the prowess of the war-like Arthur. This is
> that Arthur of whom the trifling of the Britons talks
> nonsense even today, a man clearly worthy of being

acclaimed by true history, not dreamed of in fallacious tales, who long sustained his tottering land, and sharpened the broken minds of his fellow-citizens for war. Finally, at the siege of Mount Badon, trusting in an image of the Mother of the Lord which he had sewn upon his armor, falling single-handed upon nine hundred of the enemy, he put them to flight with incredible slaughter....

But the tomb of Arthur has no-where been seen, whence ancient songs fable that he is yet to come. But the tomb of Gawaine, as I have said, was found in the time of King William by the shore of the sea.

But Geoffrey of Monmouth (himself probably a Welshman, although a good Norman vassal) made no attempt to resist the charms of "British fabling." From the pages of the *Historia Regum Britaniae,* Arthur rides out on his agelong conquest, clad in anachronistic Norman armor, with the confused history of Britain and of Troy rolled into his ancestry. Nothing thereafter could stop his romantic progress. Geoffrey, who has been accused of being "the greatest liar in history," indicates his sources clearly enough:[2]

While turning over many and various matters in my mind, I fell upon the history of the kings of Britain, and I marvelled that in the accounts which

[2] In his edition of the *Historia Regum Britaniae* (Longmans, 1929) Acton Griscom makes a strongly documented plea for the genuinely historic importance of Geoffrey's work. He calls upon archaeology and ethnology as well as upon neglected manuscripts in defence of what has been too lightly dismissed by scholars as pure imagining. "I cannot escape the conviction that when scholars return to these primary sources, early British history will be found by them to have survived in legendary or story form, and that it can be recovered by diligent search and investigation" (p. 216). The same might be said even of the romances, and many another mediaeval story.

Gildas and Bede gave of them in their fine treatises,
I find nothing concerning the kings who lived here
before the Incarnation, although their deeds are
worthy of everlasting praise, and are blithely related
from memory by many people as though they had
been written down. While I was thinking thus,
Walter, Archdeacon of Oxford, a man of great eloquence and well versed in strange histories, gave
me a very ancient book in the British tongue which
relates the deeds of all of them, from Brutus to
Cadwallader, the son of Cadwallo, in a continuous
story and in a beautiful style. At his request, although I have never made myself a fine writer by
collecting florid phrases from other authors, I con-
sented to translate that book into Latin, content
with my own homely style.

In spite of the presence of Merlin and of the giant
of Saint Michel, in spite of the glamor of Celtic names
and the charms of Guinevere, Geoffrey's book is not
romance; it is the would-be history of a realm. Arthur
is a conqueror who makes an empire and ends his career
in defeat, though he is nowhere said to be dead. At his
coronation "he was a youth of fifteen, of unequalled
valor and generosity, of such inborn goodness and
grace that he was loved by all the people." When he
took to his wars he was a general who "called his followers and said: 'My brave countrymen, you have made
Britain the queen of thirty kingdoms,'... and they all
cried with one voice that they would rather die than
leave the field while he lived." And when the traitor
Mordred took Arthur's queen and usurped his throne,
there was a great battle in which "Arthur himself was

wounded mortally, and was carried to the isle of Avalon to be cured of his wounds."

Literature owes much to anachronism. Thanks to a lack of historical perspective, the fancy of one age may transform the fact of another into something rich and strange. Writers uninhibited by too much research, and with small sense of the orderly march of events, have found it as easy to make time flow backwards as to watch it move forward. That is how a great book can cause the idealism of one age to overflow its time limits, and to fill whole centuries before and after with its own light and color, its own purpose, achievement, and failure. Chivalry as a way of life lasted for only three hundred years; it rose in the twelfth century and broke to pieces in the fifteenth, when gunpowder made the armored knight a ridiculous figure on the battlefield. At either end of this period stands a great book, widening its sway. Geoffrey of Monmouth, at the beginning, extended chivalry backward, touching the sixth century with a glamor strange to it; Malory's *Morte Dartur*, at the other end, gathered up the long traditions of chivalry, both actual and enchanted, till his work became the source for all later writers who would keep King Arthur riding down the centuries.

But between Geoffrey and Malory, the tale passed through many transformations.[3] By the time of the second Henry, *amour courtois* had entered it. The presence of this subtle, poisonously fair thing in mediaeval literature is mysterious; its roots go far back in history and are alien to European soil. It first manifested itself as a distinct movement at the Provençal court of Eleanore of Aquitaine, and as that dark queen moved to the north of France and thence to England, the "courts

---

[3] See Appendix III.

of love" followed her. Their origin is found in a fantastic blend of Roman cynicism and Oriental emotion. It was the fashion during the twelfth-century renaissance to play with Ovid, and his *Ars Amatoria* was taken a little too seriously in literature and in life. It gave a code and a form to the more subtle influences which crept into the chivalric order from Arabia through the Moorish poets of Spain, like Al Hallaj, who inspired such *trouvères* as Bernard de Ventadour. It may well be that this passionate, un-Christian travesty of the highest Christian ideals was in reality a poetic veil drawn over the Catharist heresies then rife in southern France.[4]

In any case, it was from France that "courtly love" found its way into England.[5] Chrétien de Troies, poet of Marie of Champagne, the daughter of Queen Eleanore, brought Lancelot upon the scene, and with him a fairy lake, psychological complexity, and the tragedy of stark infidelity; and once Lancelot is in the tournament, "no one can take his eyes from him, wherever he is." The castle of Joyous Guard faces Camelot. In the meantime the land of Arthur's birth had not forgotten him; from Tintagel Castle the immemorial dark pagan tale of fatality, *Tristan and Iseult,* was drawn

[4] This is the theory of Denis de Rougemont; see *Love in the Western World* (Harcourt, Brace, 1939), pp. 71 ff. This brilliant study of the "cult of passion" as expressed in the myth of Tristan and Iseult and of its religious implications, illuminates many baffling passages of mediaeval literature.

[5] For a contemporary presentation of this far-reaching "fashion," see *The Art of Courtly Love,* by Andreas Capellanus, a French priest in the service of Marie of Champagne (translated by John Jay Parry, Columbia University Press, 1941). It is hard to know whether it is irony or honesty, or sheer inconsistency that makes the author say, at the end of his lengthy, elegant and revolting book: "If you will study carefully this little treatise of ours and understand it completely and practice what it teaches, you will see clearly that no man ought to misspend his days in the pleasures of love."

into the cycle. In Wales itself the oldest versions, rooted in folklore, with Sir Kay and Sir Bedevere in their
first high places, were retold so often that some of them
crossed into Norman French and returned again, with
silken embroidery on the stark stuff of Celtic legend,
before they were written down as the *Mabinogion.*[6]
Here, Arthur is at times the lusty huntsman out for "the
great pig"; at other times, he has nothing to do but
"sit on a seat of green rushes on a covering of flame-
colored satin, with a cushion of red satin under his elbow." But the Celtic spell is on every story, sad as bird-
song in the house of the open window, grim as knives
in flesh, lovely as Olwen, in whose footsteps white tre-
foils grew.

There is another castle, Corbenic, home of the
Grail;[7] it is the center of the strangest and most passionate theme of all: the spiritual, almost mystical,
quest that lifts the already complex story to a spiritual
plane without losing any of its other elements, thus
making the romance as incongruous as real life usually
is. *Le Grand San Graal* [8] relates how Joseph of Arimathea[9] had come in a glamor of moonlight over the sea,

[6] The name given to a collection of stories in a Welsh manuscript of the
fourteenth century known as *The Red Book of Hergest.*
[7] The cause of the introduction of this intensely religious theme into such
terrestrial romance is not clearly understood. Some French scholars claim
that the *Queste del Saint Graal* is the work of Cistercian monks, based
remotely on the preaching of Saint Bernard of Clairvaux. See *Etude sur
la Queste del Saint Graal,* by Albert Pauphilet (Paris, 1921), and *La
Mystique de la Grace dans la Queste del Saint Graal,* by Etienne Gilson,
Romania L; 323-47.
[8] This is the title of the first "branch" of an enormous cycle of French
prose romances written by Anglo-Normans in the twelfth century, and
known as the Vulgate Cycle. Some are attributed to Walter Mapes. They
are largely based on earlier metrical versions, also in French, by such
writers as Béroul, de Borron and Thomas.
[9] The presence of Joseph of Arimathea in British history shows the long
influence of such apocryphal gospels as the *Descensus ad Infernos.*

riding on his own shirt. He housed the cup of the Last Supper at Glastonbury[10] and so provoked incredible adventures. Once Arthur's knights had glimpsed the cup, there was no more rest; Galahad and Parceval were in the cycle. Thus by the early thirteenth century all the elements of the tale were spinning round and round on themselves, and the later versions evolved.

LAYAMON'S BRUT

Not one of the versions so far mentioned was written in English, but at this very time an author who lived remote from every kind of court or castle wrote the first, and perhaps the greatest, version of the Arthur story in the tongue of the Saxons against whom Arthur had first fought. Unlike most writers of his time, Layamon the priest of Arnley does not mind telling his readers about himself in the charming introduction to his tremendous Chronicle. It was c.1205 when he finally laid down his feather after its journey of some 16,000 long lines over bookskin. Of the sources that he names, he blithely ignored Bede and Saint Alban and Saint Austin, and relied upon Wace.[11] But Layamon's lines were neither French nor feudal, like those of Wace. He had other sources within himself, as the poem reveals. Living near the borders of Wales, in the Arthur country, he knew floating Welsh legends unknown to Geoffrey—the elves at Arthur's christening, and the queens at his passing—but he himself was of Anglo-

---

[10] Glastonbury, where the hollows were covered by water at high tide, was the original Isle of Avalon. Here, presumably, the oldest chapel in England was built; here, too, was the disputed tomb of Arthur, but as he did not die, how could the tomb be his? Cf. the chapter called "Glastonbury" in *Men, Women and Places,* by Sigrid Undset (Knopf, 1939).

[11] Wace was an Anglo-Norman who versified the *Historia* of Geoffrey of Monmouth with courtly additions of his own.

Saxon strain. He was one in spirit with the old writer of *Beowulf*, whom he echoes time and again. In his waters "monsters bathe," there is "play of elves in the hideous pool"; his warriors are "deprived of life-day." Phrases of the old heroic poetry of the Heptarchy flash out—"trumpets sounded, breasts were spear-pierced," and "the fight was most sturdy." Above all, Arthur is a warrior king, close to his people's heart in the old Germanic way. It is fitting that the most monumental work on King Arthur in the English language should so present him, free from the languor and taint of the French romances.

Layamon's prosody, morover, is old English, though the couplets of Wace before his eyes played havoc with his forms and introduced frequent rhymes. But his defects merely give the vigor of experiment to his genius as a writer; he is a storyteller of sensitive imagination and warm heart. His interminable Chronicle glows with unspent joy in his purpose "to tell of the English their noble deeds." Only about one third of the *Brut* deals with Arthur, but it is good to see the king in his place as part of legendary English history.

A priest there was in the land,   Layamon was his name,
He was Leovenath's son   —may the Lord be gracious to him.
He dwelt at Arnley,   at a noble church
Upon Severn's banks   —good it seemed there to him—
Fast by Radstone.   There he read books.
It came into his heart,   and into his deep thought
That of the English   he would tell the noble deeds;
What they were called   and whence they came,

Who first possessed   the English land
After the flood   which from the Lord came,
That killed all here   that it quick found,
Save Noah and Sem,   Japhet and Cham
And their four wives   with them in the ark.
Layamon began to journey   wide round this land,
And gained the princely books   that he took for
    patterns.
He took the English book   that Saint Bede made,
Another he took in Latin   that Saint Alban made,
And the fair Saint Austin   who brought Baptism
    here.
A third book he took   and laid it in the midst,
That a French clerk made,   Wace was he called,
One who could well write,   and who gave it to the
    noble
Eleanore who was Queen   of the high King
    Henry.
Layamon laid down the books,   and the leaves he
    turned,
Lovingly he beheld them,   —may the Lord be
    gracious to him.
A feather he took in his fingers   and he wrote on
    bookskin,
And the true words   set he together,
And the three books   he pressed into one.
Now prays Layamon   every noble man
For Almighty God's sake,   who reads this book
And learns these runes,   that he say together
These soothfast words   for his father's soul
Who brought him forth,   and for his mother's soul
That bore him to be a man,   and for his own soul,
That it be the better.   Amen.

The tale then begins with Brutus,[12] grandson of Aeneas, who after many wars and adventures in Italy and Greece, is promised by Diana that the fair isle of Albion shall be his. He sails thither and wins it from the giants who possessed it of old. Then comes prosperity.

Brutus bethought him,   and beheld his folk,   1001
Beheld the mountains   fair and great.
Beheld he the meadows   that were very beautiful,
Beheld he the waters   and the wild beasts,
Beheld he the fish,   beheld he the fowls,—
Beheld he the leas   and the lovely wood,
The wood as it bloomed,   beheld the corn as it grew.
All he saw in the land   that was dear to his heart.
Thought he of Troy   where his kin suffered trouble,
And he journeyed through the land   and scanned the country.

He found a winsome spot   near the water
Where soon he reared   a rich burgh,
With bowers and with halls,   with high stone walls.
When the burgh was made   then was it mighty,
When the burgh was well done   he put a name on it;
He gave it for a dear name   Troy the New,
To remember the race   from whence he came.

[12] Throughout the Middle Ages, English chronicles were entitled *Brut*. The word refers to the Brutus here mentioned, eponymous founder of the British people. No wonder that mediaeval Englishmen sided with the Trojans against the Greeks! Actually the word Britain is thought to be derived from "Pretannic Isle," the name given to it by Pythias of Massila on his voyage of discovery in the fourth century B.C. The word is taken from the language of the Brythonic Celts whom he found there, and means "painted men."

Eventually this city became known as London. Generations passed and strange deeds were done by British kings, which accounts for the names of many rivers in England. At last came a king of well-known name:

Sixty years had Leir[13]   This land to wield.   1462
The King had three daughters   by his noble
     Queen;
He had no son,   whereof he was sorry,
His dignity to hold;   but the three daughters.
The eldest daughter was Gornoille,   the second
     Ragau,
The third Cordoille.   She was the youngest sister,
Fair of face.   To her father she was dear
As his own life.   Then the King grew old
And weakened in power;   and he then bethought
     him
What he might do   with his kingly realms
After his day.   He said to himself
An evil thing: "I will give my power
To all my daughters,   and give them my kingdom,
Shared among my children.   But first I will try
Which is my best friend;   she shall have the best
     share."

Gornoille and Ragau answer with lies, for they were "most wary, as women are everywhere"; and he gives them each part of his kingdom.

[13] The story of King Lear had been told in almost every century before it reached its climax in Shakespeare. It is a primeval Celtic legend put into Latin by Geoffrey, into French by Wace, and into English by Layamon, from whom it passed into a series of Chronicles. Shakespeare found it in Holinshed's *Chronicles*. He alone saw that the tale had an essentially tragic note, and he made it end accordingly. The earlier versions ended happily.

Yet would not the King   his folly leave;   1513
He bade come before him   his daughter Cordoille.
She was of all the youngest,   of a truth the wisest,
And the King loved her more   than both the
    others.
Cordoille heard the lies   that her sisters told the
    King.
She took a faithful oath   that she would not lie;
She would tell her father the truth,   were it lief
    were it loath.
Then quoth the old King   —miscounsel followed
    him—
"Now will I hear   of thee, Cordoille,
—So help thee, Apollo—   how dear is my life to
    thee?"
Then answered Cordoille,   loud and no whit still,
With game and with laughter   to her loved father:
"Thou art dear to me as my father,   I to thee as
    thy daughter;
I have soothfast love for thee,   for we are close of
    kin,
And—as I expect mercy—   I will tell thee more:
Thou art as much worth   as thou art master of,
And by as much as thou havest   so will men love
    thee;
For soon is he loathed   who has but little."
Thus said the maid Cordoille,   then she sat very
    still.
Then was the King wrathful   for he was not
    pleased,
For he weened in his thought   that it was for some
    evil
That she held him unworthy   and would not honor
    him,

As had her two sisters   who spoke lies.
Then King Leir turned as black   as a black cloth,
And his skin and his hue turned;   he was greatly
    hurt.
By his wrath he was stunned   and fell in a swoon.
Slowly he uprose   —the maiden was afraid—
Then forth it all broke;   it was evil that he spoke.
"Hearken, Cordoille,   I will tell thee my will.
Of my daughters thou wert dearest,   now thou art
    loathliest.". . .
Oft was Cordoille in woe,   never worse than then;
                                                    1552
Woe was in her heart   for her father's wrath.
She went into her bower   and often sat sore,
For she would not lie   to her loved father.
The maiden was shamefast,   her father she shun-
    ned;
She did the best she could   and abode in her bower,
And suffered heart-care   and mourned much.

Eventually Leir and Cordoille are reconciled and she
becomes the prosperous queen of all Britain.

Then the centuries move on; the scene swings up and
down England, into Cornwall and Wales, and over
the seas to Spain, to Norway, to France. Then at last
come the Romans under Julius Caesar, who here meets
with more adventures than he ever dreamed of relating
in the *Commentaries;* and then:

In Cymbeline's day,[14]   who was King in Britain,
                                                    4532
There came to this middle-earth   a maiden's Son;

[14] In his drama *Cymbeline* Shakespeare does not allude to this old belief
that word of the birth of Christ (which did actually occur in the reign of
this king) was brought at once to Britain.

Born was He in Bethlehem   of the best of all
    maids.
He is named Jesus Christ   through the Holy
    Ghost,
The joy of the whole world,   Wielder of angels.
Father He is in Heaven,   mankind's comfort,
Son He is on earth,   of the noble maiden,
And the Holy Ghost   He holds within Himself.
He gives the good spirit   to those who are dear to
    Him,
As he did to Peter   who was a poor fisher,
And made him the highest   of all mankind.
Cymbeline, Briton's King,   was a good man
    through all things;
And he lived here,   two and twenty years.
In his days there lived a man   in this land,
Strange things followed him;   he was named Teil-
    esin.
They held him as wise   for his wit-full craft,
And they all believed   what Teilesin said.
He told marvels enough,   and they all found it
    truth;
He told them each year   what was to come.
The King sent after him   twelve wise knights;
Bade them come to him,   that they should do no
    otherwise;
And they brought him soon   before the folk-King.
The King then met him   and fair greeted him.
"So help me, my head and my chin,   welcome art
    thou, Teilesin,
And liefer thy safety to me   than a thousand
    pounds."
Then answered Teilesin   and thus said to Cymbe-
    line,

"So may I thrive.   Thou shalt it well bestow."
Then was Cymbeline glad   and said to Teilesin:
"To my land there is come   strange folk-runes
From the land of Jerusalem,   things wrought in
  Bethlehem.
A little child is born   in that land,
Great and strong, with awe;   tokens are in the
  stars,
In the moon and the sun,   dread among mankind."

Eventually Christianity is established among the Britons by King Lucius, wellborn and well-beloved. He heard what Petrus had done in Rome, and what martyrdom he had suffered. So he sent to Pope Eleutherius to say that he would bend to Christ's law. And when the Pope heard this, "there was no man alive that was so blithe." Lucius set God's peace in his land.

The years passed; after bitter fighting Britain was cleansed of the Rome-folk, Saint Alban was slain in persecution, Helen,[15] King Coel's daughter, "wisest woman who knew good craft," married Constance, the Roman, and her son was Constantine the Emperor; and when Vortigern was King, "three ships good came with the flood," led by Hengest, fairest of all knights. And in the tangled reigns of Vortigern and Vortimer, Rowena, daughter of Hengest, who drank "waissal" and then poured out poison for the death of kings, passed in and out, the spirit of evil beauty, till knives were drawn under the shadow of Stonehenge (made of stones by the giants in Ireland) and chaos filled the land. Then Merlin, fatherless child, brought magic in-

---

[15] The story of Saint Helen, who found the Cross of Christ in Jerusalem in the fourth century, was especially popular in England because of the tradition that she was a British princess. See "Elene" in *Word-Hoard*, p. 213.

to Christendom, and in time Arthur, son of Uther Pendragon, was born in Tintagel Castle; and Merlin said
of him that he should live:

"As long as forever;   dead he shall be never.   9425
The while the world stands   his glory shall last,
And he shall in Rome   wield power over thanes,
All they shall bow to him   that dwell in Britain;
And of him gleemen   shall sing good things.". . .

The time came that was chosen   for Arthur to be
    born;   9627
As soon as he came on earth   the elves took him.
They enchanted the child   with enchantments
    strong,
They gave him might   to be the best knight,
They gave him a second thing,   to be a strong
    king,
They gave him a third thing,   that he should live
    long,
They gave to that king's child   gifts that were
    good,
That he might be the most generous   of all men
    living.
These things the elves gave him,   and the child
    throve.

Arthur grows up in Armorica, in ignorance of his pa-
rentage, until the death of Uther Pendragon. Then:

The Britons full soon   took Bishops three,   9941
And seven riders   strong in wisdom.
Forth they hastened   into Brittany,
And then full soon   to Arthur they came.
"Hail be thou, Arthur,   noblest of knights.
Uther greeted thee   when he came to die,

And bade that thou shouldst,   thyself in Britain,
Hold right laws   and help thy folk,
And keep this kingdom   as a good king should do,
Put thy foes to flight   and drive them from the
    land.
And he prayed to help thee   the mild son of God,
That thou mayest do well   and hold the land from
    God.
For dead is Uther Pendragon,   and thou art Ar-
    thur his son,
And dead is the other,   Aurelius his brother."
These things they told,   and Arthur sat full still.
At times he was pale   and wan of hue,
And at times he was red   and stirred in heart.
Then it all outbroke,   it was good that he spoke;
Then he spoke outright,   Arthur the noble
    knight:
"Lord Christ, God's Son,   be Thou now my
    help,
That I may in my life   hold good laws."
Fifteen years was Arthur old   when these tidings
    were told,
And all had been well spent,   for he was wisely
    taught.
Arthur forthright   called every knight,
Bade them take their weapons,   their horses saddle
With great speed,   for he would fare straight way
Into Britain.   To the sea went the thanes,
At Michael's Mount   with a great host.
The sea set them on the strand,   at Southampton
    they came to land.
Forth he went riding,   Arthur the mighty,
Right to Silchester;   there it seemed good to him.
There was the British host   boldly gathered.

Great was the bliss   when Arthur came to the burgh;
There was blast of horns,   and men most glad.
There they raised to be king   Arthur the young.
When Arthur was king   —hear a marvellous thing—
He was the most generous   of all men living,
A knight with the best,   wondrously keen.
To the young he was father,   to the old a comfort,
And to the unwise   wondrously stern.
To him was wrong loathly,   the right ever dear.
Each of his cupbearers   and his bower-thanes
And his bower-knights   bore gold on his hand,
On back and in bed   clad with gold web.
He had never a cook   who was not a champion good,
Nor any knight's swain   who was not a bold thane.

Arthur began a series of conquests, overcoming king-lets from burgh to burgh, till all Britain came under his wise and strong reign. Only King Childric resisted him:

Arthur with his fyrd   marched towards the burgh.
                                10289
And Arthur bade his knights   by days and by nights
That they should go as still   as though they would steal,
Glide over the land   and all their noise leave,
Trumpets and horns   should they all cease.
Arthur took a knight,   a bold man and bright,
And sent him to Lincoln   to his loved men,
And to them in sooth   should he say with his mouth

That Arthur would come,   the noblest king,
In the middle-night   with many a good knight.
"And ye within,   then be ye aware
That when you hear the din   the gates you unpin,
And burst from the burgh   and fell your foes
And smite down Childric   the strong and the
    mighty,
And we shall tell them   British tales."
It was in the middle-night   when the moon shone
    full bright
Arthur with his fyrd   hastened to the burgh.
His folk was as still   as though they would steal;
Forth they went gliding   till they saw Lincoln.
Then called out again   Arthur the keen man:
"Where be ye my knights,   my bold warriors?
See ye the tents   where Childric lies afield,
Colgrim and Badulf   with bold strength,
And the Alemanish folk   that has harmed us so,
And the Saxish folk   that promises sorrow."

The attack was made. Childric was defeated and fled
into hiding, whence he sent an embassy announcing his
surrender. After this, Arthur, Briton's darling,
reached out over the seas, and conquered land after land,
and for the keeping of peace the Round Table came to
be made:

It was on a Yule Day   that Arthur in London lay.
                                          11368

To him there were come   out of all his kingdom
Men of Britain,   of Scotland,
Of Ireland,   of Iceland,
And all the land   that Arthur had in hand,
All the highest thanes   with horses and with
    swains.

There were seven kings' sons   with five hundred
   knights come,
Beside the household   that followed Arthur.
Each had in heart   proud thoughts,
And thought himself better   than all his comrades.
The folk were of many lands,   there was envy
   great,
For one held himself high,   the next one higher.
Then trumpets were blown   and tables spread,
Men brought water on the floor   in golden bowls,
And then soft cloths   all of white silk,
Then sat Arthur down,   and by him Guinevere
   the Queen;
Then sat the earls   and then the barons,
And then the knights,   as each one was placed.
And men high-born   the meat then bore,
Straight forthright   to every knight,
Then towards the thanes,   then towards the swains,
Then towards the carriers   there at the board.
The men were enraged   and blows were rife.
First they threw the loaves   while they lasted,
Then the silver bowls   all filled with wine,
Then with their fists   at each other's necks.

Bloodshed ensued, and Arthur threatened dire punishment to the next offenders. The dead bodies were carried out for burial, and all then returned to the banquet.

Then men blew the trumpets   with a merry song;
                                  11437
Were they lief were they loath,   each took water
   and cloth
And then sat down   in peace at the boards,
All for dread of King Arthur,   noblest of kings.
Cupbearers in throng,   gleemen in song,

Harps rang out,   the host was in joy.
Thus full seven nights   was the host feasted.
Then is told in their tale   that the King went to
    Cornwall,
And there came to him   a crafty workman,
And he met him there   and greeted him fair:
"Hail be thou, Arthur,   noblest of kings.
I am thine own man,   to many lands have I gone;
I know wood-working,   many wondrous crafts.
I have heard told   new tidings beyond seas,
How at the board thy knights   had many fights
On a midwinter's day,   and many folk fell.
For their great pride   they wrought murder-play,
And for their high race   each would sit higher.
But I will work for thee   a board most fair,
And there may sit   sixteen hundred men,
All turn about,   and no man without,
Without and within,   man against man,
And when thou wilt ride   thou mayest take it,
And set it where thou wilt,   after thy will."

Thus was the Round Table made after four weeks, and
it brought peace and equality to Arthur's company of
knights, and soon names known through the centuries
appeared around it. "Then was Walwaine (Gawaine)
a little child, and so was the other, Mordred his brother." But still Arthur's conquests went on, and thus in
the course of battle he learned that a giant on Mont
St. Michel had carried off Helen, King Howel's daughter. He climbed the mount and watched his chance from
behind a tree:

The while came the Giant   and hastened to his fire,
                                                12964
He bare on his back   a burden great.

There were twelve swine   tied together
With great withies   all wreathed in one.
Down he threw the dead swine,   himself sat there-
    by,
His fire he built up   and great trees laid on it.
Six swine he drew to him   and laughed at the wom-
    an.
He drew out the embers,   the flesh he roasted,
And six swine he ate   ere he rose from his seat
All besmeared with ashes   —evil were the viands.
And then he roared   and rattled mightily,
And lay by the fire   and stretched out his limbs.
Let us leave now the Giant   and go to the King.
Arthur by the water   took weapons in hand,
And the Earl Bedivere,   good knight wise and
    ware,
And the third was Kay,   the king's steward and
    kin.
O'er the water they came,   weaponed with the best,
And mounted the hill   with all their might,
Until they hastened   near to the fire.
The Giant lay and slept,   the woman sat and wept.
Arthur drew near   beside his comrades,
Forbade them by their limbs   and by their dear
    lives
That none be so keen   that he should come near
Unless they saw   that there were great need.
Bedivere stood there   and Kay his comrade;
Arthur stood forth,   sturdy-mooded warrior,
Till he came to the floor   where the Giant lay and
    slept.
Ever was Arthur   void of fear,
That was clear-shown now   —strange though it
    seem—

For Arthur might there   have hewn down the
    Giant,
Slain the monster   there where he slept.
But Arthur in no wise   would touch him while he
    slept,
Lest in far-off days   he might hear upbraiding.
Then called Arthur anon,   noblest of kings:
"Arise, arise, fiend-foe!   to thy fated going!
Now shall we avenge   the death of my
    kinswoman."
Before the King   had full said this
The Giant upstarted   and grasped his great club,
And thought with a blow   to dash Arthur to
    pieces.
But Arthur drew high   his shield over his helm,
And the Giant smote thereon   till it all shivered,
And Arthur struck at him   in haste with his sword,
And whipped the chin off him   with both the jaws,
And started him behind a tree   that there stood
    near,
And the Giant smote swiftly   and hit him not,
But he smote the tree   and drove his club to bits.
And Arthur swiftly   ran about the tree.
The Giant was very heavy   and Arthur was
    swifter,
And overtook the Giant   and heaved up his good
    brand
And smote the thigh off him,   and the Giant down
    fell.
And Arthur stood and beheld,   and the foe began
    to speak:
"Lord, Lord, give me truce!   Who is it that fights?
I thought that no man   in the world's realm
Might thus lightly   lay me down in the fight,

Save it were Arthur,   noblest of all Britons;
Yet was I never of Arthur   sore afraid."
Then said to him Arthur,   noblest of kings:
"I am Arthur the King,   Britons' darling."

Then Arthur went to Rome to finish his conquest of the world, leaving his kingdom and his queen in the keeping of his nephew, Mordred. He became emperor of the universe, then turned towards home. On the way he stopped on the shore of the Channel to wait for a favorable wind.

There came in those times   a proud man riding,
                            14009
Bringing tidings   to Arthur the King
From Mordred, his sister's son;   to Arthur he was welcome,
For he thought that he brought   tidings that were good.
Arthur that long night   lay and spoke with the young knight
Who never said to him   in truth how it fared.
When it was day in the morning   and the warriors were stirring,
Arthur rose up   and stretched out his arms;
He arose and then sat   as though he were very sick.
Then asked him a fair knight: "Lord, how hast thou fared this night?"
Arthur then answered   —in heart he was uneasy—
"This night in my sleep,   as I lay in my bower
I dreamed a dream,   and sorry I am.
I dreamed that men lifted me   high on my hall;
On the hall I was astride   as though I would ride.

All the land that I have   I oversaw,
And Gawaine sat before me,   a sword he bore in
   hand.
Then came Mordred faring   with unnumbered
   folk,
He bore in his hand   a war-axe strong.
He began to hew   most hardily,
And to hew down the posts   that held up the hall.
Then I saw Guinevere,   woman dearest to me,
And the whole hall-roof   she drew down with her
   hands,
And the hall fell down   and I fell to the ground,
And my right arm broke;   then said Mordred,
'Take that!'
Adown fell the hall,   Gawaine began to fall,
And fell to the earth,   his arms broken both.
And I grasped my dear sword   in my own left
   hand,
And smote off Mordred's head,   that it bounded in
   the field. . . .
And so I have all night   thought of my dream,
                                        14056
For I know indeed   that gone is all my bliss,
For all my life   grief must I bear.
Well-a-way that I have not here   Guinevere my
   Queen!". . .
And with that word forthright   then answered the
   knight: 14077
"I say the truth, dear King,   for I am thy under-
   ling.
Thus hath Mordred done;   thy Queen he hath
   taken,
And hath set thy fair land   in his own hand.". . .
Then they sat all still   in Arthur's hall,   14088

There was heart-soreness   in the mighty King.
Then were British men   unmanned for that,
Till after a time   their voices were astir.
Wide might be heard   the cries of the Britons
That they would undo   Mordred and the Queen.

They crossed the Channel and pursued Mordred to Camelford.

That place is called Camelford   —ever more will
    last that word—   **14278**
And at Camelford were gathered   sixty thousand,
And more thousands thereto,   Mordred was their
    lord.
Then thither went riding   Arthur the mighty,
With unnumbered folk,   fated though they were.
Upon the Tambre   they drew together,
Heaved up their war-flags,   marched as one,
Locked their long swords,   laid them on helmets;
Fire sprang out,   spears splintered,
Shields shivered   and shafts were broken.
There fought all together   unnumbered folk.
Tambre was in flood   with measureless blood;
In the fight no man knew   one warrior from
    another,
Who did worst or best,   so was the battle mingled.
For each slew downright,   were he swain were he
    knight.
Then was Mordred slain,   done his life-day,
And many a knight   lay slain in the fight.
Then were slain   all the boldest men,
Arthur's household,   high and low,
And the Britons all   of Arthur's board,
And all his fosterlings   of many kingdoms.

And Arthur was wounded   with a war-spear
    broad;
Fifteen he had,   deadly wounds,
In the least of them   you might thrust two gloves.
There were no more   left from the fight
Of two hundred thousand men   that lay hewn in
    pieces,
Save Arthur the King alone,   and two of his
    knights. . . .
Then Arthur was wounded   wondrous sore. 14306
There came a young man   that was of his kin,
He was Cador's son,   the Earl of Cornwall;
Constantine was his name,   he was dear to the
    King.
Arthur gazed on him   as he lay on the ground,
And said these words   with sorrowful heart:
"Constantine, thou art welcome,   thou art Cador's
    son.
I bequeath to thee here   my own kingdom,
To guard my Britons   to thy life's end,
And keep strong the laws   that have stood in my
    day,
And all the good laws   of the days of Uther.
And I will fare to Avalon   to the fairest of
    maidens,
To Argante the Queen,   the sheenest of elves,
And she will heal   and make sound my wounds
And make me whole   with healing drenches.
Then will I come   to my own kingdom
And dwell with the Britons   in great bliss."
And after these words   there came from the sea
A short boat gliding,   cutting the waves,

And two women therein   wondrously dight;
They took Arthur anon   and bare him forth,
And soft laid him down,   and glided away.
And there came to pass   what Merlin of old said,
That great care would come   of Arthur's
    forthfaring.
Britons believe yet   that he is alive,
Dwelling in Avalon   with the fairest of elves,
And the British look still   to see Arthur coming.
There is no man born   of a noble maiden
Who can say more   in truth of Arthur.
But once was a man   whose name was Merlin;
He promised in words   —his words were true—
That Arthur would yet   come to help his English.

The *Brut* then goes on to relate the later history of the
British during the Anglo-Saxon conquest. It tells of
the formation of the Heptarchy, and of how "Gregory
felt pity—God loved him," and sent missionaries to
the Angles, "to angels most like"; and at last, in the
seventh century:

The British on every side   fared to Wales   16112
And lived by their laws   and their folk customs.
And they dwell there yet   as they shall evermore,
And the English kings   wield this land
And the Britons lost it,   this land and its peoples,
So that never more   kings were they here.
Yet that day came not,   be it henceforth as it
    may—
Happen what happen—   save through God's will.
                                        Amen.

After Layamon there were few Arthurian stories written in English, in comparison with those in other tongues. They date, generally, from the late fourteenth and fifteenth centuries, and many are of inferior quality. They deal with Merlin or Lancelot, or with the English favorite, Sir Gawaine. The latter inspired what is perhaps the finest literary achievement in metrical romance, the tale of Sir Gawaine and the Green Knight, which will be given elsewhere.[16] Arthur himself is the center of two outstanding poems with confusingly similar titles: *Le Morte Arthur* is a breezy stanzaic version, dwelling long on the fair maid of Astolat. The *Morte Arthure* is in alliterative lines, the last poem of the Arthuriad written in the Middle Ages. Although it dutifully describes the King's funeral at Glastonbury, the haunting note of immortality sounds in the closing phrase: *Hic jacet Arturus, rex quondam rexque futurus.*

MORTE DARTUR

"This book was ended in the ninth year of the reign of King Edward the Fourth (1469-70) by Sir Thomas Malory, Knight, as Jesus help him for his great might, as he is the servant of Jesus both day and night." So ends "the noble and joyous book entitled the *Morte Dartur,* which treateth of the birth, life and acts of the said King Arthur, of his noble knights of the Round Table, their marvellous enquests and adventures, the achieving of the Sangrail, and in the end the dolorous death and departing out of this world of them all." As a challenge to "ye knights of England who do but sleep

---

[16] See Chapter X. The poem is placed there, out of its Arthurian context, because of its importance in relation to the Pearl Poet.

and take your ease,"[17] the book may have fallen un-
heeded on its century, but as a synthesis, in the music
of high prose, of the whole mediaeval cycle, it has stirred writers and readers ever since.[18] The book is too
well known to need development; one scene alone will
be enough to show that the tale was perpetuated by
magic in the end, the magic of great style, and to leave
the Arthur story "looking up," for, as Ramon Lull put
it, "chivalry better agreeth to the soul than to the
body."

Book XIII, Chapters 7 and 8

And then the king and all estates went home unto
Camelot, and so went to evensong and to the great
minster, and so upon that to supper. And every
knight sat in his own place, as they were beforehand.
Then anon they heard cracking and crying of thunder, that they thought the place would all to-drive.
In the midst of this blast entered a sunbeam clearer
by seven times than ever they saw day. And all they
were alighted of the grace of the Holy Ghost. Then
began every knight to behold other, and either saw

[17] From Caxton's Preface to his edition of Ramon Lull's *Order of Chivalry*.

[18] A simple enumeration of the better-known modern versions, all of
which stem more or less directly from Malory, shows the amazing diversity
of interpretation to which the Arthuriad lends itself in ages other than that
which produced it. A significant study of contrasts is offered by: the
glimmering loveliness of unreal allegory in Spenser's *Fairie Queene* in
the sixteenth century; the ludicrous artificiality of Dryden's "heroic"
drama *King Arthur* in the seventeenth; the complete silence of the eighteenth century on the theme; the musical, expurgated, idealistic variations
on it in the Victorian *Idylls of the King,* and the raw, rowdy satire of
Mark Twain's *Connecticut Yankee* in the nineteenth; while the twentieth
century has produced already the sombre psychological beauty of E. A.
Robinson's poems and the cutting irony of John Erskine's novels. Truly
Arthur has not died.

other by their seeming fairer than ever they saw before. Then there was no knight might speak one word a great while, and so they looked every man on other, as they had been dumb. Then there entered into the hall the Holy Grail covered with white samite, but there was no one might see it, nor who bore it. And then was all the hall filled with good odors, and every knight had such meats and drinks as he best loved in this world. And when the Holy Grail had been borne through the hall, the holy vessel departed so suddenly they wist not where it became. Then had they all breath to speak. And then the King yielded thanks to God for the good grace that He had sent them. "Certes," said the King, "we ought to thank Our Lord Jesus greatly for what He has shown us this day in reverence of this high feast of Pentecost."

"Now," said Sir Gawaine, "we have been served this day of what meats and drinks we thought on, but one thing beguiled us, we might not see the Holy Grail, for it was too preciously covered. Wherefore I will make avow that tomorrow without longer abiding I shall labor in the quest of the Sangrail, that I shall hold me out a twelve month and a day, and more if need be, and never shall I return again unto the court till I have seen it more openly than it hath been seen here. And if I may not speed I shall return again, as he that may not be against the will of Our Lord Jesus Christ." When they of the Table Round heard Sir Gawaine say so, they rose up, the most part, and made such avows as Sir Gawaine had made.

Anon as King Arthur heard this he was greatly displeased, for he wist well that they might not gainsay their vows. "Alas," said King Arthur unto Sir

Liege lord of my life, I ask leave to go.

SIR GAWAINE AND THE GREEN KNIGHT

Gawaine, "you have nigh slain me with the avow and promise that you have made. For through it you have bereft me of the fairest fellowship and the truest knighthood that ever were seen together in any realm of the world. For when they depart from hence, I am sure that they shall never meet more in this world, for they shall die many in this quest. And so it forethinketh me a little, for I have loved them as well as my life. Wherefore it shall grieve me right, the departing of this fellowship. For I have an old custom to have them in my fellowship." And therewith the tears filled his eyes.

And so, like the hermit in Lull's story, the last chronicler seems to "cast out a great sigh and enter in a great thought, remembering the honor in which chivalry had been long maintained."

IV

Kings in the Kitchen

Mankind yearns for rhymes to hear
And for romances far and near.
CURSOR MUNDI

KING ARTHUR and his knights made one curious conquest which is not recorded in any story: they drove a host of English heroes from the field of literary romance into oblivion. Throughout the ages of chivalry, tales that owed little or nothing to Camelot were everywhere current, tales of kings and knights who were sturdier in character than those of the Round Table, and who became involved in even more chaotic adventures. Many of these stories originated in the confused times of the Danish invasions, and of the first Christian clashes with Islam. Perhaps because they were Teutonic in origin and antedated in their first forms the refined elements of *courtoisie*, they were gradually forced be-

low stairs in the feudal castles; perhaps because no
Malory synthesized the adventures of these forgotten
heroes into a work of art easily readable by later generations, they were not perpetuated except in the form
of a few ballads and fairy tales. They are a loss to
literature.

Many of these adventures were related in every
European language, and there are French versions even
for those of distinctively English origin. Yet the latter
have a patriotic ring; there is the suggestion of a cheer
in the voice of the narrator whenever he says "into
England they gan sail." It was the narrator who gave
unity to his sprawling tales. His song, and the under-
song of his glee-wood, held together the little circle of
listeners, though obviously he must often have broken
off with the equivalent of "continued in my next." This
sense of direct narration is too often lost in the reading
of the printed versions. By the fifteenth century the
art was settling into something approaching the "classical" correctness of the eighteenth century, and it was
this formalized type of romance, especially "tail-
rhyme," that fell under Chaucer's satire in *Sir Thopas*.[1] In earlier days the tale had gone along with unshapely enthusiasm, and with unabashed intent to edify
as well as to entertain. Even in romance, heaven and
earth were not to be severed:

[1] The tale of *Sir Thopas*, told by Chaucer in person on the road to
Canterbury, was stopped by Mine Host as "drasty rhyming." It is a
parody of the excesses of the tail-rhyme style exemplified (unfairly) as
follows:

> Sir Thopas was a doughty swain;
> White was his face as paindemain,
> His lips as red as rose.
> His cheek was like scarlet in grain,
> And I tell you, in good certain,
> He had a seemly nose.

Since the time that Jesus Christ,   1
Through His grace and His virtue,
Was born this our world within
Of a maiden without sin,
And the world to Christendom
Among mankind has now become,
Many adventures have been wrought
That all men knoweth not . . . .
To know them is fair mastery   19
To hold wisdom and leave folly.
So of an earl I shall you tell,
And how of him it befell,
And of his steward, without lying,
And the steward's son, a fair young thing.

This "fair young thing" was the hero of *Guy of Warwick* who may, in history, have been cupbearer to King Aethelstan. Romance made of him a faithful lover and a devout, pugnacious wanderer, who fought his way through most of Europe, Africa and Palestine, overcoming emperors, giants and Saracens in his efforts to become peerless in the eyes of Felice, whom he weds half through the tale in order to allow his son to carry on in the same fashion. His domestic happiness does not prevent him from turning pilgrim and even hermit. *Bevis of Hamptoun*, though better told, is even more fantastic in its bold combination of Germanic dragons, Eastern patriarchs, fairy-tale magic and good, historic King Edgar. Nobility of motive, intense human sympathy, and above all the startling lovableness of "Josian the Queen," lifts the ridiculous to the sublime. Thoroughly English in its outdoor atmosphere, sporting spirit and brotherly loyalty is *Gamelyn*, retold by

Chaucer, and the remote source of Lodge's *Rosalind* and Shakespeare's *As You Like It.*

KING HORN

This is a tale of Danish origin that came into England by an Irish route, "Westerness by the sea." The heroes are hearty Christians, the villains shadowy Saracens. In swift, uneasy, three-beat lines, the South-midland version of the story whirls young Horn through many "reversals" of concealed identity, and many an exile and return. It is "straight from the shoulder," for popular audiences. There is no courtly love, but the wandering Horn has one faithful lover to steady him. Towards the end of the poem he has been gone so long from her that the fair Rymenhild is being forced to wed another against her will. At the wedding feast Horn appears, disguised as a palmer[2] with his face blackened:

> Rymenhild rose from bench   1185
> Their thirst with wine to quench,
> After meat in the hall
> With both wine and ale.
> A horn she bore in hand
> —A custom in that land.
> Every knight and squire
> Drank there of the beer
> Save Horn alone;
> He had thereof no moan.
> Horn sat on the ground,
> In his thoughts he was bound.
> He said, "O Lady fair,
> Thou comest to me here—

[2] Pilgrims who had been to the Holy Land wore a sprig of palm in their hats to testify to the fact.

Thou givest us with the first,
For beggars be athirst."
Her horn she laid down
And from a vessel brown
Poured a gallon in his bowl,
As for a glutton's dole.
She said, "Take this cup,
And so drink it up.
Saw I never, as I ween,
A beggar that was so keen."
Horn took it from her there
And said, "O Lady dear,
Little or no wine
Save in a white cup fine.
Thou thinkest me a beggar
But I am a fisher.
Far come I from the East
To go fishing at thy feast.
My net lies near at hand
By a well fair strand;
It has been lying there
For full seven year.
I am come to see
If any fish there be.
I have come to fish;
Drink to me from the dish.
Drink to Horn from horn!
Far have I roamed, forlorn."
Rymenhild looked; behold
Her heart straightway turned cold;
She knew nought of his fishing,
And of Horn himself nothing,
But wonder made her think
Why to Horn he bade her drink.

With wine she filled the horn
And drank to the pilgrim lorn.
She said, "Drink thy fill
And after thou wilt tell
If ever thou hast seen
Horn in the woods green."
Horn drank from the horn; around
He threw his ring to the ground.
The queen went to her bower
With her maidens four;
Found what she knew of old,
A ring of graven gold
That Horn from her once had.
Sore was she adread
That Horn was dead somewhere,
For the ring was there.
Her damsel then she sent
For the Palmer as he went.
"Palmer," quoth she, "true,
The ring that there you threw,
Tell me where once it lay
And why you have come today."
He said, "By Saint Gile,
I have gone many a mile
Far beyond in the west,
Searching my very best.
I saw Horn Childe stand
By a ship in that land.
He said that he longed so
Into Westerness to go.
The ship took to the flood
With me and Horn the Good.

Horn was sick and died;
He prayed me by his side:
'Go with this ring
To Rymenhild, young thing.'
Often the ring he kissed;
To his soul may God give rest."
Rymenhild said at first,
"Heart, now mayest thou burst,
For Horn thou hast no more
For whom thou hast pined sore."
She fell upon her bed
Where a knife was hid,
To slay the King so loath
And herself both,
In that very night
If Horn came not in sight.
She set the knife to her heart
But Horn did straight upstart.
With his shirt he wiped away
The black that thickly lay
Over his neck so fair
And said, "Queen, sweet and dear,
I am Horn thine own,
And me thou hast not known?
I am Horn of Westerness,
In my arms thou gavest a kiss."
So with many another kiss
Together they made much bliss.
"Rymenhild," he said, "I wend
Down to the woods end;
There is many a knight
All ready for the fight,

Armed under cloth.
Straight they will make wroth
The king and his guests
That have come to these feasts."

Horn then summons his followers and slays the usurping king; he and Rymenhild live happily ever after.

HAVELOC THE DANE

It may be that the incidents of this athletic tale
were first elaborated by the Danes of the tenth century
to justify their position in England, but English gleemen continued to sing it for its own sake. The folk in
the kitchen were as fond of kingly romance as the lords
and ladies in the tapestried rooms above, but romance
without perfumed languor. Haveloc's adventures appear in Geoffrey of Gaimar's *Estori des Englis* side by
side with those of Hereward. He is identified in some
obscure way with Anlaf, the hero of the Battle of
Brunanburgh, fought in 937,[3] though other allusions
go back still further; Aethelwold is possibly the historic Ethelbert of Kent, baptized by Saint Augustine
in 596, and the story went through Ireland before returning by a French channel to England. The *Lay of
Haveloc* was written in the thirteenth century in the
dialect of Lincolnshire.[4] It is a swinging, wholesome,
rough-and-tumble folk epic, with overtones of history
and legend that are sounded again in a masterpiece of

---

[3] See *Word-Hoard*, p. 338.
[4] The seal of the corporation of the town of Grimsby in Lincolnshire
represents the main characters of the poem, Grim, Haveloc and Goldeburgh.

a very different kind, *Hamlet,* the drama of another Prince of Denmark.[5]

Incipit Vita Havelock, quondam Rex Anglie et Denemarchie:

Hearken to me, now, good men,   1
Wives and maidens and all men;
Of a tale I you will tell
Who it will hear, and thereon dwell.
The tale of Havelock I make it,
—While he was little he went full naked.
Havelock was a full good sort
In every company he sought.
He was the boldest man at need
That ever might ride on any steed;
All that now you soon will hear,
The tale you may now learn right here.
At the beginning of our tale
Fill me a cup of right good ale,
And I will drink it ere I tell,
That Christ may shield us all from hell;
Christ let us ever so to do
That to Him we may come too,
And, so that it may be so:
Benedicamus Domino!

The minstrel tells first how Aethelwold, the good King

[5] The story of Hamlet is drawn from remote Danish history. The earliest mention of the name is in the *Prose Edda* (compiled c. 1230) in which a much older poem speaks of the "daughters of ocean" who are "grinding Hamlet's meal." Saxo Grammaticus told the story of Hamlet and his uncle in his *History of the Danes.* Shakespeare's immediate source was a French version by Belleforest in his *Histoires Tragiques,* in which some of the incidents told of Haveloc are connected with Hamlet; for instance, the propping up of the dead soldiers with stakes during the war in England (ignored by Shakespeare). Somewhere the two stories had crossed during the interchange of tales in the Viking Ages, perhaps in the Scandinavian settlements in Ireland, in the tenth century.

of England, died, leaving his little daughter Goldeburgh to the care of Earl Godrich, who promises to
marry her to the best, fairest and strongest man in the
land. But he proves false, takes the kingdom for himself and throws her into prison. The story then goes to
Denmark where good King Birkebeyn also dies and
leaves his little son Havelock and his two sisters to the
care of Earl Godard.

When Birkebeyn was laid in grave,   408
The earl then straightway took the knave,
Havelock, that was then the heir,
Swanboro his sister, Elfled the fair,
And in a castle put the three
Where no man might come or be
Of their kin; he locked the door.
There they often grieved full sore
Both for hunger and for cold
Before they were three winters old.
Scarcely did he give them clothes,
Cared not a scrap for all his oaths,
They were not rightly clothed nor fed,
Nor did he give them a rich bed. . . .
Then anon one day he passed   447
To the tower where they were cast;
There they wailed for hunger and cold.
The knave—for he was somewhat bold—
Came to him, and on knees there
Godard he greeted thus full fair,
And Godard said: "What ails you now?
Why do you cry and make a row?"
"Because we herein hunger sore,"
Answered they, "and we want more.
We have no food, nor do we have

Herein either knight or knave
To give to us our drink and meat,
That we may have a bite to eat.
Woe is us that we were born!
Weilawei! Is there no corn
That men might make of it some bread?
We hunger so we are nigh dead."
Godard heard them wailing so,
And gave not a straw for all their woe,
But then took up each little maid,
As though it were a game he played,
As though joking he had been
—They were for hunger pale and green.
Of both he carved in two their throats,
And after cut them into groats.
It was sorrow to one and all
When the children by the wall
Lay and sprawled in their own blood.
Havelock saw it and thereby stood.
Full sorry was that simple knave,
Great dread he must then have,
For at his heart he saw a knife
For to take away his life.
But the knave that little was
Knelt before that cruel Judas,
And said: "Lord, have mercy now;
Homage, Lord, I promise you.
All Denmark to you I give
If you will only let me live."

Havelock pleads for his life so feelingly that Godard
spares him, but then gives him to Grim, an old fisherman, with orders to drown him in the sea.

In a bag then, foul and black,   555

Grim soon cast him on his back,
And bare him to his hut alive,
And gave him to Dame Leve his wife,
And said to her: "See here this knave,
So now my life thou shalt save;
I shall drown him in the sea,
For his sake we shall be free,
Have enough of gold and other fee.
Thus has my lord promised me."
When Dame Leve heard all that,
Up she started, no longer sat,
And cast the knave so hard down
That he there cracked his crown
Against a great stone where it lay.
Then Havelock might say, "Weilawei!
That ever I was a king's child!"
Was there no eagle or griffin wild,
Lion, or wolf, she-wolf or bear
Or other beast that would kill him there?
So lay the child to the middle of night,
When Grim bade Leve bring a light
That he might put on his clothes.
"Thinkest thou nought of all my oaths
That to my own lord I have sworn?
I will not be held in scorn.
I shall bear him to the sea,
Thou knowest that now it so must be.
And I shall drown him soon therein;
Rise up straight and go thou in
And blow the fire and light a candle."
But as she tried his clothes to handle,
To put them on and the fire to blow,
She saw therein a light aglow
Just as bright as it were day

About the knave there where he lay.
From his mouth there came a gleam
As if it were a sunbeam;
As light it was in all the place
As though candles burnt apace.
"Jesus Christ," quoth Dame Leve aghast,
"What light burns in our hut so fast?
Rise up, Grim, see what it may mean;
What is that light there, as you ween?"
They started both to the knave
—For a man should good will have—
Ungagged him, and then unbound,
And soon anon upon him found,
As they pulled from him his sark,
On his right shoulder a kingly mark,
Very bright, very fair.
"Goddot!" quoth Grim, "this is our heir
That shall be lord of Denmark,
He shall be king strong and stark,
He shall have us in his hand,
All Denmark and all England."

The two pay him homage and feed him well. Then with
their children, their goods and their livestock they fly
in a little boat to England. They settle in Lincoln in a
place afterwards known as Grimsby. Years later there
is a famine. Havelock, now a fine strong youth, gets
work as a kitchen scullion.

He would never take a rest   943
More than if he were a beast,
Of all men he was most meek,
Laughing always, blithe to speak,
Ever he was blithe and glad;
He hid it whenever he was sad.

He was always ready to play
With children met along the way;
With them he did all their will,
And played with them to their fill.
They loved him all, still and bold,
Knights and children, young and old.

One day Godrich comes to town, and the townspeople
gather in the castle courtyard for games to be held
in his honor.

Many a champion came to town,   1007
Many a bold lad black and brown,
And fell it so that young men,
Well about nine or ten,
Began there to play ere long;
There came the greatest and the least
That in the town were for the feast—
Champions and stark lads
And the bondsmen with their gads
As though they had just come from the plow.
There was soon gathering enow!
For there was never a horse-knave
—No matter what work he might have—
That came not thither, the sport to see.
Before their feet there lay a tree.
The stark lads, in numbers grown,
Were casting with a great stone;
The stone was big, hard to pull,
And as heavy as a bull. . . .
Havelock stood and looked at them;   1043
Nothing knew he of the game,
For never yet he saw it done,
Casting the stone, and the game won.
His master bade him go thereto

And to see what he could do.
His master bade him go ahead,
But he was full sore adread.
Thereto he started soon anon
And flipped up the heavy stone
That he must cast with, and then so
He threw it at the first go
Over all that had tried before
Twelve feet, and somewhat more.
The champions in the crowd
Nudged each other, laughed aloud;
No more would they try their hand
But said, "Too long here we stand."

Havelock, for his great strength, is married to Goldeburgh by the spiteful Godrich. At first she is very unhappy to marry a scullion, but one night she sees the
light and the kingly mark, and hears an angel say:

"Goldeburgh, let thy sorrow be,
For Havelock that has married thee
Is king's son and king's heir,
As betokeneth that cross so fair.
And more: it betokeneth that he shall
Denmark have, and England all.
He shall be king, strong and stark,
Of England and Denmark.
Thou shalt with thine eyes see
That thou shalt queen and lady be."

She rouses Havelock, who determines to go to Denmark and win back his crown, with the help of Grim's
three sons. But first he goes to church:

Before the rood straight did he fall,   1354
On Christ and the cross began to call,
And then said, "O Lord who wields

Wind and water, woods and fields,
For the holy pity of you
Have mercy on me, Lord, now,
And wreak me yet on my foe
Who before my eyes, so,
Slew my sisters with a knife
And afterwards would take my life. . . .
Bring me well to the land   1381
That Godard holds in his hand.
That is my right, every deal,
Jesus Christ, Thou knowest well."
When he had his prayer said,
His offering on the altar laid,
His leave he took from Jesus there,
And from His sweet Mother fair,
And from the Cross by which he lay
And went sore sorrowing away.

They set sail together for Denmark and ask hospitality
at the castle of Ubbe, a great lord who is devoted to
the memory of Birkebeyn. He receives them gladly,
not knowing who they are.

Above all them that therein were   1700
Havelock stood a head or more
Than any other that therein stood;
Then was Ubbe blithe of mood. . . .
When it had come time to eat   1714
Ubbe's wife came in for meat.
To her he said all playfully:
"Dame, thou and Havelock together be,
And Goldeburgh shall eat with me;
She is as fair as flower on tree.
In all Denmark is woman none
So fair as she, by Saint John."

When they were set and the board laid,
And the benison was said,
Before them came the best meat
That King or Kaiser could ever eat:
Cranes and swans and venison,
Salmon, lampreys, good sturgeon,
Spiced wine to drink and claret free,
Wine white and red, full good plenty.
Was therein no page so young
That in ale would dip his tongue.
Of those dishes all to tell,
Or of the wines, I will not dwell;
'Twould make the story overlong,
And annoy this fair throng.
When everything was served at last,
And the wassail bowl had passed,
Over their good drinks they sat long,
It was time for all to be gone.

Ubbe sends him to the house of his friend, Bernard,
and there they are attacked by a band of sixty thieves.
Havelock rushes out at them and kills seven in as
many strokes.

They rushed on him, as on a bear,   1838
As dogs rush when they want to tear,
When men play at bear-baiting;
The lads were quick and not long-waiting.
They ran to where he stood alone,
Some smote with stick and some with stone,
Some thrust their lance in back and side,
And gave him wounds long and wide
In many places, twenty or so,
From his crown right to his toe.
When he saw that, wild he grew,

Fearful was he to that crew,
For the blood ran from his sides
As water from a well glides.
Then began he straight to mow
With his bar, and thus to show
How well he could sorely smite.
Among them all was none who might
Get away, or turn his back,
But what he felt his crown crack,
So that in a little space
Twenty fell upon their face.

Havelock's prowess brings him honor and he returns
to Ubbe's house. One night in his sleep Ubbe sees the
miraculous light that betrays Havelock's identity. He
sends word all over Denmark that Birkebeyn's son has
returned.

And the folk of all the land   2316
Gave him all into his hand,
The kingdom gave him, far and nigh,
And made him king well and high.
When he was king then might men see
The greatest joy that ever could be:
Thrusting with a sharp spear,
Fencing with shields that men bear,
Wrestling with lads, throwing of stone,
Harpers and pipers, many a one,
Backgammon played, dice being shook,
Romance-reading from a book;
There might men hear the Gestes sing,
And gleemen on the tabors ding.
There might men see the bull-baiting
And the boars with hounds fighting,
Every game men might there see;

And how great Grim grew to be!
Was never yet joy more
In all this world ever before.

Godard is caught and hung with torture and rough
horse-play. Then Havelock collects an army and returns to England. He meets Godrich in open battle,
defeats him, conquers the whole land, rewards his followers, and rules with Goldeburgh for sixty years with
joy.

They had children as was seen   2978
Sons and daughters full fifteen,
Whereof the sons were kings all,
So God willed it should befall,
Queens were all the daughters fair;
Happy they who good children bear. . . .
Therefore I beseech all you   2994
That have heard this rime through,
That each of you with right good will
Would say a *Pater Noster* still
For him that did the rime make,
And thus lay many nights awake,
That Jesus Christ his soul may bring
Before His Father at his ending.

Amen.

THE NINE WORTHIES

In his preface to the first printed edition of the
Morte Dartur, Caxton speaks of "nine worthy, and
the best that ever were, to wit, three Paynims, three
Jews and three Christian men." They were a motley
company: Hector, Alexander, Caesar; Joshua, David,
Judas Maccabaeus; Arthur, Charlemagne, and God-

frey de Bouillon.[6] They appeared together through-out mediaeval literature, and only couched their arms when Shakespeare laughed them off the scene in the mock-masque at the end of *Love's Labors Lost,* where much fooling is brought to an end by bad news, and then: "Worthies, away, the scene begins to cloud."[7] For some four hundred years they had glittered in the light of a common hero-worship, and rode gaily through many an English romance. The three Jews seldom appear; of the three Paynims, Caesar is strangely neglected in "the matter of Rome le grant." But

> The Emperor Alexander, of arms high-praised,
> That noble is and renowned, and never man dreaded

had an elaborate cycle to himself. Even in the days of the Heptarchy, the geography of the East was a tempting field for magic and imagination.[8] "The hon-orable Hector who adventured to slay" appears in the interminable Troy-Books, long-winded but full of national pride as befits a record of a people descended from Aeneas. Nowhere is anachronism more frank than in Greek or Trojan tales in which dukes and knights fight for fair ladies, call each other "Sire" and "Ma Dame," and joust together under classical walls. The *Geste Historiale of the Destruction of Troy* thus relates the episode of the wooden (here brazen) horse:

> Then paid King Priam   all the pure sums   11866
> Of gold and gay silver,   and of good wheat.
> They shot it all into ship   on the sheer water

---

[6] There is an elaborate study of the nine Worthies in the alliterative *Morte Arthure,* where the King has a dream in which he sees each of his compeers overturned on the wheel of the Duchess Fortune (ll. 3220-3456).

[7] Act V, Sc. 2.

[8] See *Word-Hoard,* p. 356.

And made ready to ride   on the rough waves.
All the Greeks gathered,   the greatest and others,
With sacrifices solemn,   the singing of priests;
With professions and praises   they pulled forth
    the horse
To a side of the city,   and set it at the gates. . . .
Then the citizens, with song   and solemn
    cry   11879
Hauled forth the horse   to the high temple.
It is oftentimes said,   by many men of old:
The last joy of jolly men   joins with sorrow.
These burghers of the town   were blinded to evil;
They hauled in no horse   but their hard death.

Of the share of romance that fell to the three Christian men, King Arthur plainly has almost the monopoly, but Charlemagne was not forgotten by good Anglo-Normans. For "King Charles of France, with his twelve peers, took the Sultan of Babylon in the field, and smote off his head," is the triumphant close of *The Sowden of Babylon*. The Peers overshadow their King; Sir Firumbras, Sir Ottuel, and a somewhat belittled Sir Oliver with his Roland, move in a whirl of fire-lit, bloodstained, magic-wrought adventure controlled by entrancing Eastern maidens who murder for love, then piously crave baptism. These tales are at once lurid and devout, full of gallant gangsters and die-hard lovers. In the end:

> God give us joy of the best
> Who have read of this geste.

As for Godfrey de Bouillon, conqueror and first King of Jerusalem at the beginning of the Crusades, the romance-makers were more interested in his alleged descent from a swan than in his chivalry; no tale is more strangely preternatural than the *Chevalere Assigne.* The story slips from the heroic cycle into that of very old and ever young folk tales. Some of these stem from Christian martyrology, as the Eustace stories; some from ancient mythology, as *William of Palerme,* where the Germanic werewolf cares for a Sicilian hero; some have drifted down from a time before the separation of Arabian from Teutonic story-sources, as those of *Constance* and of *Patient Griselda,* both of whom later appear in the *Canterbury Tales.* Spain, where Moors and Christians fought and lived together for eight hundred years, was the place where many of these story-threads crossed. The English minstrels then took up the themes in their own breezier fashion.

FLORIS AND BLANCHEFLUR

This "flower-tale" from the hot East was spread all over Europe by returning Crusaders. In some countries it was heavy with the drugged sweetness of Arabia and stiff with chivalric embroidery, but a fresh wind blows through the English version, passionate as it is; the children are young and innocent, and life is their game. The poem celebrates the love of Floris, son of the King of Spain, for Blancheflur, a captive maiden. To prevent their marrying, the King sells Blancheflur into the keeping of the Admiral of Babylon,[9] who locks her up in a tower with other maidens. Floris finally wins his way to the tower and bribes the porter to let him in by giving him a huge golden cup.

---

[9] The Arabic word for sultan, *al miral,* has given the English *admiral,* commander of a fleet. Moslem chiefs were most frequently seen by Christians at the prow of a pirate ship on the Mediterranean.

The porter, to help him in his need,   **433**
Bade flowers be gathered on the meed.
He let the cup be filled with flowers
To strew in the maiden's bowers;
That was his way to help him so,
And he bade Floris in the cup to go.
Two silly girls the cup bore,
Its heaviness made them sore.
They prayed God give him evil last hours
Who filled the cup with so many flowers.
To the chamber whither they should go
The right way they did not know;
To another chamber they have gone,
Not to Blancheflur's anon.
The cup they set upon the ground,
And went and left it to be found.
A maiden came, and would be bold
The flowers to handle and behold.
Floris thought her his sweetheart bright,
Out of the cup he leapt aright,
And that maiden, in her dread,
Began to cry and almost fled.
Floris knew not where to begin
For the fear that he was in.
Into the cup he started then
And hid among the flowers again.
The maiden then bethought in truth
That it was Floris, the sweet youth;
For Blancheflur's room was near to her,
And often they together were,
And Blancheflur had oft retold
How from Floris she had been sold.
Now the maidens came running in,
Well fifteen there were therein,

And asked her what the trouble might be,
Why she had cried so terribly.
She thought, and was well aware
What best answer to make there.
"To the cup I came, and I made bold
The flowers to handle and behold.
Then outflew a butterfly
Ere I knew it, on my eye,
Then was I so sore afraid
That at once loud cries I made."
The others laughed aloud in glee
And went away and let her be.
Clarice, that maid so fair of face,
To Blancheflur then went apace,
And she said, "Sweet Blancheflur,
Wilt thou see a well fair flower?
It grew never in this land,
The flower that I bring to your hand."
"Away, Clarice," quoth Blancheflur,
"She that loveth paramour
And has joy therein, may well love flowers,
But I live in sorrow in these towers,
For I ween, undoubtingly,
That the Admiral has chosen me.
But I shall never see that day
When men, in scorn, of me shall say
That I am of love untrue,
And changed my love for someone new,
And let my old for a new love be.
Floris is true in his country;
But though, Floris, thou forgettest me,
Yet shall I never forget thee."
Clarice heard the piteous ruth,
All of trueness and of truth,

Down her face glided many a tear,
"Blancheflur," she said, "comrade dear,
Loved and sweet, my Blancheflur,
Come and see a well fair flower."
Together they go now, iwis,
And Floris has heard all this.
Out of the cup he leaps anon,
And to Blancheflur he has gone.
Each the other straightway knew,
And both their faces changed in hue.
Together without a word they leapt,
Clasped and kissed and also wept;
Their kissing lasted for a mile
Though to them it seemed a little while.

The Admiral discovers Floris, and at first is bent on killing both the children. But he finally yields to their charms and gives them a gorgeous wedding.

SIR ORFEO

In the days of Henry II, an enterprising French woman came to England and wrote poetry for noble patrons to earn her living. The best-known works of Marie de France are the *Lais,* short romances meant to be sung, all based on pre-Saxon themes. Eight poems written later on in English on the same pattern are grouped together as *Breton Lays,* though composed at widely different times and places. Chaucer's *Franklin's Tale* is an elaborate expansion of a lost lay:

These old gentle Britons in their days
Of divers adventures made their lays,
Rhymed them in their first Briton tongue,
Which lays with their instruments they sung.

They are on old Celtic motifs, maids adrift, and
knights loved by fairy queens. Loveliest of them all is
the fairy metamorphosis of the Greek tale of Orpheus
and Eurydice; romance puts no boundary between
times and places:

Sir Orfeo was a king   25
In England, a high lording,
A hardy man and stalwart too,
Kindly and courteous-also.
His father had come of King Pluto,
And his mother of King Juno
That were held as gods of old
For adventures that they told.
Orfeo most of anything
Loved the glee of sweet harping.
Sure was every good harper
To have of him much high honor.
He himself loved to harp
And laid thereon his wits so sharp.
He learned so well there never could be
A better harper than was he. . . .
This king had a queen of price
That was named Queen Herodis,
The fairest lady, be it known,
That ever was made of flesh and bone;
Full of love and of goodness,
No man could tell of her fairness.
Befell in the beginning of May
When merry and hot is the day,
And away are winter showers
And every field is full of flowers,
With blossoms bright on every bough
Everywhere waxing merry enow,

This same Queen, Dame Herodis,
Took with her two maids of price
And went once in the morning tide
To play by an orchard side,
To see the flowers spread and spring
And to hear the small birds sing.
Then they sat them down all three
Under a fair orchard tree,
And well soon this fair queen
Fell asleep upon the green.
The maids dared not her awake
But let her lie and her rest take.
So she slept till after noon
When morning tide was past and gone.
But soon her sleeping from her fled—
She cried and wildly shook with dread,
She beat together hands and feet
And scratched her face till it bled wet.
Her rich robe she tore in bits
And raved as though she had lost her wits.
The two maidens there beside
Dared no longer with her abide
But to the palace ran aright
And there told every squire and knight
That the queen was wild with fear,
They must go and look for her.
Knights then ran and ladies before,
Damosels sixty and more.
In the orchard there the queen they found,
They took her up and gathered round,
And brought her to her bed at last
And tried to hold her there full fast.
But still she cried in the same way
And would up and go away.

When Orfeo heard those tidings
Never had he heard worse things.
So he came with brave knights ten
To the chamber of the queen,
Beheld, and said with great pity,
"O dearest life, what now ails thee
That ever yet has been so still,
And now thou criest wondrous shrill?
Thy body so white, so noble born,
With thy nails is now all torn.
Alas thy face, that was so red,
Is all wan, as thou wert dead;
And alas, thy fingers small
Are all bloody and all pale.
Alas, thy lovesome eyes two
Look as a man does on his foe.
Ah, Dame, I beseech mercy,
Let be all this rueful cry;
Tell me what it is and how,
And what things may help thee now."
Then lay she still at the last
And began to weep full fast,
And said thus to the king in woe,
"Alas, my lord, Sir Orfeo,
Since we have together been
Anger has never come between.
But ever so have I loved thee
As my life, and so thou me.
But now we must part in two.
Do thy best, for I must go."

Herodis has seen the King of Faerie;[10] he has told her

[10] The word *fairy* comes through French from the Latin *Fata*. Fate
became personified as the goddess of enchantment in the fourth century.
Faerie was the realm of magic and of all preternatural beings, good or bad.

that the next day she will be carried away. This comes
to pass. In despair Orfeo leaves his kingdom and
wanders through the woods in disguise, seeking for her.

Then might he see there beside   281
Oft in the hot morning tide
The King of Faerie with his rout
Come to hunt there all about,
With dim cry and blowing,
And hounds also with him barking.
But no beast they took there,
He never knew from whence they were.
And other while he might see clear
A great host drawing near,
Well equipped, ten hundred knights,
With all the armor theirs by rights,
Of countenance fierce and stout,
With many banners streaming out.
And each held his sword outdrawn—
But he never knew where they had gone.
Again he saw another thing,
Knights and ladies came dancing
In quaint attire, cunningly,
With quaint steps, softly;
Drums and trumpets there would be,
And all manner minstrelsy.

One day Orfeo sees his wife in this fairy troupe and
follows her through a rock into fairyland.

When he had passed the rock door   349
Well three miles or even more,
He came into a fair country
As bright as sun on summer's day,
Smooth and plain and all green,

Hill or dale there was not seen.
In fields a castle standing by
Rich and royal and wondrous high.
Around it all the outer wall
Was clear and shining as crystal.
A hundred towers there were about,
Marvellous, embattled stout.
The buttresses came up from the ditch
Of red gold, arched and rich.
The vaulting was adorned all
With every manner of animal.
Within it there were dwellings wide
Of precious stones on every side.
The worst pillar to behold
Was all made of burnished gold.
All that land was ever light,
For when it should be dark and night
The rich stones began to shine
Like the bright sun at noontime.
No man may tell or think in thought
The rich work that there was wrought;
By all things he thinks it is
The proud court of Paradise.

Orfeo harps to the King of Faerie and thus wins back
his queen, and they return to his kingdom, where a
faithful steward has all in readiness for them. They
live happily ever after, as should every king and queen
of fair romance in the days of Merry England.

Of all such harpings on the glee-wood, whether in
Camelot or the kitchen:

Some be of weal and some of woe,
And some of joy and mirth also,
Some of treachery and some of guile,

And some of haps that fall be-while;
Some of game and ribaldry,
And some there be of the faerie.
But of all things that men may see,
Most of love forsooth they be.

V

In Cloister and Out

*Let your eyes be open, and your
hearts, to God's brightness.*
RULE OF SAINT BENET

BY THE END of the twelfth century a change had come
over the monasticism of England. The abbey lands
were as extensive as ever, but there was variety in the
habits of the monks and nuns who cultivated them, and
the simple lines of the buildings were beginning to rise
and sharpen to the Gothic arch. There were Cistercians, newcomers in the Benedictine family; there
were Premonstratensians, distinctive in their devotion
to the Blessed Sacrament. Then, in the early years of
the thirteenth century, came the Mendicant Orders,
Franciscans, Dominicans and Carmelites. Friars—
brown, black and white—were met on the roads and in
the towns, wherever there were people to be saved;
they were seen in the universities and libraries,

wherever there were books to be read. Manifold forms of dedication were at the choice of those who found the world too gay to live in, or too beautiful not to be offered in sacrifice.

As had been the case ever since the Fathers of the Desert, retreat to the cloister had the paradoxical effect of enriching the surrounding civilization. Wastelands were reclaimed, agriculture was improved, bookbinding became the most exquisite of crafts, the liberal and the fine arts were uplifted by the sheer exuberance of souls set free from themselves by asceticism. Culture as a by-product of prayer proved to be far lovelier than when sought for her own sake. Literature, as its nature is, reflected all these enriched arts in itself, and if civilization turned back on the monasteries and corrupted them, literature took its revenge in satire. Books written both in and out of the monasteries show the close interaction between cloister and world throughout the Middle Ages.

THE ANCREN RIWLE

Early in the thirteenth century, three young women of gentle blood and of some education made themselves a home under the eaves of a church somewhere in the south of England, possibly at Tarente in Dorset. They belonged to no specific religious Order, though they wore a habit; they were called anchoresses, though they led their life in common. They asked their director to write a Rule for them, and he did so at no small pains to himself, as he took care to tell them. So sound, so gracious and lively, so uplifting did this *Ancren Riwle* prove to be, that it soon became widely known in English, French, and Latin versions.

Its wise and friendly author is unknown. The most

convincing of the many attempts to discover his name would identify him[1] with Friar Robert Bacon, a Dominican and Professor of Theology at Oxford in 1229. Friar Robert was a close companion of Saint Edmund Rich, the lovable scholar for whom geometry was simplified by thoughts of the Three in One, and who, in an outburst of love for our Lady, put a gold ring on the finger of her statue. The brightness of such a spirit falls on the pages of his friend's book, where poetic language, racy metaphor, chuckling humor, and the insight of the true mystic blend in a work of extraordinary power and charm. Although highly original in style and artistry, it belongs in the full stream of the Church's monastic tradition. Its author was acquainted with the fifth century *Instituta Monacharum* of Caesarius of Arles, and the *Epistola ad Sororem Inclusam* of Ailred of Rievaulx, as well as with the Rules of the religious Orders then in existence and with the great homilists of the Patristic Age, while Scripture, direct and indirect, colors his work throughout. As a piece of literature, the *Ancren Riwle* furnished Middle English writers with a fund of analogues and thoughts, and molded their style for centuries; as a religious Rule, it could hardly have failed to draw its "dear Sisters" to sanctity.

"Recti diligunt te." Lord, saith God's bride to her dear-worthy Spouse, those who love Thee rightly,

---

[1] This is the theory of Father Vincent McNabb, O.P. (see *Authorship of the Ancren Riwle*, Archivum Fratrum Praedicatorum IV) who proves, from the regulations given concerning prayer, etc., that the *Riwle* was written by one who followed the Rule of Saint Augustine and who was an English Dominican (Saint Dominic based his Rule on the Augustinian). Specific references then narrow his evidence till it points to Friar Robert Bacon. Other suggested authors include Simon of Ghent, Bishop Poor of Tarente, Gilbert of Hoyland, and Saint Gilbert of Sempringham (see Hall, *Selections from Early Middle English*, II, 373).

they are upright: these live by Rule. And you, my
loved Sisters, have many a day cried out to me for a
Rule. There are many kinds of rules, but two there
are among them all which I shall speak of, at your
asking, with God's help. The one rules the heart, and
makes it even and smooth, without knot or wound of
wrong, or accusing inner-witting that says: "Here
thou sinnest," or "This is not yet bettered as well as
it ought." This rule is ever within and keeps the
heart right. *"Et hec est caritas quam describit Apos-
tolus."* . . . The other rule is all outward, and rules
the body and bodily deeds, and teaches how men
should in all things bear themselves outwardly, how
to eat, drink, dress, lie, sleep, walk. And this rule is
but the servant of the other. The other is as a Lady;
this is as her handmaid, for all that men ever do by
the other outwardly is but to rule the heart within. . . .

Now, my dear Sisters, this book I divide into eight
sections which you call parts, and each part, without
mingling them, speaks of separate things, and yet
each one follows rightly after the other, and the latter is ever tied to the former:

The first part speaks of your service.

The second is how you shall, through your five
wits, keep your heart, in which are order, and religion, and the soul's life. In this part there are five
chapters, or five sections about the five wits that keep
the heart as watchmen who are true, and it speaks
of each separately and in order.

The third part is of a kind of bird that David in
the Psalter likens himself to, as if he were an anchorite, and how the nature of that bird is like
anchorites.

The fourth part is of fleshly temptings, and of ghostly both, and of comfort against them, and of their salve.

The fifth part is of shrift.

The sixth part is of penance.

The seventh part is of a clean heart, why men ought and must love Jesus Christ, and what takes His love from us, and keeps us from loving Him.

The eighth part is all of the outer rule; first, of meat and of drink and of things that belong to them; thereafter of the things that you may receive, and what things you may keep and have; thereafter of your clothes, and of such things as have to do with them; then of dodding your hair, and of your works, and of the times when you are to be bled, and of the rule of your maidens, and at last how you should lovingly teach them. . . .

On Prayers and Devotions:

At some time in the day or in the night think and gather in your heart all the sick and all the sorry, that suffer woe and poverty, the pain that prisoners bear who lie heavy fettered with iron; think much of the Christians who are among heathens, some in prison, some in as much thralldom as an ox or an ass; have pity on those that are in strong temptations. Set all men's sorrows in your thoughts, and sigh to Our Lord that He may take care and have pity on them, and behold them with the eyes of His mercy, and if you have time, say the Psalm *"Levavi oculos meos"*. . . .

After the Mass-kiss, when the priest consecrates, there forget all the world, and there be all out of the body; there in sparkling love clasp your Beloved that is lighted down from heaven in your breast's bower, and hold Him fast, until He has granted all that ever you will. . . .

Of Speech:

First of all, when you must go to your parlor window, ask of your maiden who it is that is come, for such it may be that you should shun, and when you must go forth, cross full carefully your mouth, ears and eyes, and your breast also, and go forth with God's dread to the priest. First say *"Confiteor,"* And thereafter *"Benedicite,"* which he ought to say, and harken to his words, and sit all still, that when he parts from you he may know neither good nor evil of you, and neither can he praise or blame you. One is so well learned, another so wise-worded, that she would have him know it, and sits and speaks back at him, and gives him word for word, and becomes a master who should be an anchoress, and teaches him who is come to teach her; and she would, for her part, be known and famed among the wise. Known she is well, for through the very fact that she thinks to be held wise, he understands that she is a fool. For she hunts after praise and catches blame. For at last, when he is gone away, "This anchoress," he will say, "is of much speech." Eve held in Paradise long talk with the snake, and told him all the lesson that God had taught her and Adam of the apple, so the fiend through her words understood anon her weakness, and found a way to her loss. Our Lady, Saint Mary, did quite otherwise; she told the angel no tale, but asked him shortly what she did not know.

You, my dear Sisters, follow Our Lady, and

not the cackling Eve. For an anchoress, whoever
she may be or however much she may know, let
her keep still. Let her not have a hen's nature. The
hen, when she has laid an egg, does nothing but
cackle. And what does she get for it? Anon comes
the chough, and robs her of her eggs, and eats all
that of which she should have brought forth her
quick birds. And even so the wicked chough, the
devil, bears away from the cackling anchoress, and
swallows all the good that she has brought forth,
that should, as birds, have risen up towards heaven,
if she had not cackled. The wretched peddler makes
more noise to sell his soap than a rich mercer all his
dearworthy wares. . . .

Silence ever at meat, for if other religious do it, as
you know well, you ought to before all. And if one
of you have a dear guest, make your maiden gladden
her cheerfully in your stead, and you shall have
leave to open your window once or twice, and make
signs toward her with a glad face. . . .

Very foolish would he be who might, of his own
behoof, grind grit or wheat, if he ground the grit
and left the wheat. "Wheat is holy speech," as Saint
Anselm saith. She grinds grit who chatters. The
two cheeks are the grindstones. The tongue is the
clapper. Look to it, dear Sisters, that your cheeks
grind nought but soul-food, and your ears hear
nought but soul's heal.

Anchoresses like Birds:

But God called the good anchoresses birds of
heaven, as I said before: "Foxes have holes, and the
birds of the air their nests." True anchoresses are indeed birds of heaven that fly on high and sit singing

merrily in the green boughs; that is, they think upward, and of the bliss of heaven that never fades but
is always green. And they sit in this green singing
very merrily, that is, they rest in such thoughts and
have such mirth of heart as they who sing. A bird,
though once in a while to seek its meat for flesh's
need it lights on the ground, is never secure all the
while that it rests on the earth, but turns around
often and looks carefully all about. Even so the good
anchoress, fly she ever so high, must light sometimes
on the earth of the body to eat, drink, sleep, work,
speak, hear, where there is need, of earthly things.
But then, as the bird does, she must look well about
her and behold on each side, that she may nowhere
be mistaken, lest she be caught in some of the devil's
snares, or hurt in some wise, the while that she rests
so low.

The Seven Deadly Sins:[2]

The seven deadly sins live for the fiend, and they
are all in his hire and serve him in his court, each
one in the task that falls to him. The proud are his
trumpeters. They draw inward the wind of worldly
praise, and after with idle boast puff it out again, as
the trumpeter does to make a noise, and with a loud
sound show off their glory. And if they thought well
of God's trumpeters, and of the trumpets of the

---

[2] These finely drawn cartoons are the earliest allegorical representation
of the seven deadly sins. The subject was a favorite one with homilists
of all kinds, and it received varied and lively treatment characteristic
of the times and of the authors. In this work, cf. the realistic pictures by
Langland, pp. 319 ff. The last literary appearance of the capital sins is in
the pageant summoned up by Spenser (*The Faerie Queene,* Bk. III, Canto
18) in which there is more color than power; the age of convincing allegory was passing. The closest modern analogy to the mediaeval personification of vice appears in the pages of Bunyan.

angels of heaven that shall grimly blow at the four
corners of the world before the dreadful doom:
"Arise, dead, arise, come to the Lord's doom to be
judged, where no proud trumpeter may be saved"—
if they thought of this well they would quickly
enough blow more dimly.

Some jugglers there be who know no other glee
than to make faces and wrench their mouths and
scowl with their eyes. With this trade the unhappy
envious serve in the devil's court, to bring laughter
to their envious lord. For if anyone says well or does
well, in no wise may they look that way with the
right eye of a good heart, but they wink on the other
side, and look upward and squint. But if there is
anything blameworthy or hateful, they scowl in that
direction with both their eyes. And when they hear
anything good they turn downward both their ears,
but their hearing is ever wide open to evil. They
wrench their mouths amiss when they turn good to
evil; and if it is partly evil, through lying they
wrench it to a worse thing. These are foretellers of
their own fate, for they show beforehand how the
horrible devil shall terrify them with his grim grin-
ning, and how they themselves shall grin and snivel
and make sour faces for their great anguish in the
pain of hell. But for this they are less to be pitied
because they learned beforehand their trade of making grim faces.

The wrathful fences with knives before the fiend,
and he is his knifethrower and plays with swords and
bears them by the sharp end on his tongue. Swords
and knives are sharp and cutting words that he
throws from himself and hurls towards others. But
these show how the devil will play with them as with

sharp awls and toss them about as in a skin bag, each
toward the other, and pierce them through with hell-
swords that are keen and carving, and with fearful
pains.

The slothful lies and sleeps in the devil's arms as
his dear darling, and the devil lays his beak down to
his ear and whispers to him all that he will. For so it
surely is with him that is idle in goodness; the fiend
talks earnestly and the idle gladly receives his lore.
He that is idle and careless sleeps in the devil's arms,
but he shall grimly awake at the doomsday at the
blowing of the angel's trumpet, and in hell shall
awake with fearful amazement.

The covetous is the devil's ash-man, and lies ever
in the ashes and pokes in the ashes and stirs busily
about and rakes them together, and he putters therein and blinds himself, and makes therein figures of
augrim,[3] as reckoners do that have much to reckon.
This is a fool's bliss, and the fiend beholds all his
game and laughs fit to burst. For every wise man
understands this well, that gold and silver and all
earthly goods are but earth and ashes, and they
blind everyone that blows in them. . . .

The greedy glutton is the fiend's manciple; for
he sticks ever in the cellar or in the kitchen. His
heart is in the dishes, his thought is all on the nap,
his life is in the tun, his soul in the crock. He comes
before his lord all smutty and besmattered, a dish in
one hand and a bowl in the other; he talks with
words and wiggles like a drunken man that has a

[3] A word meaning the art of numbers. It is a Middle English form of
the Old French "algorisme," derived from the surname of a famous
Arabian mathematician of the ninth century, through whose work on
algebra the Arabic numerals came into use in Europe. Popular language
of the Middle Ages proves how far-reaching was the influence of the
Mohammedans who ringed the Mediterranean for centuries.

mind to fall. The fiend beholds his great belly, and laughs fit to burst.

In the devil's court the lecher, and all his fellows, stinks of filth, and pleases well his lord with that stinking breath, better than he should with any sweet incense. In the Lives of the Fathers it tells how he stinks before God. The angel showed this truly and openly when he held his nose when there came the proud lecher riding, and he did not so for the rotting body that he helped the holy hermit to bury. . . .

Comfort in Temptation:

Our Lord, when He suffers that we be tempted, plays with us as a mother with her young darling, who flies from him and hides herself, and lets him sit lonely and look about longingly and call "Dame, Dame!" and weep awhile. And then with outspread arms she leaps laughing towards him, and clasps and kisses him and wipes his eyes. Right so Our Lord leaves us alone now and then, and withdraws His grace and His power, that we find sweetness in nothing that we do, nor savor of heart.

The Love of Jesus Christ:

God hath won our love in all kinds of ways, and hereto belongs a tale and a veiled parable:

A Lady there was who was beset all about with foes, and her land destroyed, and she all poor within her earthern castle. Yet a mighty King's love was turned upon her, so immeasurably strong that for the wooing of her He sent His messengers one after the other, and often many together. He sent her baubles both many and fair, and means of livelihood,

and the help of His high army to hold her castle. She
took it all as a thing of no account, for she was so
hard-hearted that He could never come nearer to her
love. What wilt thou more? He came at last Himself, and showed her His fair face, that He was the
fairest of all men to behold, and spoke so sweetly
and with words so merry that they might have raised
the dead from death to life. And He wrought many
wonders and many deeds before her eyes and showed her His might. He told her of His Kingdom, and
promised to make her queen of all He owned. All
this availed nought. Is not such scorn to be wondered at? For she was never worthy to be His slave.
But through His debonaireness love had so overcome
Him that He said at last: "Dame, thou art warred
upon, and thy foes are so strong that thou mayest
in no wise without my succor flee from their hands,
lest they do thee to a shameful death. I will, for love
of thee, take this fight upon myself and save thee
from them that seek thy death. I know in sooth that
I shall receive among them wounds unto death, and
I will it heartily, to win thy heart. Now I beseech
thee, for the love that I show thee, at least to love
me dead after that death whom living thou wouldst
not love." The King did all this. He freed her from
her foes, and was cruelly ill-treated, and slain at
last. Would not that lady be of evil nature if she did
not love Him over all things thereafter?

This King is Jesus Christ, God's Son, that in
such wise wooed our souls that the devil beset. And
He, like a noble wooer, after many messengers and
many good deeds, came to prove His love and show
by knightship that He was love-worthy, as knights
used sometimes to do. He went into a tournament

He went into a tournament; the shield that covered His Godhead was His dear Body that was stretched out on the rood. ANCREN RIWLE

and for His sweetheart's sake raised His shield in fight as a keen knight pierced on every side. This shield that covered His Godhead was His dear body that was stretched on the rood, broad as a shield above in His outstretched arms and narrow beneath, for one foot, as men ween, was set upon the other foot. . . . This shield shieldeth us not only from evil, but it doth yet more; it crowneth us in heaven. But, Lord, thou sayest, whereunto? Might He not with less grief have rescued us? Yes, surely, full lightly, but He would not. Wherefor? To take from us every excuse for not giving Him our love that He so dearly bought.

Men buy lightly what they love little. He bought us with His Heart's blood—a dearer price was never —to draw our heart's love to Him that cost Him so dear. In a shield there are three things: the wood, the leather, and the painting. All these were in the shield: the wood of the rood, the leather of God's body, and the painting of the red blood that made Him fair. Again a third reason: after a keen knight's death men hang his shield high in the Church as a remembrance. And so is this shield, the Crucifix, set in church in the place where men may soonest see it, to think thereby of the knightship of Jesus Christ that He showed on the rood. His sweetheart beholds thereon how He bought her love and let His shield be pierced, that is, He let His side be opened to show her His Heart, and to show her openly how inwardly He loved her, and to draw her heart. . . .

He saith: "If thy love is to sell, I have bought it with love beyond all other. And if thou sayest that thou wilt not set it so cheap, but wilt have more, name what it shall be; set the price of my love. Thou

shalt not say so much that I will not give for thy
love much more. Wilt thou have castles and kingdoms? Wilt thou rule all the world? I shall do thee
better: I shall make thee with this queen of heaven.
Thou shalt be seven-fold brighter than the sun; no
evil shall harm thee, nothing shall vex thee; no joy
shall be wanting thee; all thy will shall be wrought
in heaven and on earth, yea, and in hell." . . .

Lo, thus Our Lord wooeth. Is she not too hard-
hearted whose love such a wooer cannot win to Himself? And especially if she thinks of these three
things: what He is, and what she is, and how great is
the love of one as high as He for one as low as she.
For thus saith the Psalm-maker: *"Non est qui se
abscondit a calore ejus."* There is none who can so
hide himself as not to love Him. The true Sun was
for this raised up on the rood in the noon-tide, to
spread over all His hot love-gleams. Thus zealous
was He, and for this He died, to kindle His love in
His lover's heart. "I am come," He says in the
Gospel, "to bring fire into earth, that is burning love
into earthly hearts, and what yearn I for but that
it blaze?" . . .

Now you have heard, beloved Sisters, how and
why God is to be mightily loved. And to enkindle
you well, gather wood thereto with the poor woman
of the town of Sarepte, which signified the kindling
of fire. "Lord," said she to Elias the Holy Prophet,
"lo, I gather two sticks." These two sticks betoken
the beam that stood upright and that other also that
went cross-wise over the dear rood. With these two
sticks you shall enkindle the fire of love in your
hearts. Look often towards them. Think if you
ought not easily to love the King of bliss, that so

spreads His arms towards you and, as begging a
kiss, bends downward His head. . . .

From the Rule for the Outward Life:

It befits not an anchoress to make herself free
with other men's alms. Would we not laugh loudly
to scorn a begger that bid men to a feast? Mary and
Martha were both sisters, but their lives were sundered. You anchoresses have taken to yourselves
Mary's part, that the Lord Himself praised. *"Maria
optimam partem elegit."* "Martha, Martha," quoth
He, "thou art in a great bustle. Mary has chosen better, and nothing shall be taken from her share."
Housewifeship is Martha's share, and Mary's share
is stillness and rest from all the world's noise, that
nothing may keep her from hearing God's voice.
And heed what God said: that nothing shall be taken
from her share. Martha has her business; let her be,
and sit you with Mary stone-still at God's feet, and
harken to Him only. . . .

My loved Sisters, you shall have no beast but one
cat. An anchoress that has cattle seems better housewife, as Martha was, than anchoress; in no wise may
she be Mary, with peacefulness of heart. For then
she must think of the cow's fodder, and of the herds-
man's hire, flatter the haywarden, take care when
the cow gets into the pound, and pay for the harm all
the same. Christ knows, this is a hateful thing when
men in the town complain of the anchoress' cattle.
Though if any must needs have a cow, take care that
it does not annoy or harm anyone, and that her
thought be not fixed on it. An anchoress ought to
have nothing to draw her heart outward. Carry on

no traffic. An anchoress that trades sells her soul to the tradesman of hell. . . .

How to Deal With Those Who Serve Outside the Cloister:

You should zealously teach them to keep their Rule, both for you and for themselves, gently though, and lovingly, for so ought woman's teaching to be: loving and gentle and seldom stern. But it is right that they should dread you and love you; but let there be ever more of love than of dread. Then shall all fare well. Men should pour both oil and wine into a wound, as God said, but more of the soft oil than of the biting wine, that is, more of gentle words than of loud, for of this comes the best thing: that is love-fear. Lightly and sweetly forgive them their guilts, when they know them and promise betterment.

So far as you may, be large with them for food and drink and clothing and other things that the flesh needs, though you be more narrow and hard on yourselves. For so does he who blows well; he puts the narrow end of the horn to his own mouth, and the wide end outward. And so do you, for you will that your prayers sound like a trumpet and a sweet noise in the Lord's ears, not only for your own but for all folk's heal; as the Lord grant through the grace of Himself, that it may be so. Amen.

When you have time, read in this book every day, less or more. For I hope that it will be helpful to you, through God's grace, if you read it often, or else I have ill-spent much of my time. God knows that I would rather set out for Rome than to begin it again after having done it. And if you find that you do as you read, thank God earnestly; and if you do it not, ask God's mercy, and go about holding it better, with your might. May Father, Son and Holy Ghost, one Almighty God, have you in His ward. May He gladden and comfort you my beloved Sisters, and for all that you endure and suffer for Him may He give you nothing less than Himself altogether. Be He ever held high, from world to world, for ever and ever. Amen.

As often as you read this book greet Our Lady with an Ave Mary for him that made this Rule, and wrote it and toiled over it. Modest enough am I to ask so little.

The devotional life reflected in the *Ancren Riwle* was bound to reach out from the religious houses to the people at large. The *Riwle* belongs to a group of widely known writings, all in the same conservative southern dialect and marked by the same rhythmic style. It includes the *Sawles Warde, Holy Maidenhood,* and three lives of saints known as the *Katherine Group.*[4]

SAWLES WARDE

There was no law of copyright in the thirteenth century to embarrass preachers or writers in their synthetic use of material. If truth was common property, why not the literary expressions of truth? In the case of the homily known as *Sawles Warde,* "John who wrote it" chose an excellent allegory[5] from among many in the works of Hugh of Saint Victor, and expanded the brief Latin into a much longer English

---

[4] It is claimed by some scholars that all these works are by the same author.

[5] *De Anima,* Bk. IV, chs. 13-15; *Patrologia Latina* CLXXVII, 185.

paraphrase, alive with vivid dialogue and arresting description. Under his pen the allegorical abstractions took on features; the household of Wit and of Will his wife fairly hums with the bustle of a mediaeval manor, without in the least losing its likeness to man's soul as it is in any century. The English version amplifies the Latin with a long description of hell, fearful enough but more restrained than many another version based upon the *Vision of Saint Paul*.[6] The description of heaven is a melodic development of brief vibrant phrases in the original such as: "So must everyone shake off his torpor, and go from fear to desire of his heavenly country." And at the end, where the Latin author gravely draws his moral, the Englishman breaks into charming doggerel. The latter method is far more persuasive.

"If the Father of the house knew at what hour the thief would come, he would certainly watch and would not suffer his house to be broken open." Our Lord in the Gospel teaches us in a parable how we ought warily to watch over ourselves against the wretched creature of hell and against his tricks. "If the lord of the house," He says, "knew when and at what time the thief would come to his house, he would be awake and would not suffer the thief to break it open." The house that Our Lord speaks of is a man himself. In this house is the house's lord, man's Wit, and the housewife. She may be called Will, and the house goes as she wills only too well, unless Wit as lord chastise her the better, and

---

[6] The original Greek version dates from the fourth century. Twenty-two later Latin MSS are extant, showing the extreme popularity of "vision literature." The treatment of this material ranged from the cheaply gruesome to Dantesque magnificence.

take from her much that she wants. And she wants
her household to follow her before all, unless Wit
forbid them, for they are all unruly and reckless
servants unless he rights them. And who are these
servants? Some are without and some within. Those
without are the man's five wits, sight, hearing,
smacking, smelling, and each limb's feeling. These
be servants under Wit, as under the house's lord,
and where he is careless there is not one of them
but behaves in an unruly manner, and often does
wrong, one in evil-seeming, another in evil deeds.
His servants be also within, busy in many a thought
how to please Will, the housewife, against God's
will, and they swear together readily and things
go their way. Though we hear nought we may be
aware of their noise and unruly bearing, until Wit
come forth and both with anger and with love chastise them the better. Because of these servants it
is never well with the house, for when Wit sleeps
or is away from home it is then that a man forgets
himself and lets his servants have their way.

This profits nought, for then the house is robbed,
and it has within it the treasure that God gave Himself to buy, that is, man's soul. For many thieves
go about by day and by night to break into the
house after that treasure that God bought with
his death, and lost His life on the rood for, wretched
spirits who with hateful deeds are set against all
good deeds. They spy around the house, God's dear
castle, that is watched over by Wit, the house's
lord. It is their evil way to seek a going-in through
the walls to murder those within. The head of them
all is the fiend, against whom and against whose

satellites the householder that is Wit guards his house thus.

Our Lord has given Wit comfort in his daughters, that is to say, the four head-virtues. The eldest is called Wareness, the second is named ghostly Strength, the third is Measure, and Righteousness is the fourth. Wit the householder, God's constable, calls Wareness forth and makes her door-warden, and she must warily look to see which are worthy to be let in or thrust out. Strength stands next to her, and if they try to come in, in spite of Wareness, she warns Strength her sister who throws them out. The third sister, Measure, takes mastery over the wilful rabble that we spoke of before, and teaches them sense, to measure through the mid-way of two evils, for that is the way to do whatever ought to be done. And she orders them all, that none of them go beyond measure. And the fourth sister, Righteousness, sits on high as the judge, and beats the guilty and crowns them that do well, and judges each with right judgment. And for dread of her each of the servants watches over his business, the eyes theirs, the mouth his, the ears theirs, the hands theirs, and each of the others watches that nothing evil shall come in. And so it is done, and all is still therein.

And Wareness fears lest one of the household should become over-confident and fall asleep and neglect his post, and she sends them a messenger that she well knows, come from afar, to make fearful those that were overhardy and those that were careless, that they might be more aware. He is taken in and gazed on by them all, for lank he is and lean, and his face deathly and pale and of strange color, and each hair on his head stands up. Wareness bade him tell first who he was and whence he came and what he sought there. "I can nowhere speak," said he, "unless I have good listening. Listen to me then. Fearful I am called, and I am death's messenger and death's reminder, and I am come before to warn you of her coming." And Wareness, who best knows how to manage her words and her works, speaks for them all and asks whence death will come, and what company she will bring with her. Fearful answers her: "I know not the time, for she said it not to me, but be on the watch, for her way is to come by stealth, sudden and unremembered, when men least ween. Of her company thou askest; I answer thee. She lights where she comes with a thousand devils. And each bears a great book full of sins written with swart, small letters, and with a huge chain bright red with fire to bind and draw to hell whoever may be shown through the book to be embroiled in sin that he with his will or his word or his work wrought in all his life, unless he has righted himself with true shrift and with death-payment."

And Wareness asked: "Whence comest thou, Fearful, death's reminder?" "I come," said he, "of hell." Then saith Wareness, "And hast then seen hell?" "Yea indeed," saith Fearful, "oft and again." "Now then," saith Wareness, "by my troth truly tell us what is hell like and what hast thou seen therein." "By my troth gladly," saith Fearful, "not what it is, for that may no tongue tell, but as best I can and know I shall relate to you. Hell is wide without measure and deep without bottom, and full of unspeakable burning. For no quick thing on earth can bear it, full of sorrow untellable, for no mouth for wretchedness nor for woe can reckon or tell it. So thick therein is the darkness that men must grope, for that fire gives no light[7] but blinds their eyes with the reek of a smothering smoke, and in that swart darkness they see swart things, as devils that trouble them with all kinds of pains, dragons grisly as devils who swallow them whole and spew them out often before and behind, and other times rend them and chew them to grit, and they after are whole again. . . . O Hell, death's house, dwelling of woe, of grief and of groaning, hateful home and hard place, loathliest land of all, and dark dwelling full of dreariness! And I am come thus," quoth Fearful, "to warn you before, and tell you these things."

Then the wilful housewife held her all still, and turned all the servants that she was wont to draw after her, truly to Wit, her lord, and to these four sisters. Then after a time Wareness spoke again and said: "I see a messenger coming, very fair of face, glad and free and garbed in lovely wise." "Let him in," said Wit. "If God wills he will bring us glad tidings, and there is much need of that, for Fearful, death's messenger, has frightened us greatly with his news." Wareness let him in and he greeted the household with laughing face, and they gave back his greeting and were all lightened of care, and were gladdened by the sight of him, for all the house shone and glimmered with his light. And he asked them if they would be pleased to hear him for a while. "Yea," quoth Righteousness, "and well it

[7] This phrase is reminiscent of the "flames that are lightless" of the Old English *Genesis B*, and the famous "darkness visible" of *Paradise Lost*. For the possible indebtedness of Milton to the earlier poem, see *Word-Hoard*, p. 82.

pleases us, and it is right and well that we graciously listen."

"Harken now then," he said, "and earnestly understand. I am mirth's messenger, and remembrance of everlasting life, and Life's Love I am called, and come right from heaven, in which I have seen, now and often before, the bliss that no man's tongue can tell of. The blessed God saw you frightened and somewhat drooping with that which Fearful told you of death and of hell, and He sent me to gladden you."

"Ah," said Wareness, "welcome, Life's Love, mirth's messenger, and for the love of God's self, if ever you have seen Him tell us somewhat of Him."

"I have seen Him oft, but not all as He is, for against the light and brightness of His face the sun's gleam is dusky and seems like a shadow, and I might not look at the brightness of His face save through a sheen mirror between me and Him that shields my eyes. So I have often seen the Holy Threeness, Father and Son and Holy Ghost, three in one, and but a little while might I bear the light. But in some wise I might behold Our Lord Jesus Christ, God's son that bought us on the rood, how He sits blissful on His Father's right hand and is ruling all things in that life lasting without limit. He is measurelessly fair and the angels are never full of beholding Him. And yet I see shining out the marks of His wounds and how He shows them to His Father to prove how He loved us, how He yielded ever to Him Who sent Him to set us free, and how He beseeches Him ever for mankind's healing. After Him I see high over all heaven that

happy maiden, His Mother Mary, sitting on a
throne so bright set with gems, and her face so full
of good that earth's light is darkness there against.
There I saw her as she besought her dear-worthy
son earnestly and inwardly for those who serve her
and He grants her blithely all that she beseeches
Him. That light I then might no longer bear.

"I looked to the angels and to the archangels and
to the others that be above them, blessed spirits that
be before God and serve Him ever and sing ever
unweariedly. Nine Orders there be, and how they
be set in order the one above the other and the task
of each one were too long to tell. So much mirth
had I at their sight that I might not for long while
look elsewhere. After them I looked toward the
Patriarchs and Prophets who make such mirth now
that they are in that land of bliss, they that before
wept for fear on earth, and now they see that all
is true which they long since said of Our Lord which
He had shown them by ghostly sight. I saw the
Apostles, poor and low on earth, full and overflowing with unmeasured bliss sitting on thrones, and
all that is high in the world is under their feet; they
are ready to judge in the day of doom kings and
kaisers and all generations of all kinds of people.
I beheld the martyrs and their unmeasured mirth,
they who here suffered pain and death for Our Lord,
and they lightly held all kinds of trifles and earthly
torments against the bliss to come that God showed
them in their hearts. After them I beheld the company of confessors who lived a good life and died
in holiness. They shine as do stars in bliss everlasting and see God in His beauty and have all
tears wiped from their eyes. And I saw the bright

and sheen company of the holy maidens most like to angels who in fellowship with them make bliss and are glad, they who when living walked over their flesh and the flesh's laws and overcame nature, leading heavenly life on earth, dwelling in mirth and in bliss. The fairness of their beauty, the sweetness of their song, no tongue can tell. All they who are there sing, but their song may none but they sing. A sweet smell follows them wherever they wend, so that one might live ever by that sweetness. He whom they pray for is most surely helped, for at their beseeching God Himself rises and all the other saints sit and hear."

"Very well," quoth Wareness, "we like what thou sayest. Now that thou hast well said of the varied happiness of each rank tell us now what bliss belongs to all alike." And Life's Love answered, "The common bliss is sevenfold: length of life, wit and love, and of that love gladness forever, merriness without measure, praise-song, lightship, secureness is the seventh." "Though I somewhat understand this," saith Wareness, "thou must unveil this more clearly and open it also." "It shall be, Wareness," saith Love's Life, "as thou willest. They live in one beauty that is brighter sevenfold and sheener than the sun, and ever in one strength to do without toil all that they will, and evermore in all good without woe, without anything that may harm or pain them, in all that ever is soft and sweet. And their life is God's sight and God's knowledge, as Our Lord said; 'that is,' quoth He, 'everlasting life, to see and know the sooth God and Him whom He has sent, Jesus Christ our Lord, for our saving.' And for this they are like Him, in the same beauty that He

is, for they see Him as He is, face to face. They
are so wise that they know all God's reads,[8] and
His runes, and His dooms that dark be and deeper
than any sea-dingle. They see in God all things,
and they know all that is and ever shall be, and
what it is, and why and wherefore and whence it
began. They love God without measure, for they
understand what He has done for them through
His great goodness, and what they owe to His dear-
worthy grace.

"And each loves the other as much as himself. So
glad are they of God who is all their bliss that no
tongue can say it, for each loves the other as himself. Each has as much mirth in the other's good as
in his own. By this you may see and know that each
has as many gladnesses as the saints are many. And
the gladness of each is as great to everyone else as
his own. Yet over all this, since each loves God
more than himself and more than all the others, he
is more glad of God than of his own gladness without any reckoning. Take heed to this: even if the
heart of one man can scarce find room for its own
joy, yet still it receives into itself the many and
great joys of others. For thus saith Our Lord to
those who have pleased Him: 'Go,' quoth he, 'into
thy Lord's bliss.' You must enter into it, for never
can it all enter into you. For this they praise God
forever and sing unwearied, ever alike lusty in their
praise-songs. As it is written: 'Blessed be they, O
Lord, who dwell in thy house, they shall praise Thee
from world unto world.' They are all as light and

---

[8] "Read" is the Anglo-Saxon word for counsel. Runes were letters of
the ancient Teutonic alphabet which, because they were often used in
pagan incantations, came to stand for hidden knowledge.

swift as the sun's gleam that shoots from the east into the west, as quick as thine eye closes and opens, for wheresoever the ghost will be, the body is there anon without letting, for nothing can stand against them; and each one is almighty to do that which he will—yea, to make heaven and earth quake with one finger." . . .

Quoth Strength: "Since it is so, what may keep us from God, or hold us from Him? I am secure in God, that life nor death nor woe nor war shall keep us from His love. But all this have we gained if we are as true treasurers who guard well His treasure, and are careful to keep us under His wing." "Get out!" quoth Wareness, "Fearful, our foe! It is not right that one house should hold these two, for where mirth's messenger is, and true love of everlasting life, Fearful is put to flight." "Now out, Fearful," quoth Strength, "thou shalt no longer live in our land."

"Now," quoth he, "I said for God all that I said, and though my tale was less merry than was that of mirth's messenger, it is not without profit for you, though it be not so fair nor so pleasing. Each of us had his time for speaking, and neither should shun the other."

"Thou warnest of woe, he tells of joy. Much need is that men most earnestly hear you both. Flit now, Fearful, while Life's Love is herein and suffer with even heart the doom of Righteousness for thou shalt full blithely be taken in as often as Life's Love ceases to speak."

Now was Will the housewife all still that ere was so wilful. And all went after Wit's ruling who was the householder, and all then were still that

were wont to be foolish and go after Will their
Lady. Now they listen to his lore and do what they
ought, through these two messengers. And now they
listen to his lore and all goes through these two
messengers that they had heard. And the four sisters
learned to keep ward against the ingoing of any
vice, and to watch truly. . . . This thought makes
man to flee all vice and draw on his heart towards
the bliss of heaven. May Our Lord give us this
through His holy grace who with the Father and
the Son and the Holy Ghost rules in Threeness ever
without end. Amen.

For holy Charity, pray a Pater Noster for John
who wrote this book.

> Whoso this writing now has read,
> And Christ has him so well sped,
> I beg through Saint Charity
> That he often pray for me
> A Pater Noster and Ave Mary,
> That my life may so here be
> That Our Lord is pleased with me.
> In youth and age may I so live
> That to Jesus Christ my soul I give.
>   Amen.

THE KATHERINE GROUP

The earliest prayers of the Church had exalted the
courage of the virgin martyrs, and this *cultus* appealed to the Anglo-Saxons, whose chivalrous admiration for women and love for things brave and strong
had been noted long before by Tacitus. From the
early *Acta Martyrum*—already more legend than history—poets and sermon writers drew thrilling stories.

When the first English monastic foundations for nuns were made in the seventh century, priestly poets wrote lives of women saints for their guidance and inspiration. The nuns, in their turn, inspired writers and scholars; they had cheered Saint Boniface, for example, by sending him books "written in gold on purple vellum." The *De Laudibus Virginitatis* composed by Aldhelm (c.680) for the nuns of Barking celebrated in rapid Latin rhyme the virtues of many saintly maidens. As the Middle Ages advanced, this spirit was heightened by the conception of our Lady as the ideal of knighthood, an ideal that grew with the chivalry of the thirteenth century.

In the same manuscripts that contain the *Ancren Riwle* and *Sawles Warde* are versions of the lives of Saint Katherine, Saint Margaret, and Saint Juliana, whose deeds speak more convincingly in honor of purity than does the *Holy Maidenhood,* included in the same group. This piece is, unhappily, by an author less broad, sympathetic and artistic than "John," and is not truly representative of the mediaeval attitude towards the subject of virginity.

Saint Katherine of Alexandria was as widely known in her day as is Saint Teresa of Lisieux in ours. Because she had been brave her banner marched with the Crusaders, and because her wisdom had defied the best pagan scholars of her time she presided in Christian schools for centuries as patron saint of higher studies. Saint Margaret of Antioch had defied the devil himself in prison, as had Saint Juliana, already celebrated in Old English days in Cynewulf's long poem.[9]

And in the five and thirtieth year of his ruling,

---

[9] See *Word-Hoard*, p. 218.

Maximinus set his kingly seat in the mother-town
of Alexander's kingdom. He sent heralds and messengers as wide as the land was, that both poor
and rich should come before him to the temple in
the court of his heathen gods, each one with his gift
to honor them with. They came all at his bidding,
each according to his means, before Maximinus himself, to honor his Mawmets,[10] the rich with sheep
and bulls as a gift, whoever could, and the poor
with quick birds.

In this same town was dwelling a maiden very
young in years, two less than twenty, fair and free
of face and of form; yet was she steadfast of true
faith within, of royal blood, an only daughter, a
rare scholar, named Katherine. This maiden was
both fatherless and motherless from childhood, but
though she was young she held her father's household wisely and warily within her heritage and the
dwelling that was hers by her birth. Not for this
did she think it good to have many under her and
to be called lady, which so many esteem, but she
was afraid both of sin and shame and of losing
and mis-spending what her forefathers had fostered.
For herself she cared nothing for the world. Thus,
lo! she kept a part of her ancestral goods for herself,
and spent all the rest on the needful and the naked.

This mild, meek maiden, this lovesome lady with
blameless bearing, loved no light play and no love
songs. She would have no songs, nor learn nor listen
to love songs, but ever she had on Holy Writ her

---

[10] A "Mawmet" was the anachronistic name given to an idol; it was a
Middle English corruption of "Mohammedan." The people uncritically
identified heathenism with Islam, thanks to current romances and pirate
encounters on the Mediterranean. Actually, idolatry was no part of the
religion of the hated "paynims"—again, a corruption of "pagans."

eyes or her heart, often both together. Her father
had set her early to belief and to learning, and she
seized it through the Holy Ghost so well that none
was her equal. Proud masters and many tested her
oft on many sides to entrap her, but not one of them
could once turn her aside with all his crafty tricks
out of the way; but she straightway gave them
such counter-strokes and turned their wiles back so
on themselves that they all acknowledged themselves vanquished and overcome, and gave her all
the mastery and all the honor.

Thus while she pondered and thought ever to keep
herself a maid in maidenhood, as she sat in a bower
of her ancestral home she heard great mirth from the
accursed temple of the Mawmets, lowing of the cattle, playing of the men, gay sound of each game to
praise and to worship their heathen gods. As she
heard this and knew not yet what it was, she sent
straight to find out what wonder it was. Soon her
messenger came again and told her the truth. She
was so kindled with wrath that she was beside herself. She summoned such of her household as she
would and went thitherward. She found very many
there, shouting and calling and howling impatiently,
with rueful cries, those that should be Christians and
believers in God's law, but who for dread of death
gave the devils gifts as the heathen did.

Who felt worse than she? Her heart was wounded
within for the wretches that she saw working wicked
works against God's will. She thought, though, as
she was gentle and patient, young thing as she was,
what would it profit if she all alone stood against so
keen a Caesar and his kingdom? She stood still a

while, and raised her heart up to the high Healer who is honored in heaven, and besought His help and hap and wisdom, as surely as all the world is wielded by His willing. Thereafter she took the weapon of true belief, and made on her breast and before her teeth and the tongue of her mouth the token of the holy Rood. Then she came leaping forth all glowing with the flame of the Holy Ghost, where the Caesar stood among the sinful slaughter of the cattle slain as gifts to the devils till each cursed altar of the wretched Mawmets ran with blood all be-blooded, and she began to cry with a loud voice: "Greeting, Caesar. It would become thee, for thy highness, if thou wouldst yield and give to the worship of God (who shaped thee and all the world) this same tribute which thou payest to devils, and which foredoes thee both body and soul."

The struggle of the virgin martyrs was carried on not only against emperors, but against the Prince of the Powers of Darkness as well. Both Saint Juliana and Saint Margaret overcame him through prayer and a woman's courage:

There appeared to Margaret in prison a cursed creature of hell in dragon's likeness, so grisly that all were aghast that saw him; that wretch glistened as though he were gold all over. His locks and his long beard shone all of gold, and his grisly teeth seemed of swart iron. His two eyes stared brighter than stars, and as gemstones broad as basins in his horned head on either side of his crooked nose. . . . (Margaret begins to pray for help:)

"Unsearchable God, full of all good,[11] whose wrath is so terrible that the dwellers in hell and in heaven, and all quick things quake before it, Thou hast wrought and Thou wieldest all worldly things. Those that praise Thee and exalt Thee in heaven, the fishes that float in the flood with fins, the flying birds that flee through the sky, and all that is wrought, work what Thy will is, but man alone. The sun goes her rounds without rest. The moon and the stars that walk through the sky stay not nor stop but stir ever more, and no whither from the way that Thou hast made for them turn they ever. Thou steerest the sea-stream that it may flow no further than Thou hast marked. The winds and the weathers, the woods and the waters bow and obey. Fiends have fear of Thee, and angels of Thy wrath. The worms and the wild beasts that dwell in the forests live after the law that Thou hast made for them. Beloved Lord, look to me and help me, Thy handiwork, for all my hope is in thee."

DEDICATION TO THE ORMULUM

Not all clerics in the monasteries had the writer's gift of letting truth shine out through beauty; some seem to have written with a wooden pen rather than with the "joy of a bird."[12] Yet many of these less gifted poets were earnest teachers, who wished to share their booklore with "the folk." While the *Ancren Riwle* was being penned in the South (c. 1325), an

[11] This passage is an extreme example of the rhythmic, alliterative prose style that had been popular in English homilies since the tenth century. Poetry is more rememberable than prose, and from primitive times had been used for direct appeals to the people.

[12] An Anglo-Saxon kenning for a quill pen. The "joy of a bird" is his feather.

Augustinian Canon in the North, probably at Elsham
Priory in Lincolnshire, was turning out thousands of
lines of impeccable verse for the benefit of the laity.
He wrote his long paraphrases of the Gospel with
enthusiasm and no genius. Each line is a perfect
septenarium[13] in a North-midland dialect sprinkled
with Scandinavian words. Its chief interest to scholars
lies in its apparently fantastic but really consistent
phonetic spelling, with doubling of consonants to indicate vowel values, but his own intention has no trace
of pedantry. He loved the Gospels and he loved his
fellow men; warmly he would share one with the
other.[14] So he dedicated his paraphrases to his dear
English people, in the person of his Brother Walter:

> Now Brother Walter, brother mine after the flesh's
>   kind,   1
> And Brother mine in Christendom through Baptism
>   and truth,
> And Brother mine in God's House, in yet a third
>   wise,
> As we two both once undertook the same Rulebook
>   to follow,
> In the same Canonhood and life such as Saint Aus-
>   tin set,
> I have done what thou badest me, and fulfilled thy
>   will,
> I have changed to English tongue the Gospel's holy
>   lore,
> According to the little wit that my Lord hath grant-
>   ed me.

[13] A seven-foot line, modelled on a Latin verse form.

[14] The charge brought against the Middle Ages of keeping the Scriptures
from the laity overlooks these frequent poetic "Englishings" of both Old
and New Testament.

Thou thoughtest that it might well to great profit
turn

If English folk, for love of Christ, would learn it
zealously,

And follow it, fulfill it all with heart, with word,
with deed.

And so for this thou didst yearn much that I should
work this work,

And I have done so at thy will, but all through help
of Christ,

And now at last we must thank Christ that it is
brought to end.

And I have gathered in this book the Gospels nearly
all

That in the Massbook may be found throughout the
year at Mass,

And aye after the Gospel stands that which the
Gospel means,

That should be told to all the folk for their souls'
need.

And yet besides, more than enough thou shalt therein find

Of that which Christ's holy people should trust and
follow well,

I have set here in this book among the Gospel words,

All through myself, many words to help fill up their
number.

But thou shalt find that these my words, wherever
they are added,

May help all those who read them here to see and
understand. . . .

Therefore the Gospel have I turned into our English speech, 151

Because blithely I could wish that all our English
people
With their ears should listen thus, and with their
hearts believe it,
With their tongues proclaim it oft, and with their
deeds so follow
That under Christendom they win, through Christ's
truth, soul's salvation,
And that we may worthy be to taste of heaven's bliss.
Amen, Amen, Amen.
I that this English book have set, English men to
teach,
I was, when I was christened first, Ormin named
by name,
And I, Ormin, full inwardly, with mouth and eke
with heart,
Herewith beg those Christian men that herein some-
times read
This book, them beg I here that they for me will
pray this prayer,
That Brother who this English book first wrote and
wrought,
That Brother, for his toil's reward, true bliss thus
may find.

Amen.

THE LAYFOLK'S MASS BOOK

The laity must be helped to do their own praying
as well as to read the Gospels, and both parish priests
and monks had their welfare at heart. If the layman
knows no Latin, a simple English commentary, half
prayer, half explanation, written in the verse forms
familiar to him from many a romance and rhyming
sermon, will be the most helpful kind of book to give

him. Somewhere in the North Midlands an unknown Dan Jeremy (unofficially canonized in two manuscripts as "Saint Jeremy") wrote such a book, presumably in French, in the days of Norman predominance. By the thirteenth century it had been translated into hearty, reverent, popular English rhymes:

A worthy thing, most of goodness   1
In all the world, is the Mass;
In all the books of Holy Kirk
That holy men in time did work,
The Mass is praised many-fold;
Its virtues never may be told.
If a thousand clerks did nought else
But that which the book tells,
And told the virtues of Mass-singing
And the profit of Mass-hearing,
They would never tell the fifth part
For all their wit and all their art,
Tell the virtues, meed and pardon
Of them that have devotion
And in cleanness and good intent
Give worship to the Sacrament.
In a book found I the same,
By one Dan Jeremy of name,
A devout man and religious,
In his book he tells thus:
That thou shalt attention take,
And at the Mass no jangling make.
Great store he sets thereto,
Why it is full holy to do.
Also he tells us the manner
In which thou shalt the Mass hear.
When the priest speaks, or if he sing,

To him give good harkening,
When he prays in privity,
Time of praying it shall be.

The poem then follows through the whole Mass, sug-
gesting thoughts in union with the liturgical prayers
and actions of the priest.

And the Mass has not ceased   596
Till time of *"Ite Missa est."*
When thou hearest thus: *"Ite,"*
Or *"Benedicamus,"* if so it be,
Then is the Mass all done.
But yet one prayer make thou soon,
And after it, then thou may
In God's name wend thy way.
God be thanked in all our works,
God be thanked by priests and clerks.

THE AYENBITE OF INWIT

Not many manuscripts tell us as much about themselves as does the *Ayenbite of Inwit* (translated as
"the biting back of our inner wit," a good dramatiza-
tion of the word "conscience"). It states that it was
written in 1340 by Dan Michel of Northgate, an
Augustinian, in the homely English of Kent spoken
by "unlearned men, fathers and mothers and their kin
again," whom the priestly author loved. He even gives
us the catalogue number of the book, that the twentieth
century may stray back and find it safe in its place,
marked CC in the "bookhouse of Saint Austin of Canterbury." One fact he neglects to mention: the whole
of his book, with the exception of the doggerel beginning and end, is a translation of a French treatise
by a Dominican, Friar Lawrence, composed in 1279

for Philip II of France and entitled *La Somme des Vices et des Vertues*. This work was very popular in England; Dan Michel's version is only one of several, in prose or verse. Finally, no less a poet than Chaucer pilfered from the wisdom of the French priest in his *Parson's Tale,* thought to be the dullest of all the Canterbury stories. Dull it is, as told by the good but unimaginative priest in Chaucer's lumbering prose, just as the tired pilgrims are watching for their first glimpse of Canterbury at the end of the long road. The treatise, under the title *Book for a King,* had the honor of being one of the first books from Caxton's printing press. But no version can equal that of Dan Michel, who is simple and often sprightly in style, and refreshing in his certainty that nothing could be more thrilling than a systematic study of the seven deadly sins, root and branch, and of the shining gifts of the Holy Ghost, flower and fruit.

Foreword:

Against the temptings of the devil, say this that follows:

"Sweet Jesus, Thy holy Blood that Thou sheddest on the rood for me and for mankind, I pray that it be my shield against the wicked fiend, all to my life's end. So be it."

This book is Dan Michel's of Northgate, written in English by his own hand. It is called the "Biting-back of our inner wit." And it is in the book-house of Saint Austin of Canterbury, with the letters CC.

Holy Archangel Michael,
Saint Gabriel and Raphael,
Bring me to the castle

Where all souls fare well.
Lord Jesus, Almighty King
That made and keeps everything,
Me, that am Thy making,
To Thy bliss Thou me bring.   Amen.

The Freedom of Grace:

The second freedom is that which the good men
of this world have, that God has freed by grace and
by virtue from the thralldom of the devil and of sin;
that they be no thralls, neither to gold nor to silver
nor to their own flesh, nor to the goods of fortune,
so that death cannot rob them. But they have their
heart so high in God that they do not prize the world
any more than a button; and they dread not king or
earl, nor any mischance or poverty, nor shame nor
death, for they are half dead, and have their hearts
so apart from the love of the world that they wait
and will for death as does the good workman for his
hire, and the gleaner for his harvest, and they that
be in woe at sea for a good port, and prisoners for
their deliverance, and pilgrims for their country. . . .

The Mild Man:

The mild man is swift and quick when the will of
God and His ruling bears him along. But when his
own will bears him and leads him, he is slack and
slothful to do well, as the star that is called Saturn
manages to run as far every day with the firmament
as the firmament bears him as he does in thirty years
in his own circle and in his own running. Lastly, the
mild man bows more than ever when he believes that
he is pleasing God, and in all things he is like the
mill-ass that as blithely bears barley as wheat and

lead as corn, to the poor as to the rich. The mild man is strong for he changes his strength for the strength of God, as saith the Prophet, wherefore there is nought that he cannot bear. For God beareth him and his burden, wherefore he bows with good will, and perseveringly. For he is never more weary than the sun that God brings forth and leads. And the more he lives the more his strength waxes, even as the little ant.

The Goodness of Alms:

There was a poor man, they say, that had a cow, and he heard his priest say in his preaching that God said in His Gospel that God would pay back a hundredfold all that men gave for Him. The good man, with the counsel of his wife, gave his cow to his priest that was rich. The priest took it blithely and sent it to the others that he had. When it came to evening the good man's cow came home to his house as it was wont to do, and led with her all the priest's cows to the number of one hundred. Then the good man said that he thought that that was the word of the Gospel that he had been repaid. And the cows were judged to be his before the Bishop, against the priest.

The Tavern of Heaven:

The great sweetness that the contemplative heart feels by the gift of wisdom in this deathly life is but a little swallow whereby men smack how God is sweet and soft, as a man tastes and smacks wine before he drinks his fill. But when men shall come into the great tavern where the tun is kept, that is, into life everlasting, where is the God of love and of peace and of bliss and of lusts and of solace, He shall be so free to each that all shall be full. As saith the Psalter: All the willing of the heart shall be fulfilled there when God shall come upon His friends in a flood of peace.

The End:

> This book is come to the end,
> Heaven's bliss God us send.   Amen.
> Now I will tell you how things went
> That this book is written in the English of Kent.
> This book is made for unlearned men,
> For fathers, for mothers, for their kin again,
> To keep them from all manner of sin,
> That in their inwit may dwell no foul stain.
> "Who is as God" is his name said
> Who made this book. God give him the bread
> Of angels in heaven, by His counsel fed,
> And receive his soul when he is dead.   Amen.

This book was finished on the Eve of the Holy Apostles Simon and Jude by a brother of the cloister of Saint Augustine of Canterbury, in the year of Our Lord's birth 1340.

When, in the interaction of the cloister and the world, corruption crept into many monasteries or walked with the Mendicant Friars from door to door along the road, literature turned upon its inspirers in satire, bitter or bantering. This trend began as early as the twelfth century, with the appearance in poetry of Golias. This legendary name stands for the loose-living, low-thinking ecclesiastics burlesqued in some caustic, indecent, riotous songs of the wandering scholars, though most of the Goliardic verse is con-

nected with the name of Walter Mapes, the cynical
and sophisticated courtier of Eleanore of Aquitaine.
The virus in them can hardly be accounted for solely
on the grounds of evident abuses among the clergy. It
is likely that a sinister undercurrent of feeling, hot
with passion from the same sources that produced the
amour courtois, blended with the boisterousness of
youth in the overgrown and undisciplined universities,
to produce the stream of Latin satire represented by
the *Apocalypsis Goliae Episcopi,* of which Browning's
Soliloquy in a Spanish Cloister is but a faint and gen-
teel echo. These poems make occult and unpleasant
reading. It is significant of the healthy spirit of the
people at large that they were not translated into the
vernacular until after the Reformation had given men
a reason for wishing to "expose" the corruptions of the
mediaeval Church.

But by the fourteenth century, when conditions
were actually at their worst, plenty of original English
satire, not stemming directly from the Goliardic literature but from the people, came to be written. Most of
it is rude and cheap. On a more literary plane Chaucer
is the flippant and humorous representative of this
trend, Langland the burningly serious. Their work
will be considered in its place. The gayer and more
popular type of satire is seen in a poem that echoes a
French *fabliau,* and whose fairy-tale touch renders it
less offensive—or effectual—than most.

THE LAND OF COCKAYGNE

Far in the sea by West Spain
Is a land called Cockaygne.
There is no land under the sky
In weal, in goodness, to it nigh.

Though Paradise is merry and bright,
Cockaygne is a fairer sight,
For what in Paradise is seen
But boughs and flowers and grass green?
And though there may be joys to suit
There is no meat there but fruit;
There is no hall nor bower nor bench,
And nought but water man's thirst to quench.
But in Cockaygne is meat and drink
Without care or trouble to think. . . .

There be rivers great and fine   45
Of oil, milk, honey and wine.
Water serveth there for nothing
But to look at, and for washing;
There is every manner of fruit,
All is solace and joy to suit.
There is a well fair abbey,
Of white monks, and of grey.
There be many bowers and halls
And of pasties are all the walls,
Of flesh and fish and rich meat,
The likeliest that man may eat.
Of flour cakes be the shingles all
Of church, cloister, bower and hall.
The pinnacles are fat puddings,
Rich meat for princes and for kings,
Man may thereof eat long,
All with right and not with wrong;
All is common to young and old,
To stout and stern, meek and bold.

There is a cloister fair and light,
Broad and long, a seemly sight,
The pillars of that cloister all

Are all fashioned of crystal
With their base and capital
Of green jasper and red coral. . . .
When the monks go to mass 114
All the windows that be of glass
Turn into crystal bright
To give the monks the more light.
When the masses all are said
And the books away are laid
The crystal turneth into glass
In the state in which it was.

A treatment of the literature of the cloister—in or out—cannot end with a fantasy. Escapism is the last resort of the satirist. Those who were most indignant with unworthy representatives of religious life knew well enough that the ideal was more real than its travesty, and the same century that produced Chaucer's friars also produced the glorious mystics and religious writers who must be given a later chapter to themselves. In the meantime, "the lay and the learned" alike knew the Rule in which Saint Benedict had laid the bedrock of Western monasticism. It was translated into English over and over again, into scholarly prose and into verse as simple as a nursery rhyme. There could be no excuse when all could read:

THE RULE OF SAINT BENET

Regula beata benedicto anglicis verbis translata

All that will truly live in land 1
As Saint Benet has ordained,
Or will give their devotion
Unto the Rule of religion,
In this book they may see set

The soothfast Rule of Saint Benet,
With many points that pertain thereto,
Night and day how they shall do. . . .
The Rule is ordained thus to read,   2481
To mend our miss and mark our meed,
And good teaching so to give
In Christ's law how we shall live,
Withdrawing from all kinds of strife
Into perfection of good life.

VI

Tales of Two Worlds

*On stormy winter nights after
supper the family gathers
around the fireplace to tell
old stories; such is the custom.*
GESTA ROMANORUM

THE WORD "STORY" is a popular shortening of the word
"history,"[1] accidental but significant. It would seem
that, by merely dropping a syllable, narrators could
extend their field from the actual to the possible, and
even to the impossible; the storyteller was set free for
wide voyaging. If the mediaeval mind was apt to be
"uncritical" of the sources of its knowledge, it was, by
way of compensation, extremely receptive. It wel-
comed, enlarged, and interchanged good stories from

[1] "Story" first appears as an English word in the *Ancren Riwle:* "I
shall, dear Sisters, tell you this story." The Anglo-Norman *estorie* was
from the Latin *historia.*

any source; it made even the most fantastic into symbols of truth on other planes. Perhaps more can be learned about the Middle Ages from story than from history, especially when the glee-wood hummed an accompaniment.

Metrical romances were not the only form of storytelling. Travellers' tales were no less romantic, and had the added attraction of at least a claim to being true, a claim not likely to be put to the test by those who listened, for actual travellers were few. Yet even the stay-at-homes were familiar with the *mappa mundi* found in learned manuscripts, a circular disc in which the known continents were geometrically divided by seas, while *oceanus* surrounded the whole in a wavy line, in which England floated like a bubble. The kind of men familiar with these maps knew well enough that the earth was round, though few had sounded out *oceanus* since the days of Lief Ericson.[2] The ignorant were still sceptical a good century after Columbus; Saint Thomas More in Renaissance days had a hard time convincing his wife of the fact.[3] Travel was constant, if difficult, through the range of the Holy Roman Empire. It was not attempted to the west; to the east and south it was rendered unduly exciting by the warlike crescent of Islam that curved dangerously up at both ends. The Crusaders broke through this curve at the sword's point, and their journeying is recorded in both poetry and prose, especially in the story of Richard the Lion-Hearted, who, on hearing:

[2] The Kensington Rune Stone, discovered in Minnesota in 1898, proves that Vikings not only crossed the ocean but penetrated to the heart of America in 1362. Its authenticity is still under investigation.

[3] See *Works*, 1557, p. 628. In a lively dialogue, Mistress Alice, under a fictional veil, rejects her husband's explanation of the roundness of the earth with a woman's arguments: "Because you go by imaginations, I will imagine with you."

Of God's need and God's loss,
For love of God took up the cross.[4]

Other men and women required a strong motive to go very far afield.

There were two such motives. Missionary zeal, which had been fully occupied from the years 500 to 1000 with the conversion of Europe itself, turned towards the pagan world when Franciscans and Dominicans appeared on the roads. Flaming souls pierced like darts through the fanatical opposition of the Moslems, and beyond into the land where the hordes of Ghengis Khan were already on the move from east to west. They gave their lives to their apostolic travels, but, with the exception of Ramon Lull,[5] they wrote little about them. The other motive was no less religious: the desire to go on pilgrimage. This carried Englishmen to Compestello, Frenchmen to Walsingham, and men of all lands to Rome. But beyond Rome lay Jerusalem. Literature is full of accounts of those who set off under vow, and of their hazardous, rewarding experiences; it is full too of ecclesiastical warnings against abuses along the way. When the palmers—whether saints or rascals—returned, men stopped them on the streets for tales, till current sermons and romances were colored as by an Eastern sunset.

[4] Ambroise, *The Crusade of Richard the Lion-Hearted,* 1.62.

[5] The Majorcan cavalier (1232-1316) was converted by a vision of the Crucified into a missionary who devoted his life to the conversion of the Saracens by courage, love and learning. He wanted a crusade with love, not hate, as its motive; he organized schools where missionaries might learn Arabic; he wrote voluminously in Catalan on mysticism and philosophy, and his treatise on *The Order of Chivalry* found its way into English literature through Caxton's translation. Lull died a martyr, stoned by the Arabs.

MANDEVILLE'S TRAVELS

It is typical of the happy irresponsibility of such tales that the best known and best "authenticated" was written by a man who probably never travelled beyond his library, a man whose very identity is a matter of dispute.[6] "Mandeville's" book, written first in French in the middle of the fourteenth century, was widely current in several English versions, and took countless readers on a vicarious pilgrimage to the Holy Land, then on a thrilling tour of the Far East to the darkest bounds of the Mongol Empire. Though the author stayed at home the while, he made skillful use of other people's travels in recounting his own imagined ones: Friar Oderico of Pordenone and William of Boldensele had covered the ground for him; romances and mythical "letters," like those of Alexander and of Prester John, filled in the empty spaces; while Vincent of Beauvais, in his *Speculum Naturale,* furnished handy descriptions of the world's marvels. All that was needed was a master storyteller to weave it all together, and such was Mandeville.

He was, however, ignorant of a far greater travel book written some fifty years before his own. It is ironical that the *Travels* of Marco Polo,[7] who wrote the truth as he had seen it, was disbelieved by his con-

---

[6] A lost epitaph in a church in Liège, together with several contradictory stories concerning the man buried there, has resulted in the following confusion: An Englishman, John de Mandeville, or "John of the Beard," known in France as Jean de Bourgoyne, "who travelled all over the world," may have written the travels that claim to be by John Mandeville, but which are attributed by scholars to his friend Jean d'Outremeuse.

[7] Marco Polo with his uncle and father journeyed through the Far East from 1275 to 1295. After his return he was imprisoned, and thus found time to write his *Travels*. His accounts sounded so exaggerated that he was nicknamed "Marco Polo of the millions," but he died repeating, "I have not told half of what I saw."

temporaries, while Mandeville seems to have gone un-challenged, perhaps because he appealed to the Pope for credit. Marco Polo, who had looked Kubla Khan in the face unblinded by Coleridge's opium spell, and whose tunic was lined with gems upon his return, might have brought about the conversion of China had his words been heeded.[8] Mandeville was apparently out for enjoyment, in spite of his piety, and he used no discrimination. He tells in a single chapter "of Saint John the Evangelist and of Hippocras' daughter transformed from a woman into a dragon," and steps from Cathay to Russia at a stride.

Prologue:

Forasmuch as the land beyond the sea, that is to say, the Holy Land that men call the land of promise or of behest, passing all other lands, is the most worthy land, most excellent, and lady and sovereign of all other lands, and is blessed and hallowed by the precious Body and Blood of Our Lord Jesus Christ, in which land it pleased Him to take flesh and blood of the Virgin Mary, to environ that holy land with His blessed feet. And there He willed of His bless-edness to be hidden in the said blessed and glorious Virgin Mary and to become man and to work many miracles, and preach and teach the faith and the laws of Christian men unto His children. And there it pleased Him to suffer many reprovings and scorns for us. And He that was King of heaven, of air, of earth, of sea, and of things that be contained in them, would only be called King of that land

[8] The Great Khan requested the elder Polos on their first journey to procure from the Pope "one hundred learned men" to come as mission-aries to Cathay. Two Friars only responded to the appeal, and these two gave up their journey in discouragement before it had well begun.

when He said: *"Rex sum Judeorum,"* that is to say,
"I am King of Jews." And that land He chose before all other lands as the best and most worthy land
of all the world, and the most virtuous. For it is the
heart and midst of all the world, witnessing the Philosopher that said: *"Virtus rerum in medio con-
sistit,"* that is to say, the virtue of things is in the
middle. . . .

Wherefore every good Christian that is of power,
and hath the where-with-all, should put himself to
pain with all his strength to conquer our right heritage and chase out all the unbelieving men. For we
be called Christian men after Christ our Father, and
if we be right children of Christ we ought to challenge the heritage that our Father left us, and do it
out of heathen men's hands. But now pride and covetousness and envy have so inflamed the hearts of the
lords of the world that they are more busy to dis-
inherit their neighbors than to challenge or conquer
their right heritage before-said. And the common
people that would put their bodies and their goods
to conquer our heritage, they may not do it without
their lords. For an assembly of people without a
chieftain or a chief lord is as a flock of sheep without
a shepherd, the which parts and scatters and knows
not whither to go. But would God that the temporal
lords and all worldly lords were at good accord, and
with the common people would take this holy voyage
over the sea. Then I trow well that within a little
time our right heritage before-said would be reconciled and put in the hands of the right heirs of Jesus
Christ.

And for as much as it is long time passed since
that there was no general passage or voyage over the

sea, and many men desire to hear the Holy Land spoken of and have thereof great solace and comfort, I, John Mandeville, Knight, albeit that I be not worthy, that was born in England in the town of Saint Albans, and passed the sea in the year of Our Lord Jesus Christ 1326, on the day of Saint Michael, and hitherto have been a long time over the sea, and have seen and gone through many divers lands and provinces and kingdoms and isles . . . shall devise you some part of the things that there be.

Chapter 18: Ethiopia

Ethiopia is divided into two principal parts; and that is into the east part and into the south part, the which south part is called Mauretania, and the folk of that country are black enough, and more black than in the other part, and they are called Moors. In that part is a well, that in the day is so cold that no man may drink thereof, and in the night so hot that no man may suffer his hand therein. And beyond that part toward the south, to pass by the sea ocean, is a great land and a great country. But men may not dwell there for the fervent burning of the sun, so is it passing hot in that country. . . .

In that country are folk that have but one foot, and they go so quickly that it is marvellous; and the foot is so large that it shadoweth all the body against the sun when they lie and rest themselves. In Ethiopia when the children are young and little they are all yellow, and when they are waxed of age that yellowness turns to be all black. In Ethiopia is the City of Saba and the land of which one of the three kings that gave presents to Our Lord in Bethlehem was king of.

From Ethiopia men go into India by many divers countries. And men call the high India Emlak. And India is divided into three principal parts, that is, India the More, a full hot country, and India the Less that is a full temperate country that stretcheth to the land of the Medes. And the third part towards the north is full cold so that for pure cold and continual frost the water becometh crystal. And upon the rocks of crystal grow the good diamonds that are of troubled color. . . . And men find many times hard diamonds in a mass that come out of the gold when men purify it and refine it out of the mine, when men break that mass into small pieces. And sometimes it happens that men find some as great as peas and some less. And albeit that men find good diamonds in India, yet never-the-less men find them more commonly upon the rocks in the sea, and upon hills where the mine of gold is. And they grow many together, one little and another great. And there are some as great as a bean, and some as great as a hazelnut. And they are square and pointed by their own kind, both above and beneath, without working of man's hand. And they grow together, male and female. And they are nourished with the dew of heaven. And they have small children that multiply and grow all the year. I have often-times essayed that if a man keep them with a little piece of the rock and wet them with May dew often-times, they shall grow every year, and the small will wax great.

And if you like to know the virtues of the diamond, that men may find in the Lapidary, that many men know not, I shall tell you, as they beyond the sea say and affirm, of whom all science and all philosophy come from. He that beareth the diamond upon him, it giveth him hardiness and manhood, and keepeth the limbs of his body whole. It giveth him victory of his enemies, in play and in war, if his cause is rightful.

Chapter 21: The Roundness of the Earth

And in the Isle of Lamary no man may see the star Transmontane, that is called the star of the sea, that is unmovable and is toward the north, that we call the Lodestar. But men see another star that is contrary to it, that is towards the south, that is called Antarctic. And right as shipmen take their advice here and govern them by the Lodestar, right so do the shipmen of those parts by the star of the south, the which star appeareth not to us. And this star that is towards the north that we call the Lodester, appeareth not to them. For which cause men may well perceive that the land and the sea are of round shape and form. For the part of the firmament showeth in one country that showeth not in another country. And men may well prove by experience and subtle compassment of wit that if a man found passages by ships that would go to search the world, men might go by ship all about the world, above and beneath.

In whatever part of the earth men dwell, above or beneath, it seems always to them that they go more right than any other folk. And right as it seems to us that they be under us, so it seems to them that we be under them. For if a man could fall from the earth into the firmament, by greater reason the earth and the sea that are so great and so heavy should fall into the firmament, but that may not be. And therefore saith our Lord God: *"Non timeas me qui suspendit terram ex nichilo."*

Chapter 24: The Great Khan of Cathay

In the Tartar City is the seat of the great Khan in a full great palace and the most passing fair in all the world, of the which the walls are in circuit more than two miles. And within the walls it is all full of other palaces. And in the garden of the great palace there is a great hill upon the which is another palace. And it is the most fair and the most rich that any man may devise. And all about the palace and the hill are many trees bearing many divers fruits, and all about there are ditches great and deep. And besides there are many pools on one side and the other, and there is a full fair bridge to pass over the ditches. And in these pools are so many wild geese and ganders and wild ducks and swans and herons that it is without number. And all about these ditches and pools is the great garden full of wild beasts, so that when the great Khan wants to have any sport or to take any of the wild beasts or of the fowls, he will have them chased and taken at the windows without going out of his chamber. The palace, where his throne is, is both great and passing fair. And within the palace in the hall there are twenty-four pillars of fine gold and all the walls are covered within with red skins of beasts that men call panthers, that are fair beasts and well-smelling, and for the sweet odor of the skins no evil air may enter the palace. The skins are as red as blood and they shine so bright in the sun that men can scarcely look at them. And many folk worship these beasts when they meet them first in the morning for their great virtue and for the good smell that they have, and their skins they prize more than though they were plates of fine gold.

Chapter 30: The Lost Tribes of Jews

Between the mountains of Scythia are enclosed the Jews of the Ten Tribes that men call Gog and Magog. And they can get out on no side. There King Alexander chased them between the mountains. And there he thought to enclose them through the work of his men. But when he saw that he could not do it nor bring it to an end, he prayed to God of nature that He would perform what he had begun. And although he was a paynim and not worthy to be heard, yet God of His grace closed the mountains together, so that they dwell all fast locked and enclosed with high mountains all about save on one side only. And on that side is the Sea of Caspia. Now some men ask, "Since the sea is on that side, wherefore go they not out by the seaside for to go where they please?" But to this question I shall answer that the Sea of Caspia goeth out by the land under the mountains and runneth by the desert on one side of the country, and after stretcheth to the ends of Persia. And although it is called a sea, it is no sea that touches to any other sea. But it is a lake, the greatest of the world. And though they should take to the sea, they know not whither they should arrive. And also they know no language but their own, and no man knows theirs but they. And therefore may they not go out.[9]

And also you shall understand that the Jews have

[9] A curious analogue to this legend has actually occurred in recent times. A boatload of Jews dispossessed by the anti-Semitic persecutions was driven from port to port on the Black Sea and was allowed to land nowhere. "And therefore they might not go out."

no proper land of their own to dwell in all the world, but only that land between the mountains. And yet they give tribute for that land to the Queen of Amazonia. . . . And yet never-the-less men say that they shall go out in the time of Anti-Christ and that they shall make great slaughter of Christian men. . . . In the time of Anti-Christ a fox shall make his tunnel and mine a hole where King Alexander had his gates made. And so long shall he mine and pierce in the earth that he shall pass through towards that folk. And when they see the fox they shall have great marvel of him because they have never seen such a beast. For all other beasts they have enclosed amongst them, save only the fox. And then they shall chase him and pursue him so straitly till he comes to the same place that he came from. Then they shall dig and mine strongly till they find the gates that Alexander had made of great stones and passing huge, well cemented and made strong for the mastery. And these gates they shall break and so go out.

Chapter 31: Prester John's Empire

The Emperor Prester John[10] holds full great land and has many noble cities and good towns in his realm, and many great divers isles and large. For all the country of India is divided into isles, for the great floods that come from Paradise that divide the land into many parts. . . . I trow that you know well why this Emperor is called Prester John. Never-the-

---

[10] This fabulously powerful and wealthy Emperor was thought by Europeans to have ruled over a huge Christian kingdom vaguely located anywhere from Abyssinia to China. The origins of the legend are probably to be found in India. In 1177, Pope Alexander III addressed a letter to *"carissimo in Christo filio Johanni illustro et magnifico indonum regi."* Later, Ghengis Khan was thought to be Prester John's grandson.

less for those that know not I shall tell you the cause.
There was a worthy and full noble prince that had
Christian knights in his company, as the one hath
that is now. So it befell that he had a great longing
to see the service in a church among Christian men.
So it happened that he came with a Christian knight
into a church in Egypt. And he heard and beheld the
service attentively. And it was the Saturday in
Whitsun Week and the Bishop gave Orders. And
he asked the Christian knight what men of degree
they should be that the Prelate had before him. And
the knight answered that they should be priests.
Then the King said that he would no longer be
called king nor emperor, but Priest, and that he
would have the name of the first Priest (Presbyter)
that went out of the Church. And his name was
John. And evermore since he is called Prester John.

Conclusion:

You shall understand, if it please you, that at my
home-coming I came to Rome, and showed my life
to Our Holy Father the Pope, and was shriven of
all that lay on my conscience of many divers points,
as man must needs that be in company dwelling
among so many divers folks of divers sects and belief as I have been. And amongst all I showed him
this treatise that I had made after information of
men that knew of things that I had not seen myself,
and also of marvels and customs that I had seen myself, as far as God would give me grace. And I
besought his Holy Fatherhood that my book might
be examined and corrected by the advice of his wise
and discreet council. And our Holy Father of his
special grace remitted my book to be examined and

proved by the advice of his said council. By the
which my book was proved for true in so much that
they showed me a book that my book was examined
by, that comprehended full much more by a hundred parts, by which the *Mappa Mundi* was made.
And so my book, albeit that many men list not to
give credence to anything but to that that they have
seen with their eyes, be the author or the person ever
so true, is affirmed and proved by our Holy Father
in manner and form as I have said.

And I, John Mandeville, Knight abovesaid, although I be unworthy, departed from our countries
and passed the sea the year of grace 1326, and have
passed many lands and many isles and countries,
and searched many full strange places, and have
been in many full good honorable company and at
many fair deeds of arms, albeit that I did none myself for my own unable insufficience. And now I am
come home in spite of myself to rest, for arthritic
gout constrains me. And I have put these things in
writing in this book, as it came to my mind, in the
year of grace 1356.

THE BOOK OF MARGERY KEMPE

In contrast to the "carpet-travellers" were the actual pilgrim-roamers who made their way "when
spring so pricked them in their hearts" from one saint's
shrine to another in Europe. Such was Dame Margery
Kempe, wife of a long-suffering burgher of Lynne and
the mother of fourteen children, who went to Rome
and Jerusalem and to most of the shrines along the
way. Half of her townsmen would have been glad to
see her imprisoned as a Lollard or burned as a witch;
the other half held her a saint. Modern critics have

found a third alternative: she was psychopathic. The question is still a matter of controversy, for *The Book of Margery Kempe*[11] tells both of adventurous wanderings and of mystical contemplation. It is a lively book, hailed at its recent discovery as "the first autobiography in English." It is like a motion picture of early fifteenth-century life, and is valuable as such. The mystic passages are couched in much the same language as those of the genuine spiritual writers of her age, but they fail to ring true. This restless, outspoken woman is too much like the Wife of Bath to be classed with Juliana of Norwich; her "boisterous weepings" disturb her present-day readers as much as they did her contemporaries. She was rather too preoccupied with the impression she made upon the friends and foes who gaped after her in church and on the highroad. But whether "this creature," as she calls herself, was a saint or no, she was a woman of spirit who could rebuke the Archbishop of Canterbury for the oaths of his lackeys, who cared for lepers and went thirsty for their sake, who held her head up on shipboard when all else were seasick. She was in the beginning converted from worldly pride:

First Book: Chapter 2

She would not leave her pride nor her pompous array, that she had used beforetime, neither for her husband, nor for any other man's counsel. Yet she knew full well that men said of her full much villainy, for she wore gold pipes on her head, and her hoods with the tippets were slashed. Her cloaks also

[11] It was written down in 1436 by a priest, from Margery's dictation. The MS was lost, and not recovered until 1934, though its existence was known from fragments of the devotional passages printed by Wynkyn de Worde in 1501.

were slashed and laid with divers colors between
the slashes, so that they should be the more staring
to men's sight, and herself be the more worshipped.

Chapter 30

Another time this creature's fellowship would go
to the Flood of Jordan, and would not let her go
with them. Then this creature prayed Our Lord
that she might go with them, and He bade that she
should go with them whether they would or not.
Then she went forth by the grace of God, and asked
them no leave. When she came to the Flood of Jordan, the weather was so hot that she thought her
feet would have burnt for the heat that she felt.

Afterwards she went with her fellowship to Mount
Quarentyne. There Our Lord fasted forty days, and
there she prayed her fellowship to help her up on
to the mount. And they said, "Nay," for they could
not well help themselves. Then had she great sorrow
because she might not come on the hill. And anon
happed a Saracen, a well-favored man, to come by
her, and she put a groat into his hand, making him
a sign to bring her on to the mount. And quickly
the Saracen took her under his arm and led her
up on to the high mount, where Our Lord fasted
for forty days. Then was she sore athirst, and had
no comfort in her fellowship. And God of His high
goodness moved the Grey Friars with compassion
and they comforted her when her countrymen would
not know her. And so she was ever more strength-
ened in the love of Our Lord and the more bold to
suffer shame and reproof for His sake in every
place where she came, for the grace that God
wrought in her of weeping, sobbing and crying,

Then she went forth by the Grace of God and asked them no leave.

BK. OF MARGERY KEMPE

which grace she might not withstand when God would send it. And ever she proved her feelings true, and those promises that God had made her while she was in England and other places also.

Second Book: Chapter 8

In Calais this creature had good cheer of divers persons both men and women, who had never seen her before. There was a good woman who had her home to her house, and who washed her full cleanly and put her on a new smock, and comforted her right much. Other good persons had her to meat and drink. . . . So they sailed forth till they came to Dover, and then each one of the company got himself fellowship to go with, if he liked, save she alone, for she could get no fellow to her ease. Therefore she took her way Canterburyward by herself alone, sorry and sad in manner that she had no fellowship and that she knew not the way. She was up betimes in the morning and came to a poor man's house, knocking at the door. The good poor man, huddled into his clothes, unfastened and unbuttoned, came to the door to know her will. She prayed him, if he had any horse, that he would help her to Canterbury and she would requite his labor. He, desiring to do her pleasure in Our Lord's name, fulfilled her intent, leading her to Canterbury.

She had great joy in Our Lord, who sent her help and succor in every need, and thanked Him with many a devout tear, with much sobbing and weeping, almost in every place she came to. Of all that it is not written, as well on yon half of the sea as on this half, on water as on land, blessed may God be. From thence she went to London, clad in a cloth of canvas, as it were a sacken apron, as she had gone beyond the sea. When she was come into London, many people took notice of her well enough. Inasmuch as she was not clad as she would like to have been, for lack of money, she, desiring to go unknown till such time as she might arrange to borrow some money, bore a kerchief before her face. Notwithstanding that she did so, some dissolute persons, supposing it was Marjory Kempe of Lynne, said so that she might hear these words of reproof: "Ah, thou false flesh, thou shalt no good meat eat." She, not answering, passed forth as if she had not heard. . . . She was so comforted in the sweet dalliance of Our Lord that she could not control herself or govern her spirit after her own will, or after the discretion of other men, but as Our Lord would lead it and measure it Himself, in sobbing full boisterously and weeping full plenteously.

For those who could not travel there was always possible "a notion voyage," made by the telling of some old tale. Such quantities of these stories were adrift that eventually many of them were gathered into more or less unified collections and fitted into an artistic framework by some author with a definite purpose in mind.

THE GESTA ROMANORUM

One practical aim for such collections was to furnish a store of *exempla* for preachers who knew the effect of a good story in driving home a *moralitas*. The influence of these pointed narratives on the development of modern literature is incalculable, though little recognized. "Preaching, and in especial the provision made for it in the way of collecting and preserving illustrative matter of all kinds, became the vehicle by which much of the lighter thought and imagination of antiquity, classical, oriental or early mediaeval, passed into the thinking and writing of the modern world."[12] The writings of Shakespeare, of Molière, of Schiller, would have been far otherwise than they are, in plot and in allusion, were it not for such collections of lore as the *Gesta Romanorum*.

It is uncertain whether this compilation was first made in England or on the Continent, but by the fourteenth century numerous Anglo-Latin manuscripts of it were in circulation, and the English translation made in the days of Henry VI was the basis of the edition "emprinted at London, in Flete Street, by me, Wynkyn de Worde," c.1510. It was probably the original compiler, be he English or French, who first shaped the not always obvious *applicacio* to the three hundred and eighty *gesta,* all of which, with magnanimous disregard for chronology, are attributed to "the Romans," whether their origins be oriental, classical, ecclesiastical, biblical, preternatural, or mere "folk-joke." Here is the tale of the bond concerning the pound of flesh, [13] with no Shylock, but with "master Virgil" in his traditional mediaeval role of necromancer;[14] here, in another tale, is the casket scene without Portia. Here are stories found in children's

[12] G. R. Owst, *Literature and Pulpit in Mediaeval England* (Cambridge University Press, 1933), p. 207.

[13] John Millington Synge, in his account of the Aran Islands, relates how he heard the tale of the pound of flesh, with literary associations current from times immemorial in East and in West, told by "an illiterate native of a wet rock in the Atlantic."

[14] The idea that Virgil was a magician, endowed with fantastic powers of conjury and prophecy, originated at Naples in the popular romances that grew up in the wake of the classics. It soon spread all over Europe.

readers today, *Androcles and the Lion, The Cat and
the Mouse.* Saints and animals shape the destinies of
knights, of kings, of those in sore distress. Virtue
triumphs and vice is punished, sometimes surprisingly,
for these are all stories "that make fair end, *ad quod
nos perducat.* Amen."

III. *Of the Magic Image:*

Diocletian was Emperor in the City of Rome, in
the empire of whom was a philosopher called Lenop-
pus, the which had by his craft set up an image,
the which put out a hand with a finger, and upon
the finger was written words: *percute hic,* that is
to say, smite here. This image stood there long, and
many a day after the death of the philosopher, and
many came to this finger, and read the superscrip-
tion, but they understood it not, and therefore they
had much marvel what it should mean. So in a
certain time there came a clerk of far countries
and oft times he saw this image, and this finger
with the scripture. And in a certain day he took a
shovel, and dug in the earth under the superscrip-
tion. And anon he found a house of marble under
the earth; and then he went down and entered into
the hall, and there he found so many rich jewels
and marvellous things that no tongue could tell.
After this he saw a board or a table spread with
rich meats enough thereupon. Then he looked afar,
and saw standing a carbuncle stone, which gave
light over all the house. And against it stood a man
with a bow in his hand, ready to shoot. This clerk
perceived right well this sight, and thought, "though
I tell this sight when I am gone hence, no man
will believe me. And therefore I will take some of

these goods in token." He started to the board, and took a fair gilt cup, and put it up. And anon the man with the bow shot towards the carbuncle so sore that it went asunder, and then was all the light gone, and the house was full of darkness. When the clerk saw this he wept sore, for he knew not how to pass out for darkness. And therefore he dwelt there still, and there he ended his life.

Morality:

Good men, this image that is thus painted is the devil, the which saith evermore, *percute hic,* smite here; that is to say, he putteth in our hearts earthly things, and biddeth us take them, but he will never speak of heavenly things. The clerk that smiteth with the shovel betokeneth the wise men of this world, who are advocates and pleaders, the which by subtlety and wickedness, get the goods of this world, and the vanities of this world. And when they have gotten them with such working they find many marvellous things, that is to say, delectable things of this world, in which they have great delectation. The carbuncle stone that giveth light is the youth of man, the which giveth to man the hardihood to have delectation and liking for worldly things. The archer that shooteth is death, the which standeth evermore ready in wait to shoot his dart. The clerk then taketh a knife—what is that? The worldly man trusteth to have all things at his own will. But in that trust the archer shooteth at the carbuncle stone, that is to say, death shooteth his shots to the youth of man, and smiteth his strength and his might. And then lieth the youth in the darkness of sin, in which darkness men oftentimes die. And therefore let us flee all lusts and all likings, and then we shall not fail of everlasting life.

XXVI. How a Greyhound Saved a Child from a Serpent:

Caesar the Emperor was a wise man reigning in the city of Rome, in whose Empire was a knight named Folliculus, the which knight loved over all things in the world jousting and tournaments. And this knight had a little babe as his son, and no more children, and he ordained for the fostering and nourishing of this child three nurses; that is, one to wash his clothes, another to feed or to pasture him, and the third to bring him to sleep with songs and rockings. Also this knight loved passingly the greyhound with the falcon, because they never failed of their prey commonly.

It happened that this knight had a tournament proclaimed in a green place nigh to his castle, and many came thereto. When the day came the knight armed him and went forth; the lady and all his household and the nurses went forth also, and left the child in the cradle; the greyhound lay by the wall and the falcon sat on a perch. There was in a certain hole of the same castle a serpent bred and brought forth, and had been there a long time, and when this serpent heard so great a noise of a people going out towards the tournament, she put out her head at the hole and saw the child by himself. She came out to slay the child; and when the falcon saw that she made a great noise with her wings, and therewith awoke the greyhound from sleep, that the greyhound might go to save the child. Then the greyhound awakened by the stirring of the falcon's wings, and shook himself and beheld the serpent, and ran fiercely to her, and the serpent was on one side of the cradle, and the greyhound on the other, to defend the child in the cradle. And they fought sore together, and the serpent bit the greyhound grievously, so that he bled strong; and the greyhound ran madly to the adder and slew her. And so with their fighting the cradle overturned, but the cradle had four feet that kept the child from the ground. And when the greyhound had slain the serpent he went to his kennel beside the wall and licked his wound.

And by that time the tournament was done and ceased. The nurses came home, and when they saw the cradle turned up-side-down and the floor bloody and the greyhound bloody also, they thought that the greyhound had slain the child. Therefore, without tarrying to go to the child, they said: "Go! Flee away, or we be dead!" And as they went the lady met with them as she came from the play, and she asked of them whither they fled. And they said: "Woe is to you and to us, for the greyhound that you love so well hath slain your son, and lies by the wall, all bloody." The lady fell down in a swoon and said, "Alas! Is my son dead?" And as she cried, the knight came from the tournament and asked the cause of her crying. Then said she, "Woe is to you and to me, for your greyhound hath slain your son." Then the knight was half mad for woe, and he entered into the hall. And when the greyhound saw his lord come he arose and, as he could, made joy with his lord as he was wont to do. But the knight anon in his madness, trusting in the word of his wife, drew out his sword and smote off his greyhound's head. And then he went to the cradle and turned it up with his hand, and saw his child safe and sound, and beside the cradle lay the serpent dead.

And by that he understood that the greyhound had slain the serpent in defense of the child. And then he cried with a high voice, "Alas! Alas! For at the word of my wife I have slain the gentle greyhound that failed never of his prey and also saved the life of my child; therefore I will take penance." And he broke his spear in three parts, and put his wife in prison, and went himself to the Holy Land. And there he lived all his life, and his son held his heritage, and so he made a fair end with the world.

The "morality" in this case is too long to quote. In it, the serpent is the devil, the greyhound is reason, the hasty sword is a "froward will," the child has been washed in baptism, and the cradle has four feet made of virtues "that his visage may not touch the earth." The conclusion of the long application is ingenious: "And therefore man, if thou hast done by instigation of the flesh, as did the knight, turn up the cradle of thy heart by meritorious works, and then thou shalt find thy soul safe; and break thy spear, that is, thy life, in three parts, that is, in prayer, fasting, and alms; and then go to the Holy Land, that is to say, to the kingdom of heaven."

THE BOOK OF THE KNIGHT OF THE TOUR LANDRY

In contrast with the vague origins of the *Gesta Romanorum* is the charmingly precise scene, laid in an April garden in France, in which the Knight of the Tour Landry made up his mind to collect a book of stories by which to train his three motherless daughters to fair womanhood. So, in less than a year, he penned for their education one hundred and forty-four chapters of good advice, pictured in tales homely, legendary, or romantic. Sin and its consequences are described without mincing words. The girls should know "how a devout man had his head cut off, and yet, on account of his fasting, lived long enough to be shriven," how "a knight refused a lady for his wife because of her forward and familiar manner." Wellbeing in heaven and on earth depends on good conduct, and the good knight's book of proofs soon spread to England, where a translation was made in the early fifteenth century, and a little later appeared a printed version "by me, William Caxton," one of the first books from the press.

Prologue:

In the year of the Incarnation of Our Lord 1371, as I was in a garden, all heavy and full of thought, in the shadow, about the end of the month of April, I but little rejoiced me in the melody and song of the wild birds. They sang there in their languages, as the thrush, throstil, the nightingale, and other birds, which were full of mirth and joy. And their sweet song made my heart to lighten, and made me to think of the time that is passed of my youth, how love in great distress had held me, and how I was in her service many times, full of sorrow and gladness, as many lovers be. But my sorrow was healed, and my service well set and quit, and he gave a fair wife, and of all good she was the flower, and I delighted me so much in her that I made for her love songs, balades, rondels, viralays, and

divers new things in the best wise that I could. But
death that on all maketh war took her from me,
the which hath made many to have a sorrowful
thought and great heaviness. And so it is more
than twenty years that I have been for her full of
great sorrow. For a true lover's heart forgetteth
never a woman that once he hath truly loved. And
as I was in the sad garden, thinking these thoughts,
I saw coming towards me my three daughters, of
the which I was joyful and had great desire that they
should turn to good and worship, above all earthly
things, for they were young and had but tender
wit. And so at the beginning a man ought to teach
his daughters with good examples. . . .

And because it is hard to know the world as it
is now, and for the reasons that I have told you, I
parted and went out of the garden, and found in
my way two priests and two clerks that I had. And
I said to them that I would make a book of examples, to teach my daughters that they might
understand how they should govern them, and know
good from evil. And so I made them extract for me
examples from the Bible and other books that I had,
as the gestes of kings, the chronicles of France, of
Greece, of England, and of many other strange
lands. And I made them read me every book. And
then I made this book. But I would not set it in
rhyme, but in prose, to abridge it, and that it might
be better and more plainly understood. And I made
this book for the great love that I had for my
daughters, the which I loved as a father ought to
love his child, having hearty joy to find ways to
steer and turn them to goodness. . . . It is a noble
and a fair thing for a man or woman to see and

behold himself in the mirror of ancient stories, which have been written by our ancestors for to show us good examples.

Chapter CV

There was a knight, a noble man that had been out in strange voyages beyond the great sea; and he had two fair nieces, whom he had nourished, and afterwards he married them off, and loved them marvellously. And in the coming homeward from his voyages he brought for each of them a gown of the best and the goodliest shape and device as at that time, and well and richly furred. And it happened he came late into the manor and place of one of his nieces, and cried and called for her, and sent unto her that she should come and see him. And she went straight into her chamber for to array her in the most fresh wise, and sent him word that she would come to him in haste. And the knight abode, and saw his niece come not, and sent again unto her, and she answered and prayed he would not think it long, for she would come unto him anon. So the knight abode so long a time that he disdained thereof, because his niece tarried so long, and came not unto him, in as much as he had been a long time in strange countries, and that she had not seen him a great while before; and he took his horse and rode his way, and went to see his other niece.

And as fast as she heard the voice of him, she knew it was her uncle that had been so long out of the country. Notwithstanding, this woman had a little before, for her pleasure and disport, taken upon her to make leaven for bread of wheat, and

with her hands as they were, plastered with the
leaven that she handled, all floury, in the state that
she was, she cometh forth with great joy, and embraced him pleasantly between her arms, and said
unto him, "My dear lord and uncle, you be right
welcome! In the same state as I heard your voice,
I am come to you, for the gladness that I have of
your presence and of your coming at this time; but
that I am come in so simple a wise before you, I
pray you to forgive it me." And the knight regarded unto the womanhood and manner of his
niece, and within himself he praised her greatly,
and he loved her much more than ever before. And
he gave her the two gowns that he had ordained
and bought for her and her sister. And because
she had come joyfully in the state that she was
before her uncle, she won two gowns; but the one
that tarried to array herself so quaintly, she lost
the grace and love of her uncle.

CONFESSIO AMANTIS

By the end of the fourteenth century a new tendency was creeping into English literature, due to a
consciousness of writing as an art to be developed
for art's sake. It is shown in the careful shaping of
great story collections by the men who might be
called our first professional writers; they fitted their
tales into a framework of artistic pattern till they became stories within a story. This device had long been
used in the East; it was familiar in England in *The
Seven Sages of Rome,* though strangely enough the
greatest of Eastern collections, *The Arabian Nights,*
did not find its way west till the eighteenth century.
Boccaccio's *Decameron* was already looking towards

the Renaissance when the *Canterbury Tales* were written.[15] It is likely that "moral Gower," had he not been overshadowed by Chaucer, might be known today as the greatest English storyteller of his age.

The effigy over the tomb of this merchant and *poeta celeberrimus* shows him lying in aristocratic ease with his chapleted head at rest upon three huge books, his own works: *Vox Clamantis,* a Latin dream-allegory on more or less current events, *Speculum Meditantis,* a French treatise on vices and virtues, and *Confessio Amantis,* his English story collection. All three are in poetry. The last was written at the command of Richard II, who met the poet one day in 1390 when their barges crossed on the Thames. His Highness offered "love" as the subject, and Gower equipped his vast compilation with allegorical "machinery" derived remotely from Alanus de Insulis. The author—here *Amans,* or any lover—is made to go on his knees in confession to Genius, the priest of the goddess of love, in an incongruous blend of mythology and theology. By way of enlightening his penitent, Genius tells him stories, smooth, lively, endless tales from all manner of sources, set in longwinded discourses, in which the figure of "the lady" is seen at times, dancing in and out of the poet's thoughts. Only after eight long books is he finally absolved. Here is the tale of *Pericles,* the source of Shakespeare's play, and here is the tale of *Ceix and Alceone,* taken from Ovid's *Metamorphoses.* It is related by Genius in proof of the fact that dreams may be of great significance to those who love. Ceix the King has been gone long on the sea. His queen prays to Juno, who sends Iris, her messenger, to

---

[15] Chaucer's work will be considered separately, in Chapter VIII.

awaken the god of sleep, that he may send a dream to
Alceone:

BOOK IV

This Iris from heaven's high stage   2977
Has undertaken the message;
Her rainy cloak she has put on,
Made in wonderful fashion
With colors of diverse hue,
A hundred more than men e'er knew;
The heavenly light unto a bow
She bent, and so she came down low
To where the House of Sleep might stand,
And that was in a strange land
That borders upon Chimerie;
For there, as saith the poesy,
The God of Sleep has made his house
In a manner marvellous.
Under a hill there is a cave
That the sun's light may not have,
So that no man may know aright
The point between the day and night.
There is no fire, there is no spark,
There is no door to creak in the dark
To cause the eyelids to unclose,
Nothing there to break repose.
And to speak of things without,
There stands no great tree nigh about
Whereon either crow or pie
May light, to call aloud or cry.
There is no cock to crow the day
Nor any beast with noisy bray.
But on the hill all around
There is growing upon the ground

Poppy, which bears the seeds of sleep,
With other herbs in such a heap.
A still water, for the nonce,
Running upon the small stones
In the bed of Lethe the river,
Under that hill in such manner
There is, which gives great appetite
To sleep. And thus full of delight
Sleep hath his house; and of his couch
Within his chamber I shall touch,
Of ebony, that sleepy tree
The boards all about be,
And that he may sleep soft
Upon a featherbed aloft
He lies with many a pillow of down.

He then sends Morpheus, who

... at night alone   3057
Appeared unto Alceone
In likeness of her own husband,
All naked, dead upon the strand.
The tempest of the black cloud,
The wild sea, the winds loud,
All this she dreamed, and saw him die,
Whereof she then began to cry,
Sleeping abed there where she lay.

Upon awakening she goes to the shore and finds him
as she had dreamed.

Anon she forth leapt to the deep   3086
And would have caught him in her arm.
This misfortune of double harm
The gods from the heaven above
Beheld, and for the truth of love

In which this worthy lady stood,
They have upon the salt flood
Her drowned Lord and her also
From death to life have turned so,
That changed to birds in shape they be,
Floating among the waves at sea.[16]

Another way in which the pulpit influenced the development of modern literature, this time in the direction of biography, was the use of saints' lives in preaching. The sermon and the "good story" were often indistinguishable when the story was of a virtuous man or woman. These stories were rooted in the liturgy, source of many cultural patterns in the Middle Ages, from cathedrals to embroidery. In the early centuries, witnesses wrote down their accounts of the sufferings of the martyrs, the first canonized saints. As the sanctoral cycle grew up beside the ferial cycle in the liturgy, it became the custom to read aloud from these *Acta Martyrum* at Mass, on the recurring feast-days. By the eighth century these *legenda*[17] were gradually transferred from the Mass (where they were replaced by the extra-liturgical sermon after the gospel) to the Office of Matins. Here they took their place in the second nocturn, between the scriptural readings and passages from the Fathers of the Church. By this time, lives of saints other than martyrs were current, beginning with the popular Saint Martin of Tours. Great cycles of *Acta Sanctorum* then developed, rooted in liturgy, amplified in the pulpits, and carried by gleeman and storyteller out of church and down the road to the fireside. Latin

[16] This legend is the origin of the phrase "halcyon weather."
[17] "Legends" were thus originally "things to be read." The extravagance of some of these saints' lives gave the word its current meaning.

collections, chronological or arbitrary in arrangement, were made on the Continent as early as the sixth century. Several times these biographies, inaccurate not to say fantastic in their unbridled credulity, were pruned in official breviaries,[18] but nothing could check the free growth of *legenda* in popular literature.[19] Vernacular renderings appeared, often in verse, for the benefit of parish priests, in which the ferial and sanctoral cycles of feasts were linked in one great chain in which some history and much devotion were blended excitingly.

THE SOUTH ENGLISH LEGENDARY

Two legendaries were completed in England towards the end of the thirteenth century, one in the North and one in the South, just as Friar Jacobus a Voragine was compiling his better-known *Legenda Aurea* in Italy. English saints such as Dunstan and Oswald stand out prominently among ancient apostles and "modern" saints like Francis and Dominic, while accounts of Saint Patrick's Purgatory and the apparition of Saint Michael read like digest novels of the supernatural. The origin of more than one current custom is to be found in these legends; drivers of automobiles today may not be as familiar as were their ancestors with the reason why their cars are equipped

[18] The word *breviarium* was first used to designate the shortened form of the Divine Office introduced by the Franciscans, in the thirteenth century. Earlier versions had grown cumbersome by the constant addition of *legenda*.

[19] The sifting of this overwhelming accumulation of saints' lives was the task undertaken by the seventeenth-century Jesuits, Heribert Rosweyde and John van Bolland, who began the critical editing of the *Acta Sanctorum*. The work is still being carried on by the group of scholars known as the Bollandists.

with a Saint Christopher medal. Some monk of Gloucester once ran the story into verse:

> Christopher lived beside the water, a hole he made
>   there;   **77**
> In his hand he bore a long pole, his staff as it were.
> When any man would go over the water, upon his
>   back he him cast
> And took his pole and bore him over, stepping
>   hardily and fast.
> For he was both strong and long, so heavy was
>   there none
> That Christopher over the deep water could not
>   bear him, everyone.
> One night over the water a voice was calling him,
> Hail! Hail! to Saint Christopher, to lead him over
>   the stream.
> Christopher rose up anon, he took his pole in his
>   hand
> And waded over the water, and found no man on
>   the land.
> Scarce had he come home again than again the voice
>   cried there;
> Christopher waded over and found no more than
>   he had ere,
> Yet it called a third time when he came back to land.
> With his rod he waded again, he saw a little Child
>   stand,
> And the Child bade him for charity to bear him over
>   the stream.
> "Come forth, if thou wilt go over," Christopher said
>   to him.
> Very lightly he took the Child and in his arms him
>   cast;

Even as he was going over, the Child began to grow
   heavy fast,
And the water waxed also, and Christopher was sore
   aghast
Of drowning the Child that was so heavy; he could
   scarcely stand at last.
Never was he so clean overcome; he gave many a
   grunt and blast,
But lest the Child should be drowned he dared not
   down him cast.
And when he had come to land—it seemed to him
   long ere—
The Child he set upon the ground, and stood up
   to rest him there.
"Who art thou that art so little, and yet so heavy be,
So heavy that I was on the point almost of drown-
   ing thee?
Though all the world were upon me laid, it ne'er
   so heavy were."
"No wonder, Christopher," said that Child, "that I
   was heavier
Than all the world, for I am more; and it no won-
   der is,
For I made all the world of nought, and everything
   that is.
And that thou mayest see the truth, pitch thy staff
   in the ground.
It shall grow leaves and blossoms soon, and fruit
   shall grow around."
The Child went forth, and Christopher took his
   staff anew,
And pitched it in the ground at dawn, and the word
   came true.

Then was he more full of faith, and loved Our
    Lord the more;
Forth he went to follow Him, and to preach His
    lore.

A few years after the *Southern Legendary* was
completed, a Canon Regular of Shropshire named
Mirk compiled his *Festial* "from the *Legenda Aurea,*
with some adding-to," for the benefit of priests "some
of whom excuse themselves by default of books and
simpleness of letters." It contains a full cycle of sermons with plentiful *narraciones,* soberly told no matter how high-wrought. Mirk's tales, like those of many
of his contemporaries, are marked by a quality difficult to describe, one that is found in the least likely
places in mediaeval writing; it might be called a phy-
sical robustness of imagination, the downright realism
of men with an uninhibited outlook upon a world
blended of matter and spirit. It could turn into frank
and revolting coarseness in many a *fabliau* like that
of Dame Sirix, and in many a tale of Chaucer; it
shocks modern readers when found in a pious context where it is reverently intended.

74. *De Miraculis Beatae Mariae*

There was one time a holy monk who loved Our
Lady wondrous much. The which monk was never
weary to praise her, and tell fair miracles of Our
Lady, and fair tales of her night and day, and so
this monk was the fairest writer that was known
in all the world. And so the Emperor of Rome had
a cousin, a companion to him, who was a young
man; and he sent after the monk and prayed him

to teach his cousin to write as well as he did, for
the reason that he was his cousin. And so the monk
taught him to write as well as he did. And then this
young man had an envy to his master, and fain
would have had him dead, for he would have himself the master of writing as his master did before;
so he cast about how he might have him dead. So
he bethought him, and made a letter to the Sultan,
and wrote therein that the Emperor would in short
time ordain to slay him and destroy all his lands.
And therefore in all the haste that he might, he
bade that he should ordain him to come and destroy
the Emperor. And so when this letter was made he
let it fall in the Emperor's hall.

And so this letter was found and read and
brought to the Emperor anon. And he marvelled
much who had written this letter. And then came
there this young man and saw his letter, and anon
he said there was no man who could write such a
letter but his master and he, and said: "You may
well wit that it was not I." And then anon the
Emperor sent after this monk and appeached him
for his letter; and he said he knew it not. And then
they showed him this letter and said it was his hand.
And he said that he never wrote it. And without any
other judgement the Emperor commanded to
smite off his arm by the elbow. And so they did
and sent him home to the abbey, and the arm with
him, and commanded the abbot to set him in prison
and let no leech-craft be done to him. And so the
abbot did.

And as he lay in prison he cried ever to Our Lady
for help, for the ache that he had on his arm as
it rotted away. And so at the last Our Lady on a

night came to him and said, "How farest thou?"
And he said, "Full sorely, for my arm is rotted
away that was wont to paint an image of thee where-
ever I went." And then she said, "Come to me and
show me thy arm." "Lady," quoth he, "it is rotted
away." "Bring it hither to me," quoth she, "and
show it to me." And so he went among the rocks
and stones where his arm lay, and brought it to
Our Lady and showed it to her. And she bade him
set it again to his arm, as it stood before. "Lady,"
said he, "it is all rotted to gobbets." "Set it again,"
quoth she, "and it shall be whole." And so he did as
she bade him, and it was as whole as ever it was.
and he wrote as ever he did before. And then he
went and rang all the bells in the abbey, and so the
abbot and all his convent rose and saw this miracle,
and thanked God and Our Lady.

THE HANDLING OF SIN

Master Robert Manning, the Prior of Brunne, had
a straightforward aim in his collection of tales. Men
"handle sin" every day; it would be better to "handle"
the consequences of sin, and from cautionary tales
learn to be virtuous. So he retells for his flock the
Manuel des Péchés of William of Waddingham:

When the year of grace fell then to be
A thousand and three hundred and three,
For unlearned men I undertake
In English tongue this book to make.
For many be of such manner
That tales and rhymes they blithely hear;
At games and feasts and at the ale
Men listen to many an idle tale.

The French original is freely expanded. It tells sad
tales, like that of the flighty carolers of Colbek who
danced in the churchyard on Christmas Eve during
the Midnight Mass, and were cursed by the priest so
that they could not stop dancing for a twelfthmonth;
in sun or snow they circled madly to the refrain:
"Why stand we? Why go we not?" Here and there
he added incidents that had happened nearer home;
he had himself known the fate of the miser-parson:

In Cambridgeshire, in a town,   **6173**
I heard tell of a parson.
Shortly to tell, at the last,
His death-evil him down cast.
Men sent after two friars
That were by chance his councilors.
These friars came, and sat to wait;
They asked him of his own state
This parson lay and stared before
At a coffer on the floor.
Thereto the friars looked, intent,
To see where his glances went;
And he looked so, ever anon,
Then lay still as any stone.
Then asked him one friar,
"What is in that coffer there?"
The parson answered no thing,
But gave a great sighing.
The friars called his men thereto,
That coffer that they might undo.
The parson's men came, everyone;
Key, they said, had they none,
But the lid they soon upcast
And broke the lock at the last.

They found the coffer to the top
Filled with the devil's crop
Of florins and of gold rings,
And of many other things
That were of silver, and vessels,
And gold and many other jewels.
The wretch saw his treasures spread,
And sat him up in his bed
And beckoned thereto with his hand.
The friar said, "I understand
That he would have some of this."
They took and filled a silver dish
Full of pence, and to him brought
To see what was in his thought.
He took and filled his fist fast,
And into his mouth the pence cast
As though he would have eaten yet,
If he might, all he could get.
And when they saw him thus do
The friars started thereunto
And took the dish out of his hand
Against his unwilling stand.
And then anon he down fell
And died in swooning, I ween well.

CURSOR MUNDI

One unknown author of the late fourteenth century
had the courage to tell the whole history of the world
in 29,555 lines of verse, from creation to doomsday,
skipping only the unprophesied parts of the future.
It was the tale of this world in terms of the next, the
whole of sacred history, biblical and legendary,
through the seven ages of the world. The author drew
on Grossetete's *Chateau d'Amour,* on Peter Come-

stor's *Historica Scholastica,* and the shifting cycles of
miracle plays, not to mention the apocrypha, while
from first to last the elaborate legend of the true
cross, from its growth in the tree that flowered on
Adam's grave to its final appearance at the General
Judgment, gleams in and out of the narrative. Fact
or fiction, the cross legend held the central paradox
of Christianity: joy through suffering. The prologue
inquires why men who love romances should not love
best the truest romance of all:

Many songs in varied rhymes,   23
In English, French, Latin sometimes,
To read and hear each one is pressed,
The things that each one likes the best;
The wise man will of wisdom hear,
To folly will the fool draw near. . . .

Therefore, I bless that paramour   69
Who, when I need, makes me secure;
Who saves me first on earth from sin,
And heaven's bliss helps me to win,
For though I sometimes am untrue
Ever is her love anew.
Her love to all is true and free,
Sweeter than honey of the bee;
On earth is found none such as she,
Mother and maiden she could be,
Mother and maiden none the less
Because of her Christ took His flesh.
Whoever loves this sweetheart true
This is the love that is ever new,
For in this life she will fail never,
And in the other she lasts forever.
Such a matter should a rhymer take,

He who skillful rhymes can make,
Of her to make a song and rhyme,
And to love her all the time. . . .

Now let the Prologue cease; herein   **265**
In Christ's name let the Book begin.
Course of the World men should it call
For it will cover almost all.
Let us make a beginning then
With Him from Whom this world began.

It is a long journey from this beginning to the end,
but finally:

Then shall be heard the trumpet blast,   **22713**
The Doomsman shall come at last
Of whom all things stand in awe;
In what form I shall you draw.
We believe, and should trust true—
Save it be Saracen or Jew—
That after the resurrection,
On the high day of His Ascension,
Jesus came to His friends sweet
As they were sitting down to eat,
And who were in dread and doubt;
With stable truth He brought them out,
Then up to heaven He was raised;
Many men stood and gazed.
His disciples, for that case,
Much joy made in that place.
A cloud they saw before Him light,
And bear Him up, wondrous bright,
Very God and man to say,
And to deem on doomsday.
In that form come shall He there
As on earth His cross He bare;

So shall He come; but this know ye:
Since the world began to be
Was never seen such sorrowful tide
As that day shall be to bide. . . .

There is no clerk may write with ink,   22745
Nor mouth may say, nor heart think.
Then one hundred thousand knights
Shall follow that Lord of many mights,
With Him to come unto that day.
Alas, what shall the sinful say?
Terror then will be his share
When he sees all burning there,
Everything in land or sea
That in this world may stand or be.
Sorrow shall the sinful fear
When all men shall the trumpet hear.
Before the face of that Caesar
Angels shall His banner bear,
His rood, whereon He once was spread,
By which to life He has us led;
He overcame the fiend before;
There is no banner dreaded more.
Was never sun shining so clear
The tenth part as that banner there;
The brightness of that cross sheen
Over the whole world shall be seen.

THE GOSPEL OF NICODEMUS

Perhaps no single piece of writing, after the Bible
itself, had a wider influence on European art and literature for twelve hundred years than the apocryphal
Evangelium Nicodemi, a vivid, spirited, dignified
pseudo-gospel. It is in two parts, the *Acta Pilati,*

dating from the fourth century, and the earlier *Descensus ad Infernos,* vaguely attributed to a certain Lucius Charinus, honored in the second century with the name of *discipulus diaboli.* Whether the devil had anything to do with his writing or not, the Church emphasized her apostolic doctrine of Christ's descent into the Limbo of the Patriarchs (loosely referred to as "hell" throughout the Middle Ages) at the Fourth Synod of Sirmium in 359, by introducing into the Creed the words *descendit ad infernos.* The apocryphal tale merely unfolded the possibilities of the scene by a use of dramatic dialogue that was bound to stimulate the imagination of writers and artists. First told in Greek, it spread in Latin versions to every country. In painting, in carving, in enamel work and stained glass, the figure of Christ victorious over the gates of hell and leading the souls of the redeemed to heaven appeared in books and in cathedrals. In Anglo-Saxon England there were versions in both prose and poetry. The earliest Middle English version is in dramatic form, echoing the triumphant dialogue of the liturgy, *Quis est iste Rex?* Every cycle of the Miracle Plays had its *Harrowing of Hell,* and the scene was eventually portrayed by Fra Angelico; it was echoed by Dante and possibly by Milton. The most powerful and poetic unfolding of the great scene of the breaking of hell will be found in the chapter on *Piers Plowman.*[20] In the following jog-trot version, Joseph of Arimathea is giving an account to the Jews of the events that took place between Good Friday and Easter, when two men who had risen from the dead told their tale of what had happened below. Scripture says, "And the graves were opened, and the bodies

[20] Cf. p. 300.

of the saints that had slept arose . . . and appeared
to many."[21] It is legend that names two of them
Lentin and Carin, in vague reminiscence of the *discipulus diaboli:*

"Of Saint Simeon well may you mean
That kept your laws full right,
And his two sons all you have seen,
Carin and Lentin they hight.
You know they both were dead indeed
And buried in your sight;
Their bodies, I know for truth and deed,
Are raised through Jesus' might.
I warrant that they both are there
Living in Arimathie,
Ever kneeling down in prayer,
And they speak not certainly.
"We will wend to them, if you so choose,
And pray them, if they will,
To tell us how from death they rose
And how are living still.
Peradventure will they in that place
Show us a sign, a skill
That they were raised by God's grace,
And what thing to fulfill."
Unto their graves went they
Where their bodies had been laid,
And found them both away,
Just as Joseph said.
Joseph, Annas and Caiphas
And Nicodemus also
Their council wholly taken have
To Arimathie to go;
And on the morning forth they pass

[21] Matthew 27.52.

To journey on that day,
From hence sixty miles it was,
Neither more nor less away.
The men in that town
Found they at the last,
On bare earth kneeling down
Praying to God full fast.
They kissed them as friend to friend
And of them were full fain.
To Jerusalem they made them wend
Straightway with them again.
Right in the temple they made them stand
And there they questioned well,
A holy relic put they in their hand
To swear the truth to tell.
"By the God of Israel,
The God Adonai,
The truth of this thing tell
That we ask you, if you may.
"And by the great God, on your oath,
That to our Fathers spake,
If it were Jesus that raised you both
Certain you must us make.
How you were raised show quickly here
That we right truth may take."
And for these words they were full of fear,
And began to tremble and quake.
To heaven both did stare,
And the token of the cross
On their mouths they made there,
And spoke with simple voice.
"Since we are conjured now to tell
What we saw through Thy might,
The marvels that oft befell

We shall rehearse full right.
All Adam's kind, we were in hell,
Full many a woeful wight,
Till on a time it so befell
Of sun we had a sight.
When we in murkness were
A light began to gleam
To us it seemed there
Like a bright sun's beam."

They then continue with the story of the Harrowing of Hell.

DEBATE OF THE SOUL AND THE BODY

Sometimes the denizens of the next world come back to this one, in warning and reproach. A lost soul may return, not only to haunt, as in ghost stories, not only in homesickness for the scene of lost joys, as in ballads of the preternatural, but as a messenger of the truth. Voices from beyond are heard in sermons, in poems, in stories. Some of these voices are reverent and powerful, others are merely gruesome; the transitions from ecstatic visions to creepy "haunting" was inevitable, once popular storytelling had taken up the theme, by a transition as natural as the changing of "all hallows' eve" into "halloween." Among the more dignified variations was a debate between a lost soul and its own dead body. The earliest version is found in Anglo-Saxon times;[22] the following is from the fourteenth century:

As I lay one winter night   1
In a drooping sleep before the day,
Forsooth I saw a strange sight,
A body on a bier lay

[22] See *Word-Hoard*, p. 172.

That had been a proud-souled knight
And little followed in God's way.
Lost was now his life's light;
The ghost was out and must away.
When the ghost had needs be gone
It went aside and there it stood,
Beheld the body it came from
So sorrowfully, with dreadful mood.

Soul:

It said: "Weila and walawoe!
Woe to thee flesh and blood bad.
Wretched body, why liest thou so,
That one time was so wild and mad?

"Thou that wert wont to ever ride
High on horse, in and out,
A knight so cunning, known so wide,
As a lion fierce and proud?
Where is all thy great pride,
And thy followers shouting loud?
Why liest thou there, so bare, aside,
Wrapped up thus in that poor shroud?" . . .

Body:

"God thee shaped by His craft,   49
And gave to thee both wit and skill.
In thy keeping was I left
To follow after thine own will.
Learned I never thy witchcraft,
Nor knew I what was good or ill,
But as a wretch both dumb and daft,
Save what thou taughtest me by thy skill.
"Set to serve thee and to please
Both at even and at morn,

I was taught to bend my knees
From the time that thou wast born.
Thou that couldst judge both our deeds
Shouldst have been aware with scorn
Of my folly, as it seems;
Through thine own fault thou art forlorn."

THE PILGRIMAGE OF MAN

If, in mediaeval storytelling, the boundary between the world where man lives and the world where he shall live is constantly crossed and recrossed in imagination, one practical question stood out from all the tales: how finally to journey in reality from "this wretched inn" to the City of Peace, there to abide. A fourteenth-century French poet, de Guileville, traced the way in his endless allegory *Le Pélérinage de l'Homme*. It is not great poetry, and still less is Lydgate's fifteenth-century translation of it, from which the following extract is taken; it is simply the metrical expression of an earnest man's thought on a great theme. Flesh-and-blood pilgrims to the earthly Jerusalem had been, throughout the Middle Ages, unwitting prototypes of many an allegorical figure. De Guileville's pilgrim dreams; he sees in a mirror the shining of the heavenly Jerusalem and sets out to find it. His adventures along the way strikingly resemble those of a later pilgrim, the well-known Christian of Bunyan's *Pilgrim's Progress;* here are the wicket gate, the scrip and armor, the guide (here Grace-Dieu) and the opposing fiend. The Baptist tinker of Bedford seems to have been more indebted than he knew to his Catholic predecessors.[23] Again, the

[23] Owst claims that it was through mediaeval pulpit traditions, perpetuated into the seventeenth century in country districts, that the figures and phrases of mediaeval allegory reached Bunyan. See *Literature and Pulpit in Mediaeval England,* pp. 97. ff.

"I" of the poem is Everyman, meeting death at the crossroads of those two worlds in which storytellers once wandered at will:

> Grace-Dieu her look then laid   24743
> Upon me, and thus she said:
> "Thou standest upon a strait passage,
> Now, as in thy pilgrimage.
> Death is present, as thou mayest see,
> From whom no man away may flee;
> He will have mercy at the last." . . .
> And then the time came on fast,   24819
> And my speech began to fail.
> I thought it folly to assail
> Grace-Dieu with questioning,
> With demands or reasoning.
> And, as I could well discern,
> Death abode at the postern,
> And his scythe began to swing,
> His cruel might on me to bring.
> Strongly did he press me on,
> For the soul must now be gone;
> And such a fear anon me took,
> Out of my sleep I then awoke.

VII

Scholars at Large

"Wisdom for sale; wisdom for sale."

THE IRISH SCHOLARS

FOR one thousand years in Western civilization the
language of prayer was also the language of learning;
such a language had necessarily to be universal. Latin,
the vernacular of the Roman Empire, developed into
the four romance[1] languages soon after the great
migrations; it would have been lost as a living tongue
had not the Church continued to pray in it as she had
done in the catacombs, and to teach in it as she had
done in the pulpits of the Western Fathers. When

---

[1] The word *romance* is derived from *Roman.* Its modern connotations
arose from the type of adventurous love-story told in the young vernaculars. To eighteenth-century critics the word was a term of contempt for
the imaginative, as opposed to the reasonable, in literature. The "romantic
movement" had its origins in an interest in the pseudo-mediaeval: ruined
towers, haunted ballads, mystery and knights of old.

Saint Jerome, in the early fifth century, gave the
Vulgate version of the Bible to Christendom, and
when the Divine Office crystallized into jewelled
prayers in the first monasteries, the perpetuity of a
living Latin was assured. When the Benedictine
cloisters became the schoolrooms of Europe, this same
prayer-tongue was used as the medium of education,
enriched by the Classics which it preserved. When,
finally, universities arose in the twelfth century, Latin
became the *lingua franca* of the new nations. Not all
the scholars who used it were cloistered; many were
the vagabonds of learning. They carried their baggage
lightly, and scattered its contents freely to the winds.
Mediaeval scholars-at-large were everywhere, buzzing
like bees from school to school, and—to borrow from
them a favorite phrase—fertilizing "the flowers of
rhetoric."[2] And these boys sang, for glee-wood could
be tuned to Latin as well as to their own tongue.

LATIN CHRONICLERS

The Venerable Bede had established a tradition of
historical writing in Anglo-Saxon days, out of love
for "the actions and sayings of our nation." The tradition lived on in the long succession of Anglo-Norman
chroniclers who, from the twelfth to the fourteenth
centuries, reviewed and extended the history of what
was still "our own nation," going lightly over the
Battle of Hastings. Their vivid, diary-like, and
usually conscientious accounts were panoramic in
sweep and sharply human in detail, and when one
chronicler let his pen fall, some brother in the same
monastery would take it up after a century or so and
go on with the story. The doings of the monastery in

² See Appendix IV, p. 525.

question were apt to loom large among national events, where a great abbot moved freely among kings and knights, his face more clearly drawn than theirs.

Roger of Hoveden was one of the busy diplomats of Henry II. On the death of his patron he retired to the North and lived in that aloof meditation on events that throws history into perspective. Like all mediaeval chroniclers, he borrowed freely from the work of other men, but he had himself seen the struggle between the King and his Chancellor, Thomas à Becket, and recorded those tense years with the vividness of an eye-witness:

1165—After these events, the Archbishop celebrated with intense fervor the Mass of Saint Stephen the protomartyr, in whose office it is said: "Princes sat and spoke against me," and he commended his cause to the High Judge, who is God. For the celebration of this Mass he was afterwards gravely accused by Gilbert, the Bishop of London, who spoke in the King's name. The Bishop laid it to his charge that he had said Mass by magical art, and in contempt of the King. For after celebrating this Mass the Archbishop placed his stole about his neck, then put on his black canonical cape, and went straight to the King's court. And at once, from everywhere, a great crowd of people gathered that they might see the end. He carried his cross in his right hand; with his left he held the bridle of the horse on which he rode. And when he had come to the King's hall he dismounted, and bearing his own cross he entered the King's house. Then he went into the outer room alone, carrying his cross. None of his own men followed him. When he had entered he found many people inside, and he sat down among them. The King was in his private room with his intimates.

Then Gilbert, the Bishop of London, came to the Archbishop in the King's name; and he rebuked him for coming into court armed thus with the cross. But Henry, Bishop of Winchester, said to the Bishop of London: "Brother, suffer the Archbishop to carry his cross; he himself must carry it well." Then the Bishop of London grew angry with the Bishop of Winchester and said: "Brother, you have spoken evilly, and evil shall come upon you, because you have spoken against the King."

Then Roger, the Bishop of York, came to him. "O, how often he would bring blandishing words, and entreat by soft persuasion" (Ovid). But the flame of ancient hatred broke out, and would not suffer him to speak peacefully. Rather he rebuked the Archbishop because he had come into court armed with the cross; and he said that the King had a sharper sword, and therefore only if he would yield to the King's counsel should he bear his cross. And one of those standing by spoke out thus:

"Believe me: if thou believe him, thou art deceived;
The reed sings sweetly, while the hunter deceives the birds.
Deadly poisons lurk in sweet honey" (Ovid).

But the Archbishop of Canterbury would not lay down his cross, but said: "If the King's sword kills the body of flesh, my sword shall spiritually smite, and send the soul to hell." And while he sat there, some men said secretly to him that the King had decreed his death.

When the threat had been carried out some years later, and Saint Thomas lay dead on the altar steps of his cathedral, the rights of the Church in its struggle with the usurping state triumphed in his death. Henry II did penance at the martyr's shrine, and, as always, literature felt the quickening touch of heroism. Innumerable lives, letters, and chronicles spread the story of Thomas through Europe; even the Icelandic tongue had its *Thomas Saga Erkibyskups*. Three centuries later, the "pilgrim way" to Canterbury was still crowded every spring, as when a company of twenty-nine rode with Chaucer from the Tabard Inn, "the holy blissful martyr for to seek."

At Glastonbury, long since glamorous with British lore, William of Malmesbury wrote histories and biographies while the rounded lines of his monastery were sharpening into the Gothic arch. Only a brief time separated him from the glory of the First Crusade, and he wrote as follows in the *Gesta Regum Anglorum* of the scene that followed the ringing speech of Pope Urban II, calling for volunteers at the Council of Clermont in 1098 with the rallying cry, "God wills it."

Book IV

The crowd of people who heard him showed their minds by a great shout, pleased with his speech, pleased with the pilgrimage. And at once, in the presence of the council, many of the nobles fell down at the Pope's knees, consecrating themselves and all that they owned to the army of God. Among them was Aimar, the powerful Bishop of Puy, who afterwards ruled the army by his prudence and enlarged it by his eloquence. In the month of November, in which the Council had been held, each went to his home. And at once the good news spread over the face of the earth, blowing like a welcome wind through the minds of Christians; and it blew so widely that there was no people so distant or so obscure who did not respond. This love stirred not only those in the Mediterranean lands but those also who had heard the name of Christ in remote islands and in barbarous countries. The Welshman left his hunting party, the Scot his fellowship with lice, the Dane his drinking-bout, the Norseman his raw fish. Fields were stripped of their laborers, houses of their dwellers, even whole cities were set in motion. Love of the necessities of life was as nothing; love of country was held cheap; God alone was before men's eyes. What was stored in granaries or concealed in treasuries to meet the hope of the farmer or of the miser, all was left behind; they thirsted only for the road to Jerusalem. There was joy for those going, sorrow for those remaining. But why speak of those remaining? The husband was seen leaving with his wife and with all his family; you would smile to see the household goods piled on a wagon, ready to set out. The road was too narrow for the traffic, the path too small for the travellers, so thickly did the long lines press together. Men's opinions varied as to the numbers, though six million migrants were estimated. Assuredly, never before were so many peoples united in one feeling, nor did such a crowd bow its stubborn passions to one and yet to no directing power. For the greatest miracle beheld was this, to see so vast a multitude pass through Christian lands without plundering, though there was no one to control them. Love of one another so burned among them that if anyone found that he had some object not belonging to him, he would expose it to be claimed for several days; and the desires of the finder were checked till the needs of the loser were satisfied.

And now came the month of March to those who longed for it, when the winter mists rolled away and the earth, clad in young spring, drew the travellers to eastern shores. They made no delay, such ardor filled their minds.

It was in the monastery of St. Albans that history-writing developed into a fine art. Here a special monk was set aside to be the historiographer. Roger of Wendover gathered the past into his *Flores Historiarum,* and his work was continued by the greatest of the chroniclers, Matthew Paris, who interpreted the thirteenth century as it passed before his eyes much in the manner of a modern editorial writer in his *Chronica Majora.* He wrote thus of the appearance of the Tartars in the East:

1238—In those days special envoys were sent by the Saracens to the French King, on the behalf of the Old Man of the Mountain,[3] who related truthfully how a monstrous and inhuman race of men had broken out from the mountains of the North and

[3] "Old Man of the Mountain" was the name given by the Christians to the chief of the tribe of the Assassins. This Arabian sect, whose peculiar tenet was secret murder, had been founded by Hassan in 1090. They lived in the mountains of Persia and terrorized the land till their power was broken by the Tartars. The word "assassin" was derived from *hashish,* the opiate by which the murderers put themselves into a state of frenzy.

had seized the wide, rich lands of the east, had de-
populated Greater Hungary, and had sent threat-
ening letters by their terrible messengers. Their
leader declared that he was the ambassador of the
High God, sent to subdue rebellious peoples. These
men have huge heads, proportionate to their bodies;
they feed on raw meat and even on human flesh;
they are incomparable archers, and cross over rivers
in portable boats of hide. They are men robust in
strength and great in body, impious, ruthless; their
language is unlike any of those of whom we have
knowledge. They abound in flocks, herds and
horses; these horses are swift, and can make a three-
days' journey in one. The men are well-armed in
front, but not behind, that they may not flee. They
have a ferocious leader named Khan. These people
dwell in the north places, in the Caspian Mountains
or near to them, and they are called Tartars from
the River Tar. They are most numerous; it seems
that they have boiled over to be a plague to men, and
this year, though they have come before, they have
debauched more fiercely than ever. Because of them,
the people of Gothland and Frisia, dreading their
attacks, did not come to Yearmouth in England
at the time of the herring fishing, to load their boats
as they usually do. For this reason, herrings were of
no value that year in England, because of their
abundance, and about forty or fifty very good ones
sold for one piece of silver, even in places far from
the sea.

    This noble and powerful Saracen messenger, who
came to the French King, had been sent in the name
of the whole people of the East to tell these things,
and to beg help from the Western nations that they

might better repress the fury of the Tartars. He
also sent a Saracen messenger to the King of England, who came to tell him all these things, and to
say that if this attack were not resisted, nothing
remained but that the Tartars would devastate the
Western lands according to the words of the poet:
"Your own house will burn with your neighbor's"
(Ovid). The messenger, therefore, asked for help
in this emergency, that the Saracens joined with
the Christians might prevent such a disaster. The
Bishop of Winchester, who was present, then broke
in sarcastically: "Let us leave these dogs to devour
each other."

THE CHRONICLE OF JOCELIN OF BRACKELOND

Saint Edmund, the young king of East Anglia, had
been martyred by the Danes in the ninth century,
"shot full of arrows like a porcupine, as Sebastian
was," because he would not yield his Christian folk
to the foes of Christ.[4] Around the place where his un-
corrupted body lay enshrined, grew up the great monastery of Saint Edmundsbury, and here in the twelfth
century ruled Abbot Sampson. At his elbow night
and day was Jocelin of Brackelond, his Boswell, a
young, inquisitive hero-worshipper. Jocelin's chronicle
of life in the Abbey from 1173 to 1190, in which "I
took care to write only what I myself saw and heard,"
centers about his hero, the Abbot. It is a story more
concerned with the temporal than with the spiritual
life of a powerful abbey at a time when the King
himself was interested in its affairs. It reveals more
of human psychology than of the workings of grace.
Yet through it the lines of the supernatural shone

⁴ See *Word-Hoard*, p. 896.

out clearly enough to be traceable by Carlyle when he read it at its first publication in the nineteenth century. He recognized in it an example of his own theory of hero-worship as a shaping force in history, and it inspired a remarkable chapter in his *Past and Present*. It revealed to him the mediaeval world, but still more the world of the spiritual life, "another world truly, and this present poor, distressed world might get some profit by looking wisely into it instead of foolishly."

Chapter 29

Abbot Sampson was of medium height, and almost completely bald; his face was neither round nor oblong; his nose prominent, his lips full, his eyes clear, and his glance penetrating; his hearing was quick; his high arched eyebrows were often shaved; he easily grew hoarse when the weather was cold. On the day of his election he was forty-seven years old and had been a monk for seventeen years. At the time of his election he had but a few grey hairs in his ruddy beard, and still fewer in his black and curling hair; but during the fourteen years following all his hair turned white as snow.

He was a most temperate man, never lazy, of good health, and fond of riding and walking till old age overcame him and checked his ardor. When he heard of the capture of the cross and the fall of Jerusalem he began to wear rough undergarments and a hairshirt, and to abstain from flesh meat. However, he still wished to have meat placed before him at table, so that the portions to be given away as alms might be greater. He liked sweet milk, honey and sweetmeats better than other food.

He hated liars and drunkards and gabblers; for virtue ever loves its like, and spurns its opposite. He blamed those who grumbled about their food and drink, and he kept to the old customs that he had followed first in the cloister. He had the virtue of never wishing to change a dish once placed before him. When I was a novice I wished to see if this were really true, and as I was serving in the refectory I got the idea of placing before him some food that would have offended any other man, in a very dirty cracked dish. When he looked at it, he seemed not to notice what it was like. Then, as there was a pause, I repented of what I had done; I seized the dish, changed the food and brought it back on a much better dish. When he saw the change, he was troubled and displeased.

Chapter 75

In the year of grace 1198, the glorious martyr Edmund willed to terrify our monastery and to teach us that his body should be more reverently and carefully watched over. There was a wooden shelf between the shrine and the high altar, where two candles burned which the guardians used to relight, and they sometimes stuck more wax on the candles and joined the parts carelessly. And under this shelf many things lay untidily together, bits of flax, thread, wax and various vessels; in fact, whatever came into the hands of the guardians was thrown there, behind the door and the iron walls.

The guardians were asleep on the night of Saint Etheldreda's[5] Feast, and part of a candle which had

[5] Saint Etheldreda was an Anglo-Saxon princess who founded the double monastery at Ely in 672. She was one of the best loved of the English saints for her high-hearted courage.

been relit fell while still burning, as we think, on the
floor covered with rags. And all the things above
and beneath it caught on fire, till the iron doors were
white hot. Lo, the anger of the Lord was kindled,
but not without mercy, as it is written, "When
Thou shalt be angry, Thou shalt remember mercy."
For just then the clock struck the hour for Matins,
and the master of the vestry arose and discovered
the fire. He ran at once and sounded the gong as
if for a death, and he cried in a loud voice that the
shrine was on fire. Then we all ran and found the
flames raging with incredible fury, enfolding the
whole shrine and mounting up towards the beams
of the church. Our young men ran for water, some
to the well and some to the clock. Some used their
hoods, and with great difficulty put out the fire.
They first stripped some of the altars. When cold
water was poured on the front of the shrine, the
stones fell and crumbled to dust. The nails with
which the silver plates were fixed to the shrine came
out of the wood which had been burned away to the
depth of my finger, and the plates hung one from
another without nails. But the golden image at the
front of the shrine and some of the stones remained
firm and intact; it was more beautiful after the fire
than before, because it was all made of gold.

The lord Abbot, who was absent at the time,
grieved greatly at the news. When he came home
he entered the chapter room and said that these
disasters, and other graver ones, had befallen us
because of our sins, and especially because of our
grumbling over our food and drink. And he laid the
blame on the whole monastery rather than on the

greed and carelessness of the guardians of the shrine.

UNIVERSITY SCHOLARS

While the monasteries were at their heyday the universities were rising. The cathedral school of Chartres gradually yielded its pre-eminence as the schools of Paris formed into a *studium generale.* The streets of Oxford and Cambridge were soon as crowded with students as the Petit Pont. These places were the uneasy melting-pots of the nations, and the forges of a new learning. The six o'clock sun surprised the scholars in their classrooms, gathering about the master of the hour. If one of them stayed in bed in his attic, it was for want of the single cloak that he shared with his fellow; it would be his turn tomorrow. Reading and disputation went on all day, till sundown sent them all to bed, "save when, on a holiday in honor of God or of His mother, they are allowed to have a fire in the hall in wintertime . . . and to make recreation with poems, chronicles of the realm, and wonders of the world."

John of Salisbury in his youth knew both Chartres and Paris; he was a university-haunter, and in the end gave to literature its first Christian treatise on political science, the *Policraticus,* and an exposition of twelfth-century education, the *Metalogicon.* He wrote from Paris to his best friend, Thomas à Becket, in 1164:

To our venerable Father, and most dear Lord Thomas, by the grace of God Archbishop of Canterbury, I, John of Salisbury, wish health and happiness. As soon as I had crossed the sea, I seemed to feel a softer air, and after the tumult of the swelling

winds I wondered at the joy and at the abundance
on every hand. . . . And when I saw the plentiful
food, the contented people, the reverent priests, the
majesty and glory of the whole Church, and the
varied occupations of the philosophers, I marvelled
at it all, as at the ladder of Jacob whose summit
touched heaven, the path for angels rising and
descending; and rejoicing in the pleasant excitement
of travel I said to myself, "Truly this is the place of
God, and I knew it not." And a line of poetry came
to my mind, "Happy is the exile to whom such a
place is given." After a few days spent in finding
lodgings and unpacking my bags, I sought the King
of France, and laid your cause before him.

Giraldus Cambrensis, Welsh Archdeacon and courtier of Henry II, had also studied at Paris, where, as
he modestly relates, he discoursed so well "that all
wondered, and knew not whether greater praise should
be given to his ornate language or to his clear arguments." He preached a crusade in Wales, and visited
Ireland for the King. The result was a book on the
geography of Ireland, which he took care to publish
widely, as he relates in *De Rebus a Se Gestis:*

Book II, Chapter 16

When he had won great name and fame for himself in the Island, Giraldus crossed from Ireland to
Wales, between Easter and Pentecost. There he put
his whole mind to finishing his *Topography.* When
it was at last finished and corrected, he did not wish
to hide it under a bushel, but to place it on a candle-
stick that it might shine out to all; so he determined
to recite it before a great crowd of hearers at Oxford, where, of all places in England, the clergy

were strongest and most eminent in learning. And as there were three parts to the book, he gave three consecutive days to the reading, a day to each part. On the first day he graciously entertained all the poor of the town, whom he invited to come together; on the next day he entertained all the doctors of the various Faculties, together with the most noted and famous of their scholars. The third day he entertained the rest of the scholars, with the knights of the town and many of the citizens. It was a splendid and costly affair, at which the authentic ancient times of the poets were relived. Such a thing has not been seen in England in present times, nor recorded in past ages.

The same comprehensive outlook that made mediaeval scholars give the name *universitas* to a center of learning, led them to compile huge books of general knowledge, often called *specula*. They held their "mirrors" not only up to nature but to their own minds. These encyclopedias may have contained haphazard learning, but they followed the progression of ideas, not of the alphabet. Isidore of Seville had set the fashion in the seventh century with his *Etymologies;* Bede's *De Natura Rerum* was the first such work in England and among the last was the *Speculum Majus* of Vincent of Beauvais, in the thirteenth century. Between them came Alexander Neckam, whose elusive person haunted the University of Paris in the years of its clamorous beginning, c.1180, and who returned to England to sift his knowledge into his own *De Naturis Rerum*. Nature, he says, "radiates her own serene majesty," and needs no ornament from him. Yet she needs interpretation, "for the upbuilding of our human ways." He opens, properly, with a mystical analysis of the first Hebrew word in Genesis; then follow eleven chapters on astronomy, including accounts of the angels and of the music of the spheres, also of the man in the moon, who is a rustic imprisoned there for stealing thorns. Of course, only the *simplex lector* will believe this last fact. Elements, plants, gems, and animals are treated in order; then comes man, treated both physiologically and morally. Faulty science can be forgiven when it is interwoven with shrewd comments on things as they are, bright pictures of life as lived, philosophical clarity, and a passionate sense of the Divine.

Chapter *XXIX: Concerning Monkeys*[6]

A monkey not only mocks men in its gestures and features, but it tries to imitate them in many ways. When the wretch sees a man covering his hands and feet with gloves and shoes, and binding his feet firmly with straps, it wants to do the same, not knowing what will happen. The crafty man then leaves these objects lying about, and hides while the silly beast tries faultily to imitate what he has seen, and is then caught, unable to run away. When once caught it is used as a cause of mirth to the vainly curious men who watch its ridiculous actions.

We grant that monkeys have many clever tricks, but never can they match the noble faculty of reasoning in men. It happened that a monkey lived among the battlements of a castle, and he used to watch the skillful work of a poor shoemaker who

---

[6] Pet monkeys were a source of entertainment in mediaeval castles. Animals and birds from the East, as well as silks and jewels, were collected by the Crusaders.

lived nearby. Whenever the shoemaker was obliged
to leave his work, the monkey would enter through
the open window, and taking his knife would cut the
leather into bits, not only annoying the poor worker
but doing serious damage to his trade. The man
pondered his grievance and longed for revenge. So
one day, when he saw the monkey watching him from
the battlement, he took up his knife and passed it
lightly back and forth across his own throat, first the
blunt edge then the sharp. Then, leaving the window
open, he went out and delayed his return on purpose.
The monkey came into the empty house, and faithfully copied the shoemaker; he passed the knife
across his throat, and soon felt the sharp blade. His
silly imitating brought its own punishment, and the
poor shoemaker rejoiced at the death of his
enemy. . . .

A monkey, at its work of amusing others and
mocking men, is a symbol not of virtue but of vice.
For do not lying superstition and hypocrisy turn
true religion into false? In habit, deed, gesture, word
and work the money-loving hypocrite simulates true
religion. . . . Woe! Woe! Man, that noble creature,
labors to become a monkey!

Chapter CLXXIII: Concerning the Liberal Arts[7]

The study of the liberal arts, though very useful
in itself, stirs up a multitude of vain questions in the
curious. For the arts are praiseworthy, but those who
abuse them are blameworthy. . . . For what is man,
liable to change and bound about with cunning

---

[7] From the time of Cassiodorus, the seven liberal arts had been the
basis of Christian education. The Trivium contained grammar, logic and
rhetoric; the Quadrivium contained arithmetic, geometry, astronomy and
music. Theology, the queen of sciences, crowned the course.

snares? Now the rose of youth blooms wide, but swiftly fades the glory of its glowing color. O would that man would consider for what he is made: to serve God, and reign with Him forever. Let man keep this before the eyes of his heart; for this end let him sigh and yearn. But, O cares, O weariness, O studies full of sweat and vanity! For the liberal arts are only of value in giving a wider, surer grasp of those things that are treated of in theology.

LYRICS

The sprawling universities were hard put to it when it came to housing the thousands of boys, technically clerical and actually irresponsible, who came and went like spring weather. Bound in a freemasonry of youth, this *ordo vagorum* spread restlessly over the land, literally singing for its supper. Without thought of what they were about, these loose-footed poets accomplished for literature what no man at his desk could have done. The sequences and hymns of the Church were ringing in their ears with the more distant lyrics of Horace and Catullus; and they shaped from the fluid medium of their colloquial Latin a haunting lyric of their own, which gradually passed into the vernaculars. Together with the contemporary Provençal troubadour and the later Renaissance man of letters, the wandering scholars were the makers of the modern lyric. The forms that they used, rhymed and stanzaic, were largely derived from the liturgy,[8] sometimes by way of

[8] Rhyme as a verse form first appears consistently in the hymns of the Church in about the tenth century. As these hymns and sequences were the part of the liturgy best known to the people at large, their patterns were gradually adapted to poetry of all sorts. It may be claimed that rhyme is among the Church's gifts to literature.

impudent parody. The thought is perennial. They were poor, and forced to beg:

> Exul ego clericus
> Ad laborem natus,

but they boasted Golias as their patron, and waxed reckless at their drinking:

> In taberna quando sumus
> Non curamus quid sit humus.

They were incurably gay,

> Gaudeamus igitur
> Iuvenes dum sumus,

yet haunted with lovelorn moodiness,

> Cum mihi sola redeo
> Haec revolvens palleo.

Most of the manuscript collection of these lyrics, such as the *Carmina Burana* (with a few pages blacked out by the censor's gall), come from Germany, but the songs themselves are international. The *Cambridge Song Book* was compiled, or at least copied, in England. The Middle English lyric would not have been what it is without its Latin counterpart, and often the two languages are woven together in macaronic form.[9]

> Thou that art so fair and bright,
> *Ave Maris Stella,*
> Brighter than the day's light,
> *Parens et puella.*

[9] Properly, macaronic verse is humorous poetry in a mixture of Latin and vernacular words with Latin endings. It was first used by Teofilo Folengo in the sixteenth century, for burlesque purposes. The word is related to "macaroni." It is now applied to any poetry in a mixture of languages.

The purely religious lyric will be studied in a later
chapter, in connection with the mystic writers who gave
soul to it; here are examples of the secular lyric, more
in tune with the voice of the *scholasticus vagabundus*.
In Merry England, the vernacular love songs are more
purely lighthearted than the Latin, which are often
heavy with the scent of Catullus' fading rose, and with
a paganism that tries in vain to forget the bittersweet
challenge of Christian austerity. The English poetry
caught the lilt of children's voices on the village green.

1.

Springtime is come with love to earth,
With blossoms and with birds' mirth
 That all this bliss bringeth.
Day's-eyes in the dales,
Notes sweet of nightingales,
 Every bird singeth.
The threstle-cock cries oooo!
Away is their winter hue
 When the woodruff springeth.
The birds sing a wondrous deal,
And look back on their winter weal,
 And all the wood ringeth.

2.

I have a gentle cock
 Croweth me day,
He makes me rise early
 My Matins to say.

I have a gentle cock,
 Come of a race great,
His comb is of red coral,
 His tail is of jet.

I have a gentle cock,
   His nature I know,
His comb is of red coral,
   His tail of indigo.

His legs be of azure,
   So gentle and so thin,
His spurs are of silver white
   To the very root within.

His eyes are of crystal,
   Enclosed all in amber,
And every night he perches him
   In my lady's chamber.

3.

Blow, Northern wind,
Send thou me my sweeting!
Blow, Northern wind,
   Blow! Blow! Blow!

I know a maid in a bower bright
That full seemly is of sight,
Gentle maiden of might,
   Fair and free of hand.
In all this great world-home
A maiden of blood and bone
Never yet have I known
   More lovesome in the land. . . .
Her fair face gleams alight
As a lantern in the night,
Her hue shines so bright,
   So fair she is and fine!
A sweet neck she has to hold,
With arms and shoulders for one bold,
And fingers very fair to fold;
   Would God that she were mine.

4.

Maiden in the moor lay,
  In the moor lay,
Sevennight full, sevennight full,
Maiden in the moor lay,
  In the moor lay,
Sevennight full and a day.

Well was her meat.
  What was her meat:
The primrose and the violet,
The primrose and the violet,
Well was her meat.
  What was her meat?
The primrose and the violet.

Well was her drink.
  What was her drink?
The chill water of the well-spring,
The chill water of the well-spring,
Well was her drink.
  What was her drink?
The chill water of the well-spring.

Well was her bower.
  What was her bower?
The red rose and the lily flower,
The red rose and the lily flower,
Well was her bower.
  What was her bower?
The red rose and the lily flower.

5.

I am of Ireland,
And of the holy land
  Of Ireland.

Good Sir, pray I thee,
Of Saint Charity,
Come and dance with me
In Ireland.

Rougher forms were used for parody or popular comedy:

1.

The man in the moon stands and strides,
On his hay-fork his burden he beareth.
No wonder it is if he downward slides,
For fear lest he fall he shuddereth and sheereth.
When the frost is fresh he has chilly fits,
The thorn-bundle keen his clothing teareth.[10]
No man in the world knows when he sits,
Nor, if it be not the hedge, what weeds he weareth.
This man up on high, whence ever he were,
Whether in the moon born and fed,
He leaneth on his fork as a grey friar;
This crooked idler is sore adread.
It is many a day that he has been there,
I guess with his errand he has not sped.
He has hewn from somewhere his bundle of briar,
Therefore with his money the hayward has fled. . . .
This man heareth me nought, though to him I cry.
I think the churl is deaf—may the devil him draw!
Though I gape up at him he will not hie;
The lazy lad knows nought of the law.
Hop forth, Hubert, you hoarse magpie!
Or you'll go into prison without delay.

---

[10] This popular idea concerning the man in the moon explains the scene in *Midsummer-Night's Dream* where the rustics, preparing their play, remark: "One must come in with a bush of thorns and a lantern, and say he comes to disfigure, or to present, the person of moonshine" (Act III, Scene 1).

Though I scold until my teeth chatter, why,
The churl won't come down till the dawn of day.

2.

Swart smoky smiths, smattered with smoke
Drive me to death with the din of their dents.
Such noise in the night men have heard never,
Such crying of knaves and clattering of knocks.
The snub-nose crook-backs cry out for coal! coal!
And blow at their bellows till their brains burst.
Huf! Puf! says one, Haf! Paf! another.
They spit and they sprawl and they tell many
　　tales;
They gnaw and they grind and they groan all to-
　　gether,
And make themselves hot with their hard ham-
　　mers.
Of bullhide are made their big aprons,
Their shanks are shackled for the fiery sparks.
Heavy hammers they have, hard to handle.
Stark strokes they strike on the steel stocks.
Lus, bus, las, das, they knock in a row;
So doleful a din would drive away the devil.
The master pulls and hammers his little pieces,
Twists them in two and strikes a treble.
Tik tak! Hic hac! Tiket taket! Tik tak!
Lus bus! Lus das! Such life they lead.
All mare-clothers, Christ give them sorrow!
No man at night may rest for these water-burners!

3.

I command all the rats that are here about
That none dwell in this place, within or without.
Through the virtue of Jesus Christ that Mary
　　bare about,

Before whom all creature ought to lout,
And through the virtue of Mark, Matthew, Luke
and John,
—All four Evangelists gathered in one—
Through the virtue of Saint Gertrude, that maid
clean,
> God grant the grace
> That no rats dwell in the place
That their names were named in.
And through the virtue of Saint Kasi,
That holy man that prayed to God Almighty
> For harm that they did
> In his mead
By day and by night,
God bade them flee and go out of every man's
sight.
Dominus Deus Sabaot! Emmanuel, the great
God's name!
I invoke in this place against rats and all other
shame.
God save this place from all other wicked wights,
Both by days and by nights! *Et in nomine Patris
et Filii.* . . .

The finger of Latin was felt even in political songs,
which are apt to be as philosophic in tone as they are
patriotic. The following three-language *Song on the
Times* is a cry of woe at the evil abroad in the reign of
Edward II:

Quand l'homme parle à Dieu, videat quae verba
loquatur;
Il doit prendre garde, ne stultios inveniatur.
Quando quis loquitur, save reason rest therein.

Derisum patitur, and little shall he so win,
Dans la sainte église sunt multi saepe priores;
Some are wise, multi sunt inferiores.
When men may most do, tunc velle suum mani-
  festat,
In donis also, si vult tibi praemia praestat.
Ingrato benefac, post haec a peine tu verra.
Pour bon vin tibi lac non dat, nec rem tibi rendra.
Sensum custodi, quasi mieux vaut-il que ta maison;
Though thou be mighty, robor nichil est sine raison.
Lex lieth down over all, fallax frans fallit ubique.
And love is but small, quia gens se gestat inique.

This *tour de force* is weighty with meaning if odd in
form. When pure political feeling broke out patrioti-
cally, as in the songs of Lawrence Minot, it moved
with muscular freedom. The *Battle of Bannockburn,*
fought in 1333, was a lusty fight:

Now to tell you will I turn
To the Battle of Bannockburn:

Scots out of Berwick and Aberdeen,
At Bannockburn were you too keen;
There slew you many guiltless, as it was seen,
And now has King Edward avenged it, I ween.
  Avenged it, I ween, well worth the while!
  Beware of the Scots, they are full of guile!

Where were you, Scots of Saint John's town?
The boast of your banner is all beaten down.
When you bid with your boasting, Sir Edward is
  bound
To kindle your care and crack your crown.
  He has cracked your crown, well worth the while!
  Shame betide the Scots, they are full of guile!

Scots of Stirling were stern and stout;
Of God and good men they had no doubt.
Now they have, the robbers, ridden about,
But at last Sir Edward rifled their rout.
He has rifled their rout, well worth the while!
But ever they are full of gawds and guile.

THE POLYCHRONICON

Returning to the schoolroom, from which scholars had carried their learning abroad till it was absorbed in the commonwealth of tradition, we find that the pen of the translator often brought Latin treatises directly into popular use. In 1387 John de Trevisa completed a translation of Higden's *Polychronicon,* a "universal history." It is one of the earliest pieces of sustained English prose, which was not yet considered a fit medium for academic writing. One passage describes the state of the language shortly before it began to be standardized; it pictures the classroom not of a great university but of a grammar school for children. They too were "scholars at large."

Chapter LIX

As it is known how many manners of people there are in this island, there are also of so many peoples as many languages and tongues. Although Welshmen and Scots that are not mingled with other nations hold well-nigh their first language and speech, yet Scots that were at one time confederate and dwelt with the Picts draw somewhat after their speech. But the Flemings who dwell in the west side of Wales have left their strange speech and speak Saxon-like enough. Also, Englishmen, although they had from the beginning three manners of speech, Southern, Northern and Middle speech in the middle of the land, as they came of three sorts of people of Germany, nevertheless by mixing and mingling first with Danes and afterwards with Normans, in many the country's language is impaired and some use strange stammering, chattering, snarling and grating teeth-grinding. This impairing of the birth-tongue is because of two things. One is that children in school, against the usage and manner of all other nations, are compelled to leave their own language and to construe their lessons and their tasks in French, and have since the Normans first came to England. Also gentlemen's children are taught to speak French from the time that they are rocked in their cradle and can speak and play with a child's bawble, and rustic men liken themselves to gentlemen, and try with great industry to speak French, to be held in greater account.

This manner was much in use before the first plague [i.e., the Black Death of 1349] and is since then somewhat changed. For John Cornwall, a master of grammar, changed the teaching in grammar-school and the construing of French into English; and Richard Pencrych learned that manner of teaching of him and other men of Pencrych so that now, in the year of Our Lord one thousand three hundred four score and five, of the second King Richard after the Conquest nine, in all the grammar-schools of England children leave French and construe and learn in English, and have thereby advantage on one side and disadvantage on another. The advantage is that they learn their grammar in less time than children were wont to do. The disadvantage is that now children of grammar-school know no more French than their left heel does, and that is harmful to them, and many must pass the sea and travel in strange lands and in many circumstances also. Also gentlemen have now almost ceased to teach their children French. It seems a great wonder that English, that is the birth-tongue of Englishmen, and their own language and tongue, is so diverse in sound in this island, and the language of Normandy hath come of another land and yet hath one manner of sound among men that speak it aright in England. Nevertheless, there are as many diverse manners of French in the realm of France as are diverse manners of English in the realm of England.

Also, concerning the fore-said Saxon tongue that is divided into three, and is scarcely left among a few rustic men, it is a wonder that the men of the east with the men of the west, as under the same part of heaven, accord more in sounding of speech than men of the north with men of the south. Therefore it is that Mercia, where are men of Middle England, as it were partners with both ends, understand better the side languages, northern and southern, than northern and southern understand each other. All the language of the Northumbrians, and especially at York, is so sharp, piercing, grating and unshaped, that southern men can scarcely understand that language. I think that that is because they are nigh to strange men and aliens that speak strangely, and also because the Kings of England dwell far from that country; for they are more turned to the south country, and if they go to the north country they go with great help and strength. The cause why they be more in the south country than in the north may be better corn land, more people, more noble cities and more profitable havens.

THE PHILOBIBLON

The title of this early fifteenth-century treatise could be applied to many book enthusiasts before the time of its author. Richard de Bury was tutor to Edward III, ambassador to the Papal court at Avignon, and Bishop of Durham, but he lives in history simply as "the booklover." His library, which followed him in five carts when he travelled, was the largest in England at the time. When he was at home, the greater part of it lay scattered about his bedroom till he could "scarcely take a step therein." The *Philobiblon* comes at the end of the Middle Ages like a summary of that passion for manuscripts which, from the cells of Monte Cassino, spread from one monastery to another, and overflowed into cathedral schools and universities until printing transformed the libraries. A scribe in the *scriptorium* (placed considerately near the kitchen or calefactory in those cold stone buildings) might write in the margin of his manuscript, "Thank God it will soon be dark," but he loved his toil. The books that came from his pen would lie in the closed presses that faced the light of the high library windows; scholars from all over Europe would come to read them, though if anyone took them away he must leave their value in gold or jewels as pledge of the safe return of what, says Richard, "infinitely surpass the riches of the world." In the glittering, allusive Latin style gained from endless reading, the Booklover pleaded the cause of his and of all libraries, in his "little treatise, which will purge from excess the love we feel for books."

Chapter I

. . . Where dost thou hide, O mighty, O chosen treasure [Wisdom]? And where shall thirsty souls

A feather he took in his fingers and he wrote on bookskin.   LAYAMON'S BRUT

find thee? Beyond doubt, thou hast placed thy tabernacle in books, where the most High, the Light of lights, the Book of life, has established thee. There, all who ask receive thee, all who seek find thee, and to those who knock the door is quickly opened. In books, the cherubim stretch out their wings, that the mind of the student may ascend and gaze from pole to pole, from the rising sun to the setting, from the north and from the sea. In books, the incomprehensible high God Himself is made comprehensible, and is clung to. In books, the nature of earthly, of heavenly, and of infernal beings is laid open; in books is revealed the law by which all states are governed; in them the offices of the celestial hierarchy are distinguished, and the tyrannies of demons are described, things that the ideas of Plato never surpassed, nor the teachings of Crato contained.

In books, I find the dead as though living; in books I foresee the future; in books, warring elements are harmonized; from books come forth the laws of peace. All things are corrupted and decay with time; Saturn never ceases to devour what he has brought forth, and oblivion would cover all the glory of the earth had not God provided mortals a remedy in books. . . .

Truth which overcomes all things, which ranks above kings, wine and women, which sanctity holds in higher honor than friends, which is a road without turning and a life without ending, to which the holy Boethius attributed a three-fold being in the mind, in the voice, and in writing, this truth seems to dwell most usefully and to fructify most abundantly in books. For the strength of the voice is lost with its sound; truth hidden in the mind is but obscure wisdom and an unseen treasure. But the truth that shines out in books desires to manifest itself to every disciplined sense. It is read by the eyes while it is heard by the ear; it offers itself even to the touch when it is transcribed, collected, corrected and preserved. . . . You alone, O books, are free and freely given; you give to all who ask, and liberate all who serve you diligently.

It is no wonder that Richard was never deterred by the price of any book, "unless the knavery of the seller is to be withstood, or a better bargain is to be expected elsewhere." When he had bought books, he respected them; and those who borrowed them must "show them once a year to the keepers."

Chapter XVII

We not only render service to God when we prepare volumes of new books, but we show holy piety if we are careful not to injure them, and if we return them unspotted to their proper places, that they may rejoice in their purity while we hold them in our hands, and rest secure when they are safe in their niches. . . .

In the first place, let there be a mature restraint in opening and closing books; they should neither be opened with undue haste, nor, when finished, be thrown down unclosed. A book should be more carefully preserved than a shoe.

There is a race of students who are badly trained, who, unless restrained by the rules of their elders, fall into endless childish habits. They act petulantly, swell presumptuously, are sure of everything while inexperienced in all. You will see, perhaps, a stiff-necked youth lounging lazily at his study. When he is pinched with winter cold his nose runs, and he does not use his handkerchief to save the book below. To such I would give a cobbler's apron instead of a book. He has an unsavory fingernail like a giant's with which he marks the places that please him. He puts many straws between the pages, which stick out to recall the passage that his memory forgets. These straws, which the book cannot digest, and which no one removes, first swell and distend the book, then rot in it. He is not ashamed to eat fruit and cheese over an open book, and to move his empty cup from side to side upon it, and because he has not his alms bag at hand he leaves the crumbs in the book. . . .

The most meek Moses teaches us in Deuteronomy XIII how to make neat cases for books where they may be kept safe from all damage. "Take this book," he said, "and place it in the side of the ark of the covenant of the Lord your God." O seemly place, and fitting for a library, which was made from incorruptible shettim wood, and was covered with gold, both within and without. But Our Savior Himself, by His example, given in Luke IV, forbids all unbecoming carelessness in handling books. For when He had finished reading a passage that held a prophecy concerning Himself, He did not return the book to the minister until He had folded it with His most sacred hands.

The fourteenth century had its Hundred Years' War, but what was a century of fighting then, compared with one year of war in an atomic age? Richard of Bury long ago added one more reason to our many for desiring world peace when he wrote, with a picture of burning libraries in his mind:

Infinite are the losses which the tumults of war have brought upon the race of books. But since the infinite can in no wise be expressed, we shall here put a boundary to our lamentation, humbly praying that the Ruler of Olympus and the most high Ruler of the whole earth, may bring an end to wars, and keep our times tranquil in His protection.

VIII

Somewhat Elfish

I was of their fellowship anon.
PROLOGUE TO THE
CANTERBURY TALES

As TIME slipped over the mid-mark of the fourteenth
century, shadows lengthened over England. The Black
Death stalked away, but the work of death is not soon
undone, and trouble trailed in its wake, trouble that
sprang from hunger and that led to revolt, that dis-
rupted economic conditions till peasant and working-
man laid their hands, for better or for worse, upon the
sources of industry. The Battle of Crécy had been
fought, but the rumble of the cannon that had been
heard there for the first time could still be heard,
longer and louder, speaking doom for the armored
knight. The Hundred Years' War allowed of no peace,
though it seemed hardly worth fighting. Worst of all,
the inner rottenness of the lives of many a churchman

and wandering friar was breaking into open corruption, and the strong hand that should have brought cleansing and healing was paralyzed; the Pope was in Avignon, not Rome, and the Great Western Schism was near. It came just as the boy-king, Richard II, took the throne of the third Edward.

In those days three great poets were living in England. It is doubtful whether they knew one another, though they may often have crossed in the streets of London; they wrote in different dialects, and their minds lived in different realms; in their hands, glee-wood spoke with full harmonies and tonic discords. They were Chaucer, Langland, and the nameless Pearl Poet. The first has been popular from that day to this; the second has been, until lately, misunderstood; the third is scarcely known. It is impossible to say which is the greatest, except that he is not likely to be the most popular.

Geoffrey Chaucer (c.1324-1400) lived where the fringes of court life brushed against the common people, and he knew both worlds. Books he knew, and the daisies opening at sunrise in the fields. He was tender, impish, petulant, now laughing like a child, now winking with the dry disillusion of a too-wise man of the world. He wrote allegories because it was the fashion; he wrote stories because he could not help it. He saw the world pass before him on the road to Canterbury. On the faces of the pilgrims he saw the shadows of his time, and its fitful sunlight. He shrugged his shoulders, called posterity to look at the surface-play of light and dark, and let the depths go unrevealed. Perhaps he would not reveal them, perhaps he could not; perhaps he did not know that they were there.

He wrote his way with relish and with irresistible charm into the front rank of English literature; he has been its darling ever since. He has been variously regarded as the last of the mediaevalists and the first of the moderns; in any case he is undoubtedly the one mediaevalist known to all moderns. Standing as he does at a crossroads in English life and language, the year 1400, he has somewhat obscured to later eyes the view of what lies behind him. As it happened, his form of speech, the Midland dialect which had become "the King's English," was in the following century gradually formed by the printing press and by social circumstances into the "standard English" of today. Chaucer's own popularity had a good deal to do with this standardization; his disciples magnified him into "the first fair finder of our language." Consequently, he can be read as he wrote, with a little effort, even today. The same cannot be said of his equally gifted contemporaries who wrote in a less fortunate dialect. It is not unnatural that after a period of relative neglect in the sixteenth century, when only the romantic-minded Spenser seems to have yielded to his fascination, he should have been erroneously hailed by Dryden at the beginning of modern times as "the father of English poetry," who lived "in the dawning of our language."[1] Dryden was an illuminating critic, but limited in his knowledge of the "monkish ages." It was some time before scholarship restored the true Chaucer

---

[1] "Preface to the Fables," *Essays of John Dryden,* ed. W. P. Kerr, (Clarendon Press, 1926), Vol. II, p. 246. Although Dryden's estimate of Chaucer is an injustice to the early English poets, anonymous or otherwise, who preceded him, it is in itself a penetrating, enthusiastic tribute to "a man of most wonderfully comprehensive nature," of whose work one can say, "Here is God's plenty."

text[2] and introduced the poet into every bookloving household.

Yet this familiarity with Chaucer is not all-inclusive. It has centered, ever since the seventeenth century, on the *Canterbury Tales,* and has neglected his other works, which have thus passed into that literary limbo where go the writings known only to university students. That was because Chaucer was a born story-teller. When Mine Host wanted a gay tale to lighten the long Canterbury road, he looked towards a hitherto silent pilgrim and asked, "What man is this? He seemeth elfish by his countenance." What Chaucer obligingly gave Mine Host was a parody followed by a "morality," the flippant *Tale of Sir Topaz,* and the dull *Tale of Melibeus.* Yet this same inscrutable man, "looking at the ground as though he would find a hare," was—as Mine Host did not seem to realize—the real author of the tales of all of those pilgrims in motley, a prince among storytellers.

Another reason for the modern partiality for the *Canterbury Tales* is the fact that they are decidedly modern in their appeal. His other works, in form at least, are completely of their day and age—which their author was not. He represents only some of the varied elements of the Middle Ages. He is, for instance, not allegorical in his outlook, yet most of his minor works are allegories. He could not put his real self into them without cracking the conventional mold. Consequently, they are not masterpieces, as are the *Tales,* with the great *Prologue* and fascinating "links." Yet they have

---

[2] The early printed editions of Middle English texts were often set from late and corrupt MSS. This is particularly true of Chaucer, and led Dryden to conclude that the poet was a poor metrist. Only in 1775 did Tyrrhwitt's edition restore Chaucer to his rightful place as a master of faultlessly musical verse.

their own significance as an indispensable part of Middle English literature. Because of this, and because of the fact that they have remained out of literary circulation for want of translation and interpretation, they will be treated here to the apparent neglect of the *Canterbury Tales*. The latter are too famous to suffer by the slight.

Lovers of Chaucer may learn much about the man himself from these so-called minor works. He is known from a miniature MS portrait, the "elfish man" who points at us with one hand and dangles a rosary from the other, but only his complete works can reveal the life behind these gestures. Their author was a child of the city streets, a page at a gay court, a diplomat in cultured foreign cities, a haunter of libraries and gardens, who lived, when home, literally on the top of a gate through which the whole world passed. His heart was warm, and he wore it on his sleeve. He deplored the bad times, judged his fellow men with shrewd affection, and lived as gayly and as gallantly as he could.

His poetry is a tapestry of fine threads, most of them imported. A study of his literary sources would involve a reading of most of the writings of the Middle Ages, in four languages. French influence was still active at a court where the kings of England had been speaking English for less than a century; Italian influence was stirring with the dawn of the Renaissance, and Chaucer had travelled into the midst of it. Latin opened to him the storehouses of monasteries and universities. It is the people of his *Tales* who are thoroughly English, and they did not find their way into his earlier work. As a poetic craftsman Chaucer was untouched by the contemporary revival of alliterative

metre, ringing with the ancient beat of English
poetry.[3] His exquisite metres and verse forms are Con-
tinental in origin. Yet, with all this, the tapestry is
woven according to his personal design; he makes his
innumerable borrowings without courtesy of quotation,
and he has no apology to offer for the oddities and dis-
proportions which are results of the mood of the moment. He has intuition and word-music; is anything
more needed to make a poet? When all is said, one is
forced to yield with Spenser, reluctantly or enthusiasti-
cally as the case may be, to:

> Old Dan Geoffrey, in whose gentle spright
> The pure well-head of Poesie did dwell.[4]

THE LYRICS

It is a characteristic Chaucerian paradox that the
lightest of his poems, the court lyrics and the fashionable ballades, should reflect a moral earnestness often
lacking in his more serious work. It is well to take
Chaucer at his face value; he meant what he said. No
one is more gravely moral than a gay youth, when
writing to a fair lady whose inconstancy has made him
a philosopher:

[3] The alliterative revival of the fourteenth century is a remarkable proof
of the long-lived virility of oral tradition. The old Anglo-Saxon metre (see
Appendix II) had apparently vanished by the middle of the thirteenth
century, but it emerged, as springs do from underground, and once more
produced literary masterpieces in the metre of *Beowulf*, freely adapted
to the changes in the character of the language. It is represented chiefly
in the work of Langland and the Pearl Poet, and also in many of the
anonymous Mystery plays and in Scottish narrative poems of the fifteenth
century. It was often combined with rhyme and stanza forms. It was
especially in country districts in the west that the pure alliterative forms
had been handed down since Anglo-Saxon times.
[4] *The Fairie Queene*, Bk. VII, Canto 7, St. 11.

Madame, for your new-fangleness
Many a servant have you put out of grace.
I take leave of your unsteadfastness,
For well I wot, while you have life's space
You cannot love full half a year in a place.
To a new thing your lust is ever keen,
Instead of blue thus may you wear all green.

This same fair lady, who seems to have had all the characteristics of the Elizabethan "merciless beauty," might profitably have also read Chaucer's *Truth—a Ballade of Good Council:*

Flee from the press, and dwell with soothfastness,
Suffice for thee thy good, though it be small,
For hoard hath hate, and climbing tickleness;
Press hath envy, and wealth blinds over all,
Savor no more than what shall to thee fall;
Work well thyself, as thou to others said,
And Truth shall deliver, be thou in no dread.

Disturb thee not all crooked to redress,
Trusting in her that turneth as a ball;
Great rest stands in little business,
And so beware, kick not against an awl;
Strive not, as doth the crock against the wall.
Subdue thyself, as thou to others did,
And Truth shall deliver, be thou in no dread.

That which is sent, receive with humbleness,
Wrestling for this world bringeth a fall.
Here is no home, here is but wilderness;
Forth, pilgrim, forth! Forth, beast, out of thy stall!
Know thy country, look up, thank God for all,
Hold the highway and by thy ghost be led,
And Truth shall deliver, be thou in no dread.

Envoy:

Therefore, thou cow, leave thine own wretchedness
Unto the world, cease now to be a thrall;
Cry mercy of Him that of His high goodness
Made thee from nought, and in especial
Draw unto Him, and pray in general
For thee and others heaven's reward instead,
And Truth shall deliver, be thou in no dread.

Explicit le bon counseill de G. Chaucer.

Whether or no his "lady dear" took his advice about dressing in green, there was one Lady dressed in blue whom Chaucer always loved, and about whom he could not banter. He rewrote, in her honor, *An A B C to Our Lady* by Guillaume de Guilville, changing the long French stanzas into his own charming "rhyme royal."[5] Poems in alphabetical acrostics had been popular since the days of Bede, and were used for the most serious subjects.

Incipit carmen secundum ordinem alphabeti:

A   Almighty and almerciable queen,
    To whom that all this world flieth for succor,
    To have release of sin, sorrow and teen,
    Glorious Virgin, of all flowers the flower,
    To thee I fly, confounded in error.
    Help and relieve, thou might Debonaire;
    Have mercy on my perilous languor.
    To vanquish me will my adversary dare.

[5] This seven-line stanza of iambic pentameter rhyming a b a b b c c was apparently invented by Chaucer, but its name of "rhyme royal" was given out of courtesy to King James I of Scotland, a "Chaucerian" and author of *The King's Quair*. See p. 514.

B   Bounty so fixed hath in thy heart his tent
     That well I know thou wilt my succor be.
     Thou canst not shun him that with good intent
     Asketh thy help; thy heart is aye so free.
     Thou art the largesse of plain felicity,
     Haven of refuge, of quiet and of rest.
     Lo! Thieves seven now are chasing me!
     Help, Lady bright, to steer my ship the best. . .

F   Fleeing I flee for succor to thy tent,
     Me for to hide from tempest full of dread,
     Beseeching thee that thou be not absent
     Though I be wicked. O help me at this need
     Though I have been a beast in will and deed
     Yet, Lady, clothe thou me with thy grace.
     Thine enemy and mine—Lady, take heed,
     Unto my death intends me so to chase.

And if, after much philosophizing and praying,
things went wrong toward the end of the poet's life, it
was only necessary for him to write *A Complaint to
My Empty Purse,* and send it to the king:

To you, my purse, and to no other wight,
Complain I, for you be my lady dear!
I am so sorry, now that you are light,
For certainly, you make me heavy cheer
Or I'd as lief be laid upon my bier;
For which, unto your mercy thus I cry,
Be heavy again, or else so must I die!

And now vouchsafe this day, ere it be night,
That I from you a blissful sound may hear,
Or see your color, like the sun so bright,
That for yellowness had never a peer.
You are my life, by you my heart will steer;

Queen of comfort, and of good company;
Be heavy again, or else so must I die!

Now, purse, that is to me as life's light,
And savior, down in this world here,
Out of this town help me by your might,
Since you will not be my treasurer,
For I am shaved as close as any friar.
But yet, I pray, unto your courtesy,
Be heavy again, or else so must I die!

Envoy to the King (Henry IV):

O Conqueror of Brutus' Albion,
Who by line and free election
Be very King, this song to you I send;
And you, who can all our harms amend,
Have mind upon my supplication!

The king not only filled the purse, but added thereto
a daily pitcher of wine, which left Chaucer still comfortable, yet poor enough to follow his own *Proverbs:*

What good in these clothes manifold,
Lo! this hot summer's day?
After great heat cometh cold;
Let no man cast his furs away.
Of all this world, the wide compass
Will not be held in my arms twain—
Whoso a great deal will embrace,
Little therefrom will he gain.

Allegory was perhaps the readiest form of literary
expression in an age that drew no sharp boundaries
between the visible and the invisible worlds, and the
type of mind that it developed (or reflected) was accustomed to seeing symbols everywhere. Naturally, it

was on the religious plane, not far below heaven, that it reached its fullest development in the fourteenth century, but in the meantime a whole world of secular allegory had grown up on a lower plane, one not too far above the sunny earth. This secular allegory borrowed the devices and often the language of its religious counterpart; but it had its own reasons for being, and its own origin had been lofty: philosophy as well as religion needed its symbols.

Boethius, lying in prison in the year 524, had been visited by the gracious figure of Philosophia herself, "a woman of full great reverence, her eyes burning and bright-seeing over the common might of men," as Chaucer himself translated from *The Consolations of Philosophy,* the textbook of the Middle Ages for a thousand years. Countless other Latin writings, in prose or in poetry, or—following the *Consolations*—in a medley of the two, were inspired by Boethius. Their authors were Christian, but the figures of pagan mythology lent themselves only too readily to this richly humanistic thought, and the way was opened for a purely secular type of allegory. Martianus Capella, earlier even than Boethius, wrote his *Marriage of Mercury,* a treatise of the seven liberal arts in allegorical form. The Platonic-minded School of Chartres in the twelfth century fore-shadowed the sixteenth-century Renaissance, with its love of nature and its anti-ascetical bias. It exalted natural virtue in questionable opposition to the monastic.

Alanus de Insulis, *"doctor universalis"* and a theologian to boot, set the type in his *De Planctu Naturae,* in which Nature appeared to him and revealed her doctrine of love, a severely moral doctrine but clothed in the riotous glamor of *amour courtois.* Such gorgeous-

ness as he described could best meet the eye in a dream,
and it became the custom for poets who followed in his
lead to fall asleep in a garden, preferably on a May
morning, and what happened to them there became a
far-reaching tradition.

THE ROMANCE OF THE ROSE

It was through this poem that the allegory of love
spread all over Europe. It is surely one of the longest
ever written, the work of two Frenchmen. Guillaume
de Lorris began it in the early thirteenth century, and
died young, before he could be disillusioned about his
lovely garden with the Rose at its heart, which the
young lover must win, with dozens of charming allegorical figures to help or hinder. Jean de Meung
took up the unfinished work some years later, and carried it through with the cynical vigor of an elderly
man of the world who is still in love with its beauty.
The philosophical undertones of the whole allegory become pronounced under his pen, and are at last expressed in a long argument concerning free will, somehow not out of place in such a flower-filled setting. The
poem was almost as much at home in England as in
France by the time Chaucer translated sections of it
into his most youthful verse, and later wove the
thoughts on free will into *Troilus and Criseyde*.
Through him, the more or less stereotyped personages
of the love-allegory were handed on to the fifteenth
century, and to the Scottish "Chaucerians," where they
came to life again for a short time before evening fell
over the allegorical garden of delights first seen in the
sunrise. The poet is wandering through the garden
when he meets a company of dancers:

And next danced Courtesy, 1251
That praised is by low and high,
For neither proud nor fool was she,
And to the dance she called me,
(I pray God give her right good grace!)
When first I came into the place.
She was not shy, not outrageous,
But wise and ware and virtuous,
Of fair speech and fair answer;
Was never man mis-spoken here.
She bore rancor to no wight.
Clear brown she was, and thereto bright
Of face, of body graceful too;
No lady more pleasant and true.
She was worthy to be seen
An empress, or a crowned queen. . . .

Fair Idleness then saw I, 1273
That to me is always by.
Of her have I already so
Told you the shape and clothing too.
For as I said, lo! that was she
That did to me that great bounty—
The garden gates she opened wide
And thus let me pass inside.
And after danced there, as I guess,
Youth, filled full with lustiness,
Who was not yet twelve years old,
With heart wild, thoughts flying bold—
Foolish she, but never meant
Harm nor slight in her intent,
But only lust and jollity,
For young folk, as well they say,
Have little thought but on their play. . . .

Ah lord! They lived there lustily!   **1319**
A great fool were he, certainly,
Who would not such a life lead here.
For this I dare say without fear,
That whoso might so well fare
For a better life would have no care;
For there is no such paradise
As to have love for a device.
Out of the place went I so,
And in the garden turned to go,
Playing along full merrily
When the God of Love full hastily
Unto Sweet-looking then did pray;
No longer would he hide away
His bow of gold that shone so bright.
He bade him bend it anon-right,
And he full soon set it on end,
And quickly it began to bend,
And took from out his arrows five,
Full sharp and ready for the drive.
Now God that sits in majesty,
From deadly wounds keep thou me free,
If he shoots with arrow fleet—
For if I with his arrow meet
It will grieve me sore, iwis!
But I, who nothing knew of this,
Went up and down full many a day;
And fast he followed me all day.

This was the type of allegory that Chaucer found
ready to his hand when he began to write. He formed
his verse style by means of it and used it to develop
his imagination and his characteristic techniques.
Through translating the *Romance of the Rose* in his

youth he steeped himself in its phraseology. He was further taught by the writings of Massault, Froissart, Deschamps. He knew the *Dream of Scipio* that Macrobius had saved for the world, and plagiarized it wholesale. He also knew the *Divine Comedy,* but the mighty conceptions of Dante broke piecemeal in his hands, and he scattered the fragments here and there over his work. He was well equipped with allegorical material.

But somehow he was never quite in earnest about his allegories, and want of earnestness is close to the root reason for his want of success. He was a realist who never cared to champion the unseen, as all the great writers of allegory have done. Only a tremendous earnestness could have welded the hundred Cantos of the *Divine Comedy* into a whole or surrounded the homely figures of *Pilgrim's Progress* with reverence. Yet even earnestness is not enough. Spenser was most earnest when he wrote that the *Faerie Queene* was a development in poetic guise of "the ethic part of moral philosophy," but he gave himself away when he added that he had "cloudily enwrapped" his precepts in allegorical devices. If all that allegory can do is to "cloudily enwrap" the truth, it has failed of its purpose, and Spenser's failure goes back to the same cause as Chaucer's. Neither had the allegorical habit of mind; to neither was the world a sacrament. Chaucer was a spectator, not an interpreter. Where he achieved unity, it is not the unity of synthesis but of psychological mood, as in *Troilus;* where he achieved vividness, it is not the vividness of spiritual conviction but that of shrewd, affectionate sympathy with men as they go along the road to a shrine, and have not yet arrived. In these fields he is great in his own way; it would be ungenerous to expect more of him. So in the end he produced interesting poems in allegorical form, which turned out to be steppingstones to poetry of a very different type. The only thing of his own that he contributed to allegory was a lively, talkative tone which finally broke the allegorical spell and left Chaucer the storyteller that he is.

THE BOOK OF THE DUCHESS

This youthful poem, abounding in good spirits, is officially a lament on the death (in 1369) of "Whyte," or Blanche, the Duchess of John of Gaunt, Chaucer's courtly patron. It is an allegory, but its figures keep walking out of their frame. At its opening, Chaucer tells his readers that he must dream; for this he must fall asleep. But he suffers from insomnia and is introspectively curious about the cause of his wakefulness. Finally he induces slumber by rehearsing at great length the tale of *Ceix and Alceone,* with its drowsy description of the god Morpheus. At last his dream comes, but so invigorating does he find the May morning that he sets off on a hunt with hounds, noticing the rabbit that "lays its hairs down all smooth" and forgetful of his purpose, until he sees the tear-bespattered figure of John of Gaunt sitting under a tree. John relates his sorrowful loss to the sympathetic poet and describes the person of his lost Blanche with affectionate and somewhat startling realism. This is no transparent personification, but a refreshingly individual lady, a little on the plump side.

As the summer's sun bright   **821**
Is fairer, clearer, hath more light
Than any planet up in heaven,
The moon, or the stars seven,

For all the world, so had she
Surmounted others in beauty
Of manner and of comeliness,
Of stature and well set gladness,
Such goodliness did she portray—
Shortly—what more have I to say?
By God and His Apostles twelve
It was my sweet, right as herself!
She had such steadfast countenance,
Such noble port and maintenance. . . .

I saw her dance so comelily,   848
Carol and sing so sweetly,
Laugh and play so womanly,
And look so debonairely,
So goodly speak, and so friendly,
That certes, I trow that nevermore
Was seen so blissful a treasure.
For every hair upon her head,
Sooth to say, it was not red,
Neither yellow or brown it was,
Methought most like to gold it was.
And such eyes as my lady had!
Debonaire, good, glad and sad,
Simple, of good size, not too wide;
And so her look was not aside
Nor yet askance, but set so fair
It drew and held men everywhere. . . .

And what a visage she had thereto!   895
Alas, my heart is full of woe
That I cannot well write of it!
I lack both English speech and wit
To describe it to the full,
And then, my spirits are so dull. . . .

And what a goodly, soft speech   919
Had that Sweet, my life's leech!
So friendly and so well grounded,
And upon reason so well founded,
Ready to treat of all good,
That I dare swear by the Rood
Of eloquence was never found
A voice so sweet in its sound. . . .

And such a fairness of a neck   939
Had that Sweet—no bone or break
There was seen, and nought mis-sat,
It was white, smooth, straight and flat,
Without hole 'or collar-bone,
As, by my seeming, she had none.
Her throat, now in my memory,
Seemed a round tower of ivory,
Of good greatness, and not too great.
And good fair White, so to relate,
That was my lady's name aright.
She was both fair and bright,
She had not been named wrong.
Right fair shoulders and body long
She had, and arms, and limbs such,
Fattish, fleshy, but not too much,
Right white hands and nails red,
Rounded form, and of good breadth
Her hips were, a straight flat back,
And nowhere was in her a lack. . . .

And Truth himself, over all,   1003
Had chosen his dwelling principal
In her who was his resting-place;
Thereto she had the most grace

To have a steadfast perseverance
And easy, temperate governance. . . .
Right on this same, as I have said,   1035
Was wholly all my love laid,
And certes, she was my sweet wife,
My sufficiency, my joy, my life,
My hap, my health and all my bliss,
My world's welfare, all of this,
I wholly hers, in every way.

The poem ends abruptly with the ringing of a bell, and the poet, impatient with his own ramblings, declares: "This was my dream, now it is done."

THE PARLEMENT OF FOWLES

This allegory, presumably in honor of the betrothal of Richard II to Anne of Bohemia (in 1381), begins with a meditation on books:

For out of old fields, as men saith,
Cometh all this new corn from year to year,
And out of old books, in good faith,
Cometh all this new science that men hear.

The old books, this time, are Boccaccio's *Teseide* and the *Somnium Scipionis*. Chaucer retells the latter tale with comments of his own, and is soon asleep, while Scipio Africanus himself leads him through a gate over which is a reversed quotation from Dante:

Through me men go into that blissful place
Of heart's heal and deadly wounds' cure;
Through me men go into that well of grace
Where green and lusty May shall ever endure.
This is the way to all good adventure.

They wander through a wood peopled with the decorous personifications of French allegory, each with a

meaning but no apparent purpose. Then, sitting in a
great temple, Chaucer sees Natura herself. She is surrounded by birds of all kinds, and suddenly the tone of
the poem changes; through the smooth conventional
verse-music breaks a crackling and a cooing, wise and
witty and a bit boisterous. The scene resembles Chanticleer's barnyard. Here are the first struttings and
winkings of the "elfish man." If the *Parlement of
Fowles* is an allegory at all, it is a personal one, and
the key to it is lost. Critics may guess at the identity of
the second tercel, but there is no identifying "a seed-
fowl, one the unworthiest," or the "kakelynge gos."
Humor and realism, and love of the common man, have
triumphed.

> For this was on Saint Valentine's Day   309
> When every fowl cometh his mate to take,
> Of every kind that men may think or say;
> And they so huge a noise began to make
> That earth and sea and tree and every lake
> So full was, that scarcely was there space
> For me to stand, so full was all the place.
> And right as Alain, in the Plaint of Kind,
> Describeth Nature in array and face,
> In such array men might her there find.[6]
> This noble Empress, so full of grace,
> Bade every fowl to take his own place
> As they were wont, always from year to year,
> On Saint Valentine's Day to stand near.
> That is to say, the birds of prey were seen

[6] This refers to the description of Natura in *De Planctu Naturae*, by
Alanus de Insulis, where superlatives were heaped up till there was
nothing more that could be said. Why should Chaucer bother? Spenser
felt the same when he met Natura in *The Faerie Queene* (Bk. VII, Canto
7, St. 9.) He refers to Chaucer's predicament, and adds: "Go seek out
that Alane where he may be found."

The highest set, and then the fowls small
That eat, as nature makes them to incline,
On worms, and things of which I tell no tale;
But water fowl sat lowest in the dale,
And fowls that live by seed sat on the green,
In great numbers, a wonder to be seen. . . .

But to the point: Nature held in her hand   371
A Formel Eagle,[7] of shape the gentlest
That ever there among her works might stand,
The most benign, and the goodliest;
In her was every virtue at its rest,
So far forth that Nature herself had bliss
To look on her, and often her beak to kiss.
Nature, the vicar of the Almighty Lord
That hot, cold, heavy, light, and moist and dry[8]
Hath knit in even number by accord,
In easy voice began to speak and say:
"Fowls, take heed of my sentence, I pray,
And for your ease, in furthering of your need,
As fast as I may speak I will me speed.

"You know well, on Saint Valentine's Day,

[7] The Formel supposedly represents Anne of Bohemia.

[8] Hot, cold, moist and dry were the four "contraries" out of which the four basic elements of earth, fire, air and water were formed. Heavy and light represent the fundamental tendencies of the elements. Casual references like this in mediaeval writings often reveal a whole philosophical or scientific system current in the thought of the age.

A quasi-scientific system of dream interpretation held that a man's dreams followed his "temperament"; e.g., a choleric man dreamed of bright and red things such as knives and foxes, a phlegmatic man dreamed of cold, wet things such as fish. See Chaucer's *Nun's Priest's Tale*. Character studies were based on the four temperaments: choleric, sanguine, phlegmatic and melancholic, which depended on the predominance of one of the four "humors"—choler (or red bile), blood, phlegm, and black bile. An understanding of this system gives meaning to many references in mediaeval and Tudor literature, up to Ben Jonson's *Every Man in His Humor*. See J. Leonard, "Ancient Humors and Modern Glands," *Irish Ecclesiastical Record,* Vol. LVI, pp. 244, 343.

By my statute, and through my governance,
You come to choose—and then flee on your way—
Your mates, as I prick you with pleasance.
But nonetheless, my rightful ordinance
I may not leave, not all the world to win,
That he that is most worthy shall begin."

She then announces that two young Tercels are competing for the hand of the Formel, and bids each plead his cause. The first says:

"Since none loveth her so well as I,   435
Although she never of love has promised yet,
Then ought she be mine through mercy,
For other bond I cannot on her set.
For never, for no woe, shall I let
From serving her, how far soe'er she wend.
Say what you list, my tale is at an end."
Right as the fresh, red, rose new
Against the summer sun so colored is,
Right so for shame began to change the hue
Of this Formel, when she heard all this;
She neither answered, "Well," or said amiss,
So sore abashed was she, until Nature
Said, "Daughter, dread ye nought, I you assure."
The other Tercel eagle spoke anon,
Of lower kind, and said, "That shall not be;
I love her better than you do, by Saint John,
Or at the least I love as well as ye;
And longer have served her, in my degree,
And if she should have loved for long loving,
To me alone had been the guerdoning."

The lesser birds get impatient at the delay, while the Formel is making up her mind.

The goose, the cuckoo and the duck also   498
So cried, "Kek, kek, kukkow, queck, queck,"
   high,
That through my ears the noise went so.
The goose said, "All this is not worth a fly!
But I can shape for it remedy,
And I will say my verdict in fair play
For water-fowls, whoso be wroth or gay."
"And I for worm-fowls," said the fool cuckoo,
"And I will, on my own authority,
For common speed, take the charge now,
For to deliver us is great charity."
"You may abide a while yet, pardee!"
Said the turtle, "if it be your will
That one may speak, he might as well be still."

The Formel refuses to make a choice while the lesser
birds continue to wrangle. Finally, Nature says that
she will give her pet another year to make up her mind.

And when this work was all brought to an end,   666
Nature bid every fowl his mate to take
By even accord, and on their way they wend.
O Lord! The bliss and joy that they make!
For each another in his wings would take
And then about the neck each other wind,
Thanking always the noble Goddess of Kind.
But first were chosen fowls who should sing,
As year by year was always their usance
To sing a roundel at their departing,
To do Nature honor and pleasance.
The song, I trow, thus was made in France,
The words were such as you may here find,
The next verse as I now have in mind.

Qui bien aime a tard oublié.

"Now welcome summer with thy sun soft
That hast this winter weather overtake
And drive away the long nights black!

"Saint Valentine, thou art full high aloft,"
—Thus sing the small fowls for thy sake—
"Now welcome summer with thy sun soft,
That canst this winter weather overtake."

Well have they cause so to rejoice them oft,
Since each of them his mate now may take,
Full blissful may they sing when they wake:
"Now welcome summer with thy sun soft,
That canst this winter weather overtake,
And drive away the long night black."

And with the shouting and the singing, too,
The fowls then all took their flight away,
I woke, and other books then took me to
To read upon, and still I read alway.
I hope, iwis, to read so some day,
That I shall dream some other thing to fare
The better; and thus to read I will not spare.

THE HOUSE OF FAME

Towards the beginning of this teasing allegory (c.1384) Chaucer pronounces a flippant malediction on readers who refuse to take him seriously. It is hard to tell how seriously he takes himself. The poem has a spacious setting; it is scattered over with echoes (which are not all parodies) of the mighty Dante, and it has classical backing from Ovid's *Metamorphoses*. It rings with under- and over-tones of philosophy and of beauty. But the disproportion of the parts to each other, the whimsy and banter of the language, are

incongruous, if delightful, and incongruity is fatal to
allegory. Chaucer himself, comical, shrewd and tender,
is peeping out from behind the elaborate scenery in
which his thoughts are dancing about.

In the poem, he delays putting himself to sleep because he is frankly curious about dreams; he discusses
various current theories concerning them, and charac-
teristically refuses to commit himself to any. When
sleep comes he finds himself in a temple of glass, full
of the statues of great personages of antiquity. The
sight of Dido sets him off to retell the fourth book of
the *Aeneid,* and causes him to reflect on Fama, the
multi-eyed goddess of reputation. Thinking thus he
wanders out into an empty plain, where:

> "O Christ," thought I, "that art in bliss,   492
> From phantom and illusion
> Save me!" And with devotion
> Mine eyes to the heavens I cast.
> Then was I ware, lo! at the last
> That fast by the sun, as high
> As I might see with my eye,
> Methought I saw an eagle soar,
> But that it seemed much more
> Than any eagle I had seen;
> But this, as sooth as death I ween,
> It was of gold, and shone so bright
> That never saw men such a sight,
> As if the heavens had just won,
> All new of gold, another sun.
> So shone the eagle's feathers bright,
> And downward it began to light. . . .

> This eagle of which I have you told,   529
> That shone with feathers as of gold,

Which so high began to soar,
I then beheld it more and more,
And saw its beauty, and the wonder,
But never was there dint of thunder
Nor that thing that flashes, lighting
On a tower, to powder smiting,
That so quickly downward bent,
Burning in its swift descent,
As this fowl when it beheld
That I was roaming in the field.
And with his grim paws strong
Within his sharp nails long
Me, fleeing, at a swoop he caught,
And up again his flight he sought
Me carrying in his claws so stark
As lightly as he would a lark,
How high I cannot tell to you.
For I went up I know not how,
For so astonished and adread
Was every virtue in my head,
What with his swoops and my dread,
That all my feelings had gone dead
And I was greatly in dismay.
Thus long in his claws I lay,
Till at the last to me he spake
In man's voice, and said, "Awake!
And be not so aghast, for shame."
He called me then by my name
In the voice of one that I could name,
And with that voice, it is plain,
My mind came back to me again;
For it was goodly said to me,
As it was never wont to be.
And with these words I squirmed around,

But in his feet he held me bound,
Till that he felt that I had heat,
And also felt my heart to beat.
And then began he to disport
And with his words to give comfort,
And said twice, "Sainte Marie,
You are troublesome to carry,
And nothing needeth it, pardee!
For, as the wise God may ever help me,
Thou shalt have no harm of this."

As they go up, the eagle explains that he is carrying
Chaucer to the House of Fame, whither every word
and rumor uttered on earth finds its way by a natural
law.

"Geoffrey," he said, "thou knowest well this,   729
That every natural thing there is
Hath a natural place,[9] where he
May best in it conserved be,
Unto which place everything,
By its natural inclining,
Moveth, that it there may come
When it is away therefrom.
Thus, lo! thou mayest all day see
Anything that may heavy be,

[9] The natural place, or "kyndly stede," is the mediaeval explanation of
the laws of gravity and of motion. A tendency towards its ultimate resting-place has been given by God to every creature, and each creature
helps to draw every other towards its end. The fundamental motion of
the universe is imparted through the "drawing" of the nine spheres which
surround the earth; the *primum mobile* is the Empyrean, the dwelling-
place of God. See the ending of the *Divine Comedy*:
    But still the will moved onward like a wheel,
    Impelled in even motion by that love
    That moves the sun in heaven and all the stars.
This conception can apply to Newton's laws as to Dante's; its philosophy will hold through any scientific discovery.

As stone, or lead, or thing not light,
Bear it to ever so great a height,
Let go thy hand, it falleth down. . . .

And for this cause thou mayest see   747
That every river to the sea
Inclined is to go by kind.
And for this reason, to my mind,
Fishes dwell in flood and sea
And trees eke in the earth be,
Thus everything, be it known,
Hath a mansion of its own
To which it striveth to go still,
And nothing can there do it ill.
Lo, this is a known truth,
Philosophers say so, for sooth,
As Aristotle and Dan Plato,
And the other clerks that know."
And then began I to look down
And beheld the plains and fields,
And now mountains and now hills,
And now valleys and now forests,
And now, but hardly, great beasts,
Now rivers and again cities,
And towns, and now great trees,
And ships sailing in the sea.
And thus soon in a while he
Had flown from the ground so high
That all the world, as to my eye,
No more seemed than a prick.

They soon fly so high that they pass among the constellations:

Then began I to look under me,   964
And beheld the aerish beasts,[10]
Clouds, mists and great tempests,
Snows, hails, rains and winds,
And the engendering of their kinds,
And all the way through which I came:
"O God," quoth I, "that made Adam,
Much is Thy might and nobleness!"
And then thought I of Boethius,
That wrote, "A thought may fly so high
With feathers of philosophy
As to pass every element."

They reach the House of Fame, crowning a great hill
of ice where the sun is already melting the famous
names cut in it. Within the hall are statues of the
great men and writers of old. Here Fama reigns as
queen, and to her come in crowds all those of earth
who wish renown. But by her side stands Aeolus, who
has two trumpets, Slander and Laud. A group of peti-
tioners ask to have their good deeds recorded.

What did this Aeolus, but he   1636
Took out his black trump of brass
That fouler than the devil was,
And began this trumpet for to blow
As though the world he'd overthrow,
So that through every land around
Went this foul trumpet's sound
As swift as pellet from a gun
When fire has through the powder run,
And such a smoke did soon outwend

[10] The signs of the Zodiac, the Bull, the Lion, etc. The signs and com-
putations of astronomy (as of astrology) were a matter of common
knowledge in the Middle Ages, when everyone told time and calendar
dates by the position of the sun and stars in the sky.

From his foul trumpet's end,
Black, blue, greenish, swartish red,
Such as where men melt their lead,
Lo, all on high from the funnel.
And thereto one thing saw I well
That, the farther that it ran,
To wax the greater it began,
As does a river from a well;
And it stank as the pit of hell.
Alas, thus was their shame rung,
—And they guiltless—on every tongue.

Another group petitions good renown, and this time
the fickle Fama commands Aeolus to blow Laud.

"Full gladly, Lady mine," said he,   1677
And out his golden trump took he
Anon, and set it to his mouth
And blew it east and west and south
And north, as loud as any thunder,
So that every man had wonder,
So broad it was, ere it stent.
And, certes, all the breath that went
Out of his trumpet's mouth smelled
As when a pot of balm is held
Amid a basket full of roses.

Chaucer finally leaves the hall in disgust. He then
comes across the house of Rumor.

And all this house, of which I said,   1935
Was made of twigs, fallow, red,
And green eke, and some were white,
As cages that men whittle right,
Or else when they baskets make
To carry out the bread they bake.

And, for the sighing through its twigs,
This house was also full of jigs,
And also full of chirckings,
And of many other workings.
And this house had open entries
As many as there are leaves on trees
In summer, when they green be,
And on the roof men yet may see
A thousand holes, and well more so
To let the sounds well outgo. . . .

And lo! This house of which I write,   1977
Certain be ye, it was not light,
For it was sixty miles in length,
And though the timber had no strength
Yet it is found to endure
While that it's pleased with adventure,
Which is the mother of tidings
As is the sea of wells and springs.

Chaucer then listens to the magnified whisperings
coming from Rumor, but when he inquires their meaning the poem breaks off. It was never finished.

THE LEGEND OF GOOD WOMEN

This collection of stories (c.1385) is the forerunner
of the *Canterbury Tales,* but because of its limitation
to one type of subject it did not give Chaucer's genius
sufficient outlet. It was probably suggested by Boccaccio's *De Claris Mulieribus,* and much of the material was drawn from Ovid. The prologue is his most
consistent and beautiful allegory, crowded with classical figures but as genuine and fresh as experience.
For once, Chaucer the realist, torn between his love
of books and of flowers, is at home in the sunrise set-

ting where he meets the god of love and his fair company. Only the opening paragraph is out of tune. It
sounds as though it had been written in annoyance at
some challenge to the orthodoxy of his Christian faith.
It has little to do with the *Legend,* unless indeed he
is claiming the same credence for the one as for the
other. The passage has opened endless controversy
as to whether Chaucer had heretical leanings. It is
more likely that he had petulant moods, and it should
no more be taken as a sign of heresy than his satirical
outbursts against monks and friars.

From the Prologue:

A thousand times I have heard men tell   1
That there is joy in heaven and pain in hell,
And I accord that it may well be so.
But all the same, this know I well also
That there is none that dwelleth in this country
That was ever known in hell or heaven to be,
Nor may he of it in other ways witen
But as he has heard it said or found it written,
For by experience no man may it know.
But God forbid that men should not believe so
More things than men have seen with their own eye!
Men should not think everything a lie
Because they saw it not once long ago.
God knows, a thing is never the less so
Though every wight may not thus it see.
Bernard the monk saw not all, pardee!
Then must we go to books that we may find
Through what those old things may be held in mind,
And to the doctrines of those old men wise
Give credence in every skillful wise,
And believe in those old approved stories

Of holiness, of reigns, of victories,
Of love, of hate, of every sundry thing
Of which I may not make rehearsing.
And if that all old books were away,
Lost were then of memory the key.
Well ought we honor and believe also
These books; we have no other way to know.
And as for me, though I have learning slight,
In reading of my books I find delight,
And to them I give faith and full credence,
And in my heart have them in reverence
So heartily that no game that I know
Away from my books will make me go,
Except sometimes on a holy day.
And certainly that when the month of May
Is come, and that I hear the birds sing,
And when the flowers forth begin to spring—
Farewell my books and my devotion!
Now am I then in such condition
That of all the flowers in the mead
Love I most those flowers white and red
Such as men call daisies in our town.[11]
To them I have such great affection,
As I said erst, when that it is May,
That o'er my bed there never dawns a day
But I am up and walking in the mead
To see this flower against the sun spread.
When it upriseth early on the morrow
That blissful sight softeneth all my sorrow,
So glad am I when that I have presence
Of it, to do all manner reverence

[11] The "cult of the marguerite" was fashionable in the court poetry of France, especially that of Machault, and this literary tradition blended well with Chaucer's genuine love for the English "day's eye."

As to her that is of all flowers the flower,
Fulfilled of all virtue and honor,
And ever the same, fair and fresh of hue,
And love it with a love ever new,
And ever shall, till that my heart die.
Though I swear not, yet I do not lie,
There loveth no man hotter in his life,
And when the eve is come, I run and strive
As soon as ever the sun is in the west
To see this flower, how it will go to rest
For fear of night, so hateth she darkness;
Her face is plainly spread in the brightness
Of the sun, for there it will unclose.
Alas! Had I but English rhyme or prose
Sufficient this flower for to praise aright! . . .

My busy ghost that thirsteth ever new   103
To see this flower so young, so fresh of hue,
Constrained with so glowing a desire
That in my heart I feel yet the fire
That made me early rise ere it was day—
And this is now the first morrow of May—
With dreadful heart and glad devotion
For to be at the resurrection
Of this flower, when that it should unclose
Against the sun, that rose as red as rose
That in the breast was of the beast that day
That Agenore's daughter led away.
And down on knees aright I then me set,
As I could this fresh flower to greet,
Kneeling always, till it unclosed was
Upon the small, soft, sweet grass. . . .

And when the sun out of the south went west,   197
And when the flower closed and went to rest

For darkness of the night—for she has dread—
Home to my house full swiftly then I sped
To go to rest, early for to rise
To see the flower spread, as I devise.
And, in a little arbor that I made,
All lined with turf freshly cut and laid,
I bade them there my bed to make,
Out of delight for the new summer's sake;
I had them strew flowers on my bed.
When I was laid, and my two eyes had hid,
I fell asleep within an hour or two
And dreamed that I was in the meadow so,
To see this flower that I so love and dread.
And from afar came walking in the mead
The God of Love, and at his hand a Queen,[12]
And she was clad in royal habit green.
A fret of gold she had about her hair,
And upon that a white crown she bare
With flowerets small, and—I do not lie—
For all the world, just as the daisies lie
Crowned with their white leaves light,
So were the frets of her crown white,
For of pearl fine and oriental .
Her white crown was so fashioned all,
The which white crown, above the green,
Made her like a daisy to be seen,
Counting also her golden fret above.
And clothed was the mighty God of Love
In silk, embroidered all with green greaves,
In with a fret of red rose leaves,
The freshest since the world was first begun.
His gilt hair was crowned with a sun

---

¹ Cupid and Alcestis, chosen as queen by the god because of her fidelity
in love.

Instead of gold, for heaviness and weight.
Therewith methought his face shone so bright
That scarcely could my eyes him behold,
And in his hands methought I saw him hold
Two fiery darts, as the coals red,
And angel-like his wings I saw him spread.
And although men say that blind is he
Yet methought that he could well see,
For sternly he began me to behold,
So that his looking made my heart turn cold.
And in his hand he held this noble queen,
Crowned with white and clothed all in green,
So womanly, so benign, so meek,
That, through all the world though men should seek
Half her beauty they could never find
In the creatures that are formed by Kind.

He then sings a ballade in praise of her beauty, after
which he sees, coming behind her, nineteen fair ladies.

I kneeling by the flower with good intent,   307
Waited to know what all these people meant,
As still as any stone, till at the last
The God of Love on me his eyes cast
And said, "Who kneeleth there?" And I answered
Unto his asking when that I had heard,
And said, "Sir, it is I," and came then near
And greeted him. Quoth he, "What dost thou here
So nigh my own flower, so boldly?
For it were more worthy, truly,
For a worm to come near my flower than thou."
"And why, Sir?" quoth I, "and it please you now."
"Because thou," quoth he, "are thereto quite unable.
It is my relique, worthy, delightable,
And thou my foe, who makes war on my folk,

For of my old servants thou hast mis-spoke,
And hindered them, with thy translation,
And keepest folk from their devotion
In serving me; and dost it folly cry
To serve Love. Thou canst not now deny,
For in plain text, without need of gloze
Thou hast translated the Romance of the Rose.
That is a heresy against my law
And makest wise folk from me to withdraw.
And of Criseyde thou hast said as thou list,
And so men have in women less trust,
When they be as true as any steel."

He then bids Chaucer make reparation by writing the
stories of true and loyal women who were faithful to
the God of Love. Of the nineteen that Chaucer pro-
posed to write, only nine were completed. Among
these "saints of love" the best-known are Cleopatra,
Thisbe, Dido, and Ariadne.

TROILUS AND CRISEYDE

The claim that Chaucer is the first of the moderns
could rest securely on one of his works: the long psychological verse-novel that tells of "the double sorrow
of Troilus." Of this remarkable work (1380)—as of
most mediaeval narrative—might be said what was
once said of Shakespeare's plays: "They use time and
place only inasmuch as they cannot get on without
them." It is a triumph of anachronism, revealing
Greek history and timeless passion in mediaeval dress
and speech. It tells a story current from the fourth
century (if not earlier) to the sixteenth. The two
main characters, Troilus the royal Trojan and Criseyde the faithless Greek, are described in the apocryphal *De Excidio Trojae Historia* by Dares the

Phrygian. Their adventures together were first detailed by Benoit de Saint Maur in his twelfth-century *Roman de Troie;* its inherent pathos and tragedy were lyrically unfolded in Boccaccio's *Filostrato,* which was Chaucer's immediate source.

The English poet, unlike the Italian, did not use the tale to express personal passion. He expanded it to tremendous length by means of what today would be called the "stream of consciousness" method, and made radical changes in the characters; his Pandarus has given us the unpleasant verb "to pander." For once he stood aloof from his work; he told his story with penetrating, ironical sympathy, with dry humor, and with tragic intensity. It moves with the slow, driving insistence of dramatic destiny. In tone, it is poles apart from mediaeval—or any—Christianity; immoral in itself and amoral in its handling, it is as unhealthily exotic as the *amour courtois* of an earlier century. Yet Chaucer was a Christian, and his poem, like all truly great works of art, is ultimately ethical in the judgment that it passes upon itself. The concluding passages, thought by some critics to be flippantly ironical or piously insincere, are in reality the only possible comment from one who has seen the truth. They are the author's own interpretation of a poem that he might well repent of having written at all.

At the end, Criseyde, summoned from Troy by her father to return to the Greek camp, has promised undying fidelity to Troilus. But as time passes, the "brittleness" of her promise becomes apparent, and the boyish and heartbroken Troilus rushes recklessly into the fight, hoping to slay his rival, Diomede. Then:

The wrath, as I began you for to say,   V,1800
Of Troilus the Greeks then bought full dear,

For thousands of them his hands made to die,
As one that was without a single peer
Save Hector in his time, as I did hear.
But wey-la-wey! saving only God's will,
Despitefully him slew the fierce Achille.

But when that he was slain in this manner,
His light ghost full blissfully then went
Up to the hollowness of the seventh sphere,
Outside it leaving every element,
And there he saw, with full discernment,
The wandering stars, making harmony
With sounds full of heavenly melody.

And down from thence soon saw he with his eyes
This little spot of earth that with the sea
Embraced is, and began then to despise
This wretched world, and held all vanity
Compared with the plain felicity
That is in heaven above, and at the last
There where he was slain his look he cast.

And in himself he laughed right at the woe
Of them that wept there for his death so fast,
And condemned all our work that followeth so
The blind lust, the which may never last,
And should all our heart on heaven cast;
And forth he went, shortly for to tell,
Where Mercury appointed him to dwell.

Such end hath, lo! this Troilus for love,
Such end hath all his own great worthiness,
Such end hath his royal estate above,
Such end his love, such end his nobleness,
Such end hath this world's false brittleness;
And thus began his loving of Criseyde
As I have told you, and in this wise he died.

O young, fresh folk, he or she,
In whom that love upgroweth with your age,
Turn ye now from worldly vanity
And upward cast the gazing of your heart
To the same God that made you at the start
To His own image. Think it but a fair,
This world that passeth soon as flowers fair.

And love Him, He who right for love
Upon a cross, our souls for to buy,
First died, and rose, and sits in heaven above,
For He will play false to no wight, dare I say,
That will his heart all wholly on Him lay.
And since He best to love is, and most meek,
What need is there for feigned loves to seek?

Chaucer's version was not the end of the tale of
Troilus and Criseyde; two very different interpretations were to bring it to conclusion. In the fifteenth
century, Henryson, a Scottish poet of staunch, unabashed morality, brought poetic vengeance to bear
upon Criseyde, whom the tender-hearted Chaucer
could only pity. She died, a repentant leper.[13] Shakespeare, with deeper wisdom and with that fine "conception of ultimates" over which Keats was to exclaim,
saw the seeds of inherent corruption in the whole story.
Troilus and Cressid is perhaps his one really bitter
play.

All the poems so far considered were written before
1386; the *Canterbury Tales,* incomplete as they are,
were the work of the last fifteen years of Chaucer's
life. His apprenticeship was over. By that time he
knew all manner of his fellow men, and he "is of their
fellowship anon," a circle into which he gladly admits

[13] See p. 582.

any latecomer who cares to join. It is for the pleasure of this friendship that the pilgrims continue to set out, year after year, "the holy blissful martyr for to seek." There is no resisting April sunshine, a good horse, good company, and one good story after another.

The pencil of the realist is here at work sketching the twenty-nine men and women, each of whom the world now knows by dress, occupation and character: the squire "with locks curled as though laid in a press"; the shipman, too far inshore, who "rode upon a rouncey as he could"; the over-portly monk "whose head was bald and shone as any glass"; the dainty nun who yet "was not undergrown"; the wife of Bath whose "hose were of fine scarlet red." Then come the twenty-five tales, and the links which weave the inimitable prologue in and out through the whole, and in which the company continue their teasing, their quarreling, and their self-revelation. Each tale, drawn from a distinct source, could be told fittingly by only one person: he whom Mine Host picks out.

There are romances, sober or gay, there are piteous deeds of love and piety, there is parody, delightful in the barnyard world of Chancticleer, raw and raucous in the underworld of weak, rascally men. The first listeners had, perforce, to hear them all. Late readers, who may choose and browse, had best take Chaucer's own advice seriously when he remarks parenthetically in the *Prologue to the Miller's Tale:*

And therefore every gentle wight I pray,   63
For God's love, deem not that I say
Of evil intent, but that I must rehearse
Their tales all, be they better or worse,
Or else make false some of my matter here.

And therefore, whoso list it not to hear,
Turn over the leaf and choose another tale.
For he shall find enough great and small
Of story-thing that touches gentleness,
And eke morality and holiness.
Blame me not if that you choose amiss.
The miller is a churl, you know well this;
So was the reeve and many another more,
And harlotry they told, both two.
Advise you, and put me out of blame,
And eke men shall not make earnest of game.

Mine Host never declared—in public—to whom the promised dinner for the best story should go. No one can make the decision for him now, but perhaps we can venture to gainsay him, just once. He cut short a mournful series of tragedies told by the otherwise cheerful monk with, "Your tale annoyeth all this company." But among the monk's tiny stories is one masterpiece, brief enough to quote in its entirety, whereas the longer ones would suffer from abbreviation. It is the work of Chaucer, the lover of men, in control of atmosphere and emotion, of sheer uninterpreted narrative that speaks for itself:

DE HUGOLINE, COMITE DE PISE

Of the Earl Hugelino the languor
There may no tongue tell, for pity;
But little out of Pisa stands a tower,
In which tower in prison put was he,
And with him were his little children three,
The eldest scarcely five years was of age.
Alas fortune! it was great cruelty
Such birds for to put in such a cage.

Damned was he to die in that prison,
For Roger, he that Bishop was of Pisa,
Had on him made a false suggestion
Which made the people up against him rise,
And put him into prison in such wise
As you have heard; and meat and drink he had
So small, that not well easily it could suffice,
And therewithal it was full poor and bad.

And on a day befell it, in that hour
When that his meat was wont thus to be brought,
The jailor shut the doors of the tower.
He heard it well, but he spoke right nought,
And in his heart anon there fell a thought
That they for hunger would make him thus to die,
"Alas," quoth he, "Alas, that I was wrought!"
And therewith the tears fell from his eyes.

His young son, that three years was of age,
Unto him said, "Father, why do you weep?
When will the jailer bring us our pottage?
Is there no morsel of bread that you do keep?
I am so hungry that I cannot sleep.
Now would to God that I might sleep forever.
Then should no hunger so within me creep.
There is no thing, save bread, that now were liefer."

Thus day by day this child began to cry,
Till in his father's bosom down it lay
And said, "Farewell, father, I must die,"
And kissed his father, and died the same day.
And when his father saw that dead it lay
For woe his two arms he began to bite,

And said, "Alas, Fortune! and weylaway!
Thy false wheel brings all my woe in sight!"[14]

His children thought that it for hunger was
That he his arms gnawed, and not for woe,
And said, "Father, do not so, alas!
But rather eat the flesh upon us two.
Our flesh you gave us, take our flesh from us so
And eat enough." Right thus they to him sighed
And after that, within a day or two
They laid them down upon his lap, and died.

Himself despaired and died for hunger sore.
Thus ended so this mighty earl of Pise
From high estate Fortune away him bore
Who so will hear of it in longer wise,
Read the great poet of Italy
Named Dante, for he can all devise
From point to point, not one word will he let be.

It is no wonder that after this Mine Host demanded
the merry tale of Chanticleer. And so the tales went on,
changing in color and in tone, until the end of the trail
drew near at four o'clock by the sun, and the somno-
lent prose of the parson sobered the company into
thought of

That perfect glorious pilgrimage
Called Jerusalem celestial,

after which: "Now taketh the Maker of this Book his
leave":

[14] This tale is an illustration of the mediaeval idea of tragedy: a fall
from the top of Fortune's wheel to its lowest revolution. The vision of
Fortune and her wheel, found in the tenth book of Plato's *Republic,* had
given the metaphorical expression of the idea. With Shakespeare, drama
returned to Aristotle's conception of tragedy as a catastrophe brought
by a great man upon himself by some flaw of character.

Now pray I to them all that harken to this little treatise or read, that if there be anything in it that liketh them, that thereof they thank Our Lord Jesus Christ, of whom proceedeth all wit and all goodness. And if there be anything that displeaseth them, I pray them also that they lay it to the fault of my uncunning, and not to my will, that would full fain have said better if I had had cunning.

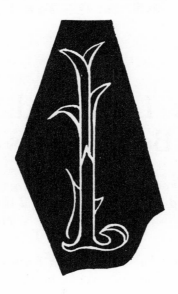

Where Love and Peace Be Masters

I that am Lord of life, love is my drink;
And for that drink today I died upon earth.

PIERS PLOWMAN

IF CHAUCER had passed William Langland while riding through the London streets, he might have noticed him as a picturesque figure among the down-and-outs; but Langland, it is quite certain, would not have bowed his gaunt head as the man from court rode by. Long Will walked those streets day and night, hungry, cold, burning now with pity, now with indignation, laughing with a wry laugh at the incongruity of evil in a world made by God, then weeping with hot passion at the superficiality of those who could not, or who would not, see the depths. He saw them, for he lived in them; and he wrote their full realism into an allegory that opens the way to the heights. The *Vision of Piers Plowman* has claimed a place in English literature as a spiritual epic as well as a mordant record of the fourteenth century, but its author will never be the darling of literature, like the man on horseback. His humor is too astringent, his sweep too vast, his illuminations too dazzling for easy enjoyment. Perhaps the love in his own great, childlike heart is too simple to win an easy return from the more sophisticated. His pilgrims do not ride lightly along a highway; they rub elbows in a narrow lane, and they are not out for Canterbury but for the next world. Langland knew that this world is full of troubles, but because he also knew it to be knit sacramentally to the next, he saw Love who is Truth abroad on all our roads even here. This street haunter wrote his tumultuous thoughts and waking dreams into a single poem. It was the work of a lifetime and the expression of a millenium, a synthesis of mediaeval Christianity by a man who lived at its crossroads.

The events of his life and even his name can only be discovered from his poem, into which they are written like an acrostic.[1] His boyhood was spent in the Malvern hills, through which he roamed pondering the learning that his hungry mind had gathered from the books in some Priory that had educated him to the

[1] "I have lived *long* in the *land*; *Long* Will men call me." (Passus XV). In one MS a marginal note to this line reads: "Nota the name of the author." From other references it may be gathered that he was born in 1332, in some village in the Malvern hills, and died in London soon after 1395.

point of taking minor orders.[2] Later he lived in London with his wife and daughter, blood-brother to the poor, buffeted by the disease and revolt then rampant among poor men. He made a living shamefacedly by singing psalms for the souls of the wealthy departed. Passionate and restless by nature, without fear or favor of the great, he might easily have made himself the pivot of a revolution.[3]

Later critics have regarded him as exactly that. Because he satirized the clergy, friars in particular, with a sharp and angry pen, and challenged all churchmen to reform, he has been hailed as the first Protestant, or at least as a Lollard. Because he writhed under economic injustice, and wrote (as many scholars think) *Richard the Redeless* to rebuke a king, he has been made into a symbol of rebellion. He was neither of these. If he saw that things were wrong, it was because he could see their twisted outlines against the pattern of things as they should be, the great design drawn in eternity and projected upon earth in the Church of Christ. Langland is not only a completely orthodox son of the Church, but he is completely obedient to the hierarchy of values in nature, in society, in government, in the Church itself. His passion was to maintain, not to overthrow, the right order. He saw both the order

[2] It would seem that Langland was a browser rather than a methodical student of the accumulated theological learning of his day. It is probable that he attended great Malvern Priory, or some other Benedictine school; it is possible that he went to Oxford; it is certain that he was thrown into constant controversy with wandering scholars of every shade of opinion. In general his thought was molded by the Franciscan School, along the lines of Duns Scotus. See C. E. Maguire, "Franciscan Influence in the Thought of Piers Plowman," in *Essays in Commemoration of Manhattanville's Centenary,* Crown Press.

[3] His poem was actually used to inflame popular feeling during the Peasants' Revolt of 1381, when John Ball's cryptic messages bade "Piers Plowman go to his work," and urged the fellows of John Trueman to "do well and better."

and the disorder, and because, as a restless contemplative, he could do nothing else to mend matters, he wrote poetry.

The lines that poured from his brooding mind are, at first sight, rough and unshapely compared to the trim lyrics and narratives of his contemporaries. He uses a South-midland dialect, and his vocabulary is as undiscriminating as was Shakespeare's after him; his words are beautiful or uncouth, colloquial or biblical, the learned terms of the Schoolmen or those coinings that come straight from the thoughts of a man talking to himself. These thoughts surged up in the long alliterative lines of the old school of song, Anglo-Saxon forms dear to the people, owing nothing to France or to the court. This rough-and-ready expression is lit throughout by an imagination as accurate as a camera and as creative as a magician's wand; it is made incandescent at moments by that intensity of feeling that changes simple utterance into glee-wood's song.

In form the poem is like a tremendous pageant, quite chaotic in its movement.[4] It consists of eleven dreams, or *visiones,* with their waking intervals, beginning or ending haphazardly in the course of the twenty *Passus* into which it is divided. The thought-lines are drawn through level after level of allegorical meaning. The characters appear from nowhere and vanish into silence; they are men and women who carry the smell of the streets on their patched coats, and each is a human being who laughs and cries and

---

[4] Langland wrote his poem three times over. The first version, written c.1362, is known as the A Text, and ends at Passus XV of the other versions. The second, or B Text, written in 1377, is three times the length of the first, expanding and completing the thought. The C Text c.1394, is simply a revision of B. The translation in this chapter is made from the B Text.

talks rudely or profoundly, yet each carries the light of another world on his face, and acts as the expression of a reality beyond his own. Readers might be tempted to exclaim with the dreamer, "This were a wicked wāy, but if one had a guide." Yet this mighty, moving pageantry can be reduced to a diagram that startles by its simple symmetry,[5] and the guide is Piers Plowman himself.

The "I" in the poem is Long Will, the dreamer, each of us. He—or better, we—find ourselves in a "field full of folk," the world as it is with its saints and its knaves and its in-betweens. Holy Church sends us all out as pilgrims to seek Saint Truth who is God. Piers Plowman the honest, symbol of a way of life,[6] is at first the layman who lives by his hands. Man is the center of interest in the first part of the poem. But in a flash there comes upon Piers the vision of a higher way, and he sets off on a search for Dowel. Remembering Piers, we children of God the Father wander in the next part through every phase of the active life, musing on theology the while. In the third part, Piers comes back on the scene, symbol of the contemplative or priestly life rising to an identification with the incarnate Son of God; he jousts with the fiend in Holy Week and emerges victor. Light conquers darkness and life death. But this tremendous climax is not the end of the story. The dreamer is a realist, and Christ has yet to live out His life till the end of ages in His Church. The last part of the poem deals with the reign of the Holy Ghost; Piers is now the symbol of Papal authority who builds the barn of Unity. The forces of

[5] See Appendix V, p. 526.
[6] This revealing interpretation of the character of Piers is that of Neville Coghill. See the Introduction to the excellent translation of the poem by Henry W. Wells (Sheed & Ward, 1945).

evil are massed against him, and in the battle Piers
vanishes, as the Pope had seemed to vanish in the Great
Western Schism even while Langland wrote. He ended his poem in a bitterly black hour, but in one last
line he reasserts that the Reality triumphant on Easter
cannot fail. Conscience is still a pilgrim who will walk
"wide as the world lasteth . . . till I have Piers the
Plowman."

The Hundred Years' War and the Black Death
seem small affairs compared to global war and whole
nations on starvation diet. But the quest of Piers
Plowman goes on from age to age; his questions and
answers are as apt and efficacious in the twentieth as in
the fourteenth century. It is a proof of the spiritual
greatness of the poem that it unfolds new aspects of
dogma and mysticism as time goes on. Contemporary
criticism, more catholic in every sense than that of fifty
years ago which considered it merely as good satire of
great historical interest, has recognized that Langland
is a realistic idealist, and that his poetry is prayer. It
reaches after God not only to know Him but to touch
and hold Him. Its message carries more easily because
literature at the present time is beginning to think and
speak allegorically once more. Mr. Antrobus is simply
a bewildered Everyman who does not know by Whom
the human race has been saved.[7] The allegory in Piers
Plowman, though at times cumbersome and confusing
through sheer exuberance, is too intensely real to be
mistaken; it lives by its own life.

At its core is the dogma of the Mystical Body, the
keynote of the spirituality of today. Here on the

[7] See *The Skin of Our Teeth*, by Thornton Wilder. This is only one of
many plays on the contemporary stage which use allegory to express the
modern approach to ancient problems.

tremendous stage of *Piers Plowman,* jostled by crowded figures who reek with realism, the spiritual drama of redemption through love is re-enacted as in a great liturgy of work-a-day life under the light of heaven. God thirsts for man's love; He seeks His food on earth. He is sated only when men "do the truth in charity" to one another, since all are "baptized and bishoped in the blood of His Heart."

Prologus. Incipit liber de Petro Plowman

In a summer season   when soft was the sun
I shaped and shrouded me   as I were a shepherd,
In habit as a hermit   unholy of works,
Went wide in this world   wonders to hear.
But on a May morning   on Malvern hills
A marvel befell me,   fairy-magic methought.
I was weary of wandering   and went me to rest
Under a broad bank   by a burn's side,
And as I lay and leaned   and looked in the waters
I slumbered in a sleeping,   so merrily it rippled.
Then began I to dream   a marvellous dreaming
That I was in a wilderness,   wist I never where.
As I beheld to the east   high to the sun
I saw a tower on a toft   well made and trimmed,
A deep dale beneath   and a dungeon therein,[8]
With deep ditches and dark,   and dreadful of sight.
A fair field full of folk   found I there between,
Of all manner of men,   the mean and the rich,
Working and wandering   as the world asks.
Some put them to the plow,   played full seldom,
In setting and in sowing   swinked they full hard,
And won what wasters   with gluttony destroy;

---

[8] This setting recalls that of the Miracle Plays familiar to Langland.

And some put themselves in pomp,   and thus were apparelled,
In showy clothing   they came disguised.
In prayer and in penance   many put themselves,
All for love of Our Lord   they lived full strait,
In hope to have   heaven-kingdom's bliss,
As anchorites and hermits   that hold to their cells,
And covet not in the country   to careen about,
For no lecherous living   to please their bodies. . . .
Bidders and beggars   rambled about   40
With their bellies and their bags   crammed full of bread,
Shammed begging for their food,   fought over their ale;
In gluttony, God knows,   they go to bed,
And rise with ribaldry,   those Robert's knaves;
Sleep and sorry sloth   follow them ever!
Pilgrims and palmers   plighted together
To seek Saint James   and the saints in Rome.
They went forth on their way   with many wise tales,
And had leave to lie   all their life after.
I saw some that said   they had sought saints;
To each tale that they told   tongues were tempered to lie
More than to say sooth,   it seemed by their speech.
Hermits in a heap   with hooked staves,
Went to Walsingham,[9]   and their wenches after them;

[9] The shrine of Our Lady of Walsingham, connected with an Augustinian monastery in Norfolk, was the scene of constant pilgrimages. So thick were the pilgrims on the road that led to it, that the Milky Way was called after it: Walsingham Way. The foundations of the chapel, destroyed in the days of Henry VIII, have recently been unearthed. There is a saying abroad that "the Faith will return to England when England returns to Walsingham."

Great lubbers and long   that were loath to swink,
Clothed them in copes   to be known from others,
And shaped themselves as hermits   to have their
    ease.
I found there friars   of all the four Orders
Preached to the people   for profit of themselves,
Glossed over the Gospel   as seemed to them good;
From coveting copes   they construed it as they
    would,
Many master-friars   must be clothed as they will,
For their money and their merchandise   march on
    together.
For since charity has turned pedlar   and prospers
    at shriving lords
Many strange things have befallen   in a few
    years;
Unless Holy Church and they   hold better
    together
The most mischief in the world   is mounting
    full fast.

An unworthy Pardoner stands in the field abusing the
faith of the people and pocketing their money. The
clergy are seeking gain in city trades while the poor go
hungry. The King, counselled by Common Sense, tries
to come to an understanding with the people. A lunatic
in the crowd cries out, "Christ save the King," and an
angel answers in Latin with advice to rulers. There
follows a vivid enactment of the fable of the Belling of
the Cat, and the conclusion is drawn that though "the
King is a child" the Commons had better let well
enough alone.[10]

Barons and burgesses   and bond-men also   216
I saw in this assembly,   as you shall hear after.

[10] A reference to the minority of Richard II.

A lady lovely of face and in linen clothed
came down from a castle.

PASSUS I, PIERS PLOWMAN

Bakers and brewers   and butchers many,
Wooldealers there,   and weavers of linen,
Tailors and tinkers   and toll-takers in markets,
Masons and miners   and many other crafts.
Of living laborers   all kinds came leaping forth,
Such as ditchers and delvers   that do their deeds ill
And spend the long day   with *"Dieu vous save,
Dame Emme!"*
Cooks and their knaves   cried, "Hot pies, hot!
Good pigs and geese,   go dine, go!"
Tavern-keepers to them   told the same tale,
"White wine of Oseye   and red wine of Gascony,
Of the Rhine and of Rochelle,   the roast to
digest."
All this saw I sleeping,   and seven times more.

Passus primus de visione

What this mountain meaneth,   and the murk
dale,   1
And the field full of folk   I shall fairly show you.
A lady lovely of face,   in linen clothed
Came down from a castle   and called me fair,
And said, "Son, sleepest thou?   Seest thou these
people,
How busy they be,   and all in a maze?
The most part of the people   that pass on this
earth,
Have they but worship in this world   they want
nothing better;
Of other heaven than here   hold they no account."
I was afraid of her face,   though she was fair,
And said, "Mercy, Madame,   what is this to
mean?"

"The tower on the toft," quoth she,   "Truth is
    therein,
And He would that you wrought   as His word
    teacheth.
For He is Father of faith,   He formed you all,
Both with skin and with face,   and gave you five
    wits
To worship Him therewith   the while that you be
    here.
Therefore He bade the earth   to help you each one
With wool and with linen,   with livelihood at need,
In measurable manner   to make you at ease."

She goes on to explain the Gospel's teaching on the
reasonable use of things, and says that Wrong lives in
the dark castle of care opposite Truth's tower.

Then had I wonder in my wit   what woman it
    was   71
That such wise words   of Holy Writ showed,
And asked her in the high Name,   ere she went
    thence,
What she was truly   that taught me so fair.
"Holy Church am I," quoth she,   "thou oughtest
    me to know;
I received thee first,   and faith taught thee,
And thou gavest me pledge   my bidding to fulfill,
And to love me loyally   while thy life lasts."

The Dreamer begs her to tell him how to reach heaven.

"When all treasures are tried," quoth she,
    "Truth is the best.   85
I appeal to *Deus Caritas*   to decide the truth;
'Tis as dearworthy a treasure   as dear God
    Himself. . . .

For Truth telleth that love   is the treacle of
    heaven,   146
No sin may be seen in him   that useth that spice;
And all his work he wrought   with love as he
    pleases.
Moses held it the best thing,   and most like to
    heaven,
And the plenitude of peace,   most precious of
    virtues.
For heaven might not hold it,   it was so heavy
    of itself,
Until it had of the earth   eaten its fill.
And when it had of this earth   flesh and blood
    taken
Was never leaf upon linden   lighter thereafter,
As pervading and piercing   as the point of a
    needle
That no armor could stop it,   and no high wall.
For this is Love the leader   of the folk of heaven's
    Lord,
And a mean, as the mayor is,   between the king
    and the commons.
Right so is Love a leader   and the law shapeth;
Upon man and his misdeeds   mercy he asketh.
And to know its nature: it cometh by right,
And in the heart, there is its head   and its high
    well.
For in kind knowing of the heart,   there right
    beginneth,
And that falleth to the Father   that formed us all.
He looked on us with love,   and let His Son die
Meekly for our misdeeds,   to amend us all.
Yet He wished them no woe   that wrought Him
    that pain,

But meekly with His mouth   mercy He sought,
To have pity on the people   that put Him to death.
Here mayest thou see example,   in Himself alone,
That He was mightful and meek,   and granted
    mercy
To them that hung Him on high   and pierced
    Him through the Heart. . . .
For thus these words   are written in the
    Gospel,   198
'Date et dabitur vobis';   thus I deal to you all.
And that is the lock of love,   and letteth out my
    grace
To comfort the care-full,   cumbered with sin.
Love is leech of life   next Our Lord Himself,
And also the strait gate   that goes into heaven;
For this I say as I said   by the very texts:
When all treasures are tried   Truth is the best.
Now I have told thee what truth is,   that no treas-
    ure is better,
I may no longer linger;   look thou to Our Lord."

Passus secundus de visione

Yet I kneeled on my knees,   and cried to her
    for grace,   1
And said, "Mercy, Madame,   for love of Mary of
    Heaven
Who bore the blissful Bairn   that bought us on
    the rood,
Counsel me by some craft   to know the False."
"Look on thy left hand, and lo! there he standeth,
Both Falsehood and Flattery   and their many
    fellows."
I looked on my left side   as the Lady taught me,

And was ware of a woman   worthily clothed
In robes fur-edged,   the finest on earth,
Crowned with a crown,   the King had no better.
Handsomely her fingers   were fretted with gold
    wire,
And thereon red rubies   red as glowing coals,
And diamonds of dearest price,   and double sap-
    phires,
Emeralds and beryls   venoms to destroy.
Her robe was full rich,   of red scarlet ingrained,
With ribbons of red gold   and with rich stones;
Her array ravished me,   such richness saw I never.
I wondered what she was   and whose wife she
    were.
"What is this woman," quoth I,   "so worthily
    attired?"
"That is Meed the maid," quoth she,   "who annoys
    me full oft,
Finds fault with my True-Love   whose name is
    Loyalty,
And lies against lords   who have laws to keep.
In the Pope's palace   she is privy as myself,
But Soothness would not have it so,   for she is a
    bastard."

A marriage is being arranged by Liar between Meed
and Falseness. Guile, Civil, and Simony hasten to the
ceremony, riding as officers of the law. The King is
told of it and commands Liar to be imprisoned.

Lightly Liar   leaped away then,   215
Lurking through the lanes,   lugged about by
    many.
He was nowhere welcome   for his many tales,
Everywhere hooted at   and sent about his business,

Till Pardoners pitied him   and pulled him into house.
They washed him and wiped him   and wound him up in clouts,
And sent him with scales   on Sunday to churches,
And gave pardons for pennies,   pounds at a time.
Then scowled leeches,   and letters they sent
That he should live with them   and look to their waters.
Spicers spoke with him   to watch over their wares
For he is clever at their craft   and knows many gums.
But minstrels and messengers   met with him once
And held him for half a year   and eleven days.
Friars with fair speech   fetched him thence,
And to hide him from comers   coped him as a friar.
But he has leave to leap out   as often as he likes,
And is welcome when he will,   and dwells with them oft.

In Passus III and IV Meed continues to corrupt those in high places with her gold and hypocritical piety till even the King advises her to marry Conscience. The latter energetically refuses, and wins Wit, Wisdom and Reason to his side. The King finally condemns Meed.

Incipit Passus sextus[11]

Thus I woke, God wot,   when I lived in Cornhill,   1
Kit and I in a cottage,   clothed as a loller,
And little enough thought of,   believe me for sooth.

[11] This biographical passage is from the C text.

Reason appears and upbraids him for a seemingly idle life.

"Certainly," I said,   "and so God help me,   22
I am too weak to work   with sickle or with scythe,
And too long, believe me,   to stoop down low,
Or working as a workman   any time to endure."
"Then hast thou lands to live by," quoth Reason,
    "or a rich family
To find thee thy food? For an idle man thou seemest,
A spender who must spend,   or a kill-time
Or forever begging   about at men's hatches,
Or falsely, on Fridays,   or Feastdays in Churches;
Which is a loller's life   that is little praised
Where Righteousness rewards,   right as men
    deserve.
        Reddit unicuique iuxta opera sua.
Or art thou broken, maybe,   in body or in mem-
    bers,
Or maimed by some mishap   whereby thou art
    excused?"
"When I was young," quoth I,   "many years
    hence,
My father and my friends   sent me to school,
Till I knew wisely   what Holy Writ meant,
And what was best for the body,   as the Book tells,
And securest for the soul,   and so I will continue.
And found I never in faith,   since my friends
    died,
A life that I liked   save in these long clothes.
If by labor I must live   and earn my living,
The labor that I learned best   by that I should
    live.
        *In eadem vocatione in qua vocati
        estis, manete.*

And I live in London   and on London both;
The tools that I labor with   and earn my living
Are *Pater Noster* and my Primer,   *Placebo* and
     Dirige,
And my Psalter sometimes   and my seven
     Psalms—
So I sing for the souls   of such as help me. . . .
And yet I hope to have   from Him that is
     Almighty   99
A gobbet of His grace,   and begin a time
That all the times of my time   to profit shall
     turn."

Passus quintus de visione

The King and his Knights   to the church
     went   1
To hear Matins of the day   and the Mass after.
Then I waked of my winking   and had woe withal
That I had not slept sounder   and so had seen
     more,
But before I had gone a furlong   such a faintness
     took me
That I could not fare a foot   all for want of
     sleeping,
And sat softly down   and said my "I believe"
And so babbled on my beads   till they brought me
     to sleep.
Then saw I much more   than I before told,
For I saw the field full of folk   that I spoke of
     before,
And how Reason arrayed himself   to preach to
     the realm,
And with a cross before the king   commenced thus
     to teach.

He proved that the pestilence   was all for pure
  sin,
And the southwest wind   on Saturday evening
Was plainly for pure pride   and no point else.
Pear trees and plum trees   were puffed to the
  earth
To show you, People,   that you should do better.
Beeches and broad oaks   were blown to the ground,
Their tails turned upward   in token of dread
That deadly sin at Doomsday   would undo them
  all.

The sermon continues until the Seven Deadly Sins
are moved to repentance.

Superbia: **63**

Peronelle Proud-Heart   plopped flat to the earth
And lay low ere she looked   and "Mercy, Lord!"
  cried,
And promised to Him   who made us all
She would unsew her shirt   and set a hair one
  there
And tame down her flesh   that fierce was to sin.
"Never high heart will have me,   but hold me low,
And suffer to be mis-said,   —so did I never.
But now I will be meek,   and mercy beseech,
For all this now   I have hated in my heart." . . .

Luxuria: **71**

Then Lechery said, "Alas!"   On Our Lady he
  cried
To make mercy for his misdeeds   between God
  and his soul.
And so on Saturdays   for seven years thereafter

He would drink with the duck   and dine but once. . . .

Invidia: **76**

Envy with heavy heart   asked for shrift
And carefully *"Mea Culpa"*   began to cry.
He was pale as a pellet,   in the palsy he seemed,
And clothed in a rough cloth,   I could not tell what,
In kirtle and short cape,   a knife by his side;
Of a friar's frock   were the foresleeves.
Like a leek that has lain   long in the sun
So looked he with lean cheeks,   louring foul;
His body bulged with wrath   and he bit his lips. . . .

Ira: **134**

Now awoke Wrath   with two white eyes,
Nivelling at the nose,   and his neck hanging. . . .
"Of wicked words I, Wrath,   made monk's dishes,   **162**
Till, 'Thou liest!' and, 'Thou liest!'   leaped out at once,
And either hit other   under the cheek;
Had they had their knives, by Christ!   they would have killed each other." . . .

Avaricia: **188**

Then came Covetousness,   I cannot describe him,
So hungry and so hollow,   he looked like Sir Harvey.
He was beetle-browed   and blabber-lipped also,
With two bleared eyes   like a blind hag,
And like a leathern purse   his cheeks lolled down
Lower than his chin;   they chivelled with age.

Like a bond-man with his bacon   his beard was
   be-slobbered,
With a hood on his head,   a lousy hat above. . . .
"Thou art an unnatural creature (Repentance
   said), I cannot assoil thee   276
Till thou make restitution   and reckon with them
   all,
And until Reason enroll it   in the register of
   heaven
That thou hast made each man good,   I cannot
   assoil thee." . . .

Gula: 304

Then began Glutton   to go to shrift
And starts off church-ward   to confess his sins.
But Beton the brewer-wife   bade him good mor-
   row,
And asked him with that   whither he was going.
"To Holy Church," quoth he,   "for to hear Mass,
And then I shall be shriven   and sin no more."
"I have good ale, Gossip," quoth she,   "Glutton,
   will you try it?"
"Hast thou in thy sack   any hot spices?"
"I have pepper and peonies," quoth she,   "and a
   pound of garlic,
A farthing-worth of fennel seed   for fasting
   days."
Glutton yields to her invitation and is carried home
drunk.

Accidia: 392

Then came Sloth all be-slobbered   with two slimy
   eyes.
"I have to sit," he said,   "or else I shall nap;

I cannot stand nor stoop,   nor without a stool
    kneel."
He belched, *"Benedicite,"*   and his breast beat,
And stretched and groaned   and snored at last.
"What, man! Awake!" cried Repentance,   "and
    get thee to confession."
"If I should die this day,   —I like not to think
    it—
I know not my *Pater Noster*   as the priest sings it,
But I know rhymes of Robin Hood   and Ran-
    dolph Earl of Chester,
But none of Our Lord and Lady,   not the least
    ever made.
I have made forty vows   and forgot them on the
    morrow,
And performed never penance   as the priest bade
    me." . . .
Then took Hope a horn   of *Deus tu*
    conversus vivificabis nos,   514
And blew with *Beati quorum*   *remissi sunt ini-*
    quitates,
Till all the Saints in heaven   sang as one.
A thousand men then   thronged together,
Cried upward to Christ   and to His clean Mother
To have grace go with them   Truth to seek.
But no wight was so wise   as to know the way,
But they blustered forth as beasts   over banks and
    hills.

They meet a pilgrim and ask him where Truth dwells.

"Nay, may so God help me," said the fellow
    then,   541
I never saw Palmer   with pike nor with scrip
Ask after him   till now in this place."

"Peter!" quoth a Plowman   and put out his head,
"I know him as naturally   as a clerk knows his
    books.
Conscience and Kindly Wit   guided me to him
And made me be sure of him,   to serve him for-
    ever,
Both to sow and to set   the while I may swink.
I have been his follower   all these fifty winters,
Sown his seed   and cared for his beasts,
Within and without   awaited his profit.
I ditch and I delve   and I do what Truth bids;
Sometimes I sow   and sometimes I thresh,
In tailor's craft and tinker's craft,   what Truth
    can devise.
I weave and I wind   and I do what Truth bids;
Though I say it myself,   I serve so as to please
    him.
I have my hire of him well,   and sometimes more.
He is the promptest payer   that a poor man
    knows.
He with-holds hire from no-one,   he has it each
    evening,
He is lowly as a lamb   and lovely of speech,
And if you will to wit   where is his dwelling
I will tell you truly   the way to his place."
"Yes, dear Piers," said the Pilgrim,   and
    proffered him hire
For to wend with them   to Truth's dwelling place.
"Nay, by my soul's health," quoth Piers,   and
    began to swear.
"I would not take a farthing   for Saint Thomas'
    shrine!
Truth would love me the less   a long time there-
    after."

The pilgrims set forth on their way.

Passus sextus

"This were a wicked way   unless we had a
    guide   1
That would follow us each foot,"   so the folk
    moaned.
Quoth Perkyn the Plowman,   "By Saint Peter
    of Rome!
I have a half acre   to plow by the highway.
Had I plowed this half acre   and sown it after
I would wend with you   and teach the way."
"That would be a long wait," quoth a lady in a veil,
"What shall we women   do in the meantime?"
"Some shall sew the sack," quoth Piers,   "lest the
    wheat spill.
And you, lovely ladies,   with your long fingers,
Have silk and sendal   to sew when it is time
Chasubles for chaplains,   churches to honor.
Wives and widows,   spin wool and flax,
Make cloth, I counsel you,   and so teach your
    daughters.
The needy and the naked,   take heed how they be,
And fashion them clothes,   for so commands
    Truth."

In the same way, Piers gives instructions to each class
of society, from the Knight down, how best to fulfill
their duty and serve Truth. Then:

Now have Perkyn and his pilgrims   fared to
    the plow.   107
To plow his half-acre   many helped him there;
Ditches and delvers   dug up the ridges.

Therewith was Perkyn pleased   and praised them
  fast.
Other workmen there were   that wrought full
  eagerly,
Each man in his manner   made himself work,
And some to please Perkyn   picked up the weeds.
At high Prime Piers   let the plow stand,
To oversee them himself;   whoso best wrought
Should be hired thereafter   when harvest time
  came.
And then sat some   and sang at their ale
And helped plow his half acre   with ho! trolli-
  lolli! . . .
"Now by peril of my soul!" quoth Piers,   "I
  shall punish you all."   173
And he whooped after Hunger   who heard him at
  once.
"Avenge me on these wasters," quoth he,   "that
  spoil the world."
Hunger in haste then   took Waster by the maw,
And wrung him by the belly   till both his eyes
  watered.
He buffeted the Britoner   about the cheeks
Till he looked like a lantern   all his life after.
He beat them both so   they nigh burst their guts;
Had not Piers with a peas-loaf   prayed Hunger
  to cease
They were dug into grave,   deem thou none other.
"Suffer them to live," he said,   "and let them eat
  with hogs,
Or else of beans and bran   baked together,
Or else milk and mean ale,"   thus prayed Piers
  for them.
Fakers for fear thereof   fled into barns

And flapped with their flails   from morning till
evening. . . .
And thereof was Piers proud   and put them
to work   200
And gave meat as he might   and measurable hire.
And then had Piers pity   and prayed Hunger to
wend
Home to his own land   and hold him there.
"For I have wrought vengeance   on wasters
through thy might
But I pray thee ere thou pass,"   quoth Piers to
Hunger,
"As to beggars and bidders   what is best to be
done?
For I know well if thou go   they will work full ill,
For it makes mischief   so meek they be now
And for default of food   this folk is at my will.
They are my blood brethren,"   quoth Piers, "for
God bought us all.
Truth taught me once   to love them each one
And to help them in all things   as they have
need."

Passus septimus de visione

Truth heard tell thereof,   and to Piers he sent   1
To take his team   and till the earth,
And purchase him a pardon   *a pena et a culpa,*
For him and for his heirs   for evermore after,
And bade him hold him at home   and plow his leas;
And to all who helped him to plow,   to set or to
sow,
Or any other task   that might avail Piers,
Pardon with Piers the Plowman   Truth has
granted. . . .

"Piers," quoth a priest then,   "this pardon
   must I read,   106
For I will construe each clause   and tell it thee
   in English."
And Piers at his prayer   the pardon unfolds,
And I behind them both   beheld all the Bull.
All in two lines it lay,   and not a leaf more,
And was written right thus   in witness of Truth:
   "Et qui bona egerunt, ibunt in vitam eternam;
   Qui vero mala, in ignem eternum."
"Peter," quoth the priest then,   "no pardon can
   I find,
But, 'Do well and have well,   and God shall have
   thy soul;
And do evil and have evil   and hope thou none
   other
But after thy death-day   the devil shall have thy
   soul.' "
And Piers in pure anger   pulled it in twain,
And said, *"Si ambulavero in medio umbra mortis,*
   non timebo mala, quoniam tu mecum es.
I shall cease from my sowing   and swink not so
   hard,
And about belly-joy   be busy no more.
Of prayers and of penance   my plow shall be
   hereafter,
And I'll weep when I should sleep,   though wheat
   bread fail me." . . .

Passus octavus de visione Petri Plowman. Incipit
Dowel, Dobet et Dobest

Thus robed in russet   I roamed about   1
All a summer season   to seek Dowel,
And questioned full often   of folk that I met

If any man knew   what inn Dowel was at,
And what man he might be   of many a man I
     asked. . . .
And thus I went widely,   walking alone   62
By a wild wilderness   and a wood-side.
Bliss of the birds   made me abide.
Under a linden in a land   leaned I awhile
To listen to the lays   the lovely fowls made.
Mirth of their mouths   made me there to sleep;
The most marvellous dream   dreamed I then
That anyone has had   in the world, as I ween.
A mighty man, methought,   and like to myself,
Came and called me   by my own name.
"Who art thou," quoth I then,   "that knows my
     name?"
"One that thou knowest well," quoth he,   "and
     no man better."

Here begins the section on Dowel:

"Know I who thou art?"   "Thought," said he then,
"I have followed thee these seven years;   hast thou
     not seen me sooner?"
"Art thou Thought," quoth I then,   "and canst
     thou tell me
Where Dowel dwells,   and make me know it?"
"Dowel and Dobet   and Dobest the third," quoth
     he,
"Are three fair virtues,   and be not far to find.
Whoso is true of his tongue   and of his two hands,
And through labor or through land   wins his liv-
     ing,
And trusty in his tallies,   taking but his own,
And is not drunk or disdainful,   Dowel follows
     him.

Dobet does right thus,   but he does much more.
He is lowly as a lamb   and lovely of speech,
And helps all men   as they may have need.
Bags and purses   he has broken them all
That Earl Avaricious held,   and his heirs,
And thus with Mammon's money   he has made
      him friends,
And has run into religion,   and rendered the Bible,
And preaches to the people   Saint Paul's words:
      Libenter suffertis insipientes, cum sitis ipsi
      sapientes:
'And suffer the unwise   to live with you.'
And with glad will does them good,   for so God
      bids you.
Dobest is above both   and bears a Bishop's cross,
Hooked on one end   to hale men from hell." . . .
Thought and I thus   went three days together, 112
Disputing about Dowel   day after day;
And ere we were aware,   with Wit we met.
He was long and lean,   like to no other,
No pride in his apparel   nor poverty either,
Grave in his seeming   and of gentle face.

In company with Wit and other characters the
Dreamer wanders from place to place, pondering many
problems of nature and of grace.

Passus nonus de visione et primus de Dowel

Losing of time,   Truth knows truly,   98
Is most hated on earth   by them that be in heaven;
And wasting of speech   that should spring from
      grace.
Speech is God's gleeman   and a game of heaven;
The Faithful Father never wants   His fiddle un-
      tuned,

Nor to have his gleeman a gadder,   a goer to
  taverns. . . .

Passus decimus de visione secundus de Dowel

Then had Wit a wife   whose name was Dame
  Study,
Lean in the face   and in the body both.
She was wondrously wroth   that Wit so taught
  me.
All-staring Dame Study   sternly said,
  "Well wise art thou," quoth she to Wit,   "wis-
    dom to tell
  To flatterers and fools   who are frantic of wit."

At her direction the Dreamer, in company with Conscience, visits Clergy and many other characters, and
has varied adventures, the outcome of them all being
a deeper understanding of truth and love, and greater
reverence for the poor.

But the care-full may cry   and call at the gates, 58
A-hungered and a-thirst,   and quaking in the chill.
There are none to take them in   and mend their
  woes,
But only to cry ho! as to a hound,   and bid them
  go hence.
Little loves he that Lord   who lends him all bliss
That so shares with the poor   a parcel in their
  need.
Were there no more mercy in mean men   than in
  the right rich
Mendicants meatless   might go to bed.

Passus XI through XV continue the discussion of
Dowel. The Dreamer is thinking aloud:

Passus undecimus

On Holy Church I thought   111
That took me at the font   for one of God's chosen;
For Christ called us all,   come if we would
Saracens and Schismatics,   and so He did the
    Jews,
Vos omnes sitientes, venite ad aquas,
Bade them suck for sin,   safely at His breast,
And drink healing for their ills,   whosoever can
    draw it;
And pray all Christians come, quoth I, and claim
    there entry,
By the blood that He bought us with,   and bap-
    tism after. . . .

*Passus quintus decimus. Finit Dowel et incipit
    Dobet*

But after my waking   it was wondrous long   1
Ere I could truly   know what was Dowel.
So my wit waxed and waned   till I was a fool.
And some blamed my life,   few approved it,
And held me a lazy wretch   and loath to reverence
Lords and ladies,   or any one else
Such as persons in furs   with pendants of silver;
To sergeants and such   I said not once,
"God keep you, Lords,"   nor lowly bowed.
So folk held me as a fool,   and in that folly I
    raved
Till Reason had pity on me   and rocked me to
    sleep,
Till I saw as by sorcery   a subtle thing withal,
One without tongue or teeth,   who told me of
    myself,

And whereof I came and of what kind.   I con-
  jured him at last
If he were Christ's creature   for Christ's love to
  tell me. . . .
"What are you called," quoth I,   "among Christ's
  people?"   21
"While I quicken the corpse," quoth he,   "called
  am I *Anima,*
And when I wish and will   *Animus* is my name;
And because I can know,   called am I *Mens,*
And when I make moan to God   *Memoria* is my
  name;
And when I make dooms   and do as Truth teaches
Then is *Ratio* my right name,   Reason in English.
And when I feel what folk tell   my first name is
  Sensus,
And that is wit and wisdom,   the well of all crafts.
And when I challenge or challenge not,   buy or
  refuse,
Then am I Conscience called,   God's clerk and
  His notary.
And when I love loyally   Our Lord and all others,
Then is leal Love my name,   in Latin *Amor;*
And when I fly from the flesh   and forsake the
  body,
Then are my spirits speechless   and *Spiritus* am I
  called." . . .
"What is Charity?" quoth I.   "A childlike thing,"
  he said,   145
*"Nisi efficiamini sicut parvuli, non intrabitis in reg-
  num celorum,*
Without childishness or folly,   a free liberal will.
Where should men find such a friend   with so free
  a heart?"

"I have lived in the land," quoth I,   "my name is
   Long Will,
And found I never full Charity   before nor
   behind. . . .
By Christ, I would that I knew him," quoth I,
   "no creature dearer."   189
"Without help of Piers Plowman," quoth he,
   "his person seest thou never."
"Do clerks know him," quoth I,   "that keep Holy
   Church?"
"Clerks have no knowing," quoth he,   "but by
   works and by words,
But Piers the Plowman   perceiveth more deeply
What is the will and the wherefore   that many men
   suffer.
   Et vidit Deus cogitaciones eorum. . . .
That knoweth no clerk   nor creature on earth 205
But Piers the Plowman,   *Petrus id est*
   Christus." . . .
God became man of a maid,   and *metropolitanus,*
                                                     544
And He baptized and bishoped   with the blood of
   His Heart
All that willed and would,   with inner-wit believe
   it;
Many a saint since   hath suffered death,
And to bring the faith there   in many countries
   died.

   Passus sextus decimus et primus de Dobet

"And yet still I wonder   what Charity means."   3
"It is a full fine tree," quoth he,   "truly to tell.
Mercy is the root thereof,   the trunk is pity,

The leaves are loyal words,　　the law of Holy
　　Church.
The blossoms are gentle-speaking　　and benign-
　　looking,
Patience is the pure tree called,　　poor, simple of
　　heart,
And so, through God and good men,　　grows the
　　fruit Charity."
"I would travel," quoth I, "to see this tree　　twenty
　　hundred miles,
And to have my fill of that fruit　　forsake all other
　　food.
Lord," quoth I, "does any man know　　whither it
　　grows?"
"It grows in a garden," quoth he,　　"that God made
　　Himself;
Amidst man's body　　is the root of that stock.
Heart is the arbor　　that it grows in,
And *Liberum Arbitrium*　　has the land to farm
Under Piers the Plowman,　　to pick it and weed it."
"Piers the Plowman!" quoth I,　　and all for pure
　　joy
When I heard his name named　　anon I swooned
　　after,
And lay long in a lone dream,　　and at last me-
　　thought
That Piers the Plowman　　showed me all the place
And bade me gaze on the tree,　　on top and on
　　root.
With three piles was it propped up,　　I perceived
　　it soon.
"Piers," quoth I, "I pray thee,　　why stand these
　　piles here?"

"For winds, if thou wilt know," quoth he,   "to
 keep it from falling;
And in blowing time they bite the flowers   unless
 the piles help.
The world is a wicked wind   to them that would
 have Truth;
Covetousness comes of that wind,   and creeps
 among the leaves,
And nigh eats up the fruit,   through many fair
 sights.
With the first pile I beat him down,   that is
 Potencia Dei Patris.
The flesh is an ill wind   and in flowering time
Through liking and lusts   so loudly it blows
That it nourishes wrong sights   and sometimes
 words.
The wicked works thereof,   worms of sin,
Bite through the blossoms   right to the bare leaves.
Then set I to the second pile,   *Sapiencia Dei
 Patris,*
That is the passion and the power   of our Prince
 Jesus.
Through prayers and through penances   and
 through God's passion in mind
I save it till I see it ripened   and somewhat fruited.
And then tries the fiend   my fruit to destroy
With all the wiles that he can,   and shakes the
 root,
And casts up at the crop   unkind neighbors,
Mischief-making back-biters,   brawlers and
 chiders,
And lays a ladder thereto,   of lies are the rungs,
And fetches away my flowers   before both my
 eyes.

But *Liberum Arbitrium*   prevents him sometimes;
He is lieutenant to keep it well,   by leave of my-
   self.
But when the fiend and the flesh   and forthwith
   the world
Menace behind me   to fetch my fruit,
Then *Liberum Arbitrium*   fetches the third pile
And beats down the fiend,   purely through grace
And help of the Holy Ghost,   and then have I
   the mastery.". . .
Then I awaked therewith   and wiped my eyes, 167
And after Piers the Plowman   pried and stared;
Eastward and westward   I awaited him fast,
And went forth as an idiot   in the country to spy
After Piers the Plowman,   and many a place I
   sought.
Then met I with a man   on mid-Lenten Sunday,
As hoar as a hawthorn,   Abraham his name.
I asked him first   from whence he came,
And whence he were,   and where he thought to go.
"I am Faith," quoth he,   "it behooves me not to
   lie."

Abraham, representing Faith, leads him to Moses,
representing Hope. Finally he sees the Good Samaritan, who represents Charity, helping the man fallen
among thieves. To the surprise of the Dreamer, Faith
and Hope flee away.

Passus septimus decimus et secundus Dobet

When I saw this I sojourned not,   but started to
   run   83
And followed the Samaritan   that was so full of
   pity,

And granted him to be his groom. "Gramercy,"
   he said,
"Thy friend and thy fellow," quoth he,   "thou
   findest me at need."
And I thanked him then,   and afterwards told him
How Faith flew away,   and Spes his fellow both,
For sight of the sorrowful man   that was robbed
   with thieves.
"Hold them excused," quoth he,   "their help may
   little avail;
No medicine on earth   may bring the man to
   health,
Neither Faith nor fine Hope,   so festered are his
   wounds,
Without the blood of a Bairn   born of a Maid.
And be he bathed in that blood,   baptized as it
   were,
And then plastered with penance,   the passion of
   that Noble,
He will stand and step,   but stalwart will be never
Till he has eaten all the Bairn,   and His blood
   drunk."

The Dreamer asks Charity concerning the Blessed
Trinity, and receives explanations in the form of
similes.

"To a torch or a taper   the Trinity is likened, 203
As though wax and wick   were twined together,
And then a fire flaming   forth out of both.
And as wax and wick   and hot fire together
Foster forth a flame   and a fair blaze,
So do the Sire and the Son   and also *Spiritus*
   Sanctus
Foster forth among folk   love and belief,

That all kinds of Christians   cleanse of their sin.
And as thou seest suddenly   sometimes a torch,
The blaze thereof blown out,   and yet burns the
    wick
Without flame or light   that burns away the
    match,
So is the Holy Ghost God,   and grace without
    mercy
To all unkind creatures   that covet to destroy
Loyal love of life   that Our Lord shaped,
And as glowing coals   gladden not the workmen
As does a rushlight or a candle   that has caught
    fire and blazed,
No more does Sire or Son   or Holy Spirit to-
    gether
Grant us grace   nor forgiveness of sins
Till the holy Ghost begins   to glow and to blaze,
So that the Holy Ghost   glows but as a coal
Until leal love   lies on Him and blows;
Then flames He as a fire   on Father and on
    Filius
And melts their might into mercy,   as men may
    see in winter
Icicles on eves   through heat of the sun
Melt in a minute-while   to mist and to water."

Passus octavus decimus et tercius de Dobet

Woolward and wet-shod   went I forth after
As a reckless fellow   that of no woe recketh,
And went forth like a loller   all my life time,
Till I waxed weary of the world   and willed after
    to sleep,
And lingered on till Lent,   and a long time I
    slept.

And of Christ's Passion and penance   that the
   people wrought,
I rested me there, and snored fast   till *Ramis
   Palmarum;*
Of children and of *Gloria Laus*   greatly I dreamed
And of Hosannah by the organ   the old folks sang.
One like to the Samaritan   and somewhat to
   Piers Plowman
Barefoot on an ass's back   bootless came pricking
Without spurs or spear;   sprightly he looked
As is the way of a knight   that cometh to be dub-
   bed,
To get him gilt spurs   or fair-slashed shoes.
Then was Faith in a window,   and cried, "Ah,
   Fili David!"
As doth a herald of arms   when adventurers come
   to joust.
Old Jews of Jerusalem   for joy there sang:
Benedictus qui venit in nomine Domine.
Then I asked of Faith   what all this doing meant,
And who should joust at Jerusalem.   "Jesus," he
   said,
"And fetch what the fiend claims,   the fruit of
   Piers Plowman."
"Is Piers in this place?" quoth I,   and he peered
   at me.
"This Jesus of his gentleness   would joust in
   Piers' arms,
In his helmet and his hauberk,   *humana natura,*
That Christ be not known here   for *Consummatus
   Deus.*
In the cloak of Piers Plowman   this pricker shall
   ride

For no dint shall daunt Him   as in *Deitate Patris."*
"Who shall joust with Jesus," quoth I,   "Jews or scribes?"
"Nay," quoth he, "the foul fiend,   and Falsedoom and Death.". . .
Then came Pilatus with much people,   *sedens pro tribunali,*   36
To see how doughtily Death should do,   and judge both their rights.
The Jews and the judges   against Jesus they were,
And all their court on Him cried,   *"Crucifige,"* sharply.
And they put Him at a pillar   before Pilate and said,
"This Jesus of our Jews' temple   jabbered, and despised it,
To undo it in one day   and in three days after
Edify it anew   —there he stands that said it—
And make it as much   in all ways as before,
Both as long and as large   as from aloft is the ground."
"Crucifige," cried a rascal,   "I warrant Him a witch."
"Tolle, tolle," quoth another,   and took of keen thorns
And began of keen thorns   a garland to make
And set it sore on his head,   and said in envy,
"Ave, Rabbi," said that ribald,   and threw reeds at Him,
Nailed Him with three nails   naked on the rood,
And poison on a pole   they put up to his lips
And bade Him drink His death-evil,   His days were done.

"And if Thou subtle be,   help now Thyself,
If Thou be Christ and King's Son,   come down
    from the rood,
Then shall we believe that Life loves Thee,   and
    will not let Thee die."
"*Consummatus est*," quoth Christ,   and began to
    swoon
Piteously and pale   as a prisoner that dies.
The Lord of Life and Light   then laid His eyes
    together,
The day for dread withdrew   and dark became the
    sun;
The wall wagged and cleft   and all the world
    quavered.
Dead men for that din   came out of deep graves
And told why that tempest   so long time dured.
"For a bitter battle,"   the dead bodies said,
"Life and Death in this darkness,   one undoes
    the other.
Shall no man know truly   who shall have the
    mastery
Ere Sunday about sun-rising,"   and sank with
    that to earth. . . .
There came forth a knight   with keen spear
    ground,   78
Named Longinus, as letters tell,   who had long
    lost his sight.
Before Pilate and other people   in the place he
    rose;
In spite of all his teeth   he was made at that time
To take his spear in his hand   and joust with
    Jesus.
For they were all unhardy   that rode on horse or
    stood,

To touch Him or taste Him,   or take Him from
the rood.
But this blind fellow then   bored Him through
the Heart;
The blood sprang down the spear   and unsealed
the Knight's eyes.
Then fell the knight upon knees   and cried for
mercy,
"Against my will it was, Lord,   to wound you so
sore,"
He sighed and said,   "Sore it grieves me
The deed that I have done;   I put me in Thy
grace.
Have ruth on me, rightful Jesus,"   and right with
that he wept.
What for fear of this marvel   and of the false
Jews,
I drew me in that darkness   to *descendit in in-
ferna*;[12]
And there I saw soothly,   *secundum scripturas,*
Out of the west coast   a wench, as methought,
Came walking in the way;   to hell-ward she looked.
That maid's name was Mercy,   a meek thing
withal,
A full benign maiden,   and buxom of speech.
Her sister, as it seemed,   came softly walking
Even out of the east,   and westward she looked,
A full comely creature.   Truth was her name;

---

[12] The following passage is the finest of the many versions of the Harrowing of Hell, See p. 212. The hell here in question is not the hell of the
damned but the limbo of the Patriarchs where all saved souls who died
before Christ's act of Redemption awaited heaven. The word "hell" is
loosely used for both states in mediaeval literature. If the distinction is
not kept clearly in mind, some passages in Langland may appear heretical.

For the virtue that followed her,　afraid was she
　never.
When those maidens met,　Mercy and Truth,
Each asked the other　of this great wonder,
Of the din and the darkness　and how the day
　dawned,
And what a light and a gleam　lay before hell. . . .
"Now suffer we," said Truth,　"I see, as me-
　thinks,
　　　　　　　　　　　　　　　　　　161
Out of the nip of the north　not far from here
Righteousness come running,　rest we the while,
For he knows more than we—　he was ere we
　both."
"That is true," said Mercy,　"and I see from the
　south
Where Peace comes playing,　clothed in patience.
Love hath coveted her long,　believe I not other-
　wise.
He has sent her some letter　as to what this light
　means
That overhangs Hell thus;　she shall tell us."
When Peace in patience clothed　approached
　these twain
Righteousness reverenced her　for her rich
　clothing,
And prayed Peace to tell them　where she was
　going,
And whom she thought to greet　in her gay
　garments.
"My will is to wend," quoth she,　"and welcome
　them all
That many a day I might not see　for murkness
　of sin.
Adam and Eve　and others more in Hell,

Moses and many more   mercy shall have;
And I shall dance thereto,   do thou so, Sister!
For Jesus jousted well,   joy begins to dawn.". . .
"What, ravest thou," quoth Righteousness,   "or
    are thou right drunk?   182
Believest thou that yonder light   might unlock
    Hell,
And save man's soul?   Sister, ween it never.". . .
Quoth Peace, "God that began all   of His good
    will   210
Became man of a maid,   mankind to save,
And suffered to be sold   to see the sorrow of dying,
The which unknitteth all care,   and beginning is
    of rest. . . .
And God went adventuring,   and took Adam's
    kind,   220
To know what he had suffered   in three sundry
    places,
Both in heaven and on earth   and now in hell he
    thinketh
To know all woe   who knows of all joy. . . .
And lo! how the sun locked   her light in
    herself   243
When she saw Him suffer   that sun and sea made!
The earth for heaviness   that He should suffer
Quaked as a quick thing   and quashed all the
    rocks.". . .
"Suffer we," said Truth,   "I hear and see both 258
How a Spirit speaks to Hell   and bids unspar the
    gates;
    Attollite portas principes vestras."
A voice loud in that light   to Lucifer cries,

"Princes of this place,   unpin and unlock!
For here comes with crown   the King of glory."
Then sighed Satan,   and said to them all,
"Such a light against our leave   Lazarus it
    fetched;
Care and cumbrance   are come to us all.
If this King come in   mankind will He fetch,
And lead it where He likes   and lightly bind me.
Patriarchs and prophets   have spoken hereof long,
That such a Lord and a light   should lead them all
    hence. . . .
Now I see where a soul   comes hitherward sail-
    ing   304
With glory and with great light;   God it is, I
    wot well.
I reed we flee," quoth he,   "fast all hence,
For we had better not be   than bide in His sight.
For thy lyings Lucifer,   lost is all our prey;
First through thee we fell   from heaven so high,
For we believed thy lying,   we leapt out all with
    thee;
And now for thy last lying   we have lost Adam
And all our lordship I believe   by land and by
    water."
Then the Light bade unlock,   and Lucifer an-
    swered:
"What Lord art Thou," quoth Lucifer,   *"quis est
    iste?"*
"Rex Gloriae,"   the Light soon said,
"And Lord of might and of main   and all manner
    virtues, *Dominus virtutum.*
Dukes of this dim place,   anon undo the gates

That Christ may come in,   the Son of Heaven's
    King."
And with that breath hell brake   for all Belial's
    bars,
Against any guard,   wide open the gates.
Patriarchs and prophets,   *populis in tenebris,*
Sang Saint John's song,   *ecce Agnus Dei.*
Lucifer could not look,   so the light blinded him,
And those that loved Our Lord   He took into His
    light,
And said to Satan, "Lo, here,   my soul makes
    amends
For all sinful souls,   to save them that be worthy.
Mine they be, and of me,   the better may I claim
    them.
Although reason recorded   in my own words
That if they ate the apple   all should die,
I promise them not here   Hell forever
For the deed that they did.   Thy deceit made it.
With guile thou didst get them   against all reason.
For in my palace Paradise,   in person of an adder,
Falsely thou fetched from there   the thing that I
    loved.
Thus like a lizard   with a lady's visage
Thievishly thou robbedst me.   The Old Law
    grants
That guilers be beguiled,   and that is good rea-
    son. . . .
For I that am Lord of life,   love is my drink,   363
And for that drink today   I died upon earth.
I fought so I thirst yet   for man's soul's sake,
May no drink moisten me   nor my thirst slake
Till the vintage fall   in the valley of Josephat,

That I drink right ripe wine,   *resureccio*
   mortuorum,
And then shall I come   as a King crowned with
   angels
And have out of Hell   all men's souls. . . .
Thus by law,” quoth Our Lord,   “lead I will
   from hence   398
Those that loved me   and believed in my coming.
And for thy lying, Lucifer,   that thou liedest to
   Eve,
Thou shalt abide it bitter,”   —and bound him with
   chains.
Astorith and all the rout   hid them in corners,
They durst not look on Our Lord,   the boldest of
   them all,
But let Him lead forth what He liked,   and leave
   what He list.
Many hundreds of angels   harped and sang,
   Culpat caro, purgat caro, regnat Deus Dei caro.
Then piped Peace   of poesy a note,
   Clarior est solito post maxima nebula phebus,
   Post inimicitias clarior est et amor.
“After sharp showers,” quoth Peace,   “most sheen
   is the sun;
Is no weather warmer   than after watery clouds.
No love dearer,   nor dearer friends
Than after war and woe   when Love and Peace
   be masters.
Was never war in this world,   nor wickedness so
   keen
That Love, if he list,   brought not to laughing,
And Peace, through Patience,   all perils stopped.”
“Truce,” quoth Truth,   “thou tellest us sooth, by
   Jesus!

Clasp we in covenant,   and each kiss the other."
"And let no people," quoth Peace,   "perceive that
     we chided,
For impossible is nothing   to Him that is
     Almighty."
"Thou sayest sooth," said Righteousness,   and
     reverently kissed her,
Peace, and Peace here   *per secula seculorum.*
Misericordia et veritas obviaverunt sibi,
Justitia et pax osculatae sunt.
Truth trumpted then and sang,   *"Te Deum*
     Laudamus,"
And then luted Love   in a loud note,
Ecce quam bonum et quam iucundum.
Till the day dawned   these damsels danced,
And men rang for the resurrection,   and right
     with that I waked
And called Kit my wife   and Calotte my daughter,
"Arise and reverence   God's resurrection,
And creep to the cross on knees   and kiss it for
     a jewel."

Passus nonus decimus. Explicit Dobet and incipit
     Dobest.

The Dreamer falls asleep at the Offertory and sees
Piers carrying a cross. Conscience tells the life of
Christ, stressing His role as conqueror.

And when this deed was done,   Dobest He
     taught,   **177**
And gave Piers power,   and pardon He granted
To all manner men,   mercy and forgiveness,
Gave might to shrive men   of all manner sins

On condition that they come   and acknowledge as
   they should
The Pardon of Piers the Plowman,   *redde quod
debes.* . . .
Thus Conscience of Christ   and of His cross
   talked,   194
And counselled me to kneel thereto,   and then
   there came, methought,
One *Spiritus Paraclitus*   to Piers and to his fel-
   lows;
In likeness of lightning   He lighted on them all
And made them to know   all kinds of languages.
I wondered what that was   and nudged
   Conscience,
And was afraid of the light,   for in fire's likeness
Spiritus Paraclitus   overspread them all.
Quoth Conscience, and kneeled,   "This is Christ's
   messenger,
And comes from the great God,   Grace is his
   name.   .
Kneel now," quoth Conscience,   "and if thou
   canst, sing.
Welcome Him and worship Him   with *Veni Cre-
ator Spiritus."*
Then sang I that song,   and so did many
   hundreds,
And cried with Conscience,   "Help us, God of
   Grace!"
And then began Grace   to go with Piers Plow-
   man,
And counselled him and Conscience   the Commons
   to summon.
"For I will deal today   and divide Grace
To all kinds of creatures   that have their five wits,

A treasure to live by   to their life's end
And weapons to fight with   that will never fail.
For Anti-Christ and his own   shall be grievous
    to the world,
And encumber thee, Conscience,   unless Christ
    help thee.
And many false Prophets,   flatterers and liars,
Shall come to be curators   over kings and earls,
And Pride shall be Pope,   prince of Holy Church,
Covetousness and Unkindness   Cardinals to lead
    him." . . .
Grace gave Piers a team,   four great oxen;   257
One was Luke, a large beast   and a mild-faced,
Mark and Matthew were two more,   mighty beasts
    both,
And joined to them was John,   most gentle of
    all—
Prize cattle of Pier's plow,   surpassing all others.
And Grace gave Piers   of his goodness four bul-
    locks,
And what his oxen plowed   they were to harrow
    after.
One was Augustine,   Ambrose another,
Gregory the great clerk   and Jerome the good.
These four, the faith to teach,   followed Piers'
    team,
And harrowed in a short while   all Holy Scripture
With two harrows that they had,   the Old and the
    New.
And Grace gave grains,   the cardinal virtues,
To sow them in man's soul,   and He told their
    names. . . .
"And when these grains," quoth Grace,
    "begin to grow ripe,   **314**

Build thee a house, Piers,   to harbor thy corn."
"By God, Grace," quoth Piers,   "you must give
  timber
And plan that house   ere you wend hence."
And Grace gave him the Cross   with the crown of
  thorns
That Christ upon Calvary   suffered for mankind.
And of the Baptism and blood   that He bled upon
  the rood
He made a mortar   and Mercy he called it;
And therewith Grace began   to make a good
  foundation,
And wattled it and walled it   with His pains and
  His passion,
And of all Holy Writ   he made a roof after,
And called that house Unity,   Holy Church in
  English.
And when this deed was done   Grace devised
A cart called Christendom   to carry Piers'
  sheaves,
And gave him horses for his cart,   Contrition and
  Confession,
And made Priesthood hayward,   while he himself
  went
As wide as the world is   with Piers to till Truth.

Pride then raises a war against Piers, and tempts
Conscience.

Quoth Conscience to all Christians then,
    "My counsel is to wend   352
Hastily into Unity,   and hold ourselves there,
And pray that we be in peace   in the barn of Piers
  Plowman,

For surely I know well   that we have nought of
strength
To go against Pride,   save Grace were with us."
And then came kind Wit   to teach Conscience,
And cried and commanded   all Christian peoples
To delve a ditch   deep about Unity,
That Holy Church stand in Unity   as on a foun-
dation.
Conscience commanded then   all Christians to
delve
And make a mighty moat,   that they might be in
strength
To help Holy Church   and them that keep it.

Passus vicesimus et primus de Dobest

During a waking interval the Dreamer meets with
Need.

When Need had reproved me thus   anon I
fell asleep
And dreamed full marvelously   that in man's
form
Antichrist came then,   and all the crop of Truth
He turned up-side-down,   and tore it by the roots,
And made Falsehood spring and spread   and
speed men's needs.
In each country that he came   he cut away Truth
And made Guile grow there,   as if it were a good.
Friars followed that fiend   for he gave them
copes,
And religious reverenced him   and rang their
bells,
And all the convent came forth   to welcome that
tyrant. . . .

Antichrist had thus soon   hundreds at his
     banner,   68
And Pride bore it   boldly about,
With a Lord that lives   to the body's liking.
Then came again Conscience   who was keeper and
     guide
Of Christian manners   and the Cardinal virtues.
"I counsel," quoth Conscience then,   "come with
     me, ye fools,
Into Unity of Holy Church   and hold ourselves
     there,
And cry we to Nature   to come and defend us,
Fools, from this fiend's limbs,   for the love of
     Piers Plowman.
And cry we to the Commons   that they come to
     Unity,
And there abide and bicker   against Belial's chil-
     dren.
Nature heard Conscience   and came out of the
     planets,
And sent out his foragers,   fevers and fluxes,
Coughs and spasms,   cramps and toothaches,
Colds and running sores,   and dirty scabs,
Boils and tumors   and burning agues;
Frenzies and foul evils,   foragers of Nature,
Had picked and preyed   on the heads of the
     people,
Till a large legion   straight lost their lives.
There was, "Harrow!" and, "Help!   Here
     comes Nature!
With breath that is dreadful   to undo us all."
The Lord that lived for lust   then aloud cried

To Comfort, a knight,   to come and bear his ban-
    ner.
"Alarm, alarm!" quoth that Lord,   "let each keep
    his life."
And then these men met   ere minstrels could
    pipe
Or heralds at arms   had called their lords aloud.
Old Age the hoary   was in the vanguard
And bore the banner before Death,   by right he
    claimed it.
Nature came after   with many keen sores,
As pox and pestilence,   and struck many people;
So Nature through corruption   killed full many.
Death came driving after   and all to dust pashed
Kings and knights,   kaisers and popes;
Learned nor lay,   he let no man stand,
And what he hit evenly   stirred never after.
Many a lovely lady,   and lovers of knights,
Swooned away and died   for sorrow of Death's
    dints. . . .
Then Old Age came after me,   and went
    over my head,   182
And made me bald before   and bare on the crown.
So hard on my head he went   it will be seen ever.
"Sir evil-taught Age," quoth I,   "ill-manners go
    with thee!
Since when does a road lead   over men's heads?
Hadst thou been civil," quoth I,   "thou wouldst
    have asked leave."
"Yea, my dear Lord," quoth he,   and laid on more
    age,
And hit me under the ear,   scarce could I hear
    more,

And buffeted me about the mouth,   and beat out
    my teeth
And grieved me with the gout;   I may not go at
    large. . . .
And as I sat in this sorrow   I saw how
    Nature passed   198
And cried to Nature   out of care to bring me.
"Lo, Old Age the hoary   hath attacked me.
Avenge me, if you so will,   for I would be hence."
"If thou wilt be avenged,   get thee into Unity,
And hold thee there ever   till I send for thee,
And look thou learn some craft   ere thou come
    hence."
"Counsel me, Nature," quoth I,   "What craft is
    best to learn?"
"Learn to love," quoth he,   "and leave all other."
"How shall I get money then   to clothe and feed
    me?"
"If thou truly love," quoth he,   "thou shalt lack
    never
Meat nor worldly weeds   while thy life lasts."
And there by counsel of Nature   I commenced
    to roam
Through contrition and confession   till I came to
    Unity;
And there was Conscience constable   all
    Christians to save,
And besieged soothly   by seven great giants
That with Antichrist   held hard against
    Conscience.
Sloth with his sting   a hard assault he made,
Proud priests came with him   more than a
    thousand

In jackets and pointed shoes   and ruffians' long
     knives,
Came against Conscience;   with Covetousness
     they held.
"By Mary," quoth a shrewish priest   of the land
     of Ireland,
"I count Conscience no more—   as long as I catch
     silver—
Than I do to drink   a draft of good ale!"
And so said sixty   of the same country,
And shot against him with shots   many a sheaf of
     oaths,
And broad-hooked arrows,   God's heart and his
     nails,
And almost brought Unity   and holiness down.
Conscience cried, "Help, Clergy,   or else I fall
Through imperfect priests   and prelates of Holy
     Church."
Friars heard him cry   and came to help him,
But they knew not their craft   and Conscience
     forsook them.

In the confusion Piers Plowman has disappeared.
Peace is made the porter of Unity. Hypocrisy wounds
Contrition, and Friar Flatterer comes posing as a
physician to help him.

He came to where Conscience was   and knocked
     at the gate.   **327**
Peace unpinned it,   the porter of Unity,
And in haste asked   what his will were.
"In faith," quoth the Friar,   "for profit and for
     health

I would talk with Contrition and therefore came
 I hither."
"He is sick," said Peace, "and so are many
 others.
Hypocrisy has hurt them; it is hard to
 recover." . . .
But Smooth-Speech bade Peace open the
 gates,   346
Let in the Friar and his fellows and make
 them fair cheer.
"He may see and hear, and so it may befall
That Life through his lore may leave Covetous-
 ness,
And be adread of Death and withdraw from
 Pride,
And accord with Conscience, and each kiss the
 other."
Thus through Smooth-Speech entered the Friar,
And came in to Conscience with courteous greet-
 ing.
"Thou art welcome," quoth Conscience, "canst
 thou heal the sick?
Here is Contrition," quoth Conscience, "my
 cousin, wounded.
Comfort him," quoth Conscience, "and take care
 of his sores.
The plasters of the Parson and his powders bite
 too sore.
He let them lie overlong and is loath to change
 them.
From Lent to Lent he let his plasters bite."
"That's overlong," said the Limitor, "I shall
 amend it."

And he went and felt of Contrition   and gave him
    a plaster
Of "a little private payment,   and I shall pray
    for you
And all that are dear to you   all my life-time,
And make you my Lady   at Mass and at Matins,
As the Friars of our Fraternity   —for a little
    silver—"
Thus he goes and gathers   and lies where he
    shrives,
Till Contrition had clean forgotten   to cry and to
    weep
And wake for his wicked works   as he was
    wont to do.
For comfort of his confessor   he left contrition,
The most sovereign salve   for all kinds of sins.
Sloth saw that,   and so did Pride,
And came with a keen will   to assail Conscience.
Conscience cried out   and bade clergy help him,
And also Contrition   to keep the gate.
"He lies and dreams," said Peace,   "and so do
    many others.
The Friar with his physic   has enchanted this folk,
And plastered them so easily   that they dread
    no sin."
"By Christ," quoth Conscience then,   "I will be-
    come a pilgrim
And walk as wide   as the whole world stretches
To seek Piers the Plowman   that can destroy
    Pride,
And that Friars may have provision   who flatter
    now for need

And oppose me, Conscience.   Now may Nature
    avenge me
And send me hap and heal   till I have Piers
    the Plowman."
Then he cried out for Grace   until I awoke.

Explicit hic dialogus Petri Plowman.

x

Pearl-Poetry

So fare we all in love and song,
As kings and queens in courtesey.

PEARL

THERE is another fourteenth-century poet worthy to
form a triumvirate with Chaucer and Langland. That
a single age could produce three writers of such vastly
different temperament and technique says much for
the vigor and variety, the height and the depth, of its
culture. The word *altus* means both high and deep,
and the surest way of understanding the depths is to
look at the heights. Readers who have been refreshed
by the storyteller and stirred by the epic-maker will
be lifted up by the Pearl Poet.

He is called by that name because his other name
has been lost, and because he wrote pearl-poetry. His
work is brilliant, clean-cut, precious, and it catches fire.
Jewels are used for the adornment of the gay or for

the enhancing of sacred things; they answer to the light. Jewel-poetry sparkles with humor or glows with the reflected flame of candles on the altar; it is always lovely, and allows of no mingling with the sordid or the dark. We know nothing of this master craftsman except what can be perilously guessed from the one thing that he has left behind him, a manuscript[1] containing four poems in a north-western dialect. Even such conjectures rest upon the assumption (which has so far met the tests of scholarship) that the poems are by a single author. Though very different, they are stamped with a particular quality of genius hardly divisible among four men. One man of wide culture and experience could have written a brilliant Arthurian romance, *Sir Gawaine and the Green Knight,* two captivating verse homilies, *Patience* and *Cleanness,* and the spiritual dream-allegory, *Pearl.* There are also interlinking references, especially to pearls, and the language and technique in the four are similar.

It is tempting to reconstruct from the poems the life of their author. He would be of an old and knightly family of Lancashire, living in a castle not too far from some monastery with its rich library, where a nobleman's son with intellectual tastes could steal an education otherwise unneeded for his position in life. In the surrounding countryside, among bookloving men, traditions of the older literature of England would be strong, its alliterative metre and its memory of heroes. He would ride and hunt far afield, through the Arthur country to the south-west. He would become ac-

---

[1] MS Cotton Nero AX is in a late fourteenth-century script, and thus nearly contemporary with the author of the poems, which can be dated from internal evidence as belonging to the second half of the century. The dialect is that of North Lancashire. The MS is illustrated throughout with full-page drawings, crude but lively in execution.

quainted with the gallantries of court life, possibly as
a page. He would have travelled then to London, perhaps beyond, and have moved in literary circles where
the names of Boccaccio and Dante were spoken, and
where Provençal metres were played with. Driven by
increasing awareness of spiritual values, did he become
a monk? Or did he marry, and become the father of
a daughter who died young? He may have become a
monk after married life—or never at all. Let readers
of *Pearl* decide for themselves.

As for the Pearl Poet's relation to his age, he is as
precise about its dress and manners as is Chaucer, he
is as convinced of its spiritual values as is Langland,
but he never sets out to portray or reflect it. He leaves
contemporary troubles alone. If he has remained rela-
tively unknown to later generations, the fact is largely
due to the difficulty of his language, archaic, highly
wrought and remote from the more readable speech of
London, and to his apparent aloofness from the other
men of his times. Through books and through experience he travels into fairyland, into lands of the Bible,
or into heaven, but no matter where he goes he meets
and loves people, and the people are those of his century—and of ours.

SIR GAWAINE AND THE GREEN KNIGHT

This tale is a detached episode of the Arthurian
cycle. Its artistic finish, its unity of plot, its moral
earnestness, and the clean, breezy joy that blows
through it set it apart from the formless ramblings of
many metrical romances. As Lancelot was the favorite
knight of French story-listeners, and Parcival of the
German, so was Sir Gawaine the hero of the English.
He was such a perfect blend of the best elements in

chivalry that this story of his adventures is also an allegory on the knightly virtue of courtesey, and "as pearls to white peas" is Gawaine to the rest of knights. Moreover, in spite of the magic drawn from Celtic sources, and the romantic glamor that clings to every Arthurian name, this tale is so true to human nature, with its funny, adventurous, brave and tender characters, that it blends reality with romance, and is completely up to date, as far as fourteenth-century dress and castle architecture are concerned. Its metrical form is curious; long stanzas of alliterative lines end with a "bob-and-wheel" of short rhyming lines. This bold and effective blend of the old accentual metre of the Anglo-Saxons with the quantitative, patterned forms of French (and remotely of classical) origin, is characteristic of the Pearl Poet.

Sir Gawaine opens, as should all good English "histories," with the origins, the coming of Brutus from Troy. Then:

Of all that here built   of Britain's kings   25
Aye was Arthur the noblest,   as I have heard tell.
An adventure on the earth   I intend telling,
Such that a marvel   some men hold it,
A strange adventure   of Arthur's wonders.
If you will listen to this lay   but a little while
I will tell it as fine   as in town I heard it
            With tongue,
    As it is told in writing
    In story stiff and strong,
    With true letters linking
    In land as has been long.[2]

This King lay at Camelot   at Christmas tide,

---

[2] A reference to the revival of alliterative metre.

With many lovely lords,　ladies of the best,
Courteously of the Round Table,　all the courtly
　　brothers
With rich revel aright　and reckless mirth.
There tourneyed the gallants　full many a time,
Jousted full jollily,　these gentle knights,
Then careered to the Court　their carols to make.
There the feasting was the same　full fifteen days,
With all the meat and the mirth　that men could
　　devise,
Such glad noise and glee,　glorious to hear,
Festal din by day,　dancing by night.
All was high happiness　in halls and chambers
With lords and with ladies　as each was most lief.
With all the weal of the world　they dwelt there
　　as one,
The best-known knights　under Christ Himself,
And the loveliest ladies　that ever had life,
And the comeliest King　that the Court holds.
For all this fair folk　was in its fresh age,
　　　　　And still
　　The luckiest under heaven,
　　King of the highest will—
　　It now were hard to reckon
　　So hardy a troop on hill.

The Court is gathered one day for a feast, with King
Arthur, Queen Guinevere, Sir Gawaine, and other
favorites at the high table. An elaborate meal is spread
before them.

But Arthur would not eat　till all were served,　85
He was so jolly in his joyousness　and somewhat
　　boyish.
A cheerful life he liked;　he loved the less

Either to long lie   or to long sit,
So busied him his young blood   and his brain wild.
And another manner   moved him also
That he through nobleness had taken: he would
     never eat
Upon such a great day,   unless there were devised
An unknown tale   of some adventure,
Of some mighty marvel   that he might believe in,
Of his ancestors, of arms,   or of other adventures;
Or someone besought him   for a sure knight
To join with him in jousting,   in jeopardy to meet
And risk life for life,   granting each to other
As fortune would give them   to gain the
     advantage.
This was the King's custom   when he held court
At each recurring feast   among his free followers
               In hall.
          Therefore with haughty air
          He stands proud and tall,
          Full fresh in that New Year
          Much mirth he makes withal. . . .

Now will I of their service   tell you no more,   130
For everyone well knows   no want was there.
Another noise full new   swiftly drew near,
That the Prince might have leave   to support life
     with food.
For scarce had the noise   for a while ceased
And the first course in the court   fittingly served,
Than there comes in at the door   a ghoulish
     creature,
The mightiest on earth   for his high measure,
From the neck to the waist   so square-built and
     thick,
And his loins and his limbs   so long and so great,

Half giant on the earth   I judge that he were.
The hugest of men   he must have been,
And the merriest in his size   that might ride
    abroad,
For in back and in breast   was his body strong,
Yet was his waist   worthily small,
And his features fitting   the form that he had
        Full clean.
    Wonder at his hue men had,
    So was his semblance seen.
    He fared as one proud and glad,
    And over all bright green.

And all garbed in green   this fellow in his weeds,
A tight coat full strait   that stuck to his sides,
A merry mantle above,   adorned within
With fur of the finest   as lining full clean,
With white fur full bright,   and his hood too
Freed from his locks   and laid on his shoulders,
Neat-fitted hose   of the same green
Spanned on his calf,   and the clean spurs under
Of bright gold upon silk strips   barred full rich,
Pointed shoes neath his shanks   when the man
    rides,
All his vesture verily   like sheer verdure,
Both the bars of his belt   and other bright stones
That were richly ranged   in his clean array,
About himself and his saddle   upon worked silk.
It were troublesome to tell   of half the trifles
Embroidered above   with birds and flies,
With gay gaudy green,   gold amid it.
The pendants of his trappings,   the proud cropper,
His bit-studs, and all metal   were enamelled
    therewith.

The stirrups that he stood in   were stained with
    the same,
His saddle-bows after,   and the fine tail-pieces
Glimmered and gleamed   all of green stones.
The horse that he hied on   was all the same,
        Certainly;
      A green horse great and thick,
      A steed full strong was he,
      In a broidered bridle quick,
      With his rider to agree.

The Green Knight then throws out a challenge. He asks for a knight who will strike off his head with the great green axe that he carries, and who in return will receive a like blow from the Green Knight. Sir Gawaine courteously steps forward and accepts the challenge.[3]

The Green Knight upon the ground   readily
    lights,   416
Bows a little his head,   the flesh he uncovers,
His long lovely locks   he lays over the crown,
Lets his naked neck   show for the business.
Gawaine grips his axe,   gathers it on high,
The left foot on the floor   before him he sets.
He let it down lightly   to light on the naked neck,
So that the sharp edge   shivered the bones
And shrank through the sheer grease   and
    sundered it in twain.
The fair head from the shoulders   hit to the earth;
Many kicked it with their feet   as it rolled forth.
The blood ran from the body   and gleamed on the
    green,

[3] This episode comes from a Celtic source. A beheading challenge is found in the Middle Irish romance, *Bricriu's Feast.*

But neither faltered nor fell   the fellow for all
     that,
But stoutly he started forth   upon stiff shanks,_
And roughly he reached out   there where the men
     stood,
Caught at his lovely head   and straight lifted it up.
Then he turns to the horse,   the bridle he catches,
Steps in the steel bows   and straddles aloft.
His head by the hair   he holds in his hands,
And as sedately   he sat in his saddle
As if no mishap ailed him,   though he headless
     were
          In that place.
     He turned his trunk about
     And the ugly head still bled,
     Men were in fear and doubt
     By the time his say was said.

For the head in his hand   he holds up even,
Towards the dearest lady on the dais   he dressed
     the face
And it lifted up its eyelids   and looked full broad,
And spoke thus with its mouth,   as you may now
     hear:
"Look, Gawaine, be thou prompt   to do what
     thou hast promised,
And seek me loyally   till thou, man, find me,
As thou hast promised in this hall   with these
     knights listening.
To the Green Chapel go,   I charge thee, to get
Such a dint as thou hast dealt,   thou hast deserved
     it,
To be duly dealt   on New Year's morn."

The Green Knight rides away, and the Christmas revels go on.

Then the Yule went by   and the year after,   500
And each varied season   followed the other.
After Christmas   comes the crabbed Lent,
That tries flesh with fish   and with food more
    simple.
Then the weather of the world   against winter
    struggles,
The cold shrinks down,   clouds are uplifted,
Sheer sheds the rain   in showers full warm,
And falls on the fair flats;   flowers there show.
Both the ground and the groves,   green are their
    garments.
Birds are busy to build   and brightly sing
For solace of the soft summer   that follows after
              By the bank,
     And blossoms swell for bloom
     Where the rich hedges stand,
     Noble notes are soon
     Heard in the proud woodland.

Then the season of summer   with the soft winds,
When Zephyrus sighs   on the seeds and herbs.
Very fair are the roots   that wax thereout
When the dampening dew   drops from the leaves
To bide a blissful gleam   of the bright sun.
Then hies the harvest,   hardens them soon,
But warns them for the winter   to wax full ripe,
Drives with drought   till the dust rises
From the face of the fields   to fly full high.
Wroth wind of the welkin   wrestles with the sun,
Leaves loosen from the lime trees   and light on the
    ground,

And grey grows the grass   that was once green.
Then all ripens and rots   that rose at first,
And thus runs on the year   with yesterdays many.
Winter winds back again   in the way of the world,
      Indeed
      Till Michaelmas moon
      Was come with wintry speed
      Then thinks Gawaine full soon
      Of his anxious deed.

He then is clad in his most magnificent armor and
mounts on his great horse Gringolet. On his shield is
the Pentangle called "Overall," symbolizing perfection. He is the Knight of Courtesey. He takes farewell
of Arthur and his court.

He climbed over many cliffs   in strange coun-
    tries   **713**
Far wandering from his friends   as a stranger
    he rode.
At each bank or water-course   where the warrior
    passed
He found a foe before him,   as it ever befell,
So foul and so fierce   that he needs must fight it.
So many marvels in the hills   did the knight meet
    with
That 'twere too long to tell   of the tenth part.
Sometimes he wars with dragons   and with wolves
    also,
And now with the wood-trolls   that lurk in the
    gnarled crags;
With wild bulls and bears,   and with boars also,
With ogres that puffed after him   from the high
    precipice.

Had he not been doughty and brave and served the
   Lord   doubtless he had been dead and undone
   full often.
Though the warring were grievous   yet worse
   was the winter,
When the clear cold water   showered from the
   clouds
And froze ere it fell   on the faded earth.
Nigh slain with the sleet   he slept in his armor,
While clattering from the crests   the cold brooks
   ran down
And hung high o'er his head   in hard icicles.
Thus in peril and in pain   and in sore plight
The knight roamed the country-side   till Christ-
   mas Eve
                   All alone,
         And in that weary tide
         To Mary made his moan
         That she would be his guide
         Into some shelter soon.

By a mount in the morning   merrily he rides
Into a forest full deep   and fiercely wild,
High hills on each hand   and holtwoods under
Of huge hoary oaks   standing by hundreds;
The hazel and the hawthorn   were tangled
   together
With rough ragged moss   rampant over all,
And many birds unblithe   upon the bare twigs
Piteously piped there   for pain of the cold.
The knight on Gringolet   rode beneath them
Through mire and through marshes,   a lonely
   man
Troubled lest he fail   to serve fairly

The noble Lord   who that selfsame night
Had been born of a maid   to make our peace.
And therefore sighing he said: "I beseech Thee, Lord,
And Mary, that is mildest   Mother so dear,
For some harbour where highly   I might hear Mass,
And Thy Matins tomorrow,   meekly I ask.
And thereto I pray   with Pater and Ave
        And Creed."
    He rode on in his prayer,
    Grieving for each misdeed.
    He signed himself often there,
    Saying, "Christ's Cross be my speed."

He had not signed himself,   this knight, but thrice
When he was ware in the wood   of a dwelling by a moat
Above a lawn on a hill,   locked under boughs
Of many tremendous tree-trunks   about by the ditches. . . .
He paused on a bank   where his horse pawed, 785
By the deep double ditch   drawn round the place
The wall reached to the water   wondrously deep,
Then hugely high   it towered aloft,
Of hard hewn stone   up to the cornice,
With horn-work under battlements,   in the best manner,
And with turrets full gay   geared between,
With many lovely loops   that looked full clean.
Finer defences   the knight had ne'er looked on.
And within he beheld   the hall full high,
Towers planted between   thickly adorned,
Fitted pinnacles   fair and long
With carven tops   craftily made.

Chalk-white chimneys   saw he enough
Upon tower-roofs   that twinkled white.
So many painted pinnacles   were powdered
    everywhere,
Among castle embrasures   they clambered thick,
So that pared out of paper   purely it seemed.
The fellow on the horse   thought it fair enough
If he might but come   within the cloister,
To harbor in that hostel   for the holy-days
       As they went.
    He called and soon there came
    A porter most pleasant;
    From the wall he asked his claim
    And hailed the knight-errant.

The drawbridge is lowered and Gawaine rides across
to be received with eager courtesey by retainers who
lead him to a magnificent room. The Lord of the castle
soon appears to greet him.

Gawaine glanced at the man   who greeted him
    goodly,

       842

And thought him a bold lord   that owned the
    burgh,
A huge noble for the nonce,   at the height of his
    years.
Broad and bright was his beard,   beaver-hued,
Stern, stiff in his stride   on stalwart shanks,
A face fierce as fire,   free of his speech,
And able seemed he for sooth,   as the knight
    thought,
To hold lordship   over goodly lieges.
The lord led him to a chamber   and loudly
    commanded
That a man be given him   to serve him lowly.

There were ready at his bidding   servants enough
Who brought him to a bright bower   where the
     bedding was noble,
With curtains of clean silk   with clear gold hems,
And coverlets full curious   with comely panels
Of bright fur above,   embroidered besides,
Curtains running on ropes,   red gold rings,
Tapestries on the walls   of Toulouse and Tarsia,
And under foot on the floor   fitting carpets.
There was despoiled,   with speeches of mirth,
The knight of his byrnie   and his bright weeds.
Rich robes full promptly   were brought to him
To take and to change   and to choose the best.

Dinner is then served by the open fire in his room, after which he goes to the chapel for Vespers. Coming out, he meets the beautiful young wife of the Lord of the castle accompanied by an ugly old woman. Gawaine is invited to spend Christmas week with his new friends, and the Lord promises to show him the Green Chapel on New Year's morn. Christmas passes happily, and one evening the Lord announces his intention to go hunting the next day.

"Yet first," quoth the Host,   "a bargain we'll
     make.   1105
Whatsoever I win in the woods   it will be yours,
And what you achieve here,   change with me for it.
Sweet one, we shall swap,   swear me so truly,
Whether it happens to be   worthless or better."
"By God," quoth Gawaine the good,   "I grant
     it to you.
Whatever pleases you   is a pleasure to me."
"Bring us a beverage!   This bargain is made!"

So said the Lord of the place;   they laughed each
   one,
They drank and they dallied   and they revelled
   light-hearted,
These lords and ladies,   as long as they liked.
Then with fresh faces   and many fair speeches
They stood and stopped,   and spoke stilly,
Kissed full comely   and took their leave
With many light words;   and with gleaming
   torches
Each to his bed   was brought at last
            Full soft
     And yet for a little space
     Recalled promises oft.
     The old Lord of that place
     Could well hold sport aloft.

At dawn the next day the Lord is off to the deer-hunt.
He spends the whole day in an exciting and successful
chase. Meanwhile at home:

Gawaine lingered while the daylight   gleamed on
   the walls   1180
Under a cover full clear,   curtained about,
And as he slid into slumbering   slyly he heard
A little din at the door   that deftly opened,
And he heaved up his head   out of the clothes,
A corner of the curtains   he cast up a little
And waited warily   what it might mean.
It was the Lady,   loveliest to behold,
That drew the door after her   secretly and
   still. . . .
Then he unlocked his lids   and looked in
   wonder,   1201
And signed himself   the Savior to honor

Aright.
With chin and cheek full sweet
Of mingled red and white,
Lovely was she to greet
With small lips laughing bright.

The Lady then proceeds to flirt with him, but Gawaine
treats her with perfect courtesey and reserve. He
allows her to give him one kiss. In the evening the Lord
returns with a splendid catch of deer.

"All I give you, Gawaine,"   quoth the Lord
    then,   1383
"For by accord of our covenant   you may crave it
    as your own."
"That is truth" quoth the Knight,   "I say the
    same,
What I have worthily won   within these walls
Iwis with as good will   it shall be yours."
He clasps his fair neck   within his arms
And kisses him as comely   as he can devise.

The next day the Lord hunts a wild boar. At home
the Lady again flirts with Sir Gawaine, and gives him
two kisses. In the evening the Lord faithfully receives
the kisses from the Knight, in return for the boar's
head. The third day:

After Mass a morsel   the Lord and his men took.
                                                             1690
Merry was the morning;   he asked for his mount,
And all the hunters that on horses   should follow
    after
Were soon on their steeds   before the hall gates.
Very fair was the field,   for the frost clung;
Fiery red on cloud-drifts   rose the sun

And skirted full clear   the clouds of the welkin.
Hunters loosened their hounds   by a holt side;
Rocks rang in the woods   for the cry of their
    horns.

This time the Lady gives Gawaine three kisses and
begs him to accept a gift. This he refuses to do, but at
last she shows him a green lace girdle.

"Will you forsake this silk,"   said the Lady
    then,   1846
"Because it is simple in itself?   And so it well
    seems.
Lo, it is so little,   and less is it worthy;
But whoso knew the qualities   knit into it
Would appraise it at more price,   peradventure.
For a man that is geared   with this green lace,
While he has it neatly   fastened about him
There is no hero under heaven   that can hew him
    down,
For he may be slain   by no means on earth."
Then the knight thought,   and it came to his heart
'Twould be a jewel in the jeopardy   that was
    adjudged to him
When he got to the Chapel   to fetch his blow;
If he got through unslain   'twere a fine thing.
Then he suffered her pleading   and let her speak.

He ends by accepting the lace and concealing it on his
person. That evening he gives the Lord the three kisses
but says nothing of the lace. After the merry-making
that night they say farewell, as Gawaine is to leave
early next morning for the Green Chapel.

Now nighs the New Year   and the night passes,
                                                                    1998

Day breaks in the dark   as the Lord bids it,
But wild weathers of the world   were awake
    thereout,
Clouds casting keenly   the cold to the earth
With harm enough from the North,   bringing
    pain to the naked.
Snow shivered down sharply,   nipping the wild
    things;
The warbling wind   whipped from on high
And drove each dale   full of great drifts.
The knight listened full well   that lay in his bed.
Though he locked his lids   full little he slept;
By each cock that crew   he knew full well the time.
Swiftly he dressed   ere the day sprang,
For there was light from a lamp   lit in his
    chamber.
He called to his chamberlain   that answered
    promptly,
And bade bring his byrnie   and saddle his horse.
So the other got up   and fetched his garments,
And got Gawaine ready   in fine fashion.
First he clad him in his clothes   to keep out the
    cold,
And then in his harness   that was kept hand-
    somely,
Both his paunce and his plates   polished full clean,
The rings rubbed of their rust   in his rich byrnie,
And all was fresh as at first.   He said fair thanks
                For the deed.
        He had on every piece;
        Cleaned full well each weed.
        The gayest from here to Greece,
        The Knight called for his steed.

Gawaine rides through the snowy countryside with his retainer, who does his best to dissuade him from encountering his foe. As they come near to their destination the retainer bids him goodbye and rides away. Gawaine looks about for the Green Chapel.

Soon away in a field a hill he saw,   2171
A swelling mound by a bank of a brimming
  stream,
By the falls of a flood that flowed there.
The burn blubbered therein as if it were boiling.
The Knight turned his horse and came to the hill,
Lighted down gracefully and to a limb tied
The reins of his steed, to a rough branch.
Then he hied to the hill, about it he walked,
Debating with himself what it might be.
It had a hole on the end and on the other side,
Overgrown with grass in patches everywhere.
All was hollow within, an old cave
Or a crevice of an old crag, he could not deem
  which,
     Or dream.
  "Wey! Lord!" quoth the gentle Knight,
  "Is this the Chapel Green?
  Here, about midnight,
  Might the devil at Matins be seen."

"Now indeed," quoth Gawaine, "it is grim
  enough here.
This oratory is ugly, with herbs overgrown.
Well it beseems the creature clothed all in green
To make his devotions in the devil's wise.
Now I feel it is the fiend in my five wits
That has staked his chance to strike me here.

This is a chapel of mischance,   may bad luck
    mar it!
This is the cursedest kirk   that ever I came in."
With high helm on head,   his lance in his hand,
He roamed up to the rock   of the rough dwelling.
Then heard he from a high hill   on a hard rock
Beyond the brook, on a bank,   a marvellous
    great noise.
What! It clattered on the cliff   as though to
    cleave it,
As if on a grind-stone   a scythe was ground.
What! It roared and whetted   as water at a mill;
What! It rushed and roared   with a ringing
    sound.
Then, "By God," quoth Gawaine,   "that gear,
    as I guess,
Is a fine greeting   to give to a Knight
                On this spot.
        Let God work! Weh lo!
        Sighing will help me not.
        My life though I forego
        Noise frightens me no jot."

Then the good Knight   called full high:
"Who is master in this place   to keep his promise?
For now Gawaine the Good   is come right here.
If anyone wills ought,   come hither fast—
It is now or never—   his need to speed."
"Abide!" quoth one on the bank   above his head,
"Thou shalt have all in haste   that I promised
    once."
Yet the noise went on rushing   roughly a while,
As he turned to his whetting   ere he would light.
Then he came by a crag   out of a hole,

Whirling out of a nook   with a fierce weapon,
A Danish axe new dight   to give the dint with,
With a huge edge   level with the handle
Filed on the grind-stone,   four feet large.
It was no less by the lace   that gleamed full
   bright,
And the man in green,   geared as at first,
The face and the legs,   the locks and beard,
Save that fair on his feet   he kept to the earth.
He set the steel on the stone   and stalked beside;
When he came to the water   he would not wade,
He hopped over on his axe   and quickly strode
Stoutly fierce on a field   that broad lay about them
         On the snow.
    Sir Gawaine the Knight did he meet,
    Who bowed nothing low.
    The other said, "Now, Sir Sweet,
    Thou'lt keep thy word, I trow."

Gawaine then bows his head for the blow. The other
raises his axe and brings it down, only to draw it back.
Gawaine had winced. A second time he whirls the great
blade, and withdraws it just before it entered the
Knight's neck.

Gawaine full angrily   with wrath then said: **2299**
"Why, thresh on, thou fierce man,   thou
   threatenest too long,
I expect thou art afraid,   thine own self."
"Forsooth," quoth the man,   "so boldly thou
   speakest,
I will no longer linger   or delay thy business
         Right now."
    Then he stands firm for the blow
    And frounces both lip and brow,

No marvel if the other mislike
Who looked for no rescue now.

He lifted lightly his blade   and let it down fair
With the barbed edge that bit   on the bare neck;
Though he struck hard   he hurt him no more,
But nicked him as he dallied,   and severed the
     skin.
The sharp edge shrank to the flesh   through the
     sheer grease,
Sheen blood over his shoulders   shot to the earth.
And when the Knight saw the blood   gleam on
     the snow,
He sprang forth, span-foot,   more than a spear-
     length,
Took hastily his helm   and on his head cast it,
Shot both his shoulders   under his fair shield,
Drew out a bright sword   and boldly spoke.
Never since the man   had been born of his mother
Was he ever in this world   half so blithe:
"Cease, man, thy blows,   bid me no more!
In this place I have taken   a stroke without strife.
If you give me any more   I shall quickly requite,
And pay them back again   —trust you in that—
          And fierce ones, lo!
     But one stroke was here to fall,
     The covenant was made so,
     Formed in Arthur's hall,
     Therefore, good Sir, now ho!"

The Green Knight leans on his axe and laughs, then
explains the strange situation:

"First I threatened thee merrily   with one blow,
          2345

And withheld it with no sore; this I gave thee
For the bargain that we made on the first night.
Thou didst keep to the truth, and truly pay me,
Gavest me all the gain, as a good man should.
The other blow for the morn, man, I pretended
 to give thee,
When you kissed my clear wife, the kisses you
 gave me.
For both these I dealt thee but two bare strokes
   Without blow.
  A true man truly brave
  You need have feared no woe.
  But that last tap I gave
  Since you failed at the third go.

For it is my weed you are wearing, that woven
 girdle,
My own wife weaved it, I know it for truth.
I knew well thy kisses and thy ways also,
And the wooing of my wife —I wrought it
 myself.
I sent her to try thee, and truly methinks
Thou art the most faultless man that walks on
 his feet.
As a pearl by white peas is of more price,
So is Gawaine, in good faith, by other knights.
But you lacked a little, Sir, and wanted loyalty,
But for no wicked work nor wooing either
But for love of your life— the less I blame you."

Gawaine bows his head in shame; the Green Knight
laughs and says that he is Bercilak de Hautdesert,
Lord of the castle, and Gawaine's host. The whole adventure had been planned by the old woman who is in
reality Morgane the Enchantress, who had hoped by

it to terrify Queen Guinevere, whom she hates. He
begs Gawaine to return to the Castle with him. The
Knight refuses, but begs leave to keep the green lace
in memory of his adventure. He rides back to Arthur's
court, shows the lace before the whole court, and confesses his unknightly deed in concealing it.

The King comforted the Knight,　　and the court
　　also　　　　　　　　　　　　　　　　　　　2513
Laughed loudly thereat;　　and accorded in lovely
　　wise
The Lords and Ladies　　who belonged to the
　　Table,
That each of the brotherhood　　a bauldric should
　　have
Bound obliquely about him　　of bright green,
And for the sake of the Knight　　to wear it as
　　he did.[4]
And honor it had　　for ever more after
As it is written　　in the best books of romance.
Thus in Arthur's day　　this adventure befell,
And the Brut books　　bear witness thereof,
Since Brutus the bold man　　abode here first
When the siege and the assault　　had ceased at
　　Troy.
　　　　　　　　　　Iwis
　　　　Many adventures borne
　　　　Have befallen such ere this;
　　　　Now may He that wore crown of thorn
　　　　Bring us to His bliss. Amen.

　　　　Hony soyt qui mal pence.

[4] This episode may be connected with the foundation of the Order of
the Garter, c.1845. The proverb with which the poem closes is the motto
of the Order.

CLEANNESS

Mediaeval writers were frankly eager to "adorn a moral and to point a tale." The didactic and the pleasurable elements of art were felt to be inseparable; a successful blending of the two depended upon the artist. In *Sir Gawaine,* the poet let the rapid interest of good narrative bring home his lesson concerning the attractiveness of cleanly courtesey. In his two homiletic poems he began with the lesson, then pictured its truth in narrative. Each of these lengthy, lively sermons in verse is written in the old alliterative metre, but its usual formless movement is here cut sharply into quatrains.

Cleanness is a study in God's treatment of sinful man. The prologue declares that God is "so clean in His court" that all who come before Him must be found clad "in weeds full bright," as Christ said in the parable of the marriage feast, and so, "Thou mayest become pure through penance, till thou art a pearl." Three great scenes from the Old Testament are presented to bear out this truth: the deluge, the destruction of Sodom and Gomorrah, and Belshazzar's feast —each with dramatic possibilities. They are woven together with other illustrations, and with charming, casual and convincingly theological comments. The Vulgate is the poet's main source, but not a little of the color and light that plays over his earnestness comes from his acquaintance with *Mandeville's Travels,* the *Book of the Knight of the Tour Landry,* and Clopingel's *Clean Rose.* He strikes at sin with honest abhorrence of its essential discourtesey to "our lovely Lord," and with equally honest delight in the exciting stories, whose pictures and persons are drawn with the sureness of a literary Giotto.

Old Abraham in his land   alone he sits,   601
Even before his house door,   under an oak green.
Bright glittered the beams   of the broad heaven;
In the high heat thereof   Abraham bided.

He was sheltered by shadows   under sheer leaves
When he was aware on the way   of three noble
    beings.
That they were gracious and free   and fair to
    behold
It is easy to believe   by what came to pass.

For the man that there lay   under the leaves,
When he had sight of them,   hastened straight-
    way,
And as to God the good man   got up before them,
And hailed them in One-head   and said,
    "Gracious Lord,

"If thy servant on earth   has deserved merit
Linger with him a little,   I lowly beseech.
Pass not by thy poor one,   if I dare pray it,
Ere thou hast bided with him   and under boughs
    rested.

"I shall willingly bring you   a little water
And fast fare about   to wash your feet.
Rest here by this root,   and I shall make ready
And bring a morsel of bread   as balm to your
    heart."

"Fare forth," quoth they,   "and fetch as thou
    sayest;
By the bole of this broad tree   abide we here."
Then hurriedly into his house   he hied to Sarah,
Commanded her to be clever   and quick for once.

"Three measures of meal   mingle and make cakes,
Under ashes full hot   hide them straight.
While I fetch something fat   stir thou the fire,
Prompt at this point   to make some pottage."

He went to the cow house   and brought a calf
That was tender and not tough,   and tore off the hide
And bade his servant   fast to boil it,
And he at his word   deftly did it.

The man then made haste   to bare his head,
Took a clean cloth   and cast it on the green,
Threw thriftily thereon   three unleavened cakes,
Brought butter withal   and by the bread set it.

Meet measures of milk   he put between,
And then the pottage   in a fair platter.
As a steward in goodly wise   he served them fair,
With serious and sweet manner,   of such as he had.

And God as a glad guest   made good cheer,
Was fain of His friend   and the feast praised.
Abraham all hoodless,   with arms folded,
Ministered meat before Him   Who all might wields.

God then foretells to Abraham the destruction of Sodom and Gomorrah. Abraham asks that his brother Lot may be spared, and God promises to warn him.

His message into Sodom   was sent in that time,
     781
That very evening,   by angels twain
Moving meekly together   as merry men young,
As Lot at his lodge desk   leaned all alone

In a porch of that place,   nigh to the gates,
Royal and rich   as the owner himself.
As he stared into the street   where strong men
    played
He saw walking together   those sweet men twain.

Fine youths were they both   with beardless chins,
Royal, rolling hair,   like to raw silk;
Of hue as the briar-flower   was their bright skin,
Full clean was the look   of their clear eyes.

Proud white were their robes,   and well became
    them,
In all features full fine,   and faultless both,
Nought awry in either,   for angels they were,
As soon he understood   who sat in the gates.

Rapidly he rose   and ran to meet them,
And lowly he bowed down,   Lot, to the ground,
And then said soberly,   "Sirs, I beseech you,
Light at my lodge   and linger therein.

"Come to your servant's cot,   I crave it this once;
I shall fetch you a vessel   to wash your feet.
I long for you one night   nigh me to linger,
And in the merry morning.   you may take your
    way."

And they said nay,   for they wanted no house,
But still in the street   where they were standing
They would linger the long night   and lodge
    thereout;
House enough for them   was the heaven above.

Lot urged them so long   with loving words
That they granted him that   and grudged no
    longer.

Into his building   he brought them straight,
Royally arrayed,   for he was rich ever.

That night the angels warn Lot's household that they
must flee.

The angels by the hand   had them out of the
     gates,   941
Preaching the peril,   bidding them pass fast,
"Lest ye be taken in the fall   of the tyrants here,
Bow to my bidding   and hasten hence."

And they argued not,   but swiftly they flew;
Early, ere heaven-gleam,   they came to a hill.
The great God in grimness   began above
To waken wild weathers,   the winds he called.

And they wrathfully wafted up   and wrestled
     together,
From earth's four corners,   quarrelling loud.
The clustering clouds   were cast up in towers,
Where the thick thunder blasts   pierced them
     through.

The rain reeled down,   sifted thick
With flashes of fire   and flakes of sulphur,
All in smoldering smoke,   smacking full ill
It swathed Sodom   on every side.

It struck into Gomorrah   and loosened the
     ground,
Abdama and Sybeym,   these cities all four
Be-rolled in the rain,   roasted and burned,
And fearfully were the folk   afraid in those
     lands.

For when hell heard   the hounds of heaven,
It was fain thereof,   and unfolded straight.

The great bars of the abyss   it burst up at once,
All the regions were riven   in rifts full great.

And cloven all in little clouts   were the cliffs
     everywhere,
Like loosened leaves of a book   that is torn in
     twain;
The breath of the brimstone   blended with it
And the lands and cities   sank into hell.

In the epilogue, the poet returns to the homely, fundamental, gracious *moralitas* that he has been unfolding:

Thus in three ways   I have shown you through-
     out   1805
That uncleanness cleaves deep   into the dear heart
Of that delightful Lord   Who dwells up in
     heaven,
Entices Him to anger   and wakes up His wrath.

And cleanness is His comfort,   and courteous
     ways He loves,
And they that seemly are,   shunning softness, see
     His face.
May He send us this grace: to go gay in our gear,
That we may serve in His sight,   where solace
     never ends.

PATIENCE

One day the poet, as he tells us in the prologue to
this "divine comedy," was at High Mass on a holyday,
and heard how Our Lord taught us that "poverty and
patience are playfellows." The thought of Jonas leaped
to his mind. So he tells the tale of the restive prophet
who learned by the hard way that submission to
God's will is best, and the sooner the better. The word

"patience" then meant more than it does now; it included the philosophic notion of "receiving the action of another"; agent and patient, action and passion are fundamental notions in Saint Thomas. Jonas must be shaped by God into an instrument fit for His hand. He kicks at first, and the events recorded in the Bible are the result. They are paraphrased by the poet with daring, sympathetic humor, with a pictorial vividness that anticipates modern realism, and with words that rise to great music. He shows God coming close, in loving familiarity to His naughty children, even good-humoredly using their racy colloquialisms.

It befell on a time   in the land of Juda   61
That Jonas was enjoined therein,   —gentle prophet.
God's call came to him,   unglad it made him;
Harshly was the word   whispered in his ear.

"Rise rapidly," He said,   "and go forth straight;
Take the way to Nineveh   without more talk,
And in that city sow   my sayings all about
At the point in that place   that I put in thy heart.

"For iwis they are so wicked   that live in that dwelling,
And their malice is so much   that I may not abide it,
But must venge me on their villainy   and venom at once;
Now go thither swiftly   and say this errand."

When the voice was still   stunned was his mind.
He grew wrathful in his wit   and wildly he thought:
"If I bow to His bidding   and bring this tale,

And be taken to Nineveh,   my troubles begin.

"He tells me those traitors   are tip-top shrews.
If I come with these tidings   they'll take me
    straight,
Pin me in a prison,   put me in stocks,
Torture me in tight fetters,   take out my eyes.

"This is a marvellous message   for a man to
    preach
Among enemies so many   and miserable fiends!
But if my gracious God   such grief wills for me,
For the sake of some sin   wants me slain,

"At all perils," quoth the Prophet,   "I approach
    it no nearer,
I shall go some other way   that He watches not
    over.
I shall take me to Tarsus   and tarry there a while,
And lightly, when I'm lost,   He'll leave me alone."

Then he rises rapidly   and goes at once,
Jonas towards the port Japha,   jangling with
    temper;
For nothing would he put up   with any of those
    pains,
Though the Father that formed him   made cheap
    of his weal.

"Our Sire sits," he said,   "on a seat so high
In His glowing glory,   and is little gloomy
Though I be taken in Nineveh   and naked
    despoiled,
On a rood sadly rent   by many ribalds."

Thus he passes to the port   his passage to seek,
Finds he a fair ship   ready for faring,

Matches with the mariners,   makes their pay
To tow him to Tarsus   as quick as they might.

Then he took to the deck   and they handled their
   tackle,
Caught up at the cross-sail,   cables they fastened,
Nimbly at the windlass   they weighed their
   anchors,
Spread sprightly to the bow-sprit   the spare bow-
   line.

They gathered up the guide rope,   the great cloth
   falls.
They laid in on larboard,   they luffed about;
The blithe breath at their back   the broad sail fills
And swings the sweet ship   swift from the haven.

Was never so joyful a Jew   as Jonas was then,
That the danger of the Lord   was so doughtily
   escaped.
He fancied that the One   that all the world
   formed
Had no might in that sea   any man to grieve.

Lo, the witless wretch,   since he would not suffer
He has put himself in plight   of a worse peril.
'Twas a foolish fancy   that he felt in his mind,
Though he were safe from Samaria,   that God
   saw no further. . . .

For the Wielder of wit,   wise in all things,   129
Ever wakes and waits;   at will He has ways.
He called on the creatures   He carved with His
   hand;
They wakened wrathfully,   for with wrath He
   called.

"Eurus and Aquilon,   that in the east sit,
Blow both at my bidding   upon wan waters."
Then was there no time   between His tale and
    their deed,
So ready were they both   to work His will.

Anon out of the north   the noise begins,
When both breaths blew   on the wan waters.
Rough rack rose   with redness thereunder,
The sea sighed full sore,   a marvel to hear.

The winds on the wan waters   so wrestled to-
    gether,
And the waves full wild   weltered so high
And then bowed to the abyss,   that frightened
    fishes
Durst no where for the roughness   rest at the
    bottom.

When the wind and the water   and the boat met,
It was a joyless brig   that Jonas was in,
For it reeled around   on the rough waves,
And the gale bore it aft   till it burst its gear.

Then were hurled in a heap   the helm and the
    stern.
First crashed many ropes   and the mast after,
The sail dipped to the sea,   then had to drink
Their craft of the cold water,   and then the cry
    rose.

Then cut they the cords   and cast all there out,
Many lads forth leaped   to lave and to cast,
To scoop out the wild water   that fain would
    escape;
For though man's lot be loathsome,   life is sweet.

They were busy overboard   their bales to cast,
Their bags and their feather-beds   and their
    bright weeds,
Their chests and their coffers   and their casks all,
To lighten the ship   if a chance should offer.

The sailors in desperation pray to their various gods,
and then decide to cast lots to see who is guilty of
crime, that they may cast him overboard.

There failed no man   that they might find   181
Save Jonas the Jew   who slept in the shadows.
He had fled for fear   of the flood sounds
To the bottom of the boat,   and on a board lay,

Holding on to the edge,   against heaven's
    vengeance,
He had slipped in slumber;   slobbering he snored.
A fellow poked him with his foot,   bade him
    perk up,
May Raguel[5] in his chains   raise him from dreams!

By the hair he took him   and held him then,
Brought him up by the breast,   and on the board
    set him,
Arraigned him full roughly,   what reason he had
In such straits of sorrow   to sleep so fast.

Soon they took their lots   and dealt them
    severally,
And aye the lots fell   at last on Jonas.
Then quickly they turned   and asked full loud,
"What the devil hast thou done,   doting wretch!"

---

[5] Raguel was the name of a popular devil in the Mystery Plays. Warlow,
occurring a few stanzas later, is another.

He acknowledges that he is a Hebrew, and confesses
his sin. They pity him and try to save the ship without
sacrificing him.

But in blubber of the black flood   burst their
     oars,   221
They had nought in their hands   to help them
     then,
No comfort and no counsel   could they find either
But to adjudge Jonas   to his justice straight.

By top and by toe   they took him then,
Into that loathly lake   they lurched him out;
No sooner had he tumbled in   than the tempest
     ceased,
And the sea grew meek   as soon as it might. . . .

Now is Jonas the Jew   adjudged to drown,   245
From the shattered ship   men shoved him out;
A wild wallowing whale,   as Wyrd[6] shaped it,
That was beaten from the bottom,   floated by the
     boat.

He was aware of the man   that sought the water,
And swiftly swung round   and opened to swallow.
While they still held his feet   the fish took him;
Without touch of tooth   he tumbled in his throat.

Then he swings and sways   to the sea-bottom,
By many rocks full rough   and shifting sands,
When the man in his maw   dazed with dread—
Little wonder it was   if he felt woe.

[6] *Wyrd* was the pagan Anglo-Saxons' name for Fate or Destiny. After
their conversion it came to mean Divine Providence, shaping human life.
Shakespeare found the word still in use in Scottish dialect, where it had
come to mean "magical," and his "weird sisters" gave it the current meaning of "strange or uncanny."

For had not high Heaven-King   through His
   hand's might
Warded the wretched man   in Warlow's guts,
Who might live there,   by law of any kind,
Or any life go on   so long within him?

But he was succored by that Sire   that sits so high,
Though hopeless of help   within that fish,
So driven through the deep,   in the dark
   wallowing.
Lord, cold was his comfort,   and his care huge!

For he knew each case   of what had come to him,
How from the boat in the blubber   a beast had
   caught him
And threw him in at his throat   without threat
   more,
As a mote through a minster door,   so wide were
   his jaws.

He glided in at the gills,   through gluey filth,
Reeling in by an opening   that seemed like a
   road,
Heels over head,   hurtling about
Till he stumbled into a space   as broad as a hall.

There he fastened his feet   and fumbled about,
And stood up in his stomach   that stank like the
   devil,
There in fat and in filth   that savored as hell
Was built his bower   who willed not to suffer. . . .

And as he sailed on   ever he heard   **331**
The great waters above,   beating at his side.
Then a prompt prayer   the prophet then made,
In this wise, as I ween;   his words were many:

"Lord, to Thee have I called   in cares full strong.
From the hole Thou hast heard me   in the depths
    of hell.
I called, and thou knewest   my hoarse voice;
Thou hast dipped me in the dim heart   of the deep
    sea.

"The flow of Thy flood   has folded me round,
All the moving gulfs   and the groundless deeps,
And Thy striving stream   of many strengths
In a dashing dam   are driving over me.

"Yet I said as I sat   on the sea-bottom,
Care-full, I am cast out   from Thy clear eyes,
And severed from Thy sight;   yet surely I hope
To tread again in Thy temple,   and keep tryst
    with Thee.

"I am wrapped in water,   to my stunned woe;
The abyss binds the body   that I abide in.
The pure rippling water   plays on my head;
I am fallen down   to the feet of the mountains. . . .

"When the access of anguish   was hid in my
    soul,   325
Then I remembered   my mighty Lord,
Praying Him for pity   to hear His prophet,
That into His holy House   my orison may
    enter." . . .

Then Our Father to the fish   gave fierce
    bidding   337
To spit him out straightway   on dry ground.
The whale went at His will   and found a shore
Where he brought up the man   as Our Lord
    bade him.

Then he drifted to the sand   in his soiled clothes;
It may well be that he needed   to wash his mantle.
The banks he beheld   and bided beside
Were of the very regions   that he had renounced.

Then a wind of God's word   reproached him
      there:
"Wilt thou never go to Nineveh,   no way at all?"
"Yes, Lord," quoth he,   "lend me but Thy grace
To go at Thy pleasure;   nought else pleases me."

Further lessons are taught him in Nineveh, and when
God spares the city, after all his preaching, the
Prophet at last learns the meaning of true patience.
God's final advice is:

"Be not so gruff, good man,   but go forth thy
      ways;
                                                              524
Be proved and be patient,   in pain and in joy.
For he that is too ready   to rend his clothes
Must sit down in worse ones   to sew them to-
      gether."

PEARL

At first reading, *Pearl* dazzles by its sheer brilliance
and intricacy; it is a necklace of rare design wrought
by "a gentle jeweller." The vocabulary flashes with
contrasting words, French and Scandinavian blended
with sterling Anglo-Saxon, words homely and remote, learned and popular, book-words and heart-
words. The stanza form, more elaborate even than
Spenser's, is probably Provençal in origin. It consists
of twelve lines in four-beat alliterative metre, with the
caesura almost obliterated, woven together by the
amazing rhyme-scheme of *a b a b a b a b b c b c*. The
one hundred and one stanzas fall into groups of five,

bound together by a common refrain in the last line, the key-word of which is caught up in the opening line of the following stanza; and these twenty clusters fall into a perfect pattern when the last line of the poem takes up the key-word of the first. The necklace is clasped.

The matter of the song is as brilliant as its manner, revealing the high cultivation of the author. Like a good Anglo-Norman he has wandered in the gardens of the *Romance of the Rose;* his opening stanza is guarded by Love-Danger, that allegorical figure that stood for aloofness between a man and his beloved. Like a good Anglo-Saxon he is steeped in the traditions that flow from the days of the Heptarchy; he knows Providence by its primeval name of *Wyrd*. Like a good European, in the days when the Holy Roman Empire made Europe one, he is widely read. Whether or no he borrowed from Dante, he was led to heaven by a maiden; Pearl was his Beatrice, who is also heavenly Wisdom. Whether or no he borrowed from the *Fourteenth Eclogue* of Boccaccio, he knew the comfort of a human face smiling at him from near Paradise; Pearl was his Olympia. There is no doubt of his borrowing from the Scriptures, and from the theological and homiletic learning of the Schools, for the Psalter, the Parables of the Gospel, and above all the Apocalypse, are the stuff of his thought and the color of his sight. Most of all, like a good mediaevalist, allegory was his natural language.

But in speaking that language he was not conventional but highly personal. Independently, he falls asleep in August, not in May, and the story of what he dreamed is in the nature of a confidence. He tells of his sorrow at the loss of Pearl, of her radiant appearing to him, of her words of wisdom on the things that matter most, of the glimpse she granted him of the New Jerusalem. Finally, he tells of his mad attempt to cross the severing streams before his time had come, and of his awakening, wise and comforted and submissive.

Modern interpreters of his hidden meanings have asked themselves: is this poem an allegory, or an elegy, or both? Is the poet actually the bereaved father of a little girl who died at the age of two, and who appears to him in the ageless maturity of her heavenly life? Or is he a monk who has lost, after two blissful years, the sweetness that he had clung to in prayer, and who is taught peace in dryness through a vision of the glory to come? Or is he a preacher who wishes to teach, through this dream-device, lessons of the spiritual life and of the workings of grace?[7]

These questions may never be answered, but the poem remains. Catholic poetry is a many-dimensional thing, and its dimensions are no more separable than the length and breadth and height of a cube. Earthly events may well be the groundwork of mystical experience, and both are but revealings of immutable doctrine. Pearl has been claimed as a poem of Our Lady, a poem of the Blessed Sacrament, a poem on grace and free will. It is all of these, and is also a personal poem. It is the poem of a man, and thus a lyric *Everyman*. For whether the poet is a bereaved father

[7] All the early editors and critics assumed the literal interpretation, that the poem is the elegy of a bereaved father. Chief in interest and importance among more recent interpretations is that of Sister Madeleva, given in *Pearl: A Study in Spiritual Dryness*. She discards the elegiac theory; the poem is an allegory of the state of soul of a monk, "a perfectly consistent exposition, revelation, and ecstatic climax of spiritual 'blues'," studied against a richly documented background of mediaeval spiritual writings.

or a cloistered mystic finding his way through dark
purifications, the path that he takes is the same. It is
the path from grief to peace, from earth to heaven,
along which Everyman is stumbling.

Chaucer smiled mischievously at evil; Langland
stormed and wept over it. Was the Pearl Poet an
escapist, dreaming of a land bright enough to blind
him to trouble? Hardly. From his poem emerges a
central truth, one upon which the theology and spirituality of today are concentrating—the truth of the
Mystical Body:

> Members of Jesus Christ are we.
> So is each Christian soul a limb
> Joined to His Body full certainly.

In that unity with Christ, the poet lonely for Pearl in
his arbor of death is one with those who have suffered
loss; the eager poet drawn on by loveliness to Love
till he crosses the separating stream, is all those who
will take rebuke, be cleansed, do God's will. And when
he sees the New Jerusalem in a light more bright than
sun or moon, he is all those who know that heaven is
more real than earth. The Pearl Poet saw it so.

> Pearl, pleasant for princes' play,   1
> Cleanly closed in gold so clear,
> Out of Orient, I dare say,
> Found I never her precious peer;
> So round, so radiant in every way,
> So small, so smooth her facets were,
> Wherever I judged of jewels gay
> Apart I set her, single and dear.
> Alas, I lost her in an arbor here
> Through grass to ground; I found her not.

I pine away in love and fear
For my own Pearl without a spot. . . .

From such a spot must spices spread;   25
Where such richness to rot has run
Blossoms pale and blue and red
Now shine full sheen against the sun.
Flower and fruit have never fled
Where it drove down in the mould dun,
For grass must grow from grain that is dead,
Else no harvest were ever won.
Each good from good is aye begun;
So seemly a seed will fail us not,
And springing spices will ne'er have done
From that precious Pearl without a spot.

And in that spot of great renown
I entered, in an arbor green,
In August, in high season
When corn is cut with curved blades keen.
The hill where my Pearl had fallen down
Was shadowed with foliage sheer and sheen,
Gillyflowers, ginger and gremillon
With peonies powdered in between—
Place seemly for her it must have been,
A floating fragrance failed it not.
She dwells there worthily, I ween,
My precious Pearl without a spot.

Hands clasped, before that place I lay;
In care and cold was my soul caught,
A deafening din in my heart astray,
Though reason held the peace I sought.
I mourned for my Pearl that was shut away
With reckless words that fiercely fought.

In Christ Himself my comfort lay,
But my wretched will wrongfully wrought.
I fell upon the flowers, distraught;
Their odors through my senses stole.
I slid into slumbering that brought
Dreams of my Pearl, spotless, whole.

From that spot my spirit sprang in space,
Adream on the mound left my body, free.
My ghost had gone, by God's grace,
Adventuring where marvels be.
In this world I knew never such a place,
But I know that cliffs rose toweringly.
Towards a forest I turned my face
Where the rich rocks I could see.
Men scarce might think such a light could be,
The gleaming glory that glowed there;
For webs were ne'er woven more wondrously
Nor half so rich as that splendor fair.

Fair are all the down-sides
With crystal cliffs that climb on high;
A holt-wood bright about them bides
With boles as blue as Indian dye.
Like burnished silver each leaf slides,
Quivering on boughs they thickly lie;
When the glinting gleam against them glides
With shimmering sheen they shine on high.
The gravel I ground on the strand thereby
Was all of Orient pearls rare.
Dim and dark were sunbeams nigh
To the glowing of that splendor fair. . . .

The splendors of the fair stream deep   **109**
Were its precious banks of beryl bright.

Sweetly rushing, the waters' sweep
Made a whispering sound in their wandering flight.
The water-depths the clear stones keep
That gleamed as through glass; they glowed alight,
As streaming stars when earth-men sleep
Stare in the welkin on winter night.
For every pebble in the pool so bright
Was emerald, sapphire, or gem rare,
Till all the water shone with the light,
So wondrous was that splendor fair. . . .

More marvels then adaunted me.   **157**
I saw beyond that merry stream
A crystal cliff rise shiningly;
Royal rays shone out, agleam.
At its foot sat a child, fair to see,
A maiden of grace, full debonaire.
Dazzling white was her robe so free;
I knew her well, I had seen her ere.
As glistening gold, refined and rare,
So shone that sheen one by the shore.
Long I looked upon her there,
And ever I knew her more and more.

The more I gazed on her fair face
That gracious form I seemed to know,
And a gladdening glory came to embrace
Me who had little known but woe.
I longed to call her name of grace
But wonder gave my heart a blow;
To see her in so strange a place
Made my heart too stunned to know.
She lifted up her face aglow,
White as ivory by the shore;

It stung my wild heart straying so,
And ever the longer ever the more.

More than I wished my dread arose;
I stood full still and dared not call.
With open eyes and mouth held close
I stood as quiet as hawk in hall.
A ghostly meaning it would disclose;
I dreaded what might then befall,
Lest she escape me whom I chose
Ere I could hold her for good and all.
That gracious gay one without gall,
So smooth, so small, so seemly and slight,
Rose up in array royal
As a precious thing in fair pearls dight.

Pearls set right royally
Favored men might there have seen,
When she, fresh as a fleur-de-lys,
Down the bank came like a queen.
All glistening white her garments free,
Open at sides and bordered clean
With the merriest pearls set generously,
The loveliest that have ever been;
Sleeves large and hanging, as I ween,
Bedecked with double pearls of white;
Her kirtle of the same rich sheen
With precious pearls was all bedight.

She wore a crown, that lovely girl,
Of margarites and no other stone,
High pinnacled of clear white pearl
With figured flowers wrought thereon;
No other head-piece save the curl
Of soft hair hanging down, long-grown.

Her look was grave, like a duke or earl,
Her skin more white than whale's bone,
As shorn gold sheer her hair shone
Upon her shoulders soft and light.
Her glowing beauty deep in tone
Set off her pearls with richness dight. . . .

So dight in pearls that precious piece   229
Beyond the water walked toward me.
No gladder man from here to Greece
Than I was then; I knew that she
Was nearer to me than aunt or niece.
The greater was my joy to be
When that precious creature spoke with peace,
Inclining low, so womanly.
She raised her rich crown, fair to see,
And hailed me with a gesture light.
Well was it then with happy me
To answer that Sweet in pearls dight.

"O Pearl," quoth I, "in pearls bedight,
Art thou my Pearl for whom I long
And mourn for all alone at night?
Much have I missed thee, grieving strong
Since in the grass thou hast slipped from sight;
Pensive, broken, in pain so long,
And thou in a life of joy and light,
Paradise, without strife or wrong!
What Wyrd snatched my Jewel from the throng
And tore us thus apart? Since we
To one another should belong,
A joyless jeweller must I be."

That Jewel then, in gems fair,
Lifted her face with its eyes of grey,

Put on her crown of Orient rare
And gravely then began to say:
"Sir, thy tale is misread there,
To say your Pearl has gone away,
Who in her coffer of precious ware
Lives in this garden of grace so gay,
Herein to dwell forever and play
Where miss and mourning never were;
Here is thy treasure all the day,
Wert thou but a gentle jeweller.

"But, gentle Jeweller, if thou lose
Thy joy for a gem that was dear to thee,
Methinks but madly thou dost choose,
And ruest thy loss unreasoningly.
For what thou hast lost was but a rose
That flowered and failed, as its kind must be,
But a precious casket must now enclose
What is to a pearl changed peerlessly.
Thou hast called thy Wyrd a thief, but He
Whom thou blamest in thy wild anger
From thy undoing brings light to thee;
Thou art but a graceless jeweller!"

He then pours out the tale of his suffering and
struggles and begs to be allowed to come to her beyond
the stream. She gently rebukes and then comforts him;
he asks her to tell him about her life.

"A blissful life here have I led,   409
The state thereof I will not hide.
Thou knowest well when thy Pearl lay dead
I was full young, by age untried.
But my Lord the Lamb, through His Godhead
Has taken me to be His bride,

Crowned me Queen in His fair homestead
For length of days in bliss to bide.
My heritage reaches far and wide
As His dear one. I am wholly His;
His praise, His price is all my pride
And the root and ground of all my bliss."

"Blissful," quoth I, "may this be true?
Be not displeased if I speak error.
Art thou the Queen of heavens blue
To whom this world must do honor?
We trust in Mary from whom grace grew,
Who bare a Child from Virgin Flower;
Who could her sovereignty undo
Save one who is higher in favor?
And for the peerlessness of her
We call her Phoenix of Araby,
Who perfect flew in high honor,
Like to that Queen of Courtesey."

"Courteous Queen," that sweet one said—
Kneeling to ground she bent her face—
"Matchless Mother, merriest Maid,
Blessed beginner of every grace!"
Then rose she up and a little stayed,
Speaking towards me across that space:
"Sir, men have joy here unafraid,
For no supplanters are in this place.
Our Empress has all heaven's grace,
And earth and hell she holds in fee.
None from her home will she displace,
For she is Queen of Courtesey.

"The court of the kingdom of God alive
Has a property of its own being:

Each soul that may therein arrive
Of all the realm is queen or king.
And none shall another e'er deprive,
But each is glad of the other's having,
And would that their crowns were worth five,
If possible were their enhancing.
But my Lady of whom Jesus did spring
Holds empire over all that be,
And she displeases us in no thing,
For she is Queen of Courtesey.

"As says Saint Paul, by courtesey
As head or arm or leg of Him
Members of Jesus Christ are we.
So is each Christian soul a limb
Joined to His Body full certainly.
To the Master of might we all belong.
Lo now, what hate or guile can be
Between the limbs that are knit so strong?
The head feels neither grief nor wrong
If on arm or finger a ring it see;
So fare we all in love and song
As kings and queens in courtesey." . . .

"That courtesey is too free of deed,   481
—If this be true which thou dost say—
Two years in our land was life thine to lead;
Thou couldst neither please God nor pray,
Thou couldst neither say Pater nor Creed,
And now made a Queen on the first day!
I cannot believe—so God me speed—
That God would work in so strange a way.
To a countess or damozel, *par ma fay,*
'Twere much in heaven to even come nigh,

Or else a lady of less degree,
But a Queen! That is a goal too high."

She answers his problems by explaining the parable
of the laborers in the vineyard, and says that innocence
is as precious in God's eyes as penance.

"You know that God made mankind meet   **637**
To dwell in bliss and perfect light.
Our first father lost that seat
When the apple tempted him to bite.
We were all damned for that meat
To die in dolour, far from delight,
Thence to wend into hell's heat
Therein to dwell in his despite.
But soon there came our ransom right,
Rich blood ran on rood so rough
And winsome water; in that plight
The grace of God waxed great enough.

"Enough there rose from out that well,
Blood and water from the broad wound;
The blood has bought us from bale of hell,
From the second death has saved us sound.
The water is baptism, sooth to tell;
It followed the sword so grimly ground,
And washed us till that guilt fell
That us with Adam in death nigh drowned.
Now is there nought in the world round
Between us and bliss; He withdrew His rod.
For all that was lost has now been found,
And great enough is the grace of God."

She speaks long on this theme of the Redemption and
love; then the dreamer resumes his questions:

"O spotless Pearl in pearls rare,   745
Who bears," quoth I, "the pearl of grace,
Who formed for thee thy figure fair?
Who wrought thy robe? Full wise he was.
Thy beauty came not from nature's share,
Pygmalion painted not thy face,
Nor did Aristotle of wisdom rare
Write of thy virtues in any place.
As the fleur-de-lys thy color; I trace
Thy angel-bearing gracious and clean.
Tell me, Bright One, of thy peaceful grace
That bears the pearl of spotless sheen."

"My spotless Lamb who makes all complete,"
Quoth she, "my own dear Destiny,
Chose me as His mate, although unmeet
Might such a union seem to be.
When I left your world of tears and sleet
In goodliness He called to me,
'Come hither, my own true love sweet,
For mote or spot is none in thee.'
He gave me might, and my beauty;
In His blood He washed my robe anew,
Crowned me in clean virginity
And set me with pearls of spotless hue.". . .

"Of Jerusalem I now may tell,   793
If thou wilt know what kind is He,
My lamb, My Lord, my dear Jewel,
My Joy, my bliss, my Sweetheart free.
Isaias said of Him so well,
—Of His debonaireness in great pity—
'That Glorious Guiltless whom they will fell
Without any cause for villainy,
As sheep to the slaughter led will be,

Like a Lamb that the clipper comes to claim.
He shall close His mouth at each query
When Jews judge Him in Jerusalem.' . . .

"This Jerusalem Lamb had never a stain   841
Of any other hue save white;
No mark or touch had ever lain
On the white wool so rich and bright.
And each soul that spotless can remain
Is to the Lamb a worthy wife,
And though each day he bring more again
Among us is never ill-will or strife.
We wish that every one were five,
The more the merrier, so may God bless!
In company will our love thrive,
In honor the more and never less."

She continues her description of the New Jerusalem
until he begs to be allowed to at least see it, even if
he cannot enter it yet.

"Spotless maiden, meek and mild,"   961
Then said I to that lovely flower,
"To that blissful dwelling bring me, Child,
And let me see thy blessed bower."
That sheen one said, "Thou art too wild,
Thou mayest not enter within God's tower,
But a sight of His dwelling undefiled
The Lamb will give thee, by great favor.
From without thou shalt see that clean cloister,
But within it one foot thou comest not;
To walk in that street thou hast no power
Save thou wert clean without a spot.

"If thou wilt have me this place unhide,
Go where the river rises free,

And I along the other side
To that distant hill will follow thee."
No longer then would I abide;
Neath leafy branches quietly
I walked till on a hill I spied
A burgh, and then gazed wonderingly.
Beyond the brookside, far from me,
With rays more bright than sun it shone,
As in the Apocalypse we see
Pictured by the Apostle John.". . .

A description of the New Jerusalem follows that is
a close paraphrase of the Apocalypse, till at last he
sees into the heart of the City.

They had no need of sun or moon,   1045
The very God was their lamplight,
The Lamb their lantern, like the noon;
Through Him the City gleamed so bright.
Through walls and dwellings my look pierced soon,
It was so clear nought hindered sight.
The throne stood there, its splendor strewn
With rich adornment, of great height.
John the Apostle in that light
Saw the High God Himself thereon.
A river ran from the throne outright;
Brighter than sun or moon it shone. . . .

The moon there may not grow in might,   1069
For spotty is she, of form too grim;
And in that place is never night—
Why should the moon her course there trim
And vie with that more worthy light
That shines upon the brook's brim?
The planets are in too poor a plight,

And the sun itself is far too dim.
About that water trees fair of limb
Bear the twelve fruits of life full soon;
Twelve times a year they bear for Him,
Their fruit renewing every moon. . . .

Right as the mighty moon will rise   1093
Before the day-gleam dies away,
So suddenly, in wondrous wise,
I saw a procession wend its way.
This noble City, this rich prize,
Was suddenly full, a fair display
Of virgins in the same guise
As was my Blissful in queen's array.
Crowned were they all in the same way,
Set off in pearls and robes of white.
On the breast of each was bound that day
The blissful pearl with great delight.

With delight they fared together there
On golden streets that gleamed as glass,
Hundreds of thousands I know there were
And all alike their livery was;
'Twere hard to choose those of gladdest cheer.
They saw the Lamb then proudly pass
With seven horns of red gold clear
Robed in pearl-white, as one who has
All precious things. Many a gracious lass
Pressed to the throne, before His sight;
Mild as modest maidens at Mass
So drew they on with great delight. . . .

Delighted on this Lamb to gaze   1129
My mind marvelled wonderingly.
Best was He, blithest, most to praise

Of any that we know to be.
White His robes were, simple His ways
And calm His looks. But I could see
A wound wide and wet always
Over His Heart, rent terribly.
From His white side the blood poured free.
Alas, thought I, who did that spite?
Burned alive should that foe be
Ere therein he had taken delight.

The Lamb's delight we well may ween,
Though He was hurt, and wide wounds had.
In His fair face pain was never seen,
Glorious was His glance, and glad.
I looked among His servants sheen,
Fulness of life was on them laid.
And there I saw my little Queen
Who I thought was nigh me in the glade.
Lord, much of mirth she there made
Among her comrades clothed in white.
Across the stream I longed to wade
For love-longing and great delight.

Delight so drove me, eye and ear
That with maddening thoughts my soul was tried.
When I saw my Precious I would be there
Beyond the water, by her side.
There was nothing that I would not dare,
Nothing held me; to rise and stride
Into the stream was all my care,
And to swim the rest although I died.
But I was halted in good tide.
When I started in the stream, astray,

I was recalled and bidden bide,
For that was not my Prince's way.

It pleased Him not that I rashly flew
To the marvellous stream, mad, unafraid;
A thing so rude and wild to do
That swiftly was my running stayed.
For just as to the bank I drew
I was startled from my dream-glade;
I woke in the arbor that I knew,
My head upon the hill was laid
Where once my Pearl to the ground strayed.
I roused myself and in dismay
Sighing to myself I said,
"Now may all be my Prince's way."

It pleased me ill from that fair place
To be cast out so suddenly,
From all those brave sights full of grace.
A longing held me heavily
And ruefully I cried a space:
"O Pearl," quoth I, "so rich to see,
How dear the presence of thy face
In this true vision given to me.
If it be true, and verily
Thou goest in a garland gay,
In this dungeon it is well with me
That thou pleasest thy Prince in His own way."

Had I been bent my Prince's way,
Yearned but for what He gave to me
And held me in His will to stay,
As my Pearl prayed me earnestly,
Into God's presence drawn that day
I would have pierced His mystery.

But oft men seize and bear away
More bliss than is theirs lawfully.
And so my joy was wrest from me,
An outcast from those high realms still.
Lord, mad are they who strive with Thee
Or reach for ought against Thy will.

To please that Prince is an easy way
For a Christian soul in peace to be,
For I have found Him night and day
A God, a Lord, a Friend to me.
Upon this hillside where I lay
Longing for Pearl so pensively,
I gave her into God's way,
In Christ's dear blessing, willingly,
Whom the Priest shows daily. It is He
Under the form of Bread and Wine;
And as servants in His home may we
As pleasant pearls before Him shine.

Behind the Signs

These were God's darlings.
THE LADDER OF PERFECTION

THE fourteenth century was an age of extremes; its restlessness kept men moving in one direction or another, and literature reflects their journeyings. Some friars landed in taverns, thorough scoundrels; satire quickly caught up with them, and sketched them in the act of selling their quack indulgences. Some laymen found their way into the court of heaven, and shining dream-allegories reflected their joy. All the while a small company of men and women, neither mendicants nor dreamers, lived apart and found reality behind the signs of the times. These were the contemplatives who travelled into "the cloud of unknowing," where literature followed them with a sure step.

It would require a more profound searching of Church History than can be here attempted to find

reasons for the flowering of mystical experience and
expression that occurred in many countries during
this paradoxical century. Suffice it to say that by some
law of compensation the worst and the best are usually
found to grow side by side in human grain fields. The
Babylonian Captivity and the Great Western Schism
—causes and effects of the current corruption of the
salt of the earth—produced confusion and discord
enough. They, also, in spite of themselves, produced
saints like Catherine of Siena to undo the mischief.
In England the ambiguous lives of Wycliffe and his
Lollards were counterbalanced by the strenuous and
lovable virtue, the unearthly clarity of life seen in
many a hermitage where recluses were writing books
because what they had to say was too good to keep
to themselves, and because "speech is God's gleeman,
and a game of heaven."

Though some of these writers "knew no letter," and
none of them made much of what learning they had,
their books represent an important phase in the history
of the development of mystical theology, stemming
back through Saint Augustine to pre-Christian philosophy, and reaching forward through the later Spanish mystics to our own day. Plato, the most poetic of
ancient philosophers, is at the starting-point of this
line of tradition. His parable[1] concerning "the world
of shadows and reality" was a symbolic expression, on
the plane of natural truth, of the problems concerning
that immediate perception of the divine by which
Christian contemplatives would later transmute theology into mysticism:

[1] *Republic,* Book VII.

If beings who have been chained in a cave with their backs to the light, accustomed to mistaking shadows on the wall for realities, are brought out into the day, they will not at first see. . . . When one of them approaches the light his eyes will be dazzled and he will not be able to see anything at all of what are now called realities. He must needs first grow accustomed to the upper world. And he will see the shadows best, next the reflections of men and other objects in the water, and then the objects themselves. Then he will gaze upon the light of the moon and the stars and the spangled heavens, and will he not see the stars by night better than the sun and the light of the sun by day? Last of all he will be able to see the sun, and not mere reflections of it in the water, but he will see it in its own proper place and not in another, and he will contemplate it as it is.

The lofty conceptions of Plato, transmitted by the writings of Plotinus and other neo-Platonists, molded the mind of Saint Augustine even before his conversion, and in him they were baptized. Augustine's philosophy, intensely intellectual as it was, burned with the ardor of his own passionate desire for God; constantly it overstepped the limits of the merely rational into realms of mystical experience where images yield to the uncreated Light, and where "in the flash of one trembling glance it arrived at That which Is." In his pages the great principles of mystical theology were first shaped to expression: the three "ways," the purgative, the illuminative, the unitive; the three kinds of visions, corporeal, imaginative and intellectual. Until the coming of Saint Thomas Aquinas eight centuries later, the love-shot lyrical thought of Saint Augustine

dominated the philosophy and the spiritual life of
Europe, where contemplatives who longed, like him,
"to love what they saw and possess what they loved,"
fed their minds on such passages as the following:

Late have I loved Thee, Beauty so old and so
new, late have I loved Thee! Behold, Thou wert
within, and I without; and there I sought Thee, and
I, so unlovely, fell on the lovely things that Thou
hast made. Thou wast with me, and I was not with
Thee. Those things kept me far from Thee, things
which, hadst Thou not been in them, would have had
no being. Thou didst call and cry out, and break in
on my deafness; Thou didst flash and shine, and
scatter my blindness. Thou wert fragrant; I have
breathed Thee and now I pant for Thee. I have
tasted, and I hunger and thirst. Thou hast touched
me, and now I burn for Thy peace.[2]

But shortly after Saint Augustine's day another influence came into western Europe from the East,
through the writings of the mysterious personage
known as the pseudo-Dionysius.[3] It was he who gave
to mystical theology one of the most widely used of all
its metaphors—the darkness into which the soul must
enter to find light:

O Trinity, super-essential, super-divine and super-
excellent, guide of the God-seeking thought of

[2] *Confessions*, Book X, Ch. 58.
[3] In the early ages, the works of this unknown writer were attributed
to Dionysius the Areopagite, mentioned in the *Acts of the Apostles*.
Later criticism has shown that he was probably a Christian neo-Platonist,
a Syrian of the sixth century. His works became current in Europe
through the Latin translation of Scotus Erigena, and Saint Thomas
Aquinas made extensive use of them. They include *Mystical Theology*,
Celestial Hierarchy, *Ecclesiastical Hierarchy*, *The Divine Names*, and
six letters.

Christians, lead us to the heights of those hidden and mystic places beyond knowledge and beyond light, where the simple, absolute and immutable mysteries of theology are revealed in that darkness-more-than-light of a silence that tells secret things, a silence that in darkness filled with shadows shines out with something more than light, and fills intangibly and invisibly with the splendors of the ultra-beautiful those minds whose eyes are held. . . . We long to come into this darkness beyond light, and by emptying of sight and knowledge to see and to know that which exists above vision and knowledge.[4]

The knowledge of the pseudo-Areopagite had been spread in the twelfth century by the "Victorines," Hugh and his disciple Richard, who were Augustinians of the Abbey of Saint Victor in Paris, a center of theology and mysticism at a time when the foundations of scholasticism were being laid at the University of Paris. Richard wrote of "that grade of love in which the mind of man is rapt into the abyss of divine light, so that, utterly forgetful of all exterior things, it knows not itself and passes wholly into its God."[5] At the same time Saint Bernard was fighting heresy, calling Crusades, and singing aloud to *"Jesu Dulcissime"* and to His beautiful Mother. It was the simple, piercing lyricism of Saint Bernard, moving along the same lines of allegory and exegesis as the more formal theologians, that stirred the mystics of the fourteenth century most effectively, for even the "unlettered" could understand the outpourings of the lover who knew of God's presence "only by the movement of my heart."

[4] *Mystical Theology I and II.*
[5] *De Quatuor Gradibus Violentiae Caritatis.*

In the meantime, the greatest theologian of them all had come, and had done for Aristotle what Saint Augustine had done for Plato, but it took time for the more austere writings of Saint Thomas Aquinas to permeate the familiar thought of the wayside contemplatives, and the influence of the *De Veritate* is less evident in their works.

The influence of this long line of spiritual writers flowered simultaneously in many lands in the fourteenth century, especially in Germany and the Low Countries. Blessed John Ruysbroeck, under his beech-tree in the Green Dale, learned how "when the intellect stops short, love advances and goes in." The Dominicans, John Tauler and Blessed Henry Suso, preached and wrote how "no created light can reach or shine into this divine ground, for it is the dwelling-place of God and His sanctuary." These men all used the vernacular as did their fellow-mystics in England where manuscripts were penned, confidentially, for "ghostly friends" in English as homely as that of the *Canterbury Tales,* and with imagery and vision that rise to the transcendent. A mystic, who must express the inexpressible, is necessarily thrown back upon symbolism which Belloc has called "the language of high and hidden things," and the transparent, vibrant speech of these writers is richly image-starred, in itself a sign of the Signified. Each writer is highly individual, yet they have in common the paradoxes in which mysticism abounds; they reflect the vast unknowable in tiny, precise pictures, sketched from the kitchen or the fields of spring; they seek after "the naked divinity," and find it in the sacred Humanity of their dear "knight Jesus." Their fresh and homely words, their merriment, their friendliness, invite the world at large to enter the intimate loneliness of their life with God.

WRITINGS OF RICHARD ROLLE

When the hermit Richard Rolle died in 1349, the Cistercian Nuns of Hampole were so sure of his immediate canonization that they compiled an Office, with long *legenda* recounting his life and miracles:

Pange lingua graciosi Ricardi preconium,
Pii, puri, preciosi, fugientis vitium,
Celsi, sancti, gloriosi, felicis per premium.

As a young man Richard fled from Oxford because of the dryness of secular learning, but he was so steeped in the writings of Saint Augustine and Saint Bernard that their thoughts were his own. He made himself an anchor's robe from two of his sister's dresses, one grey and one white, and topped the costume with his father's rainhood. He lived in a hermitage on the estate of Sir John Dalton till he reached the state of prayer in which the very thought of Jesus was "heat, song and sweetness" to him; then he took to the roads, and led any soul who cared to follow him "stalwartly, devoutly and sweetly" into contemplative ways. He wrote in Latin *Incendio Amoris* and *Emendatio Vitae,* with some commentaries on the Scriptures; and in strong Yorkshire English *The Form of Perfect Living, The Command of the Love of God,* and a number of brief treatises, meditations and lyrics. Much that he never wrote is attributed to him, for his disciples tried not only to pray but to write in his free and glowing manner.

The Form of Perfect Living:

But now may thou ask me and say, "Thou speakest so much of love, tell me, what is love? And where is love? And how shall I love God verily? And how may I know that I love Him? And in what state may I most love Him?" These are hard questions to teach, for a feeble man and fleshly as I am. But nevertheless therefore I shall not leave off to show my wit, as I think it may be. For I hope in the help of Jesus, who is the well of love and peace and sweetness.

Thy first asking is, "What is love?" And I answer: Love is a burning yearning in love, with wonderful delight and secureness; God is light and burning. Light clarifies our skill; burning kindles our covetousness, that we desire nought but Him. Love is a life, coupling together the lover and the loved. For meekness makes us sweet to God, purity joins us to God. Love makes us one with God; love is fairhead of all virtues. Love is the thing through which God loves us, and we God, and each of us the other. Love is desire of the heart, ever thinking on that which it loves; and when it has what it loves, then it joys, and nothing can make it sorry. . . . We must force ourselves to clothe ourselves in love as the iron or the coal does in the fire, as the air does in the sun, as the wool does in the hue. The coal so clothes it in the fire that all is fire; the air so clothes it in the sun that all is sun; the wool so substantially takes the hue that it is like it. In this manner shall a true lover of Jesus Christ do: his heart shall so burn in love that it shall be turned into the fire of love and be as it

were all fire, and he shall so shine in virtue that no
part of him shall be murky in vice. . . .

Contemplative life has two parts, a lower and a
higher. The lower part is meditation on Holy Writing, that is, God's words, and in other thoughts good
and sweet that men have of the grace of God, and
also in loving God in psalms and hymns, or in
prayers. The higher part of contemplation is in beholding and yearning for the things of heaven, and
joy in the Holy Ghost. Men have that oft, even
though it be that they are not praying with the
mouth, but only thinking of God and of the fairhead of the angels and of holy souls. Then may I
say that contemplation is a wonderful joy of God's
love, the which joy is the loving of God that may
not be told; and that wonderful loving is in the soul,
and for abundance of joy and sweetness it ascends
into the mouth, so that the heart and the tongue accord in one, and body and soul joy in the living God.

A man or a woman that is ordained to contemplative life, first God inspires them to forsake this
world, and all the vanity and the covetousness and
vile lust thereof. Then He leads them away alone
and speaks to their hearts, and, as the Prophet says,
He gives them to suck of the sweetness of the beginning of love, and then He sets them in will to
give themselves wholly to prayers and meditations
and tears. Then, when they have suffered many
temptations, and when the foul annoyance of
thoughts that are idle and of vanities that will encumber them that cannot destroy them are passing
away, He makes them gather their hearts within and
fix them only on Him, and He opens to the eyes of
their souls the gates of heaven, so that the same eyes

look into heaven; and then the fire of love verily lies in their hearts and burns therein, and makes them clean of all earthly filth, and thenceforward they are contemplative men, ravished in love. For contemplation is a sight, and they see into heaven with their ghostly eyes. But thou must know that no man has perfect sight of heaven while he is living in the body here; but as soon as they die they are brought before God, and see Him face to face and eye to eye, and dwell with Him without end. For Him they sought and Him they coveted, and Him they loved with all their might.

Lo, Margaret, I have shortly told thee the form of living, and how thou mayest come to perfection, and to love Him that thou hast taken to thee. If it do thee good and profit thee, thank God and pray for me. The grace of Jesus Christ be with thee and keep thee. Amen. . . .

Treatise on the Holy Name:

"Oil outpoured is Thy name." The name of Jesus comes into the world, and as soon it smells as of oil poured out. It is taken as oil, for everlasting salvation is hoped from it. Soothly, "Jesus" is as much to mean as Savior, or heal-full. Therefore, what means "oil outpoured is Thy name," but that Jesus is Thy name? This name is oil outpoured, for Jesus, the Word of God, has taken man's kind. Jesus, Thou fulfillest in work what Thou art called in name; soothly thou art He whom we call Savior, therefore Jesus is Thy name. Ah! Ah! That wonderful name! Ah! That delightful name! This is that name that is above all names, name the highest of all, without which no man hopes for healing. This name is in my

ears a heavenly sound, in my mouth honey-full
sweetness. Therefore, no wonder that I love that
name, which gives comfort to me in all anguish. I
cannot pray, I cannot have ought in mind, but what
sounds of the name of Jesus. I savor no joy in which
Jesus is not mingled. Whereso I be, whereso I sit,
whatso I do, the savor of the name of Jesus departs
not from my memory. I have set the memory; I have
set it as a token upon my arm, for love is strong as
death. As death slays all, so love overcomes all.
Everlasting love has overcome me, not to slay me
but to quicken me. But it has wounded me, that it
may teach me. It has pierced through to my heart to
the marrow ere it be healed. And now, overcome, I
fail. Scarce do I love for joy, nearly I die, for I
suffice not for most delicious sweetness, and to be
ever thus drunken. It cannot be that the flesh fail not
when the soul in such joys is ravished by joy. But
whence unto me such joy but for Jesus? The name
of Jesus has taught me to sing, and enlightened my
mind with the heat of unmade light.

Meditation on the Passion:

When thou hast thought over all the pains that
Jesus suffered for thee, think in thy soul that thou
standest by Him in that place, and seest what they
do to Him. Speak then to Thy Lord the words of
Saint Bernard, "God my Lord, sweet Jesus, what
hast Thou done that Thou, so bloody, hangest on
the rood, that never did evil, but ever did good?"
Guiltless, they do Thee to death; woe is me therefore, for I am guilty of Thy death, and against law
and reason it is to slay Him that never did amiss,
and let him pass free who did the harm. For this, you

wretched Jews, take me, for I am the sinful one that has done evil and followed the fiend's counsel. I pray you, let this Innocent pass, and do me to death, for I have trespassed. Think also inwardly how He said on the rood before He yielded the ghost—for it may stir thee to have sorrow for thy sins and rue on His death that was so pained for thee, and so wreak His death on thyself—that He thus on the rood cried, *"Consummatum est,"* that is "All is fulfilled," as if He said, "I am fulfilled of sorrow, both in body and soul." In body: for all was pained from the crown of the head to the sole of the foot. In soul: through our unkindness, that gives Him no thanks for His good deed, but does what is in us ever to renew His pain. And that over-passes all His pains that He before suffered; for this He said at the end: "I am fulfilled of sorrow." And at this word He bent down His head and said to His Father, "Into Thy hands my soul I yield.". . . And think on the stinging sorrows of His Mother, that was with Him aye to the death, and beheld all that they did with her child. Never bore martyr as much as she bore! For martyrs were pained in body, and God's mother in soul, that may not die. For all the pains that her Son bore were thrust through her soul, and she yearned through sorrow to die, and no sorrow might slay her.

THE LADDER OF PERFECTION

Walter Hilton passed his life as an Augustinian Canon in Thurgarton Priory, Nottinghamshire, a dignified and ample home of books, of business, and of contemplation. He wrote his own great book, *The Ladder of Perfection,* for a "ghostly sister in Jesus

Christ," and the rubric of one manuscript states all that is directly known about him: *"Magister Walterius Hylton, qui fuit homo venerabilis scientia et vite sanctitate, composuit hunc librum plenum catholica doctrina et edificacione."* If he is less subjective and emotional, perhaps less poetic, than "blessed Richard, Hermit," he is more ordered, more steadily luminous and easier to follow, for "from the lowest to the highest a soul may not suddenly start, no more than a man that will climb upon a high ladder, and setteth his foot upon the lowest rung, may at the next fly up to the highest." Lowly examples serve him for the highest truths: the fervent soul kept at the boiling-point will withstand temptation, for how can flies light on the edge of a bubbling pot? His whole work is Christocentric. He begins with the first stages on the ascetic road and follows it dutifully, but he is so possessed by a "soothfast desire and clean love longing" for the "homely and peaceful presence of the blessed man, Jesus Christ," that his feet fly over the hard stones towards the entrance into vision. In the last chapters the gates stand open, "by touching of His gracious presence."

Book II, Chapter 21

There was a man that would go to Jerusalem; and for he knew not the way he came to another man that he hoped knew the way thither, and asked whether he might come to that city. The other man said to him that he might not come thither without great trouble and much travail, for the way is long and perils are great of thieves and robbers, and many other lettings there be that fall to a man in the going. . . .

Then saith the pilgrim: If it be so that I may

have my life safe and come to that place that I
covet, I charge not what mischief I suffer in the
going; and therefore say me what thou wilt, and
soothly I promise to do after thee. That other man
answers and says thus: Lo, I set thee in the right
way. This is the way, if thou keep the lesson that I
teach thee. What so thou hearest or seest or feelest
that should let thee in thy way, abide not with it
wilfully, tarry not for it restfully, behold it not,
like it not, dread it not; but aye go forth in thy way,
and think that thou wouldst be at Jerusalem. For
what thou covetest, that thou desirest, and nought
else but that. And if man rob thee and despoil thee,
beat thee, scorn thee and despise thee, strive not
again if thou wilt have thy life. But hold thee with
the harm that thou hast and go forth as nought
were, that thou take no more harm. And also if men
will tarry thee with tales and feed thee with false-
hoods, to draw thee to mirths and to leave the pilgrimage, make deaf ear, and answer not again, and
say nought else but that thou wouldest be at Jerusalem. And if men proffer thee gifts and will make
thee rich with worldly good, attend not to them;
think aye on Jerusalem. And if thou wilt hold this
way and do as I have said, I undertake thy life that
thou shalt not be slain, but thou shalt come to that
place that thou covetest.

Ghostly to our purpose, Jerusalem is as much to
say as "sight of peace", and betokeneth contemplation in perfect love of God. For contemplation is
not else but a sight of Jesus, which is very peace.
Then if thou covet for to come to this blessed sight
of very peace and be a true pilgrim to Jerusalem-
ward, though it be so that I were never there, never-

theless as far forth as I can I shall set thee in the way thitherward. The beginning of the high way in the which thou shalt go is reforming of faith, grounded meekly in the faith and in the laws of Holy Church, as I have said before; for trust securely, though thou hast sinned here-before, if thou be now reformed by the sacrament of penance after the law of Holy Church, that thou art in the right way.

Now then, since thou art in the sure way, if thou wilt speed in thy going and make good journeys thee behoveth to hold these two things often in thy mind: meekness and love. That is, I am nought, I have nought, I covet nought, but One. Thou shalt have the meaning of these words in thine intent and in habit of the soul lastingly, though thou have not specially these words aye formed in thy thought, for that needeth not. Meekness saith, I am nought, I have nought. Love saith, I covet nought but One, and that is Jesus. These two strings well fastened with the mind of Jesus, maketh good accord in the harp of the soul, when they be craftily touched with the finger of reason; for the lower thou smitest upon that one, the higher soundeth that other. . . .

Right as a true pilgrim going to Jerusalem leaveth behind him house and land, wife and child, and maketh himself poor and bare from all that he hath, that he might go lightly without letting: right so if thou wilt be a ghostly pilgrim, thou shalt make thyself naked from all that thou hast, that are both good deeds and bad, and cast them all behind thee, that thou be so poor in thine own feeling that there be nothing of thine own working that thou wilt lean upon restingly, but aye desiring more grace of love and aye seeking the ghostly presence of Jesus. And

if thou do thus, then shalt thou set in thy heart
wholly and fully that thou wouldest be at Jerusalem
and at none other place but there. And that is, thou
shalt set in thine heart wholly and fully, that thou
wouldest nothing have but the love of Jesus, and
the ghostly sight of Him as He will show Him; for
to that only thou art made and bought and that is
thy beginning and thine end, thy joy and thy
bliss. . . .

Book II, Chapter 23

But if there be a worldly thing that behoveth
needs to be done to thyself or to thine even Christian, speed thee soon of it, and bring it to an end
that it hang not on thy heart. If it be another thing
that needeth not, or else it toucheth not thee, charge
it not, jangle not therewith, nor anger thee not,
dread it not, like it not, but smite it out of thy heart
readily. And say thus: "I am nought, I have nought,
nought I seek or covet but the love of Jesus." Knit
thy thought to this desire. . . .

Book II, Chapter 25

Then, since this murkness and this night is so good
and so restful, though it be but short, that standeth
only in desire and longing to the love of Jesus with
a blind thinking on Him, how good then, and how
blessed it is to feel His love and to be illumined with
His blessed unseeable light to see soothfastness, the
which light a soul receiveth when the night passeth
and the day springeth. . . . That is, light of grace
sprang and shall spring to them that dwell in the
shadow of death, that is, in this murkness that is like
to death. For as death slayeth a living body and all

How blessed to be illumined with His light, the
which light a soul receiveth when the night
passeth and the day springeth.

THE LADDER OF PERFECTION

fleshly feelings of it, right so desire to love Jesus felt in this murkness slayeth all sins, all fleshly affections and all unclean thoughts for the time, and then nighest thou fast to Jerusalem. Thou art not yet at it, but by small sudden lightings that glide out through small crannies from that city shalt thou be able to see it from far, ere that thou come thereto. For wit thou well, though that thy soul be in this restful murkness without troubling of worldly vanities, it is not yet where it should be, it is not yet clothed all in light nor turned all into fire of love; but it feeleth well that there is somewhat above itself that it knoweth not nor hath not yet, but it would have it, and burningly yearnest for it. And that is nought else but the sight of Jerusalem.

Book II, Chapter 46

But then with the help of the angels, the soul seeth yet more. For knowing riseth above all this in a clean soul; and that is to behold the blessed kind of Jesus. First of all His glorious manhood, how it is worthily raised above all angels kind; and then after of His blessed Godhead, for by knowing of creatures is known the Creator. And then beginneth the soul for to perceive a little of the privities of the blessed Trinity. It may well enough, for light of grace goeth before and therefore she shall not err as long as she holdeth her with the light. . . .

Wondrous great love feeleth the soul with heavenly delight in beholding of this soothfastness, when it is made through special grace; for love and light go both together in a clean soul. There is no love that riseth of knowing and of special beholding that may touch so near our Lord Jesus as this love may;

for this knowing only is worthiest and highest in itself of Jesus, God and man, if it be specially showed
by the light of grace. And therefore is the fire of this
flaming love more burning than is the knowing of
any creature bodily or ghostly.

And all these gracious knowings felt in a soul of
the university of all creatures, in manner before
said, and of our Lord Jesus, maker and keeper of
all this fair university, I call them fair words and
sweet speakings of our Lord Jesus to a soul which
He will make His true spouse. He showeth privities
and proffereth rich gifts of His treasure, and array-
eth the soul with them full honestly. She need not be
ashamed with the company of her fellows to appear
afterwards to the face of Jesus her spouse. All these
lovely dalliances of privy speech between Jesus and
a soul may be called a hid word, of which Holy Writ
saith thus: "Soothly to me is said a hid word, and
the veins of his whispering mine ear hath perceived."
The inspiration of Jesus is a hid word, for it is
privily showed to His lovers; through which a clean
soul perceiveth readily the veins of His murmuring,
that are specially showing of His soothfastness, felt
with inly savour and ghostly delight, a privy whispering of Jesus in the ear of a clean soul.

It behoveth him to have great cleanness in soul, in
meekness and in all other virtues, and to be half deaf
to noise of worldly jangling, that should wisely perceive these sweet ghostly whisperings. This is the
voice of Jesus, of which David saith thus: "The
voice of our Lord Jesus making ready harts, and
He shall show the thicket." That is: the inspiration
from Jesus maketh souls light as harts that start
from the earth over bushes and briars of all worldly

vanity; and He showeth to them the thicket, that are His privities, that may not be perceived by sharp eyes. These beholdings, soothfastly grounded in grace and in meekness, make a soul wise and burning in desire for the face of Jesus. These are the ghostly things that I spoke of before, and they may be called new gracious feelings. And I do but touch them a little, to make wise thy soul. For a soul that is clean, stirred by grace to use of this working, may see more in an hour of such ghostly matter than might be written in a great book.

REVELATIONS OF DIVINE LOVE

On the south side of the chancel of the Church of Saint Julian in Norwich the foundations of an anchorite's cell may still be seen, and in the church wall is the "squint" through which Dame Juliana heard mass. The scribe of one manuscript of *The Revelations of Divine Love* tells us briefly of her: "Here is a vision showed by the goodness of God to a devout woman, and her name is Julian, who is a recluse at Norwich, and is yet in life, A.D. 1413. In the which vision are full many comfortable words, and greatly stirring to all them that desire to be Christ's lovers." She was then over seventy years old. She had entered young into her anchorhold and striven much for God, for Our Lord once said to her, "I thank thee for thy travail, namely that of thy youth." She spent the long years that followed in pondering over what God had shown her in one day and one night, "a revelation of the love that Jesus Christ, our endless bliss, made in sixteen showings." She wrote the story of these showings, "for in all this I was greatly stirred in charity to mine even-Christians, that they might all see and know the same

that I saw, for I would it were comfort to them. . . .
For it is God's will that you take it with great joy and
liking, as if Jesus had showed it unto you all." She
would have her readers "leave the beholding of the
wretch that it was showed to, and mightily, wisely and
meekly behold God," yet we cannot but see at the same
time Juliana herself, so humble, refreshing, wise and
witty, "lovely and homely," like the Lord she loved,
an exalted mystic and a sensible, winning woman. Her
account has brought to thousands the simple comfort
that she wished, and it has brought to students of the
spiritual life clear examples of the three manners of
vision outlined in Saint Augustine, and elaborated
later in the writings of the great Spanish mystics of the
sixteenth century. Juliana calls them simply: "bodily
sight, word formed in my understanding, and ghostly
sight." Her account of them is in the simple language
of experience:

This is a Revelation of Love that Jesus Christ,
our endless bliss, made in Sixteen Showings, or
Revelations particular.

These Revelations were showed to a simple creature that could no letter the year of our Lord 1373,
the Eighth day of May. Which creature desired
afore three gifts of God. The First was mind of His
Passion; the Second was bodily sickness in youth, at
thirty years of age; the Third was to have of God's
gift three wounds.

As in the First, methought I had some feeling in
the Passion of Christ, but yet I desired more by the
grace of God. Methought I would have been that
time with Mary Magdalene, and with others that
were Christ's lovers, and therefore I desired a bodily

sight wherein I might have more knowledge of the bodily pains of our Saviour and of the compassion of our Lady and of all His true lovers that had seen, that time, His pains. For I would be one of them and suffer with Him. Other sight nor shewing of God desired I never none, till the soul were departed from the body. The cause of this petition was that after the shewing I should have the more true mind in the Passion of Christ. . . .

These two desires, of the Passion and the sickness, I desired with a condition, saying thus: "Lord, thou wottest what I would, if it be Thy will that I have it; and if it be not Thy will, good Lord, be not displeased: for I will nought but as Thou wilt."

For the Third gift, by the grace of God and teaching of Holy Church I conceived a mighty desire to receive three wounds in my life: that is to say, the wound of very contrition, the wound of kind compassion and the wound of wilful longing toward God. And all this last petition I asked without any condition.

These two desires aforesaid passed from my mind, but the third dwelled with me continually.

And when I was thirty years old and a half, God sent me a bodily sickness, in which I lay three days and three nights; and on the fourth night I took all my rites of Holy Church, and weened not to have lived till day. . . .

My Curate was sent for to be at my ending, and by when he came I had set my eyes, and might not speak. He set the Cross before my face and said: "I have brought thee the image of thy Maker and Saviour; look thereupon and comfort thee therewith."

Methought I was well as I was, for my eyes were set uprightward into Heaven, where I trusted to come by the mercy of God; but nevertheless I assented to set my eyes on the face of the Crucifix, if I might; and so I did. For methought I might longer dure to look evenforth than right up.

After this my sight began to fail, and it was all dark about me in the chamber, as if it had been night, save in the image of the Cross whereon I beheld a common light; and I wist not how. All that was beside the Cross was ugly to me, as if it had been mickle occupied with the fiends. . . .

Then came suddenly to my mind that I should desire the second wound of our Lord's gracious gift: that my body might be fulfilled with mind and feeling of His blessed Passion. For I would that His pains were my pains, with compassion and afterward longing to God. But in this I desired never bodily sight nor showing of God, but compassion such as a kind soul might have with our Lord Jesus, that for love would be a mortal man: and therefore I desired to suffer with Him.

The First Showing:

In this suddenly I saw the red blood trickling down from under the Garland hot and freshly and right plenteously, as it were in the time of His Passion when the Garland of thorns was pressed on His blessed head that was both God and Man, the same that suffered thus for me. I conceived truly and mightily that it was Himself showed it me, without any means.

And in the same Showing suddenly the Trinity fulfilled my heart most of joy. And so, I understood, it shall be in heaven without end to all that shall come there. For the Trinity is God: God is the Trinity; the Trinity is our Maker and Keeper, the Trinity is our everlasting lover, everlasting joy and bliss, by our Lord Jesus Christ. And this was showed in the First Showing and in all: for where Jesus appeareth, the blessed Trinity is understood, as to my sight. . . .

In this He brought our blessed Lady to my understanding. I saw her ghostly, in bodily likeness: a simple maid and a meek, young of age and little waxen above a child, in the stature that she was when she conceived with child. Also God showed in part the wisdom and the truth of her soul: Wherein I understood the reverent beholding that she beheld her God and Maker with, marvelling with great reverence that He would be born of her that was a simple creature of His making. And this wisdom and truth—knowing the greatness of her Maker and the littleness of herself that was made—caused her to say full meekly to Gabriel: "Lo me, God's handmaid!" In this sight I understood soothly that she is more than all that God made beneath her in worthiness and grace; for above her is nothing that is made but the blessed Manhood of Christ, as to my sight. . . .

The Eighth Showing:

Here saw I a great oneing betwixt Christ, and us, to mine understanding: for when He was in pain, we were in pain.

And all creatures that might suffer pain, suffered with Him: that is to say, all creatures that God hath made to our service. The firmament, the earth, failed for sorrow in their kind in the time of Christ's dying. For it belongeth kindly to their property to know Him for their God, in whom all their virtue standeth: when He failed, then behoved it needs to them for kindness to fail with Him, as much as they might, for sorrow of His pains.

In this time, I would have looked up from the Cross, but I durst not. For I wist well that while I beheld in the Cross I was sure and safe; therefore I would not assent to put my soul in peril: for beside the Cross was no sureness, for fear of fiends.

Then had I a proffer in my reason as if it had been friendly said to me: "Look up to heaven to His Father." And then saw I well, with the faith that I felt, that there was nothing betwixt the Cross and Heaven that might have dis-eased me. Either me behoved to look up or else to answer. I answered inwardly with all the might of my soul, and said: "Nay, I may not, for Thou art my heaven." . . .

The Fourteenth Showing:

But oftentimes when our falling and our wretchedness is showed us, we are so sore adread, and so greatly ashamed of our self, that scarcely we wit where we may hold us. But then willeth not our courteous Mother Jesus that we fall away, for Him were nothing lother. But He willeth then that we use the condition of a child: for when it is dis-eased, or adread, it runneth hastily to the mother for help, with all its might. So willeth He that we do, as a meek child saying thus: "My kind Mother, my gracious Mother, my dearworthy Mother, have mercy on me: I have made myself foul and unlike to Thee, and I nor may nor can amend it but with

Thy privy help and grace." And if we feel us not then eased forthwith, be we sure that He useth the condition of a wise mother. For if He see that it be more profit to us to mourn and to weep, He suffereth it, with ruth and pity, unto the best time, for love. And He willeth then that we use the property of a child, that even more kindly trusteth to the love of the mother in weal and in woe.

And He willeth that we take us mightily to the Faith of Holy Church and find there our dearworthy Mother, in solace of true understanding, with all the communion of the blessed. For one single person may oftentimes be broken, as it seemeth to himself, but the whole Body of Holy Church was never broken, nor never shall be, without end. And therefore a sure thing it is, a good and a gracious, to will meekly and mightily to be fastened and oned to our Mother, Holy Church, that is, Christ Jesus. For the food of mercy that is His dearworthy blood and precious water is plenteous to make us fair and clean; the blessed wounds of our Saviour be open and enjoy to heal us; the sweet, gracious hands of our Mother be ready and diligently about us. For He in all this working useth the office of a kind nurse that hath nought else to do but to give heed about the salvation of her child.

The Sixteenth Showing:

And from that time it was showed I desired oftentimes to witten what was our Lord's meaning. And fifteen years after, and more, I was answered in ghostly understanding, saying thus: "Wouldst thou witten thy Lord's meaning in this thing? Wit it well: Love was His meaning. Who showed it thee?

Love. What showed it thee? Love. Wherefore
showed it He? For Love. Hold thee therein and thou
shalt witten and know more, nor witten therein other
thing without end." Thus I learned that Love was
our Lord's meaning.

Mistress Margery Kempe[6] called at Dame Juliana's
window one day. She claimed, perhaps too loudly, that
she too had been favored with mystical vision, but as
her spiritual writings are ambiguous, to say the least,
they will not be considered here. But if "this creature"
made herself singular, many another contemplative
with better right than she to speak of spiritual things
lived so hidden a life that even their names have been
lost. Their books speak for them. Some are translations, witnesses to the flow of spiritual teaching from
one country to another through monastic foundations.
Such is *The Mirror of Simple Souls,* rendered from
French into English by an unknown M. N. who carefully glossed his translation to save unlearned readers
from the danger of quietism that lurked in the thir-
teenth-century original.[7] It was written for "souls
touched of God, severed from sin, in the first estate of
grace, who ascend by divine grace into the seventh
estate of grace where the soul hath her fullhead of perfection by divine fruition in a life of peace. And among
you, actives and contemplatives, that to this life may
come, hear now some mites of the clean love, of the
noble love, of the high love of free souls, and how the
Holy Ghost hath His sail in His ship."

[6] See page 180.
[7] The author was a Frenchman, possibly a Carthusian, whose work is
a steppingstone between the twelfth-century theologians and the Flemish
mystics of the fourteenth century. It is in dialogue form, like the writings
of Saint Catherine of Genoa.

THE CLOUD OF UNKNOWING

Among the anonymous treatises is a group of seven writings traceable to the same completely unknown author. Of these, *The Cloud of Unknowing,* complemented by its sequel, *The Book of Privy Counselling,* stands out as perhaps the most remarkable book on contemplation in the English language.[8] Both are addressed to a "young disciple in God's school" in vigorous, colloquial language of the North Midlands, dashed with humor and strongly rhythmic in movement. The writer avoids all display of his own wide reading, yet makes no claim to be an innovator, for, "I mean the thing that all our old Fathers have written and taught before us, and the thing which is the fruit and flower of all Holy Scripture." He then weaves into his own highly original pattern the teachings of Dionysius, Saint Augustine, Saint Gregory, Saint Bernard, Richard of Saint Victor, and the nearly contemporary author of *De Adhaerendo Deo;* and he anticipates some of the most characteristic features of Saint John of the Cross, for he had experienced the "dark night" and the "living flame of love." He knew that his subject was high and difficult, open to misinterpretation by the "fleshly janglers, glosers and blamers," of whom his country was full at the moment. "I pray thee," he wrote, "that thou let none see the book but such as thou thinkest is like the book." But those who are called to "a meek blind stirring of love and a naked intent unto God," let them "lift up the foot of love and step towards that state." To enter the cloud of luminous darkness, infused contemplation, they must

* The other works are *The Epistle of Prayer, The Epistle of Discretion of Stirrings, Of Discerning of Spirits, Denis Hid Divinity, Benjamin Minor.*

"leave the working of natural wit," which "may be called in comparison of this but feigned folly formed in fantom, as far from the very soothfastness when the ghostly sun shineth as is the darkness of the moonshine in a mist in midwinter from the brightness of the sunbeam in the clearest time of midsummer day." His cloud is the same as "the good murkiness, the rich nought" of Hilton, for "this nought and this night is a great ease for the soul that loveth Jesus."

Chapter IX

For one thing I tell thee: it is more profitable to the help of thy soul, more worthy in itself and more pleasing unto God and to all the saints and angels in heaven—yea, and more helpful to all thy friends, bodily and ghostly, quick and dead—such a blind stirring of love unto God for Himself, and such a privy love-place upon this cloud of unknowing; and better it were for thee to have it and to feel it in thy ghostly affection than it is to have the eye of thy soul open in contemplation or beholding of all the angels or saints in heaven, or in hearing of all their mirth and the melody that is among them in bliss.

Chapter XXVI

Do on then fast! Let see how thou bearest thee. Seest thou not how God stands and abides thee. For shame! Travail fast but awhile, and thou shalt soon be eased of the greatness and the hardness of this travail. For although it be hard and strait in the beginning, when thou hast no devotion, nevertheless yet after when thou hast devotion it shall be made full restfull and light unto thee that before was full hard, and thou shalt have little travail or none. For then will God work sometimes all by Himself; but not always, nor yet for a long time together, but when He likes and as He likes, and then will it seem to thee merry to let Him alone. Then will He sometimes, peradventure, send out a beam of ghostly light, piercing this cloud of unknowing that is betwixt thee and Him, and show some of His privity, of which man may not or cannot speak. Then shalt thou feel thine affection inflamed with the fire of His love, far more than I can tell thee, or may, or will at this time. For of that work that falleth to God alone, dare I not take it upon me to speak with my blabbering, fleshly tongue; and shortly to say, although I durst, I would not.

The Book of Privy Counselling:

Unclothe thyself of all manner of feeling of thyself, that thou be able to be clothed with the gracious feeling of God. And this is the true condition of a perfect lover, only and utterly to despoil himself for the thing that he loveth and admit or suffer to be clothed but only in that thing that he loveth; and that not only for a time but endlessly to be lapped about therein, in full and final forgetting of himself. This is the work of that love that none may know but him that feeleth it. This is the lesson of Our Lord when He saith, "Whoso will love me, let him foresake himself," as he who saith, "Let him despoil himself of himself if he will be verily clothed in Me Who am the wide garment of love and of lasting that never shall have end." . . .

RELIGIOUS LYRICS

The cells of hermits were not solitary for long at a

time; burdened pilgrims came to the outer windows
and went away lighthearted.

> Merry it is in May morning,
> Merry ways to go.
> And by a chapel as I came
> Met I with Jesus to churchward gone,
> Peter and Paul, Thomas and John,
> And his disciples everyone,
> Merry it is!

It was inevitable that the spiritual joy overflowing
from souls of prayer should break out into lyrics sung
and recited far and wide among the people. Hundreds of these religious songs fill the great manuscript collections of the thirteenth and fourteenth centuries.

The earliest vernacular hymns go back to Godric,
the twelfth-century hermit of Finchale, who was the
first to transpose Latin metres into English. Legend
has it that each of these three brief songs was revealed
to him in a vision:

Saint Mary, Virgin Queen,
Mother of Jesus Christ the Nazarene,
Take shield, help thy Godric mightily;
Take him; bring him, glorious, into God's realm
    with thee.
Saint Mary, Christ's bower,
Maiden's cleanness, mother's flower,
Blot out my sins, rule my heart's love,
Bring me with joy to God Himself above.

Christ and Saint Mary as on a footstool have me led,
That I need not on this earth with my bare foot
    tread.

Saint Nicholas,[9] God's friend dear,
Build us a fair, bright house here.
By thy birth, by thy death knell,
Saint Nicholas, bring us there safe and well.

It was Richard Rolle who led the chorus of religious lyric singers in the fourteenth century. The *Cantus Amoris* is a loosely rhythmic passage from *Ego Dormio*. "Now," he says in the midst of his prose, "I write a song of love that thou wilt delight in when thou art loving Jesus Christ":

My song is in sighing
My life is in longing
Till I see Thee, my King,
So fair in Thy shining.

So fair in Thy fairhead:
Into Thy light me lead,
And in Thy love me feed.
In love make me to speed,
That Thou ever be my meed. . . .

I sit and sing
Of love longing
That in my breast is bred,
Jesus, Jesus, Jesus,
When am I to Thee led?

Full well I know
Thou seest me below;
In love my thought is stead;
When I Thee see

[9] Saint Nicholas, Bishop of Myra in the fourth century, was tremendously popular throughout the Middle Ages in both the Eastern and Western Church. Legends are rife concerning him and he is, by popular acclaim, patron of travellers and of children. As Santa Claus, he still holds sway.

And dwell with Thee,
Then am I filled and fed.

Jesus, my dear and my darling,
Delight art Thou to sing,
Jesus, my mirth, my melody,
When wilt Thou come, my King?

Jesus, my heal and my honey,
My strength and my comforting;
Jesus, I covet to die
When to Thee it is pleasing. . . .

And I Thy love shall sing
Through sight of Thy shining
In heaven without ending.   Amen.

The following is one of the lyrics of Rolle that set
the pattern for a whole school of poets:

Love is life that lasts for aye, which to Christ will
   hold,
For weal nor woe may change it not, as wisest men
   have told.
Thy night it turns into a day, thy labor into rest;
If thou wilt love thus as I say, thou mayest be with
   the best.

Love is thought with great desire of a fair loving,
Love I liken to a fire that slacken will for nothing;
Love will cleanse us of our sins, love reward will
   bring,
Love the King's own heart may win, love of joy
   may sing. . . .

Jesus is love that lasts for aye; to Him is our
   longing.

Jesus the night turns into day, the dawn to day-
    spring.
Jesus, think on us now and aye, for Thee we hold
    our King,
And give us grace, as Thou well may, to love Thee
    without ending.

Rolle's song was caught up and echoed in haunting,
anonymous little poems such as the following:

All other love is like the moon
That waxes and wanes as flower in plain,
As flower that falls and fades so soon,
As day that showers and ends in rain.

All other love begins by bliss,
In weeping and woe it makes ending.
No other love our whole joy is
But what arises in Heaven's King,

Whose love is new and ever green,
And ever full without waning.
His love makes sweet with no pain,
His love is endless, like a ring.

Franciscan influence is strong in many of the lyrics,
for the romanticism of the Poor Man of Assisi, lover
of Lady Poverty and brother of all things lovable,
had spread far and wide through his Mendicant sons.
Through him a note of intensely personal compassion
had come into men's thoughts of the Passion. Realistic
crucifixes had but lately replaced the older Byzantine
type which had portrayed Christ as King of Glory
rather than as the Man of Sorrows.

I sigh when I sing
    For sorrow that I see,

When I with weeping
  Behold upon the tree,
And see Jesus the sweet
  His Heart's blood let
For the love of me.
His wounds wax wet;
  Mary reweth Thee.

High upon a down
  Where all folk may it see,
A mile from the town,
  About at mid-day,
The rood is upreared,
His friends are all afraid,
  They cling like clay.
The rood stands in stone,
Mary is alone;
  Her song is Weylaway!

     · · · · · · · ·

Now goeth sun under wooded place,
Me reweth, Mary, thy fair face;
Now goeth sun under tree,
Me reweth, Mary, thy Son and thee.

     · · · · · · · ·

Lord, Thy Passion!
Whoso thinks aright thereon
Tears come,
Eyes are swollen,
Cheeks are wet
And the heart grows sweet.

     · · · · · · · ·

Lovely tears of lovely eyes—
Why dost thou me such woe?

Sorrowful tears of sorrowful eyes—
 Thou breakest my heart in two.

Thou sighest sore;
Thy sorrow is more
Than man's tongue can tell;
Thou singest of sorrow,
Mankind to borrow
Out of the pit of hell.   (Refrain)

I, proud and keen,
Thou meek and clean
Without woe or wile;
Thou art dead for me,
And I live for Thee,
So blessed be that will.   (Refrain)

Thy mother seeth
How woe thou beest,
Therefore she yearns apart;
To her thou speakest,
Her sorrow Thou slakest—
Sweet prayer won Thy Heart. (Refrain)

Thy Heart is rent,
Thy body is bent
Upon the rood tree;
The tempest is spent,
The devil is schent,
Christ, by the might of Thee.

Lovely tears of lovely eyes—
 Why dost Thou me such woe?
Sorrowful tears of sorrowful eyes—
 Thou breakest my heart in two.

It was Saint Francis, too, who had made the first Christmas Crib, while liturgical drama familiarized the scenes of Bethlehem:

Lullay, lullay, little Child,
Thou that wert so stern and wild
Art now become so meek and mild
    To save what was lost before.

But for my sin I wot it is
That God's Son suffers this;
Mercy, Lord, I've done amiss,
    Iwis I will no more.

Against my Father's will ere long
I chose an apple, rueful wrong!
Wherefore my heritage is gone,
    And now Thou weepest therefore.

An apple took I of a tree,
But God it had forbidden me,
Wherefore I should damned be
But for Thy weeping here.

Lullay for woe, little thing,
Thou little Baron, Thou little King;
Mankind is cause of Thy mourning,
    That Thou hast loved so dear.

        . . . .
As I lay upon a night
Alone in my longing,
Methought I saw a wonder sight,
A maiden child rocking.

The maiden would without a song
Her Child asleep bring;

The Child thought she did Him wrong
And bade His Mother sing.

"Sing now, Mother," said that Child,
"What shall me befall
Hereafter, when I come to age,
So do mothers all.

"Every mother that truly
Can her cradle keep,
Is wont to lullen lovely
And sing her child to sleep. . . .

"Mother," said that sweet thing then,
"I shall teach thee to sing
What shall come upon me here,
My deeds and suffering. . . .

"I shall be so simple
And to men so knowing
That most part of the people
Shall will to make me King."

"Sweet Son," then said she,
"No sorrow will it bring
If I may yet see that day
When Thou art made a King."

"Do way, Mother!" said that Sweet,
"Therefore came I nought,
But to be poor, and cure the pain
That mankind has brought.

"When two and thirty years be done,
And a little more,
Mother, thou shalt make much moan
And see me die sore. . . .

"For shamefully shall I die
Hanging on the rood,
For man's ransom shall I pay
My own Heart's blood."

"Alas, Son," said that maid,
"Since that it is so,
How shall I abide that day,
To bear Thee to this woe?"

"Mother," said He, "take it lightly,
I shall live again
In human nature, through my might,
Or else I wrought in vain. . . .

"All this world I shall judge
At the doom-rising;
Sweet Mother, here is all
That I will now sing."

Certainly this sight I saw,
This song heard I sing,
As I lay this Yule Day
Alone in my longing.

The thought of Christ as a Knight brought all the
idealism and much of the romance of chivalry into the
sanctuary. The first of the following poems shows the
ease with which the words of Scripture, made vivid
by the liturgy of Holy Week, found their way into
popular poetry.[10] The second, the imagery of knighthood, blends with the mysteries of religion in a haunting enigma.[11]

What is He, this lordling, that cometh from the
    fight

[10] See *Isaias* 63.
[11] The Feast of Corpus Christi was introduced into the Church in 1264.

With blood-red weed, so grisly dight,
So fair accoutred, so seemly in sight,
So stiffly He goeth, so doughty a Knight?

I it am, I it am, that speaks nought but right,
Champion to heal mankind in the fight.

Then why is Thy shroud with blood arrayed,
As treaders in the vineyard with wine all
    be-sprayed?

The vineyard have I trodden, myself alone,
And of all mankind there was no other one.
I have them trodden in wrath and pain
And my weed is sprinkled with their blood again,
And all my robe fouled, to their great shame.
The day of vengeance lives in my thought,
The year of payment forget I nought.
I looked all about for a helping one,
I sought all the rout, but there was none.
It was my own strength that this cure wrought,
My own doughtiness that help there brought.

Of God's mercy will I bethink me,
And praise Him in all things that He gives me.

      . . . .
Lully, lully, lully, lully,
The falcon hath borne my mate away.

He bare him up, he bare him down,
He bare him into an orchard brown.

And in that orchard there was a hall
That was hung with purple and pall.

And in that hall there was a bed
That was hung with gold so red.

And in that bed there lies a knight,
His wounds bleeding day and night.

By the bedside kneels a maiden bright,
And she weeps both day and night.

And by that bedside stands a stone,
"Corpus Christi" written thereon.

England was Our Lady's dower, and she its crowned
Queen. The simplest and loveliest of its songs were
laid at her feet.

I sing of a maiden
　That is mateless;
King of all kings
　For her son she chose.
He came all so still
　Where His mother was
As dew in April
　That falls on the grass.
He came all so still
　To His mother's bower
As dew in April
　That falls on the flower.
He came all so still
　Where His mother lay
As dew in April
　That falls on the spray.
Mother and maiden
　Was never none but she;
Well may such a lady
　God's mother be.

. . . .

In a tabernacle of a tower
As I stood musing on the moon,

The crowned queen of most honor
Appeared in ghostly sight full soon
There complaining all alone,
For man's soul was wrapped woe:
I cannot leave mankind alone,
Quia amore langueo. . . .

Mother of mercy for thee was I made,
Who needs mercy but thee alone?
To give thee grace I am more glad
Than thou to ask; why wilt thou none?
When said I no? Tell me, tell on!
Never yet, to friend or foe.
When thou askest nought, then make I moan,
Quia amore langueo. . . .

My child is outlawed, pleader for thy sin,
His body was beaten for thy trespass;
It pricks my heart that one near of kin
Should be despised, O Son, alas.
Thou art His brother, thy mother am I,
He sucked my breast He loved thee so.
He died for thee, my heart thou hast,
Quia amore langueo. . . .

Now Son, said she, wilt thou say nay
When man would mend him of his miss?
Thou lettest me never in vain yet pray.
Then sinful man, look thou to this:
What day thou comest, welcome thou art.
These hundred years though astray thou go
I take thee full fain, I clasp, I kiss,
Quia amore langueo.

Now will I sit and say no more,
But live and look with great longing;

When man will call I will restore;
I love to save him, my offspring,
No wonder my heart still hangs on him.
He is my neighbor, what may I do?
For him I had this worshipping,
Quia amore langueo.

Why was I crowned and made a queen?
Why was I called of mercy the well?
Why should an earthly woman be
So high above angels in heaven's realm?
'Tis for thee, man, sooth to tell.
Ask my help and it shall be so;
I was ordained to save thee from hell,
Quia amore langueo.

Now man, have mind on me forever,
Look on thy love thus languishing.
Let us part from each other never,
My help is thine own, creep under my wing.
Thy sister is queen, thy brother a king,
Thy heritage ready, come soon thereto.
Take me for thy bride and learn to sing
Quia amore langueo.

This poem has its counterpart in another, in honor
of Our Lord, based on the *Canticle of Canticles,* in
which the same haunting refrain occurs:

In the valley of restless mind
I sought in mountain and in meed,
Trusting a true love for to find.
Upon a hill then took I heed,
A voice I heard (and near made speed)
In great dolor complaining so—

"See, dear soul, my sides bleed,
Quia amore langueo."
Upon this mount I found a tree,
Under this tree a man sitting;
From head to foot wounded was **He**,
His Heart's blood I saw bleeding,
A seemly man to be a king,
A gracious face to look unto.
I asked **Him** how **He** had paining,
He said, *"Quia amore langueo.*

"I am the love that false was never;
My sister, man's soul, I loved her thus.
Because I would in no wise dissever,
I left my kingdom glorious.
I bought her a palace full precious;
She fled, I followed, I loved her so
That I suffered these pains so piteous,
Quia amore langueo. . . .

"**My** sweet spouse, will we go play?
Apples be ripe in my garden;
I shall clothe thee in new array,
Thy meat shall be milk, honey and wine.
Now, dear soul, let us go dine,
Thy sustenance is in my skrip, lo!
Tarry not now, fair spouse mine,
Quia amore langueo. . . .

"Long and love thou never so high,
Yet is my love more than thine may be.
Thou gladdest, thou weepest, I sit thee by,
Yet might thou, spouse, look once at me.
Spouse, should I always so feed thee
With child's meat? Nay, love, not so!

I pray thee, love, with adversity,
Quia amore langueo.

"My spouse is in chamber, hold your peace!
Make no noise, but let her sleep.
My babe shall suffer no dis-ease;
I may not hear my dear child weep.
For at. my breast I shall her keep.
No wonder though I tend her so;
This hole in my side had been never so deep
But *Quia amore langueo.*"

WRITINGS ON DEVOTION TO THE SACRED HEART

The following *Querela Divina* is found in one of the popular anthologies[12] of Rolle and his imitators:

O mankind, have in mind
My pains' smart.
Behold and see, that is for thee
Pierced my Heart.

The verses are accompanied by a rough drawing of Christ, who points with one hand to His side, while beneath the other hand is a large heart with a gaping wound, around which is written: "This is the measure of the wound that our Jesus Christ suffered for our redemption." Similar representations were appearing at this time all over England, not only in manuscripts but in carvings of wood and stone, in metal work, in stained-glass windows. It was the earliest manifestation in art of a devotion that had been growing in the Church from the earliest times, to become graphic in the fourteenth century under the same impulses that produced the mystic writers.

[12] MS B.M. add. 37049.

Saint John the Beloved—"and we know that he speaketh true"—tells how he saw the Heart of Christ opened on the cross. From this starting-point in Scripture, strong lines of dogma reached out through the Patristic Ages, and flowered into devotion in the ages when faith found leisure for prayer in the monasteries. "The side of the dead Christ was struck by a lance that the Sacraments might flow forth from which the Church is formed,"[13] wrote Saint Augustine; and six hundred years later Saint Anselm, contemplating this wounded side, found his way within, "for that opening reveals to us the riches of his goodness and the love of His Heart."[14] From then on "that devotion, the keenest edged," grew strong in the cloisters, especially in France where the first hymn to the Sacred Heart, *Ave Regis Cor Aveto,* was probably written, and in Germany where, in the monastery of Helfta, Saint Gertrude in her visions saw heaven poured out on earth through that splendid Heart. The devotion overflowed among crusaders and troubadours, and the unknown poem-makers of the people.[15] As time moved on towards the centuries of upheaval and disunion, the devotion would become more ascetic, more astringent, more forceful as a bond of unity, while never losing its prayerful and mystical character. After the time of Saint Margaret Mary it would gradually receive full papal sanction, and take its place in the cycle of the liturgy, becoming, in our own days, a driving force in Catholic Action, and the ex-

[13] *In Joannis Evangelium,* P.L. XXXV, 1463.

[14] Meditation X, P.L. CLVII, 761.

[15] The prevalence of the Devotion in Middle English writings can be seen from many passages already given in this book, showing how it permeated the thought of the people. See *Ancren Riwle,* p. 133, *Piers Plowman,* p. 342, and *Pearl,* p. 416.

pression of the sense of corporateness inherent in the doctrine of the Mystical Body. The writings of fourteenth-century England represent a very simple, tenderly human phase in the development of the devotion to the Sacred Heart, as expressed in the anonymous *Meditation on the Wounded Heart:*

Behold specially the five most notable wounds: two in His blessed hands, and two in His blessed feet, and the most open wound in His right side. Into these wounds of Christ's most blessed hands and feet, with Thomas of India put in thy fingers, that is to say, thy most subtle thoughts and desires. And in the wound of Christ's blessed side, since it is the largest and deepest, put in all thy hand, that is to say, all thy life and all thy works, and there feel Christ's Heart so hot loving thee, and also there feel Christ's blessed heart-blood shed for thee, and to ransom thy soul; also there feel the water of Christ's side streaming as of a well of life, for to wash thee and all mankind of sin. And there fetch up water of everlasting life without end of those five most open wounds of Christ as out of five wellsprings. . . .

Out of the largest and deepest well of everlasting life in the most open wound of Christ's blessed side, fetch up deepest and heartliest water of joy and bliss without end, beholding there inwardly how Christ Jesus, God and man, to bring thee to everlasting life, suffered that hard and hideous death on the cross, and suffered His side to be opened, and Himself to be stung to the Heart with that grisly spear; and so with that doleful stroke of the spear there gulched out of Christ's side that blissful flood of water and blood to ransom us, water of His side to wash us, and blood of His Heart to buy us. For love of these blessed wounds creep into this hot bath of Christ's heart-blood, and there bathe thee, for there was never sin of man nor of woman, thought nor wrought, that was laved with lovely sorrow and heartly repentance, that there was not in this well full remission to buy it, and water of life fully to cleanse it and wash it. There rest thee here, comfort thee here, live in Christ's Heart without end. Amen.

In the meantime, Juliana of Norwich beheld in the tenth of her "showings," "how good and how happy it is to dwell in Thy Heart."

The Tenth Showing:

Then with a glad cheer our Lord looked unto His Side and beheld, rejoicing. With His sweet looking He led forth the understanding of His creature by the same wound into His side within. And then He showed a fair, delectable place, and large enough for all mankind that shall be saved to rest in peace and in love. And therewith He brought to mind His dearworthy blood and precious water which He let pour all out for love. And with the sweet beholding He showed His blissful heart even cloven in two.

And with this sweet enjoying, He showed unto mine understanding, in part, the blessed Godhead, stirring then the poor soul for to understand, as it may be said, that is, to think on the endless Love that was without beginning, and is, and shall be ever. And with this our good Lord said full blissfully: "Lo, how that I loved thee," as if he had said: "My darling, behold and see thy Lord, thy God that is thy Maker and thine endless joy, see what liking and bliss I have in thy salvation; and for my love enjoy now with me."

And also, for more understanding, this blessed word was said: "Lo, how I loved thee! Behold and see that I loved thee so much ere I died for thee, that I would die for thee; and now I have died for thee and suffered willingly that which I may. And now is all my bitter pain and all my hard travail turned to endless joy and bliss to me and to thee. How should it now be that thou shouldst anything pray that liketh me, but that I should full gladly grant it thee? For my liking is thy holiness and thine endless joy and bliss with me."

This is the understanding, simply as I can say, of this blessed word: "Lo, how I loved thee." This showed our good Lord for to make us glad and merry.

XII

Drama on Wheels

We purpose plainly to have stillness in this press,
The people to please with plays full glad.

COVENTRY BANNS

THE late Roman Empire and the early Fathers of the Church thought alike on at least one point: they had no use for actors. The ragged, brazen *mimi,* tragic play-folk who made the populace roar with laughter, were declared *infames* by civil law and were excommunicated by the Church.[1] There was reason for this sweeping severity, for Western drama was at its lowest ebb, morally and artistically. It had come a long

---

[1] It was decreed in several local councils that actors must give up their calling upon conversion to Christianity. In case of relapse *"sacro communio cum ceteris Christianis non dari."* Saint Augustine, while condemning the theatre of his day, defended the study of the higher forms of classical drama. See *The City of God,* II, 8.

way from its high religious origins at the altar fires of Greece; in the fifth century, only the débris of Roman comedy was left to wash over Europe with the tides of barbarian conquest. But men must still laugh and be entertained, and here the classic *mimus* met the Teutonic *scop* on common ground; the mediaeval minstrel blended the two traditions.

Thus the lighthearted found expression and the heavyhearted found relief in an offhand kind of drama that needed no stage for its acting. The rope walkers, tumblers, pantomimers, bear and monkey trainers, and the singing, dancing jongleurs were welcome anywhere, singly or in troupes. All that was needed was an open space, an audience, and the sound of the glee-wood.

In the villages, the pulse of undying custom beat on in the folk-plays which came as regularly as the seasons they remotely symbolized. Memories of unrememberable heathen ways lived on in the sworddances, where winter died to give rise to spring at the word of an oddly practical doctor. In these plays the blackened faces of the Morris-dancers bespoke the neighborhood of Moors, while the Eastern legend of Saint George was drawn into the Teutonic folk festivals to form the mummer's play, still acted as late as the nineteenth century as a Christmas revel. Earlier, it had been on Hock Tuesday or Plough Monday, in the first warmth of spring, that the mummers came knocking, dancing and begging:

> In comes Saint George
> The champion bold.
> With my bloody spear
> I have won ten thousand pounds in gold.

> I fought the fiercest dragon
> And brought him to a slaughter.
> And by that means I gained
> The King of Egypt's daughter.[2]

Invariably there followed a fight, a cure, a rough-and-ready matchmaking, a begging for pennies, and a game ending with a comforting reflection such as:

> Ashes to ashes and dust to dust,
> If God won't have you the devil must.

LITURGICAL DRAMA

While folk-drama and the remnants of the classic *scenici* went their spontaneous way without much development at the hands of the simple people who revelled in them, high drama came once more into being, again near an altar fire. The Church which had condemned a theatre fallen from dignity, created a new one in which her own ministers became actors. As her liturgy was essentially dramatic, expressing in color, sound, movement and fragrance the inner meaning of a divinely human action, it was natural to linger and enlarge here and there, till lesser plays grew out of the unchanging drama. It happened first in the great monastic churches at Easter time, when, after the Introit, the Mass paused for a moment while clerics representing the Three Marys were solemnly saluted by boys in white, standing as angels to left and right of the altar:

Angeli:

Quem quaeritis in sepulchro, O Christicolae?

[2] From the Plough Play of Bassingham. The text of these folk-plays is only extant in eighteenth- or nineteenth-century versions.

Mulieres:

Jesum Nazarenum crucifixum, O coelicolae.

Angeli:

Non est hic, surrexit sicut praedixerat;
ite, nuntiate quia surrexit de sepulchro.

Chorus:

Alleluia, surrexit Dominus de sepulchro qui
pro nobis pependit in ligno, alleluia.

Thus in the ninth century a playlet came out of a trope;[3] it spread from church to church, and grew in length with repetition, till it became by the twelfth century a whole cycle of Easter plays, distinct from the liturgy but still bound up with it. A corresponding cycle grew out of the Christmas Mass, longer and richer than the first; it began with Old Testament prophecies and eventually drew in the shepherds, the kings, Herod and his court, the slaughtered children and their mourning mothers. Independent plays for feast-days were added to a dramatic pageantry that soon reached into the future, portraying Antichrist and the end of the world. Scriptural prose broke into elaborate poetry; the sacerdotal actors donned vivid dress; not only the sanctuary but the nave and transept of the church formed the stage for vigorous acting and lusty Latin song. The liturgical drama was at once prayer and spectacle. Its underlying principle was

---

[3] Thus Christian drama had its origin in the music of worship. A trope is a verbal amplication of a passage in the liturgy, which grew out of the practice of fitting words to the elaborate Gregorian melodies by which final syllables were prolonged, especially the last *a* of the Alleluia. Notker Balbulus, a monk of Saint Gall in the ninth century, is credited with the earliest tropes.

sound, but without the restraint of formal liturgy it tended to run riot. But before defeating its own end, it gave rise to another type of drama, acted in the streets and market-squares by laymen in their every-day speech.[4]

MYSTERY PLAYS

The transition was made during the thirteenth century, and in each country the newly secularized drama took on, with the vernacular, a distinctive form. In England the plays, while remaining religious, became a civic affair; the trade-guilds undertook to act them. When the Feast of Corpus Christi was established in 1264 the outdoor procession became the rallying-point which set the whole city in motion, and drama was put on wheels.

If one stood long enough in the warm June air at some street corner, say in York, he would see the whole cycle of religious mysteries unroll before his eyes.[5] One by one the double- or triple-deck pageants would lumber up, and pause. On the first, manned by the farmers, God would sit in His spangled heaven atop the scaffolding, while His disobedient angels fell down their ladders into the smoky mouth of hell, mercifully "lapped in cloth" on the lowest landing. On the next, the plasterers would form heaven and earth out of nothing. The cardmakers saw to the forming of Adam

[4] Extant texts of liturgical plays are rare in England, although every type was surely represented there.

[5] Four Cycles are extant in English in fifteenth-century manuscripts. They are: the Chester plays, the York plays, the Townley (or Wakefield) plays, and the Hegge plays (or *Ludus Coventriae*). From the account books of various guilds, interesting facts about the "properties" used in these plays can be gathered, "gloves for God," "powder to set the world on fire," "two worms of conscience."

and Eve; then in the fourth play, in the Garden of
Paradise, the fullers spoke as follows:

Deus:

> Adam and Eve, this is the place   1
> That I have granted of my grace
>   To have your dwelling in.
> Herbs, spices, fruit on tree,
> Beasts, fowls, all that you see
>   Shall bow to you within.
> In this place called Paradise
>   Your joys shall begin,
> And if that you be wise,
>   Turn not away by sin.
> All your will here shall you have,
> Living things, to eat or save,
>   Fish, fowl or fee.
> You may take them as your own,
> All other creatures that are known,
>   Your subjects, shall they be.
> Adam, over more and less
> Lordship in earth here grant I thee,
> This place that worthy is,
>   Keep it in honesty.
> Look that you keep it carefully.
> Multiplied shall creatures be,
>   Each one in fitting hour.
> Look that you both save and set
> Herbs and trees, for nothing let,
>   So that you may procure
> Life for every beast and man,
>   And fowl of each stature.
> Dwell here now, if you can;
>   Your labor shall endure.

Adam:

O Lord, loved be Thy name,
For now is this a joyful home
   That Thou hast brought us to,
Full of mirth and solace sweet,
Herbs and trees, fruit to eat,
   With many spices new.
Lo, Eve, now are we brought
   Both unto rest and peace,
We need to take no thought
   But make it all increase.

Eve:

Loved be ever such a Lord,
Who has given us great reward,
   To govern both great and small,
And made us after His own thought
   Among these mirths all.
Here is a joyful sight,
   This place where dwell we shall,
We love Thee, Most of Might,
   Great God, on Thee we call.

Deus:

Love my name with good intent,
And hearken to my commandment,
   And do my bidding humbly.
Of all the fruit in Paradise,
Take you thereof in every wise,
   And make you right merry.
The tree of good and ill,
   What time you eat of this,
You speed yourselves to kill,
   And be brought out of bliss.

All things are made, man, for thee now,
All creatures shall to thee bow
That is brought to thee nigh.
On earth I make thee lord of all,
And beasts shall be to thee in thrall;
Thy kind shall multiply.
Therefore this tree alone,
Adam, this out-take I,
Of fruit of it eat none,
For if you do you die.

Adam:

Alas, Lord, that we should do so ill!
Thy blessed bidding we shall fulfill,
Both in thought and deed;
We shall not near this tree nor its bough,
Nor eat the fruit that grows there now,
Therewith our flesh to feed.

Eve:

We shall do Thy bidding,
We have no other need,
Thy fruit shall still be hanging,
Lord, that Thou hast forbid.

Deus:

Look that you do as I have told,
Be pleased with all that you now hold
For here is wealth at will.
This tree that bears the fruit of life
May neither thou nor Eve, thy wife,
Thy hands therewith fill.
And now this tree that I out-take,
Keep it strictly, for my sake,

> That nothing may come near.
> All others at your will shall be,
> I out-take nothing but this tree,
> To feed you with in fear.
> Here shall you lead your life
> With dainties that are dear;
> Adam, and Eve thy wife,
> My blessing have you here.

The Townley Cycle of plays counts among its anonymous writers a man of genius, with a nine-line stanza of his own. His hand appears in the play of Noah, acted by the water carriers. There was nothing to check comedy, here in the open air, and nothing to prevent comedy from blending with reverent, luminous piety, here among a childlike crowd of believers in the homeliness of God.

Noah:

> Now my gown I will cast off   and work in my
>   coat;   262
> I will make the mast   ere I stir one foot.
> Ah, my back is breaking fast!   This is a sorry
>   note.
> It is a wonder that I last,   such an old dote.
>   I am sold
> To begin such a work,
> My bones are so stark
> No wonder they shirk.
>   For I am full old. . . .
> Window and door,   even as He said,   280
> Three rows of chambers,   they are well made;
> Pitch and tar full sure   thereupon laid;

This will even endure;   I am pleased and well
 paid.
 For why?
It is better wrought
Than I could have thought;
Him that made all of nought
 I thank only.
I must not be sluggish   but hie me some-
  whither
My wife and my household   bring also hither.
Come here quickly, wife,   and consider now
  whether
We must hence flee,   all of us together
 At last.

Uxor:

Why, Sir, what ails you?
Who is it assails you?
To flee it avails you,
 And you are aghast.

Noah:

There is other yarn   on the reel, my dame.

Uxor:

Tell me the whole thing   or else be to blame.

Noah:

He that our cares can heal   —blessed be His
  name—
He has promised for our weal   to shield us
  from shame,
 And said
All this world about

With floods so stout
That run in a rout
   Shall be overlaid.

He said all that be slain   save only we,
Our obedient bairns   and their wives three;
A ship He ordained   to help us get free.
Thus with might and with main   let us
      thankful be,
   For He betters our bale.
Hie now, fast go we thither.

Uxor:

I know never whither,
In a daze and a dither
   For fear of thy tale. . . .

Their three sons help to load the ark, whereupon
Noah's wife refuses to enter it.

Noah:

Dame, ever and still   must we abide grace.   334
Therefore, Wife, with good will   come into this
      place.

Uxor:

Sir, for Jack nor for Jill   will I turn my face
Till I have on this hill   spun for a space
   On my spindle.
Woe to him who would get me.
Now will I down set me;
Let no man upset me
   Lest my wrath kindle.[6]

[6] The supposition that Noah's wife was a stubborn scold is an early
piece of mediaeval humor. The Junius MS (c.1000) has a drawing which
represents her standing with arms akimbo before the gangplank of the
ark.

Noah:

Behold in the heaven　　the cataracts all
Are open now, even,　　the great and the small,
And the planets seven　　have left their stall.
Thunder and lightning　　are causing to fall
　Full stout
Halls and bowers,
Castles and towers.
Full sharp are these showers
　Raining about.
Therefore, Wife, have done;　　come into ship
　fast.

Uxor:

Yea; go sole thy shoes　　—the better will they
　last.

Prima Mulier:

Good Mother, come soon,　　all is overcast,
Both the sun and the moon.

Secunda Mulier:

　　　　　　　　And many winds blast
　Full sharp.
Floods run in a din.
Therefore, Mother, come in.

Uxor:

In faith, I will spin;
　All in vain ye carp. . . .

She persists in her refusal till the water reaches her,
when she suddenly takes to the gangplank. There

again she stops and argues, till Noah loses his patience
and threatens to beat her.

Uxor:

> Spare me not, I pray thee,   but do as thou
>   think.   379
> These great words shall not flay me.

Noah:

>   Abide, Dame, and drink.
> For thou shalt be beaten   with this staff till thou
>   stink.
> Are strokes good? Tell me!

Uxor:

>   What say ye, Wat Wink?

Noah:

> Speak!
> Cry me mercy, I say.

Uxor:

> Thereto say I nay.

Noah:

> Do it, by this day,
>   Or thy head shall I break. . . .

Each then appeals to the audience to chastise their
husbands and wives respectively, to teach them dis-
cipline betimes. They then turn on each other.

Noah:

> I shall make thee still as a stone,   beginner of
>   blunder!   406

I shall beat thee back and bone,   and break all
    in sunder.
(They fight.)

Uxor:

Out! Alas!   I am gone! Out upon thee, man's
    wonder!

Noah:

See how she can groan   and I lie under.
    But wife,
In this haste let us go,
For my back is nigh in two.

Uxor:

And I am beaten so blue
    That I may not thrive.
(They enter the ark.)

Primus Filius:

Ah, why fare ye thus,   Father and Mother
    both?

Secundus Filius:

Ye should not be spiteful,   standing as though
    loth.

Tertius Filius:

These floods are so hideous,   dangerous and cold
    both.

Noah:

We will do as ye bid us,   we will have no more
    wroth,
    Bairns dear!

Now with helm in hand
My ship I'll command.

Uxor:

See in the sky stand
    The seven stars near. . . .

They float about in the ark till the rains cease and the hills appear. The raven and the dove are sent and return with their message.

Primus Filius:

These floods are gone,   Father behold.   **523**

Secundus Filius:

There are left now none,   of that be ye bold.

Tertius Filius:

As still as a stone   does our ship hold.

Noah:

That land we were on   would I were told,
    My children dear.
Sem, Japhet and Cham,
With glee and with game
Let us go all the same,
    And no longer stay here.

Uxor:

He have we been, Noah,   long enough now,
With grief and anger   and very great woe.

Noah:

Behold, on this green   neither cart nor plow

Is left, as I ween,　　nor tree nor bough,
　　Nor any other thing.
But all is away,
Many castles, I say,
Towns great of array
Have fled in this flowing.

Uxor:

These floods, with no fright,　　all this world
　　　　so wide
Have moved with their might,　　on every side.

Noah:

Dead are they aright,　　who were puffed up
　　　　with pride,
Every man living　　that ever was spied
　　With sin.
They are all slain
And put into pain.

Uxor:

From thence again
　　May they never win?

Noah:

Win? No, iwis,　　unless He that might has
Would amend their miss　　and admit them to
　　　　grace;
As He in bale is bliss,　　I pray Him in this
　　　　space,
In Heaven high with His　　to provide us a
　　　　place,
　　That we
With His saints in sight

    And His angels bright
    May come to His light,
      Amen, for charity.

From the York Cycle again is this scene of the sacrifice of Abraham:

Abraham:

Nay, Son, this deed must needs be done;   **197**
My Lord God will I not gainsay,
Nor ever make mourning and moan
To offer thee to Him this day.

Isaac:

Father, since God our Lord alone
Vouchsafed to send, when you did pray,
A son to you when you had none,
And now wills that he wend his way,
Therefore so must you do,
Offer me on this place;
But first I shall tell you
By counsel in this case.
I know myself, in course of Kind,
My flesh in dread of death will stand.
I am afraid that you shall find
My force your order will withstand.
Therefore it best is that you bind
In bands fast both feet and hand,
Now, while I am in might and mind.
Thus safely will your offering stand.
For, Father, when I am bound
My might may not avail;
Here will no fault be found
To make your promise fail.

For you both old and weakened be,
And I am strong and wild of thought.

Abraham:

To bind him that my strength should be!
But for God's will that would I nought.
But lo! Here shall no force be,
So shall God have what He has sought.
Farewell, my Son! I shall thee yield
To Him that all this world has wrought.
Now kiss me heartily, I pray;
Isaac, I take my leave of thee.
My blessing hast thou now today;
I must thee miss!
And I beseech God Almighty
To give thee His.
Thus do we both assent
Unto Thy words wise.
Lord God, to this intent
Receive Thy sacrifice.
This to me is a peerless pain
To see my own dear child undone!
I had rather that I were slain
Than see the sight thus of my son.
It is God's will, it shall be mine;
His bidding will I never shun.
To God's command I shall incline,
That in me fault there may be none.
Therefore, my Son so dear,
If thou wilt anything, say;
Thy death now draws near—
Farewell, for once and aye. . . .

Isaac:

Now farewell, earth so broad!
Flesh waxes faint for fear.
Now, Father, take your sword;
Full long you tarry here.

269

Abraham:

Nay, Son, I beseech thee yet;
That do I not without fear.
Thy words make my cheeks grow wet,
And change, Child, full oft my cheer.
Therefore, lie down, hands and feet;
Now may thou know thy end is near.

Isaac:

Ah, Father dear, life is full sweet;
The dread of death troubles me here.
As I am now your son,
To God I give me still.
Now am I laid here—
Do with me what you will.
I ask one thing, in my despite,
Father, but one word will arise:
I beseech you, ere you smite,
Lay this kerchief on my eyes;
Make your offering aright,
And the work will thus be wise.
My soul to God, in offering,
My body to be burned away.
Now Father, fail not in this thing,
But smite as fast as well you may.
Farewell, in God's dear blessing

Abraham:

> And mine, forever and aye.
> That peerless Prince I pray,
> My offering here to have it.
> My sacrifice this day,
> I pray Thee, Lord, receive it.

Angelus:

> Abraham! Abraham!

Abraham:

> Lo! Here, iwis.

Angelus:

> Abraham, abide, and hold thee still;
> Slay not thy son, do him no miss.
> Take here a sheep, thy offering still,
> Is sent thee from the King of bliss.
> Faithfully His will is done,
> He bids thee make offering of this,
> Here at this time, and save thy son.

Abraham:

> I praise that Lord with full heart here
> That of His love this loan has lent
> To save my son, my darling dear,
> And sent this sheep to this intent.
> We shall offer it to Thee here.
> So shall it be as Thou hast meant.
> My Son, be glad and make good cheer,
> God has us good comfort sent.

The Townley Cycle contains two versions of the Shepherd's Play. The second is a rough-and-tumble comedy, coarse, funny and shrewd enough in its open-

ing scene to have been overheard on the English downs
where chilly shepherds chaff one another. Mak, the
scoundrel, plays a trick on his fellows by putting a
stolen sheep in his baby's cradle, but he is caught and
soundly tossed in a blanket. The shepherds are at this
rough sport when *Gloria in Excelsis* breaks on their
ears. They hurry to Bedlam, mimicking the angels'
song on the way, but once they are before the holy
Child all is love:

Primus Pastor:

> Hail, comely and clean, hail, young Child;   710
> Hail, Maker as I mean of a maiden so mild.
> Thou hast cursed, I ween, the devil so wild;
> The false worker of evil, now goes he beguiled.
>   Lo—He merries!
> Lo—He laughs, my Sweeting;
> A well fair meeting!
> My promise I'm keeping;
>   Have a bob of cherries!

Secundus Pastor:

> Hail, Sovereign Savior, for Thou hast us sought;
> Hail fair Child and Flower that all things has
>   wrought.
> Hail, I kneel and I cower. A bird have I brought
>   To my bairn from afar.
> Hail, little tiny thing,
> Of our creed Thou art King.
> I would drink and sing,
>   Little Day-Star.

Tertius Pastor:

> Hail, darling dear, full of Godhead,
> I pray Thee be near when that I have need.

Hail, sweet is Thy cheer! My heart would bleed
To see Thee sit here in such a poor weed
  With no pennies!
Put out Thy hand and call,
I bring Thee but a ball.
Have it, and play withal,
  And go to the tennis.

Maria:

The Father of Heaven, God Omnipotent,
That set all in sight, His Son has He sent;
He named me by name, came to me ere He went;
I conceived Him full even, through might as He
    meant,
  And now is He born.
He will keep you from woe;
I shall pray Him so.
Tell of Him as you go
  And remember this morn.

Primus Pastor:

Farewell, Lady, so fair to behold
With thy Child on thy knee.

Secundus Pastor:

But He lies full cold.
Lord, well is me. Now we go; behold.

Tertius Pastor:

Forsooth, already it seems to be told
  Full oft.

Primus Pastor:

What grace we have found!

Secundus Pastor:

Come forth, now we are sound.

Tertius Pastor:

To sing are we bound:
Take it aloft.

The pageant of the Assumption Play (from the York Cycle) carries the scene back to the heights of heaven, though acted by stablemen:

Jesus:

Mine angels that are bright and sheen,   1
On my message take your way
Unto Mary, my Mother clean;
That maid is brighter than the day.
Greet her, holy, as is well seen,
And to that fair one you shall say:
Of heaven I have her chosen Queen,
In joy and bliss that last for aye.
I bid you say what I have thought,
And why it is that now you wend:
I will have her body to me brought
To dwell in bliss without an end.
My flesh was formed out of her own;
Unseemly thing it were, iwis,
That she should bide there all alone
And I dwell here so high in bliss.
To her shall you go therefore
Full friendly for to fetch her hither;
There is nothing that I love more,
In bliss then shall we dwell together.

Primus Angelus:

O blissful Lord, now most of might,
We are ready with all our might
Thy bidding to fulfill.
To Thy Mother, that maiden free,
Chosen fount of chastity,
As it is Thy will.

Secundus Angelus:

Of Thy message we are full fain.
We are ready with might and main
Both by day and night;
Heaven and earth now glad may be,
That lovely maiden they may see
In whom Thou once did light.

Tertius Angelus:

Lord Jesus Christ, our Governor,
We are ready at Thy bidding;
With joy and bliss and great honor
We shall Thy Mother bring.

Scene:

Near Mary's grave.

Quartus Angelus:

Hail, thou daughter of blessed Anne,
Who once conceived through the Holy Ghost
And then brought forth both God and man,
He who beat down the fiend's boast.

Quintus Angelus:

Hail, root of Jesse, that forth brought
The blessed Flower, our own Saviour,

He who made mankind of nought
And brought him up into His tower.

Sextus Angelus:

Of thee alone He would be born
Into this world of wretchedness,
To save mankind that was forlorn
And bring them out of great distress.

Primus Angelus:

Thou mayest be glad, both day and night,
To see thy Son, our own Savior,
He will crown thee, Lady bright,
Thou blessed Mother and fair Flower.

Secundus Angelus:

Mary, Mother and maiden clean,
Chosen by thine own Child,
Of heaven and earth thou art queen,
Come up now, Lady meek and mild.

Tertius Angelus:

Thy Son has sent us after thee
To bring thee now into His bliss,
There shalt thou dwell and blithe be,
Of joy and mirth thou shalt not miss.

Quartus Angelus:

For in His bliss without end
Thou shalt all kinds of solace see,
Thy life in liking thou shalt spend
With thy dear Son in Trinity.

Maria:

Ah, blessed be God who above all stands;

Himself knows best what is to do.
I thank Him with my heart and hands
That He His bliss will take me to.
And you also, His angels bright,
That by my Son to me are sent.
I am ready with all my might
To fulfill His commandment. . . .

Scene:

The heights of heaven.

Primus Angelus:

Jesus, Lord, and Heaven's King,   81
Here is Thy Mother for whom Thou sent.
We have brought her at Thy bidding,
Take her to Thee as Thou hast meant.

Jesus:

Hail be to thee, maiden bright,
Thou art my Mother and I thy Son.
With grace and goodness thou art dight;
With me this bliss thou hast won.
Now shalt thou have all joys so light,
The time is past of all thy care,
Thee shall worship angels bright,
Of sorrow thou hast no more share.

Maria:

Jesus, my Son, loved mayest Thou be;
I thank Thee heartily in my thought
Who in this wise ordains for me,
And to this bliss Thou hast me brought. . . .

Jesus:

Before every other creature   145
I shall give thee grace and might,
In heaven and earth to send succor
To all that serve thee day and night.
I grant them grace with all my might
Through the asking of thy prayer
Who call on thee by day and night
In what mis-ease they may be ere.
Thou art my dear and my liking,
My mother and my maiden sheen.
Receive this crown, my dear darling;
Where I am King thou shalt be Queen.
My angels bright, a song ye sing
In honor of my Mother dear.
And here I give you my blessing,
Holy now, together here.

MIRACLE PLAYS

Beside the cycles of Mysteries, there were the
Miracles, independent plays concerning special saints.
The ever popular Saint Nicholas was the subject of
Latin playlets in which, as early as the twelfth century,
he is seen playing his future role of Santa Claus, rais-
ing schoolboys to life, giving gifts to dowerless
maidens. *The Conversion of Saint Paul* is one of the
few Miracle plays extant in English. It was played
at three separate *stationes* surrounded by movable
"mansions" in some small town. The first station is
Jerusalem; Saul is "goodly to see, like an adventurous
knight"; he asks the High Priest for letters while his
servant makes rowdy horseplay at the inn and demands "a peck of oats and a bottle of hay." The first
scene ends with a dance, and an epilogue:

Poeta:

Finally, of this station thus we make
    conclusion,   155
Beseeching this audience to follow and succeed
With all your diligence this general procession.
To understand this matter, who so lists may read
The Holy Bible for the better speed.
There shall he have the perfect intelligence;
And thus we commit you to Christ's magnificence.

At the second station, Damascus, "here cometh Saul
riding in with his servants":

Saulus:

My purpose to Damascus fully I intend.   169
To pursue the disciples my life I apply.
For to break down the churches thus I conde-
    scend;
None shall I suffer them to edify.
Perchance our laws they might harm thereby,
And the people also turn and convert,
Which should be great heaviness into my
    heart. . . .

"Here cometh a fervent flame with great tempest,
and Saul falleth down off his horse; that done, God
speaketh in heaven":

Deus:

Saul, Saul, why dost thou me pursue?   183
It is hard to prick against the spur!
I am thy Savior that is so true,
Which made heaven and earth and each creature.
Offend not my goodness, I will thee re-cure.

Saulus:

> O Lord, I am afraid! I tremble with fear.
> What wouldst Thou I did? Tell me here!

Deus:

> Arise, and go thou with glad cheer
> Into the city a little here beside,
> And I shall thee succor in every fear,
> That no manner of ill shall betide.
> And I will there for thee provide
> By my great goodness what thou shalt do.
> Hie thee as fast thither as thou mayest go.

Saulus:

> O merciful God, what aileth me?
> I am lame; my legs are taken from me so,
> My sight likewise, I may not see.
> I cannot tell whither to go.
> My men have forsaken me also.
> Whither shall I wend, or into what place?
> Lord, I beseech Thee, help me of Thy grace.

Primus Miles:

> Sir, we be here to help thee in thy need
> With all our allegiance; we will not cease.

Saulus:

> Then in Damascus I pray you me lead,
> In God's name, according to my promise.

Secundus Miles:

> Put forth your hand with promptness.
> Come on your way. We shall you bring
> Into the city without tarrying. . . .

The soldiers lead Saul to one of the *Mansiones,* and then depart for Jerusalem.

Saulus:

> Lord, of Thy comfort much I desire,   262
> Thou mighty Prince of Israel, King of Pity,
> Who me has punished as Thy prisoner,
> That has neither eaten nor drunk these days three.
> But, gracious God, for Thy visitation I thank
>   Thee.
> Thy servant I shall be as long as I have breath,
> Though I therefor should suffer death.

"Here cometh Ananias to Saul."

Ananias:

> Peace in this place, and goodly mansion!
> Who is within? Speak in Christ's holy name!

Saulus:

> I am here, Saul. Come in, in God's benison.
> What is your will? Tell, without any blame.

Ananias:

> From Almighty God, certainly, to thee sent I am,
> And Ananias men call me, where I dwell. . . .

Saulus:

> His mercy to me is right welcome;   290
> I am right glad that it is thus.

"Here the Holy Spirit shall appear above him."

Ananias:

> Be of good cheer, and perfect jubilation,
> *Descendit super te Spiritus Sanctus,*

Which hath with His grace illumined us.
Put forth thy hand and go with me,
Again to thy sight here I restore thee.

Saulus:

Blessed God, thanks to thee ever be!
The scale is fallen from my eyes twain.
Where I was blind and could not see,
Lord, Thou hast sent me my sight again.
From sobbing and weeping I cannot refrain,
My pensive heart is full of contrition,
For my offenses my body shall have punition. . . .

Ananias:

I christen you with mind full perfect   **325**
Receiving you into our religion,
Ever to be steadfast and never to deflect,
But ever constant without variation.
Now is fulfilled all our observation,
Concluding, thou mayest know it then,
In nomine Patris et Filii et Spiritus Sancti,
    Amen.

Saulus:

I am as glad as a bird in the air
That I have received this blessed Sacrament.

Ananias:

Come on your way, Saul, let nothing make you
    fear.
Take you some comfort for your body's
    nourishment.

In the third scene, two bombastic devils "rage and
roar with thunder and fire" because:

> Our special friend, my chosen Saul,
> Is become servant to the high God eternal.

But for all their sputtering, Saul, now Paul, preaches
a long sermon on the deadly sins, and disappears over
the wall in a basket as the play ends.

These Miracle plays allowed for a freer intermingling of comic and spectacular elements than did the
Mysteries. The *Play of Mary Magdalene* in fifty-two
scenes featuring fifty-five characters and four mobs,
moves from Bethany to Marseilles, from hell to heaven,
with a shipwreck thrown in. It is a tumultuous, reverent, exciting drama in which the step from the sublime
to the ridiculous is short but avoidable, if only the
author's epilogue be taken seriously:

> If anything amiss be
> Blame cunning and not me.
> I desire the readers to be my friend,
> If ought is amiss, that to amend.

MORALITIES

Allegorical figures appear among the angels and
saints and sinners who crowd the scene of *Mary
Magdalene;* the Morality plays were coming into their
own. A drawing in the MS of *The Castle of Perseverance* gives the scene: a tower in the center, for Mankind, with four adjacent scaffolds, one for God, to the
east; one for the world, to the west; one for the flesh,
to the south; while to the north Belial plays on his own
scaffold, "with gunpowder burning in pipes in his
hands and ears." And "Mankind's bed shall be under
the castle, and there shall the soul be under the bed
till he shall rise and play." Mankind is assaulted by
good angels and bad; his castle is stormed in one war-

like scene after another. He yields to a life of sin, and then comes relentless Death. Lying on his bed under the tower, Mankind must die, but his last words are: "I put me in God's mercy." Then "the soul crawls from beneath the bed" and turns to his good angel, who can do nothing for him.

Bad Angel:

> Ya! Why would thou be covetous   3072
> And draw thee again to sin?
> I shall thee brew a bitter juice,
> In swelling bonds thou must then burn.
> In high hell shall be thy house,
> In pitch and tar to groan and grin.
> Thou shalt lie drowned like any mouse,
> From that no man can thee turn:
> It was thy very will.
> That day the ladies[8] thou forsook
> And to my counsel thou then took,
> Thou wert better hung up on a hook
> Upon a jibbet hill. . . .
> Now jog we hence at a dog-trot;   3000
> In my dungeon I shall thee spear.
> On thee is many a sinful spot,
> Therefore this shame I shall thee shear
> When thou comest to my nest. . . .
> Boy, on this back I bring;   3122
> Speedily thou must spring;
> Thy *Placebo* I shall sing!
> To devil's dell
> I shall thee bear to hell.
> I will not dwell;
> Have good day! I go to hell. . . .

[8] These "ladies" are the Virtues which, in an earlier scene, had tried to win *Humanum Genus* to God.

But Mercy has not forgotten the soul's last prayer. She appears before God, as His "dear daughter young":

Mercy:

> Lord, though that man hath done more miss than
> good,   3367
> If he die in very contrition,
> Lord, the least drop of Thy blood
> For his sin maketh satisfaction.
> As Thou died, Lord, on the rood,
> Grant me my petition.
> Let me, Mercy, be his food,
> And grant him thy salvation,
>   *Quia dixisti "misericordiam amabo."*
> Mercy shall I sing and say,
> And *Miserere* shall I pray
> For mankind ever and aye,
>   *Misericordiam domini in eternum cantabo.*

The prayer is granted, the long play is ended, and the audience sent away from the street corners where, under the open sky, one and all had seen their fate enacted on a wooden cosmos, in earnest doggerel. And at the end God says to them:

> Thus ends our game,
> To save you from sinning;
> Ever at the beginning
> Think on your last ending!
>   *Te Deum Laudamus.*

There were moral plays stiff with unrelieved dignity, whose high aim was undone by wooden metre and prolix platitude. Such was *A Morality of Wisdom* in which the title-character appears in "rich purple cloth

of gold . . . with a gold beard curled," and enlarges
upon Scripture, to its detriment. But even here lines
of bare, lucid loveliness are found, like those spoken by
Anima who, "as a maid in white cloth of gold . . . with
a rich chaplet laced behind, hanging with two knots of
gold and side tassels, kneeling down to Wisdom, thus
saith":

> *Hanc amavi et exquisivi.*
> From my youth thee have I sought,
> To have for my spouse most specially;
> For a lover of your shape am I wrought.
> Above all health and beauty that ever was sought
> I have loved Wisdom, as for my light;
> For all goodness with him is brought.
> In Wisdom I was made all beauty-bright.

But there were other plays loud with buffoonery
and indecency in which the moral purpose is frittered
away in slapstick. Such was *Mankind* where Mercy,
the constant friend of the erring, proves no match for
New-Guise, Now-a-Days, and Naught, nor for, Titi-
villus, the sauciest devil of them all, the incarnation of
lightness, the least of whose imprecations is:

> Go your way, a devil's way, go your way, all!
> I bless you with my left hand; foul you befall!

Gradually the Moralities gave way before the Interludes that carried mediaeval farce into the dining-
halls of Tudor noblemen. The Mysteries, long held in
suspicion by the graver sort of Bishop, were finally
banned by the Reformation. Fragments of the broken
plays were swept into the Renaissance tide as it rose
in the inn-yards of London. Elizabethan drama absorbed the earlier elements, with no acknowledgement.

Drama on wheels, with its religious soul, its liturgical inheritance, its popular accent, its texture as of rough grass freshened under dew, its jocularity and its high, sweet, childlike seriousness, had gone.

EVERYMAN

But one great thought remained, to be repeated without change "in manner of a moral play" through centuries to come. The same land and time that produced the leering caricature, *Mankind,* also produced *Everyman.* The grave, bell-toned lines still ring familiar. "Here beginneth a treatise of how the high Father sendeth Death to summon every creature to come and give account of their lives in this world." Death has given his message; Everyman, aghast, has received absolution, and stands at length by his open grave.

Everyman:

> Alas, I am so faint I may not stand;   786
> My limbs under me doth fold.
> Friends, let us not turn again to this land,
> Not for all the world's gold;
> For into this cave I must creep
> And turn to earth, and there to sleep.

Beauty:

> What! Into this grave? Alas!

Everyman:

> Yea, there shall ye consume, more and less.

Beauty:

> And what? Should I smother here?

Everyman:

Yea, by my faith, and never more appear.
In this world live no more we shall,
But in heaven, before the highest Lord of all.

Beauty:

I cross out all this! Adieu, by Saint John!
I take my cap in my lap, and am gone.

Everyman:

What, Beauty? Whither will ye?

Beauty:

Peace, I am deaf, I look not behind me,
Not if thou wouldst give me all the gold in thy
chest! (Exit)

Everyman:

Alas! Whereto may I trust?
Beauty goeth fast away from me!
She promised with me to live and die.

Strength:

Everyman, I will thee also forsake and deny;
This game liketh me not at all.

Everyman:

Why then, ye will forsake me all?
Sweet Strength, tarry a little space.

Strength:

Nay, Sir, by the rood of grace!
I will hie me from thee fast,
Though thou weep till thy heart burst.

Everyman:

Ye would ever bide by me, ye said.

Strength:

Yea, I have thee far enough conveyed!
Ye be old enough, I understand,
Your pilgrimage to take on hand.
I repent me that I hither came.

Everyman:

Strength, you to displease I am to blame,
Yet promise is debt, this ye well wot.

Strength:

In faith, I care not!
Thou art but a fool to complain.
You spend your speech and waste your brain.
Go! Thrust thee into the ground! (Exit)

Everyman:

I had weened surer I should you have found.
He that trusteth in his strength
She him deceiveth at the length.
Both Strength and Beauty forsaketh me;
Yet they promised me fair and lovingly.

Discretion:

Everyman, I will after Strength be gone.
As for me, I will leave you alone.

Everyman:

Why Discretion! Will ye forsake me?

Discretion:

> Yea, in faith, I will go from thee.
> For when Strength goeth before
> I follow after evermore.

Everyman:

> Yet I pray thee, for love of the Trinity,
> Look in my grave once, piteously.

Discretion:

> Nay, so nigh I will not come.
> Farewell, everyone. (Exit)

Everyman:

> O, all thing faileth, save God alone,
> Beauty, Strength, and Discretion.
> For when Death bloweth his blast
> They all run from me full fast.

Five Wits:

> Everyman, my leave now of thee I take.
> I will follow the others, for here I thee forsake.

Everyman:

> Alas, then may I wail and weep,
> For I took you for my best friend.

Five Wits:

> I will no longer thee keep.
> Now farewell, and there an end! (Exit)

Everyman:

> O Jesu, help! All hath forsaken me!

Good Deeds:

Nay, Everyman, I will bide with thee;
I will not forsake thee indeed.
Thou shalt find me a good friend at need.

Everyman:

Gramercy, Good Deeds! Now may I true friends
see.
They have forsaken me, everyone;
I loved them better than my good deeds alone.
Knowledge, will ye forsake me also?

Knowledge:

Yea, Everyman, when ye to Death shall go,
But not yet, for no manner of danger.

Everyman:

Gramercy, Knowledge, with all my heart!

Knowledge:

Nay, yet I will not from hence depart
Till I see where ye shall be come.

Everyman:

Methink, alas, that I must be gone
To make my reckoning, and my debts pay,
For I see my time is now spent away.
Take example, all ye that do here, or see,
How they that I loved best do forsake me,
Except my Good Deeds, that bideth truly.

Good Deeds:

All earthly thing is but vanity.

Beauty, Strength and Discretion do man forsake,
Foolish friends, and kinsmen that fair spake.
All fleeth save Good Deeds, and that am I.

Everyman:

Have mercy on me, God most mighty,
And stand by me, thou mother and maid, Holy
Mary!

Good Deeds:

Fear not, I will speak for thee.

Everyman:

Here I cry God mercy!

Good Deeds:

Shorten our end, and minish our pain,
Let us go, and never come again.

Everyman:

Into Thy hands, Lord, my soul I commend.
Receive it, Lord, that it be not lost.
As Thou boughtest me, so me defend,
And save me from the fiend's boast,
That I may appear with that blessed host
That shall be saved at the day of doom.
In manus tuas, of mights most
Forever, *commendo spiritum meum.*

Good Deeds:

Now hath he suffered what we all shall endure;
The Good Deeds shall make all sure.

Now hath he made ending.
Methinks that I hear angels sing,
And make great joy and melody
Where Everyman's soul received shall be.

XIII

Shadows of Change

The passing of great melody,
And flutes full of harmony.
REASON AND SENSUALITY

THIS CHAPTER is brief, for it deals with echoes. The first printing press in England began its clatter in 1477, and from then on books were "not written in pen and ink, to the end that every man may have them at once." Caxton the printer, whose "eyes dimmed with overmuch looking on the white paper," was modestly unaware that he had marked the end of the Middle Ages. Aristocrats, somewhat ashamed of the cheap appearance of the new books, set their out-of-work scribes to ruling lines under the print to make it look like handwriting, but they could not turn back the sundial. The machine began its reign in books.

The variety of books printed by Caxton[1] mirrors the wide taste of an age of transition that had no particular enthusiasms of its own. The country, worn out with the War of the Roses and overbusy with commercialism, gave itself up to the Tudors. The Renaissance was upon it, but the fact caused no more immediate excitement than the discovery of America. The creative forces of a new age were let loose only in the next century. From the death of Chaucer till the reign of Henry VIII, old and new trends moved along together without much clash, chilled into a common formalism. Middle English changed unobtrusively into Modern, as "standard English" subdued the dialects.[2]

The best of what was written in the fifteenth century was either a repetition or an anticipation. The melodic prose of Malory was a summation of past romance; the alert verse of the Miracle Plays was the people's translation of old prayers. But writers such as Pecock and Fortescue shaped their prose to meet the demands of the New Learning, while Barclay and Skelton versified their way into the Tudor Age. The minstrel's glee-wood changed into the lute of the Elizabethan courtier. There is only time, here in a last brief chapter before the change, to hear a few snatches of the transitional song.

[1] Representative among them are are: Jean de Vigny, *The Game and Play of Chess; The Sayings of the Philosophers;* Boethius, *The Consolations of Philosophy;* Cicero, *Of Old Age; Reynard the Fox;* Chaucer, *The Canterbury Tales;* Malory, *Morte Dartur; Legenda Aurea; The Book of Good Manners; Blanchardyn and Eglantine.*

[2] The south-Midland dialect, spoken at the increasingly important capital, and used by Chaucer, the most popular writer, gradually became the accepted standard. The printing presses of London sent it to every part of the country, and tended to fix the fluidly phonetic spelling. Rapid changes in pronunciation and grammatical structure made Middle English almost unreadable by the sixteenth century.

Some of it is flatly mundane and practical, commercialized facts put into poetry on the Dryden principle that a good thing can be better said in verse than out of it. The *Libel of English Policy* exhorts "all England to keep the sea environ, and namely the narrow sea, showing what profit cometh therefrom":

Also over all Scotland the commodities   244
Are skins, hides, and of wool the fleece.
All this must pass by us away
Into Flanders by England—this is no nay.
And all her wool is draped for to sell
In the towns of Popering and of Belle,
Which the Duke of Gloucester in great ire
For her falsehood set all on fire.

This was the policy of wealth, but city life ground out a type of poverty that could laugh at itself in *London Lickpenny:*

Then came the Taverner and took me by the
    sleeve   105
And said, "Sir, a pint of wine would you essay?"
"Sir," quoth I, "it may not grieve
For a penny may do no more than it may."
I drank a pint, and for it went to pay;
Sore hungered, away I went indeed,
For well London Lickpenny for once and aye.
For lack of money I may not speed.

If poetry rose above this level, it was because some author followed with perilous closeness in the footsteps of Chaucer, that "dear Master." Lydgate, overfacile and overlong, closed the Garden of the Rose in *Reason*

and Sensuality. He translated the *Dance Macabre,* a
French poem which reflected, as did art and even
popular games, the morbid interest in the grave following in the wake of the Black Death. It pictures a
skeleton leading men of all conditions in a fantastic
dance; the fifteenth century, like the eighteenth it
resembles in so many ways,[3] had its graveyard school:

> Ah, mercy, Jesu! How mankind is frail   **233**
> And little time in this world abiding.
> No man of this life hath charter or seal;
> Therefore it may be likened in everything
> Unto a flower so amorously flourishing,
> Which with a frost beginneth right soon to fade
> When cruel death his message lists to bring;
> A lively thing he bringeth in the shade.

It was in Scotland that the best poetry was written
by men who were true "Chaucerians," and more. King
James I himself, when prisoned in an English tower,
wrote *The King's Quair* in hearty amorous allegory:

> And therewith cast I down my eyes that day,
> Where as I saw, walking beneath the Tower,
> Full secretly new come there to play,
> The fairest or the freshest young flower
> That ever I saw, methought, before that hour.
> And for that sudden sight, there soon did start
> The blood of all my body to my heart.

---

[3] Briefly, these resemblances are: a fondness for didacticism, attention
to ornate forms, a sceptical tone. These are not the best qualities of either
age! Paradoxically, the eighteenth century started a reaction against
classical formalism by falling under the spell of pseudo-mediaevalism.

Dunbar, the moody, impish, skeptical court-haunter, has a new way of his own with ancient themes. In his *Seven Deadly Sins* the Vices are having a merry dance:

> First of all in dance was Pride
> With bare wild back and bonnet on side.

His May garden in *The Golden Targe* is still very much alive:

> The roses young, now spreading at their tops,
> Were powdered bright with heavenly beryl drops
> Through beams red, burning as ruby sparks.
> The skies rang for shouting of the larks.

His faith is strongly happy, in spite of the fickleness of men:

> Done is a battle on a dragon black,
> Our champion Christ confounded hath his force.
> The gates of hell are broken with a crack;
> Raised is the sign triumphant of the Cross.

Henryson closed the tale of Troilus and Criseid with stern pity. In his *Testament of Cressid,* the fickle heroine dies a leper:

> This royal ring set with a ruby red   582
> Which Troilus with love once made my own,
> To him again I leave it when I'm dead
> To make my piteous death unto him known.
> Thus I conclude shortly, and make an end;
> My spirit I give Diana where she dwells
> To walk with her in wasted woods and wells.

There is one kind of poetry associated with the fifteenth century that was none of its making; balla-

dry blew through it like a wind from elsewhere, pick-
ing up a vocabulary along the way. Extant Scottish
and English ballads were shaped, for the most part, in
that otherwise unpoetic age. But the origins of the
ballad lie far behind in the singing, dancing folk-
groups of the mediaeval village. Oral transmission is
the very law of being of a ballad; no matter how local,
the tale it tells cannot belong to any one age. In their
lingering, leaping way, with their lonesome refrains,
they passed through the sophistication of the Renaissance and reached America with the first colonists.
There, they blazed a new trail of song from the Ap-
palachian Mountains, along rivers and railroads, to
the cowboy ranches of the West. But the form in
which the traditional ballad appears in print is that of
the fifteenth century, while its spirit is the spirit of
romance. The greenwood outlaws are alive in them:

> Now Robin Hood is to Nottingham gone
> With a link a down, and a day,
> And there he met with a silly old palmer
> Was walking along the highway.

Ghosts and knights, and stout Scots lords, unhappy
lovers and queens of fairyland are abroad in them;
voices heavy with grief and the foreboding of beauty
speak in them:

> I saw the new moon late yestreen
> Wi' the auld moon in her arms;
> And if we gang to sea, Master,
> I fear we'll come to harm.

The age of *Glee-Wood* ended, not with a military
clash like the Norman Conquest that had closed the

age of *Word-Hoard,* but with the dire coincidence of
two subtle forces—the Renaissance and the Reformation. The two fell together upon England, and the
dust of confusion rose so high that Middle English
literature all but vanished behind it.

Epilogue

One man looked through the confusion with steady eyes. In 1534 Sir Thomas More, Chancellor of the realm, went to the Tower because he was willing to pay with his blood for the faith of Merry England. Now this wise and witty man, genial friend of Renaissance cynics, was looked upon in his own day as a light going before the steps of new learning. Later ages have placed him among the great Humanists, the type of what a Christian Renaissance could have been, and may yet be. *Utopia* is one of the most provocative and most "modern" books of the sixteenth century. Sir Thomas More was the man of the future, checked by untimely death.

But Saint Thomas More was also the man of the past, and his death proved that the spirit of that past was deathless. His *Dialogue of Comfort in Tribulation,* written in the Tower, is the epilogue of Middle English literature. Its style is that of the homilists and mystics before him; its familiarity with the unseen is that of the allegorists. The notes of glee-wood are all heard in it: gayety, homeliness, romance, forthright language, love of earth and nostalgia for heaven, the realities that do not change with literary fashion, and most of all the vibrant truth that is in love with Love. For His sake the author lost his head on the block, and left his heart behind him in a book. He knew then:

How wonderful huge and great those spiritual heavenly joys are, of which our carnal hearts have so feeble and so faint a feeling, and our dull worldly wits so little able to conceive so much as a shadow of the right imagination. Of that heavenly joy Our Lord will give to the martyrs a special kind. "To him that overcometh I will make him a pillar in the Temple of my God and he shall go no more out thereof." The martyrs are the pillars of the Church. They are so because they have suffered. But their sufferings are not to be compared to the glory to come. Saint Paul, who had suffered so much, said this same short and momentary tribulation of ours that is in this present time, worketh within us the weight of glory above measure on high, we beholding not those things that we see, but those things that we see not. For these things that we see, be but temporal things: but those things that are not seen are eternal. Now to this great glory can there no man come headless. Our head is Christ, and therefore to Him must we be joined, and as members of His must we follow Him, if we will come thither.

The Middle English Language

Middle English is not a consistent or unified language:

1. The Old English dialects—Northumbrian, Mercian and West Saxon—developed into three distinctive forms of Middle English, each with many local variations: Northern (including Lowland Scots), Midland, and Southern (including Kentish).

2. An influx of French words and forms resulted in a rapid "grammatical decay," so that many of the Old English inflectional endings were worn down to a nondescript final *e*. This process was much more rapid in the Midlands than elsewhere. The western forms of each dialect remained the most archaic.

3. As spelling was purely phonetic, and the scribes of each time and locality reflected current usage, there is no such thing as "standard" Middle English. Gradually, after the fourteenth century, the dialect of London (southeast Midlands) developed into a unified modern English.

The following examples will give some idea of the characteristics of this fluid tongue. Translations of each will be found in the text, at the pages indicated:

A. From the *Ancren Riwle,* Southern, c.1225. See
   p 135.

> ʒe, mine leove sustren, ne schulen habben no
> best bute kat one. Ancrene þet haveð eihte
> puncheð bet huswif, ase Marthe, was, þen ancre;
> ne none weis ne mei heo beon Marie mid griðful-
> nesse of heorte. Vor þeonne mot heo þenchen of
> þe kues foddre, and of heordmonne huire, oluh-
> nen þene heiward, warien hwon me punt hire,
> and ʒelden þauh þe hermes.

B. From Haveloc the Dane, Midlands, c.1300. See
   p. 97.

> Hwan Birkabeyn was leyd in grave,
> þe erl dede sone take þe knave,
> Haveloc, þat was þe heir,
> Swanboro his sister, Helfled þe toþer,
> And in þe castel dede he hem do,.
> þer non ne micte hem comen to
> Of here kyn, þer þei sperd wore.

C. From *Sir Gawaine and the Green Knight,*
   Northern (Lancastrian), c.1370. See p. 380.

> Thenne þe knyʒt   con calle ful hyʒe:
> "Who stiʒtlez in þis sted,   me steven to holde?
> If any wyʒe oʒt wyl,   wynne hider fast,
> Oþer now oþer never,   his nedez to spede."
> "Abyde" quoth on on þe bonke,   aboven over
>   his hede,
> "And þou schal haf al in hast   that I þe hyʒt
>   ones."

D. From Chaucer's *Monk's Tale,* London, c.1390.
See p. 296.

Of the erl Hugelyn of Pyse the longour
Ther may no tonge telle for pitee;
But litel out of Pyse stant a tour,
In whiche tour in prison put was he,
And with him been his litel children three.
The eldeste scarsly fyf yeer was of age.
Allas, fortune! it was greet crueltee
Swiche briddes for to putte in swiche a cage!

The Development of English Prosody

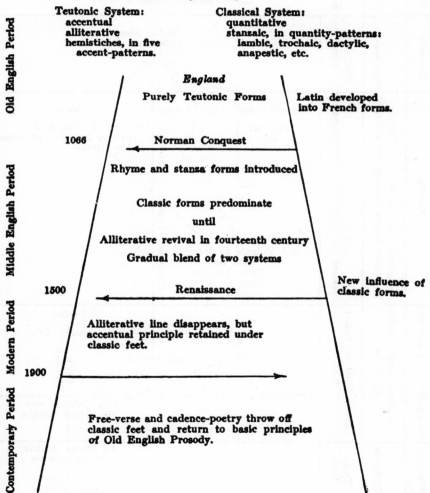

Indo-European Origins

Teutonic System:
accentual
alliterative
hemistiches, in five
accent-patterns.

Classical System:
quantitative
stanzaic, in quantity-patterns:
iambic, trochaic, dactylic,
anapestic, etc.

England

Purely Teutonic Forms

Latin developed
into French forms.

1066 — Norman Conquest

Rhyme and stanza forms introduced

Classic forms predominate

until

Alliterative revival in fourteenth century

Gradual blend of two systems

1500 — Renaissance

New influence of
classic forms.

Alliterative line disappears, but
accentual principle retained under
classic feet.

1900

Free-verse and cadence-poetry throw off
classic feet and return to basic principles
of Old English Prosody.

Old English Period

Middle English Period

Modern Period

Contemporary Period

Growth of the Arthurian Cycle

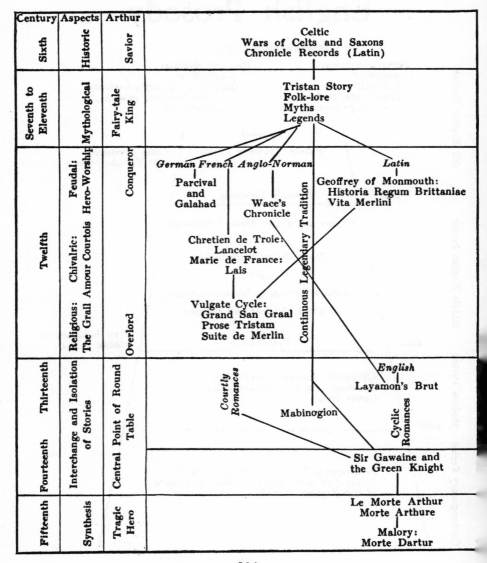

Century	Aspects	Arthur			
Sixth	Historic	Savior		Celtic Wars of Celts and Saxons Chronicle Records (Latin)	
Seventh to Eleventh	Mythological	Fairy-tale King		Tristan Story Folk-lore Myths Legends	
Twelfth	Feudal: Hero-Worship Chivalric: Amour Courtois Religious: The Grail	Conqueror Overlord	*German French Anglo-Norman* Parcival and Galahad Chretien de Troie: Lancelot Marie de France: Lais Vulgate Cycle: Grand San Graal Prose Tristam Suite de Merlin	Wace's Chronicle	Continuous Legendary Tradition	*Latin* Geoffrey of Monmouth: Historia Regum Brittaniae Vita Merlini
Thirteenth	Interchange and Isolation of Stories	Central Point of Round Table		*Courtly Romances*	*English* Layamon's Brut
Fourteenth				Mabinogion	Cyclic Romances
					Sir Gawaine and the Green Knight
Fifteenth	Synthesis	Tragic Hero			Le Morte Arthur Morte Arthure Malory: Morte Dartur

Influence of Church Latin on Middle English Literature

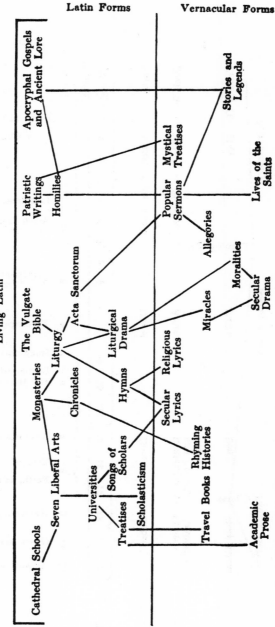

Latin Forms   Vernacular Forms

Living Latin

Cathedral Schools — Seven Liberal Arts — Universities — Songs of Scholars — Scholasticism — Treatises — Travel Books — Rhyming Histories — Academic Prose — Secular Lyrics — Chronicles — Monasteries — Liturgy — Hymns — Liturgical Drama — Acta Sanctorum — The Vulgate Bible — Religious Lyrics — Miracles — Moralities — Secular Drama — Allegories — Popular Sermons — Patristic Writings — Homilies — Mystical Treatises — Apocryphal Gospels and Ancient Lore — Lives of the Saints — Stories and Legends

Transition from Latin to the vernacular in each type of literature was gradual. The two forms existed side by side through the thirteenth and fourteenth centuries.

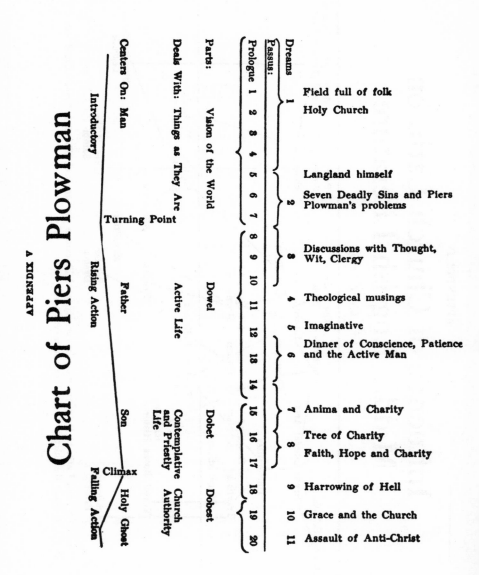

APPENDIX V

Chart of Piers Plowman

Dreams	Passus:				
1	Prologue 1				Field full of folk
	2				Holy Church
	3				
	4				
	5				Langland himself
2	6				Seven Deadly Sins and Piers Plowman's problems
	7				
3	8				Discussions with Thought, Wit, Clergy
	9				
4	10				Theological musings
5	11				Imaginative
6	12				Dinner of Conscience, Patience and the Active Man
	13				
	14				
7	15				Anima and Charity
8	16				Tree of Charity
	17				Faith, Hope and Charity
9	18				Harrowing of Hell
10	19				Grace and the Church
11	20				Assault of Anti-Christ

Parts:
Vision of the World | Dowel | Dobet | Dobest

Deals With: Things as They Are | Active Life | Contemplative Church and Priestly Life

Centers On: Man | Father | Son | Holy Ghost

Introductory | Rising Action | Falling Action
Turning Point | Climax

526

Sources of Translations

TEXTS USED, AND THE MANUSCRIPTS UPON WHICH
THE TEXTS ARE BASED

1. "L'Estori des Engles"; Rolls Series 237; MS Royal A XXI.
2. "The Worcester Fragment"; Hall, J., *Selections from Early Middle English*, Oxford Press, 1920; MS Worcester Cathedral 174.
3. "Vita Wulfstani"; Camden Series 40; MS Cotton Claudius A V.
4. "The Peterborough Chronicle"; Rolls Series 43; MS Laud 636.
5. "Robert of Gloucester's Chronicle"; Emerson, O., *Middle English Reader*, Macmillan, 1905; MS Cotton Caligula A 11.
6 "The Proverbs of Alfred"; Hall; MS Jesus College 29.
7. "The Bestiary"; *ibid*; MS B.M. Arundel 292.
8. "The Owl and the Nightingale"; Atkins, J., Cambridge Press, 1922; MS Jesus College 29.
9. "De Nugis Curialium" of Walter Mapes; Camden Series 50 (O.S.); Bodleian MS.
10. "Chronicle Records of King Arthur"; (1) Nennius, *Historia Britonum*, Mommsen, *Munumenta Historica Germaniae*, Berlin, 1898; (2) *Annales Cambriae*, Rolls Series 31; MS Harleian 3895; (3) *De Rebus Gestis Regum Anglorum*, Stubbs I., 8.
11. "Historia Regum Britaniae" of Geoffrey of Monmouth; ed. Griscom, A., Longmans, 1929; MS Cambridge 1706.
12. "Layamon's Brut"; ed. Maddon, L., 1847; MSS Cotton Caligula A IX, Otho C XIII.
13. "Morte Dartur"; Caxton's Edition reprinted by H. Oskar Sommer, London, 1889.

14. "Guy of Warwick"; Early English Text Society 42 (E.S.); Auchinleck MS.
15. "King Horn"; E.E.T.S. 14 (O.S.); MS Cambridge Gg 4, 27, 2.
16. "Haveloc the Dane"; E.E.T.S. (E.S.); MS Laud Misc. 108.
17. "Geste Historiale of the Destruction of Troy"; E.E.T.S. 39 and 56 (O.S.); Hunterian MS.
18. "Floris and Blancheflur"; E.E.T.S. 14 (O.S.); MS Cambridge Gg 4, 27, 2.
19. "Sir Orfeo"; Sisam, K., *Fourteenth Century Prose and Verse;* Clarendon Press, 1921; Auchinleck MS.
20. "Ancren Riwle"; Camden Series 57 (O.S.); MS Cotton Nero A XIV.
21. "Sawles Warde"; Hall; MSS Bodleian 34, Royal 17 A 27.
22. "The Katherine Group"; Hall; MS Royal 17 A.
23. "Ormulum"; Emerson; MS Junius I.
24. "Layfolks' Mass Book"; E.E.T.S. 71 (O.S.); MS Caius College Cambridge 84.
25. "Ayenbite of Inwit"; E.E.T.S. 23 (O.S.); MS Arundel 57.
26. "The Land of Cockaygne"; Cook, A., *A Literary Middle English Reader,* Ginn, 1915; MS Harley 913.
27. "Rule of Saint Benet"; E.E.T.S. 120 (O.S.); MS Cotton Vespasian A 25.
28. "Mandeville's Travels"; E.E.T.S. 153 (O.S.); MS Cotton Titus C XVI.
29. "The Book of Margery Kempe"; E.E.T.S. 212 (O.S.); Bowdon MS.
30. "Gesta Romanorum"; E.E.T.S. 33 (E.S.); MSS Harley 7333, Cambridge Kk 1.6.
31. "Book of the Knight of the Tour Landry"; E.E.T.S. 33 (O.S.); MS Harley 1764.
32. "Confessio Amantis"; ed., Macaulay, G. C., *Works of John Gower,* Vol. II, Oxford Press, 1901; MS Fairfax 3.
33. "South English Legendary"; E.E.T.S. 87 (O.S.); MS Laud 108.
34. "Mirk's Festial"; E.E.T.S. 96 (E.S.); MS Bodleian Gough Eccl. Top. 4.

35. "The Handling of Sin"; E.E.T.S. 119 (O.S.); MS Harley 1701.
36. "Cursor Mundi"; E.E.T.S. 57 (O.S.); MS Cotton Vespasian A 3.
37. "Gospel of Nicodemus"; E.E.T.S. 100 (E.S.); MS Digby 86.
38. "Debate of the Soul and Body"; Emerson; MS Laud 108.
39. "The Pilgrimage of Man"; E.E.T.S. 92 (E.S.); MS Cotton Vitellius C XIII.
40. "Chronicle" of Roger of Hovedon; Rolls Series 138; MS Reg. 14 C 1.
41. "Gesta Regum Anglorum" of William of Malmesbury; Rolls Series 236; MS Regis 13 D 2.
42. "Chronica Majora" of Matthew Paris; Rolls Series 154; MS Corpus Christi XXVI, Cambridge.
43. "Chronicle" of Jocelin of Brakelond; Rolls Series 246, MS Harleian 1005.
44. "Letter of John of Salisbury"; Migne, P. L. CXCIX.
45. "De Rebus a se Gestis" of Giraldus Cambrensis; Rolls Series 32; MS Cotton Tiberius B XIII.
46. "De Naturis Rerum" of Alexander Neckam; Rolls Series 93; Magdalen College MS.
47. "Springtime Is Come"; Cook; MS Harley 2253.
48. "I Have a Gentle Cock"; *ibid;* MS Sloane 2593.
49. "Blow Northern Wind"; Cook. Böddeker, p.168.
50. "The Maid in the Moor"; Sisam; MS Rawlinson D. 913.
51. "The Irish Dancer"; *ibid;* MS Rawlinson D. 913.
52. "The Man in the Moon"; Brown, C., *English Lyrics of the Thirteenth Century,* Oxford Press, 1932; MS Harley 2253.
53. "The Blacksmiths"; *ibid;* MS Arundel 292.
54. "Rats Away"; *ibid;* MS Rawlinson C 288.
55. "Song on the Times"; Camden Series 6 (O.S.); MS Regis 12 C XII.
56. "Battle of Bannockburn"; Sisam; MS Cotton Alba E IX.
57. "The Polychronicon" of Higden; Emerson; MS Cotton Tiberius D 7.

58. "The Philobiblon" of Richard of Bury; ed. Thomas, C., London, 1888; MSS collated.
59. "Against Women Unconstant"; ed. Skeat, W. W., *Complete Works of Geoffrey Chaucer*, Clarendon Press, Vol. I; MS Harley 7578.
60. "Truth—A Balade of Good Counsel"; *ibid;* Ellesmere MS.
61. "The A.B.C. to Our Lady"; *ibid;* MS Cambr. Ff 5.30.
62. "Complaint to His Empty Purse"; *ibid;* MS Fairfax 16.
63. "Proverbs of Chaucer"; *ibid;* MS Fairfax 16.
64. "The Romance of the Rose"; *ibid;* Glasgow MS.
65. "The Book of the Duchess"; *ibid;* MS Fairfax 16.
66. "The Parlement of Fowls"; *ibid.*
67. "The House of Fame"; *ibid,* Vol. III; MS Fairfax 16.
68. "The Legend of Good Women"; *ibid;* MS Fairfax 16.
69. "Troilus and Criseyde"; *ibid,* Vol. II; MS Corpus Christi Cambr. 16.
70. "Prologue to the Miller's Tale"; *ibid,* Vol. IV; MSS collated.
71. "The Monk's Tale"; *ibid.*
72. "Piers Plowman"; ed. Skeat, W. W., Oxford Press, 1888; MSS collated.
73 "Sir Gawaine and the Green Knight"; ed. Tolkein and Gordon, Oxford Press, 1935; MS Cotton Nero A X.
74. "Cleanness"; ed. Gollancz, I., Oxford Press, 1921; *ibid.*
75. "Patience"; E.E.T.S. 1(O.S.); *ibid.*
76. "Pearl"; ed. Gollancz, Chatto and Windus, 1921; *ibid.*
77. "The Form of Perfect Living" of Rolle; Horstman, C., *Richard Rolle of Hampole,* I. 1896; MS Cambridge Dd V.64.
78. "Treatise on the Holy Name" of Rolle; E.E.T.S. 20; Thornton MS.
79. "Meditation on the Passion"; Horstman, I.; MS Arundel 507.
80. "The Ladder of Perfection" of Hilton;* ed. Underhill, E., London, 1923; MS Harley 6579.
81. "Revelations of Divine Love" of Juliana of Norwich;* ed. Hudleston, Dom Roger, Burns & Oates, 1935; MS Sloane 2499.

82. "The Cloud of Unknowing"; E.E.T.S 218 (O.S.); MS Harleian 674.
83. "The Book of Privy Counselling"; *ibid.*
84. "Godric's Hymns"; Hall; MS Royal 5 F.
85. "Cantus Amoris" of Rolle; Horstman, I.; MS Cambridge Dd V. 64.
86. "Love Is Life"; ed. Brown, C., *Religious Lyrics of the Fourteenth Century*, Oxford Press, 1924; MS Cambr. Univ. Dd 5.64.
87. "All Other Love"; *ibid;* MS Eton Coll. 36.
88. "I Sigh When I Sing"; Cook, Böddeker, pp. 210-2.
89. "Now Goeth Sun"; ed. Brown, C., *English Lyrics of the Thirteenth Century*, Oxford Press, 1922; MS Selden 74.
90. "Lord, Thy Passion!" *ibid;* MS St. John's Coll. Camb. 62.
91. "Lovely Tears"; *ibid;* Advocates Lib. 18.7.21.
92. "Lullay, Lullay, Little Child"; *ibid;* MS Advocates Lib. 18.7.21.
93. "As I lay upon a night"; *ibid;* MS Grimestone.
94. "Who is He?" *ibid;* MS Phillipps 8336.
95. "The Falcon hath borne my mate away"; Cook; MS Oxford Balliol, 354.
96. "I sing of a maiden"; *ibid;* MS B.M. Sloane 2593.
97. "Quia Amore Langueo" to Our Lady; Brown, *Religious Lyrics of the Fourteenth Century;* MS Douce 322.
98. "Quia Amore Langueo" to Our Lord; Cook; MS Camb. Univ. Lib. Hh 4.12.
99. "Meditation on the Wounded Heart"; Horstman, II; MS Univ. Coll. 97.
100. "The Play of Paradise"; *The York Cycle*, ed. Smith, L. C.; MS Ashburnham 137.
101. "The Play of Noah"; E.E.T.S. 71; Townley MS.
102. "The Play of Abraham"; *York Cycle;* MS Ashburnham 137.
103. "The Play of the Shepherds"; E.E.T.S. 71 (E.S.); Townley MS.
104. "The Play of the Assumption"; *York Cycle;* MS Ashburnham 137.

105. "The Conversion of Saint Paul"; E.E.T.S. 70 (E.S.); Digby MS.
106. "The Castle of Perseverance"; E.E.T.S. 91 (E.S.); Macro MS.
107. "A Morality of Wisdom"; E.E.T.S. 70 (E.S.); Digby MS.
108. "Everyman"; ed. Adams, J. Q., *Chief Pre-Shakespearian Dramas*, Houghton Mifflin, 1924; ed. from the printed edition of John Scot.
109. "The Libel of English Policy," Hammond, E., *English Verse Between Chaucer and Surrey*, Duke University Press, 1927; MS Harley 4011.
110. "London Lickpenny"; *ibid;* MS Harley 367.
111. "The Dance of Death"; E.E.T.S. 187 (O.S.); MSS Ellesmere 26 A 13, Lansdowne 699.
112. "The King's Quair"; ed. Lawson, A., Black, 1910.
113. "Lyrics" of Dunbar; ed. MacKenzie, W. M., *Poems of William Dunbar*, Edinburgh, 1932, MSS collated.
114. "Testament of Cressid" of Henryson; ed. Wood, H., *Poems and Fables of Robert Henryson*, Edinburgh, 1933, Charteris text.
115. "Dialogue of Comfort in Tribulation" of Saint Thomas More; ed. Bowden, H. S., *Crumbs of Comfort*, Burns & Oates, 1915.

* As it was impossible to obtain any text of the original of this selection, the translation used is that of the editor of the above edition.

Select Bibliography

Allen, H. E.; *Richard Rolle's English Writings;* Clarendon Press; 1931.

Andreas Capellanus; *The Art of Courtly Love;* Columbia University Press; 1941.

Benham, A. R.; *English Literature from Widsith to the Death of Chaucer;* Oxford University Press; 1916.

Bennett, H. S.; *England from Chaucer to Caxton;* Harcourt, Brace; 1928.

The Book of Margery Kempe; ed. Butler, B. W.; Devin Adair; 1944.

Brown, C. F.; *A Register of Middle English Religious and Didactic Verse Forms;* Oxford University Press; 1916.

Brusendorff, A.; *The Chaucer Tradition;* Oxford University Press; 1925.

Bryan, W. F., and Dempter, G.; *Sources and Analogues of Chaucer's Canterbury Tales;* Modern Language Association of America; 1941.

Cambridge Songs; ed. Breul, K.; Cambridge University Press; 1915.

Chambers, E. K.; *Arthur of Britain;* Sidgwick & Jackson; 1927.

——————.; *The English Folk Play;* Clarendon Press; 1933.

Chambers, R. W.; *Thomas More;* Harcourt, Brace; 1935.

Chaucer, G.; *Canterbury Tales;* tr. Nicolson, J. V.; Covici-Freide; 1934.

Child, F. G.; *English and Scottish Popular Ballads;* 10 vols.; Little, Brown; 1857. Condensed edition: Kittredge and Child; Houghton, Mifflin; 1904.

Chronicle of Jocelin of Brakelond; ed. Lane, L. C.; London; 1922.

Comper, F. M.; *The Life and Lyrics of Richard Rolle*; Dent; 1929.

Contemporary Civilization Source Book; Part I, sections 2-4; Columbia University Press; 1941.

Coulton, G. G.; *Chaucer and His England*; London; 1908.

——————.; *Medieval Panorama*; Macmillan; 1940.

Crusade of Richard the Lion-Hearted; tr. Hubert and La Monte; Columbia University Records of Civilization; Columbia University Press; 1941.

Florence of Worcester's Chronicle; Bohn Library; London; 1854.

Fowke, F. R.; *The Bayeux Tapestry*; Bell; 1898.

Geoffrey of Monmouth; *Historia Regum Britaniae*; ed. Griscom, A.; Longmans; 1929.

Gerould, G. H.; *The Ballad of Tradition*; Oxford University Press; 1932.

The Golden Legend; ed. Ryan, G., and Ripperger, H.; Longmans; 1941.

Gordon, R. K.; *Troilus*; Longmans; 1934.

The Great Rejected Books of the Biblical Apocrypha; Vol. XIV of "The Sacred Books and Early Literature of the East"; ed. Horne, C. F.; New York and London.

Griffin, N. E.; *Dares and Dictys*; Baltimore; 1907.

Hammond, E. P.; *English Verse Between Chaucer and Surrey*; Cambridge University Press; 1927.

Homans, G. C.; *English Villagers of the 13th Century*; Harvard University Press; 1941.

Houston, Mary G.; *Mediaeval Costume in England and France*; Black; 1939.

Ingulph's Chronicle; London; 1854.

Jespersen, O.; *Growth and Structure of the English Language*; Blackwell; 1935.

John of Salisbury; *Frivolities of Courtiers and Footprints of Philosophers*; ed. Pike, J. B.; University of Minnesota Press; 1943.

——————.; *The Statesman's Book of John of Salisbury*; ed. Dickenson, J.; Knopf; 1927.

Ker, W. P.; *Epic and Romance*; Macmillan; 1908.

Langland, W.; *Vision of Piers Plowman*; tr. Wells, H. W.; Sheed & Ward; 1945.

Lathrop, Henry B.; *Translations from the Classics into English from Caxton to Chapman;* University of Wisconsin Press; 1933.

Leonard, J.; "Ancient Humours and Modern Glands"; *Irish Ecclesiastical Record,* Vol. LVI, 244, 343.

Lewis, C. S.; *The Allegory of Love;* Oxford University Press; 1938.

Loomis, R. S.; *Celtic Myth and Arthurian Romance;* Columbia University Press; 1927.

Lounsbury, T. R.; *Studies in Chaucer;* 3 vols.; Harper; 1892.

Lowes, J. L.; *Goeffrey Chaucer and the Development of His Genius;* Houghton, Mifflin; 1934.

Madeleva, Sister; *Pearl; A Study in Spiritual Dryness;* Appleton; 1925.

Mapes, W.; *de Nugis Curialium;* ed. and tr. Tupper, F., and Ogle, M.; Chatto and Windus; 1924.

Mathew Paris' Chronicle; 4 vols. Bohn Library; London; 1852.

More, St. Thomas; *English Works;* facsimile and reprint, ed. Campbell, W. C.; Eyre and Spottiswoode; 1931.

Nicoll, A.; *Masks, Mimes and Miracles;* Harcourt, Brace; 1931.

Owl and the Nightingale; ed. Atkins, J. W.; Cambridge University Press; 1922.

Owst, G. R.; *Preaching in Medieval England;* Cambridge University Press; 1926.

——————.; *Literature and the Pulpit in Medieval England;* Cambridge University Press; 1933.

Paston Letters 1422-1509; ed. Gairdner, J.; London; 1872-75.

Plimpton, G.; *The Education of Chaucer;* Oxford University Press; 1935.

Pollard, A. W.; *English Miracle Plays;* Clarendon Press; 1927.

Raby, F. J. E.; *History of Christian Latin Poetry of the Middle Ages;* Oxford University Press; 1927.

——————.; *History of Secular Latin Poetry of the Middle Ages;* Oxford University Press; 1934.

Representative Medieval and Tudor Plays; ed. Wells, H. W., and Loomis, R. S.; Sheed & Ward; 1942.

Rashdall, H.; *The Universities of Europe in the Middle Ages;* 3 vols.; Clarendon Press; 1936.

Roger of Wendover; *Flowers of History;* Bohn Library; London; 1849.

Schlauch, M.; *Medieval Narrative;* Prentice-Hall; 1940.

Schipper, J.; *History of English Versification;* Cambridge University Press; 1910.

Scuddery, V. D.; *Morte d'Artur of Mallory;* Dent; 1921.

Sir Gawain and the Green Knight; ed. Gordon and Tolkein; Clarendon Press; 1930.

Spurgeon; *Chaucer Criticism and Allusion;* Cambridge University Press; 1925.

Thompson, J. W.; *The Medieval Library;* University of Chicago Press; 1939.

Thorndike, L.; *University Records and Life in the Middle Ages;* Columbia University Press; 1944.

Travels of Marco Polo; ed. Kornroff, M.; New York; 1926.

Troilus and Criseyde; ed. Root, R. K.; Princeton University Press; 1839.

Waddell, H.; *Mediaeval Latin Lyrics;* Holt; 1933.

——————.; *The Wandering Scholars;* Houghton, Mifflin; 1927.

Ward, B.; *Early Lives of St. Edmund of Canterbury;* Sands; 1903.

Wells, J. E.; *A Manual of Writings in Middle English,* with 8 Supplements; Yale University Press; 1927.

Winn, H. E.; *Select English Writing of Wycliffe;* Oxford University Press; 1923.

Young, K.; *The Drama of the Medieval Church;* Clarendon Press; 1933.

Vulgate Version of Arthurian Romance; ed. Sommer, H. O.; Carnegie Institute of Washington.

Chronological Tables

LITERATURE AND ART

Twelfth Century Renaissance
School of Chartre—Victorines
University of Paris
Wandering Scholars
Rise of Gothic architecture
Classical metres introduced
Latin Chroniclers
"Amour Courtois"
Goliardic verse
Records and poems in Anglo-Saxon Chronicle
"The Silent Century" in English
Development of Arthurian Cycle
Breton Lais

c. Worcester Fragments
Rise of Hereward Cycle
Ingulf's Chronicle
L'Estori des Engles
William of Malmesbury: Histories
Vita Wulfstani
End of Peterborough Chronicle
Proverbs of Alfred
Geoffrey of Monmouth: Historia Regum Britaniae
Vita Merlini
c. Rise of Oxford & Cambridge
Anglo-Norman writers:
Marie de France
Wace
Thomas & Beroul
Vulgate Cycle
Latin writers:
Walter Mapes
Giraldus Cambrensis
John of Salisbury
Jocelin of Brakelond
Alexander of Neckham
Owl and Nightingale
Rise of Robin Hood cycle

ENGLISH HISTORY

Planting of "new forests"　　　Rise of free cities
Anglo-Saxons subdued by　　Struggle between Church and State
Normans　　　Civil War　　　Conquest of Ireland

Norman Conquest
William I
Hereward's Rebellion
Lanfranc
War with Malcolm
Bp Wulfstan
Domesday Book
William II
Henry I
Contest with St. Anselm
Stephen
Henry II
m. Eleanor of Aquitaine
Martyrdom of St. Thomas of Canterbury
Richard I
c. Robin Hood
John

CHURCH HISTORY

Eastern Schism　　　Latin Kingdom of Jerusalem
Struggle against lay-investiture
First Crusade　　　Second Crusade　　　Third Crusade

St. Gregory VII
Canossa
Urban II
Council of Claremont
Jerusalem taken
Cistercians
Gilbertines
St. Bernard
Teutonic Knights
Innocent III

1066
1078
1087
1095
1099
1100
1135
1148
1154
1170
1189
1198
1199

LITERATURE AND ART

High point of: Universities, trade guilds, scholastic philosophy & Gothic architecture
Latin liturgical plays
      Rise of vernacular miracle plays
Moorish influence through Spain
Debate literature—Roman de la Rose and secular allegory
Platonic philosophy   Aristotelian philosophy
      Apocryphal gospels: Harrowing of Hell
Spread of metrical romances   Rise of balladry
Religious allegory   Eastern stories, spread by Crusaders
Gradual blend of French & English languages

Layamon's Brut
Ormulum
Ancren Riwle, Sawles Warde
Katherine Group
Bestiary
Matthew Paris' Chronicles
Foreign romances:
Floris & Blancheflur
Troy Cycle
Carolingian Cycle
English romances:
King Horn
Haveloc
Bevis of Hamptoun
Guy of Warwick
Mabinogion (Welsh)
University writers:
Roger Bacon
Grossetete
Alexander of Hales
William of Ockham
Lay Folks' Mass Book
Summa of St. Thomas
Robert of Gloucester's Chronicle
Vernacular lyrics:
Secular
Religious
South English Legendary

ENGLISH HISTORY

          Mendicants in England
Interdict   Conquest of Wales & Scotland
        Civil War

Stephen Langton
Magna Carta
Henry III
English Proclamation
Reforms of Simon de Montfort
Edward I
Jews exiled
Model Parliament

CHURCH HISTORY

Papacy at height of temporal power
        Papal opposition to Semitic persecution
Albigensian Crusade   Inquisition established
        Missionaries in the Orient

4th	5th	6th	7th	8th
Crusade	Crusade	Crusade	Crusade	Crusade

Jerusalem taken
Franciscans
Dominicans
Children's Crusade
Carmelites
Feast of Corpus Christi
Council of Lyons
Boniface VIII "Clericos Laicis"

1200 1209 1215 1247 1264 1272 1296

LITERATURE AND ART

Use of paper introduced

Early Italian Renaissance
Art center in Florence

Religious lyrics—Influence of Devotion to the Sacred Heart
Satirical verse
Sermon and story collections compiled

Alliterative revival
Miracle plays
Revival of vernacular prose

Ramon Lull
Dante's Divine Comedy
Handling of Sin
Cursor Mundi

Richard Rolle:
Treatises
Poems

Political Songs:
Laurence Minot

Ayenbite of Inwit
Gesta Romanorum (Latin)

Influence of:
Boccaccio
Petrarch
Mandeville's Travels
Richard of Bury's Poly-
chronicon
Wycliffe

Contemplative writers:
Walter Hilton
Juliana of Norwich
"Cloud of Unknowing"
Langland's Piers Plowman

c. Pearl Poet:
The Green Knight
Cleanness
Patience
Pearl

Trivisa's Polychronicon

Chaucer:
Lyrics
Book of the Duchess
Parliament of Fowls
House of Fame
Legend of Good Women
Troilus
Canterbury Tales

Gower's Confessio Amantis

ENGLISH HISTORY

Rise of manufacture & commerce
Hundred Years' War
Economic unrest

Edward II

Edward III

Independence of Scot-
land

b. of Crecy
Black death
Statute of laborers
b. of Poitiers

Wycliffe movement
Richard II

Peasants' Revolt

Henry IV

CHURCH HISTORY

Great Western Schism

"Babylonion captivity" at Avignon

"Conciliar Theory"

Scandals & abuses

Great Jubilee
Clement V
Papacy at Avignon

John of Monte
Corvino in China

Urban V

St. Catherine of
Siena

Papacy returns to
Rome

Wycliffe con-
demned

1800	
1827	
1849	
1862	
1876	
1881	

LITERATURE AND ART

Art of the Quattrocento; Humanism

Renaissance

Rise of standard English

Spread of printing
Columbus: discoveries

"Chaucerianism" Didactic poetry
"Dance of Death" motif
Rise of Mortality Plays Extant texts of ballads
  Court plays and interludes
Rise of academic prose Rise of secular drama

Mirk's Festial
c. Extant texts of:
  Mystery cycles: York
    Townley
    Wakefield
    Hegge
  Anon: Flower and Leaf
    London Lickpenny
    Libel of English
    Policy
  Lydgate and Occleve
  Arthurian romances
  The King's Quair
  Miracles: Conversion of
    St. Paul
    Mary Magdalene
  Gesta Romanorum (English version)
  Book of the Knight (English version)
  Book of Margery Kempe
  Introduction of printing
  Caxton's translations.
  Moralities:
    Castle of Perseverance
    Mankind
    Wisdom
    Everyman
  Prose Writers: Pecock
    Fortesque
    Translators
  Malory's Morte Dartur
  Duke Humphrey's library opened
  Scottish: Dunbar
    Henryson
    Border ballads
  Skelton, Hawes, Barclay
  Michael Angelo & St. Peter's
  Dialogue of Comfort

ENGLISH HISTORY

English explorers

Renewal: Hundred Years' War

Wars of the Roses

Northern Rebellion

Henry V
b. of Agincourt

Henry VI

Jeanne d'Arc

Edward IV

Caxton's Press

Richard III
Henry VII

Henry VIII

Henry VIII breaks with Rome
Martyrdom: St. Thomas More

CHURCH HISTORY

Abuses of Indulgences Spanish Inquisition Missionaries in
Hussite Heresy Papal interest in Renaissance New World
  Crusades against Turks Reformation

Council of Constance

Martin V, end of Schism

Brief reunion of east and west
Fall of Constantinople

Leo X

Luther's Revolt

Year
1400
1414
1417
1422
1430
1439
1453
1461
1477
1483
1492
1500
1518
1535

Index

Index

545

DATE DUE